Rosemary Ingham and **Liz Covey** have both spent most of their adult lives working in the theatre. Ms. Ingham did graduate work in playwrighting and costume design at the Yale University School of Drama. After many years spent designing and constructing costumes in regional theatre, she is now Assistant Professor of Design in the Theatre Department of Southern Methodist University. Ms. Covey was born in Leicester, England, was trained at the Leicester College of Art, and worked in every phase of costume design and construction at most of the major theatres in London before coming to the United States. She is now a free-lance designer whose costumes have been seen from coast-to-coast at such theatres as the American Conservatory Theatre, the Seattle Repertory Theatre, the Milwaukee Repertory Theatre Company, the Hartford Stage Company, and the Indiana Repertory Theatre.

THE COSTUMER'S HANDBOOK

How to make all kinds of costumes

Rosemary Ingham
Liz Covey

A SPECTRUM BOOK

PRENTICE-HALL, INC., Englewood Cliffs, N.J.   07632

Library of Congress Cataloging in Publication Data

Covey, Liz.
  The costumer's handbook.

  (A Spectrum Book)
  Bibliography: p.
  Includes index.
  1. Costume.   I. Ingham, Rosemary, joint author.
II. Title.
TT633.C67 1980   646.4'7   79–14893
ISBN 0–13–181263–7
ISBN 0–13–181255–6 pbk.

© 1980 by Prentice-Hall, Inc., Englewood Cliffs, New Jersey 07632

Editorial/production supervision
by Shirley Covington and Donald Chanfrau
Page layout by Jim Wall
Cover design by Howard Leiderman
Manufacturing buyer: Cathie Lenard

A SPECTRUM BOOK

10 9 8 7 6 5

Printed in the United States of America

Prentice-Hall International, Inc., *London*
Prentice-Hall of Australia Pty. Limited, *Sydney*
Prentice-Hall of Canada, Ltd., *Toronto*
Prentice-Hall of India Private Limited, *New Delhi*
Prentice-Hall of Japan, Inc., *Tokyo*
Prentice-Hall of Southeast Asia Pte. Ltd., *Singapore*
Whitehall Books Limited, *Wellington, New Zealand*

Contents

Acknowledgments

So many people have contributed to the contents of this book that the following list of persons and organizations, to whom thanks is especially extended, is surely incomplete. The authors apologize in advance for any oversights.

Frances Aronson
June and Bennet Averyt
Jo Brenza
Richard Bryant
Michael J. Cesario
Shan Covey
Laura Crow
John Dillon
Deborah M. Dryden
Katie Duckert
Carl Eigsti
Linda Fisher
Claudia Gleason
Amlin Gray
Robert Ingham
Nagle Jackson
Joanne Karaska
Marna King

Ellen Kozak
Barbara Murray
Barbara Nieft
Sara O'Connor
John Olon
Holly Olsen
Berl Orr
Susan Perkins
Rose Pickering
Peggy Rose
Rose-Marie Seck
Larry Shue
Liza Stewart
Joe Tilford
Therald and Ann Todd
Susan Tsu
James Watson

We also thank:

The Juilliard School
The Milwaukee Repertory Theater
The Theatre Department, Beloit College
The Theatre Department, Southern Methodist University
The Theatre Department, University of Minnesota
The Theatre Department, University of Wisconsin-Milwaukee
The Tyrone Guthrie Theatre

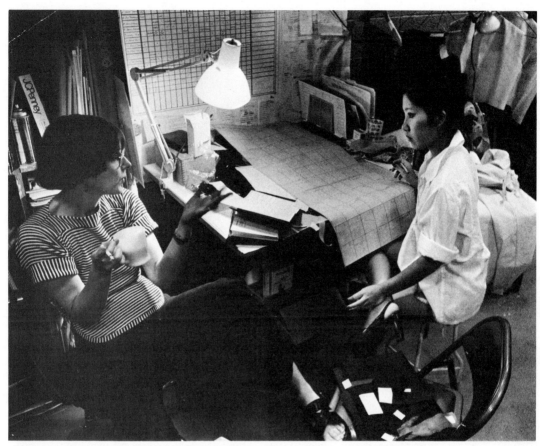

Costume shop manager Rosemary Ingham and costume designer Susan Tsu confer in the costume shop at the Milwaukee Repertory Theater. (Photograph by Mark Avery.)

1

The Costume Shop: Machines, Equipment, Supplies

Theatrical costumes can be constructed in almost any available space: in church basements, in barns, in rooms no larger than broom closets, in theatre lobbies, in someone's living room, and in well-equipped shops. Beautifully designed and meticulously executed costumes may emerge from any of these places, but it is always a frustrating experience to work long hours in a disorganized room without proper machines or supplies. Costume technicians—professional, student, or amateur—who produce consistently fine stage clothing deserve no less than adequate space and appropriate equipment.

The purpose of this chapter is to provide some basic advice for equipping and stocking a costume shop. Organizing each particular work space, however, presents unique problems that call for individual solutions. No one is better equipped to recognize and offer solutions for these problems than a costumer who has built costumes in a wide variety

of environments. No theatre organization should undertake to build or convert an area for the purpose of constructing costumes without consulting such a person.

The standard for space, equipment, and supplies which has been adopted in this chapter, and indeed throughout this book, is particularly relevant to regional professional theatres and to college and university theatre departments that offer professional training in the costume field. Amateur theatre groups, high schools, and small liberal arts colleges can operate nicely with far less space and specialized equipment. At the end of the chapter there are three lists of suggested equipment and supplies: one for the very small, or part-time, theatrical producing group; one for the medium-sized, low-budget group; and one for the large, fully staffed professional company or professionally oriented university theatre department.

Unfortunately, even though a great many

new theatre facilities are built each year in this country, these theatres are no more likely to have adequate costume shops than a converted summer barn theatre or a community theatre organization that uses the local high school auditorium for mounting its productions. Far too many times, costume shop requirements receive low priority when a new theatre is being planned. When budget and space cuts must be made, the costume construction area is often the victim. This is an attitude that has left many new theatres with inconveniently located, poorly lit, and badly ventilated costume shops in which mazes of electrical extension cords, in clear violation of building codes, are necessary in order to operate machines. Only the recognition that both costume staff efficiency and

FIGURE 1.1(a) & 1.1(b)   *Two views of the costume shop at the Tyrone Guthrie Theatre in Minneapolis. (Photograph by Rod Pilloud.)*

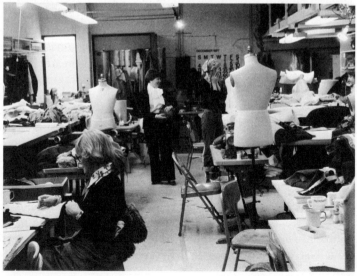

the quality of the costumes produced are closely related to a well-planned work space can change the prevailing attitude.

The ideal costume shop probably exists only in the imaginations of costume designers and technicians. There are, however, many excellent costume shops all over the country that illustrate what can be accomplished if care is taken and money spent wisely. The costume shop at the Tyrone Guthrie Theatre in Minneapolis is an outstanding example of a well-planned and rather costly area. On a much more limited scale, the costume shop at Beloit College, a small liberal arts institution in Wisconsin, is indicative of what can be done with equally careful planning and far less money.

FIGURE 1.2 *The costume shop at Beloit College. (Photograph by Therald Todd.)*

LIGHTING THE COSTUME SHOP

Natural light is both a tremendous asset and a real rarity in a costume shop. The majority of shops in both professional and university theatres are situated below ground level or in the interior of a building—without windows. Natural light is as important to the costumer as it is to the painter. Costume technicians are constantly engaged in matching subtle fabric colors and textures. They spend hours dyeing a piece of fabric the exact shade the designer wants and more hours painting and shading the completed costume. Architects would never think of planning a painter's studio without allowing for natural light, preferably a northern exposure; sadly, the same thought does not go into the location of costume shops. It has been suggested that theatre planners are still tied to the nineteenth-century garment industry belief that if windows were provided in the shops, the workers would waste valuable time gazing at the scenery! If this notion is still alive, every effort must be made to dispel it. Student costume technicians at the University of Montana, in Missoula, enjoy a breathtaking view of the mountains without suffering a noticeable loss of efficiency. Every costume shop would benefit from a natural light source and some sort of view, even if it is only the neighboring rooftops.

Since natural light is impossible to provide once the building has been built and the costume shop situated in the basement, the next most important consideration is the kind and quality of artificial lighting. Far too many shop spaces suffer under fluorescent rather than incandescent light. Fluorescent tubes *always* alter color to some extent, and they flatten out textures. If fluorescent lights cannot be exchanged for incandescent fixtures, supplement the fluorescents with clip-on lamps, small floods, or spots, which can be focused on specific work areas. When planning or remodeling a costume construction area, consider installing light tracks with incandescent fixtures that can be moved and adjusted.

CUTTING SPACE

Every costume construction area must have an adequate cutting space. Ideally, it should be a flat, sturdy table, wide enough to lay out a 45-inch-wide piece of fabric, and somewhat more than six feet long. It should stand about waist high. (A dining room table is about ten inches too low for comfortable cutting.) The top should be made of some material into which straight pins, push pins, T-pins, or thumbtacks can be stuck.

The cutting table in Figure 1.3 was designed by a cutter at The Juilliard School and built in their scene shop. It has a cork top and several shelves and drawers underneath for storage. A much less expensive cutting table can be constructed from two by fours and plywood. Lay a sheet of fiberboard (also called building board or homosote) on top of the plywood and cover it with muslin, brown paper, or plastic sheeting. Fiberboard is far less expensive than cork, and it is quite serviceable.

Temporary cutting tables can be contrived by putting folding banquet tables or ping-pong tables up on wooden blocks (or bricks or cinder blocks) to raise them to a suitable height. A sheet of covered fiberboard can be laid on top.

FIGURE 1.3   *A cutting table in the costume shop at The Juilliard School. (Photograph by Frances Aronson.)*

Position cutting tables in the construction area in such a way that they are accessible from all four sides. The cutter may have to move around the table to cut large capes or trained skirts. A shelf under the cutting table is useful for holding fabrics, long rulers, squares, and curves.

SEWING TABLES AND CHAIRS

All sewing machines should rest on sturdy tables that do not shake when the machine is running. A wobbly table is hard on the machine and distracting to the operator. Table drawers that can hold bobbins, needles, and cleaning tools are nice but not essential. Most of the tables and cabinets sold with domestic machines are not sturdy enough for costume shop use. Purchase only the machine and place it on the stoutest table you can find or build. Industrial sewing machines must be installed in industrial sewing tables.

Costume technicians spend many hours sitting at their sewing machines. In order to prevent unnecessary fatigue and, particularly, strain on the back and shoulder muscles, it is important that each machine have a sturdy chair that is the correct height and that the technician maintain an erect, relaxed seated posture. The type of chair used by typists and telephone operators, with adjustable back and height, is a good choice. These chairs usually come equipped with casters, a convenient feature, although threads will have to be snipped from the wheels at regular intervals in order to keep them rolling.

Equip each sewing machine with a pair of thread snipping scissors. Industrial thread nippers wear well and are inexpensive. Tie the nippers to the machine or tack them to the table, with a ribbon short enough so the nippers will not hit the floor if dropped. Each machine should also have some kind of protective cover to put on it when it is not in use.

Plan a comfortable hand-stitching area somewhere in the shop. An old kitchen table with chairs around it might be sufficient. Consider a tailor's sewing bench. In *Tailoring Suits the Professional Way,* author Clarence Poulin says, "In handsewing, the best posture to adopt is the traditional cross-legged one, used from time immemorial in the trade. The tailor sits on his bench, his work supported on his knees, which are at just about the most comfortable distance from his eyes and his hands. Contrary to general opinion, this is a much more comfortable posture than the bent and cramped one that must be assumed in sitting on a chair." Costume technicians who have accustomed themselves to working in this position recommend it highly.

FIGURE 1.4 *A domestic sewing machine in use. (Photograph by Susan Perkins.)*

PRESSING AREA

The pressing area should be located near the sewing machines. Make sure there is a shelf or a table near the ironing surface on which various pressing aids can be kept. Purchase an industrial ironing board if at all possible. Domestic ironing boards are never quite sturdy enough for a costume shop and even the heaviest of them will tip over under sufficient provocation. Many industrial ironing boards have a basket underneath which helps to keep trains, floor length skirts, capes, and long pieces of fabric from dragging on the floor. Some shops use an ironing table, either in addition to, or instead of, an ironing board. An ironing table can be converted from an old wooden dining table, or it can be built to size specifications in the scene shop. Pad the surface with a blanket and cover it with muslin. All the small pressing boards and the tailor's hams can be used on top of an ironing

FIGURE 1.5 *An industrial ironing board in the costume shop at the Milwaukee Repertory Theater. (Photograph by Mark Avery.)*

table. It is an especially convenient surface for pressing long lengths of fabric and large garments.

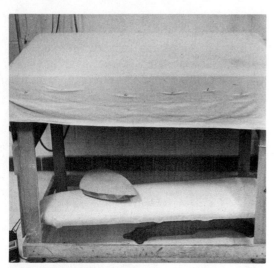

FIGURE 1.6 *An ironing table. (Photograph by Frances Aronson.)*

FIGURE 1.7 *Pressing equipment. (Photograph by Richard Bryant.)*

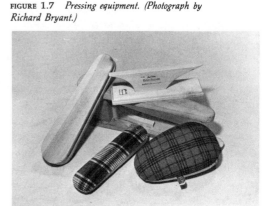

SUPPLIES STORAGE

Storage places for cutting supplies, sewing notions, and stock fabrics should be conveniently located and, insofar as possible, covered against dust. Medium-sized metal or wooden drawer units are excellent for pins, needles, tracing paper, elastic, seam binding, and so forth. These units can generally be bought secondhand at office supply stores or from office liquidation sales. Old metal drawers will open and close smoothly if they are treated with silicone.

Store spools and cones of thread on shelves or on nails or spikes driven into the wall; they will stay neater than if they are put in a drawer. Frequently used fabrics, such as muslin, lining and interlinings, and large quantities of trim, will be more accessible on shelves than in boxes. Take the time to roll stock fabrics on cardboard tubes before storing them and they will be less wrinkled and easier for the cutter to handle.

In the hand-stitching area, keep a supply of small containers to hold pins, thimbles, hooks and eyes, and buttons. If these items are in containers, they are less apt to end up on the floor, and it is easier to return them to the storage area once the work is complete. Cover bars of hard soap with pieces of fabric to form practical pin and needle cushions; soap helps to keep the points sharp.

STOCK STORAGE

Ideally, the stock storage area should be adjacent to, but separate from, the work area. If space permits, there should be one area for hanging stock and another for boxed stock. Both areas should be dry and protected from extremes in temperature. Dampness is particularly damaging to fabrics.

Enclosed wardrobes for hanging costumes

are excellent, but very few theatres have them. Banks of pipe racks are common. Racks on which full length period garments are to be hung should be about six feet from the ground, and even then the trains on long dresses will have to be pinned up. Lower racks can be used for men's suits, trousers, and jackets. Rolling racks are necessary for moving costumes from place to place.

Shoes and boots are more accessible if they are stored on relatively shallow shelves rather than in boxes or bins. Shoes should be carefully sorted as to size and pairs should be tied together. Separate men's shoes from women's shoes.

The box storage area should have shelves on which boxes for small items such as undergarments, socks, neckties, aprons, and so forth may be placed. Adjustable metal shelving is ideal for this purpose. Storage boxes should never be so large that they cannot be handled easily. Boxes with close-fitting tops are particularly nice. Shoe boxes make good containers for gloves and collars. Divide similar stock items into two or more boxes rather than pack one box so tightly that it is impossible to find an item in it. Label all boxes clearly with their contents. It is essential to have a chart or legend, showing where specific items are located, hung in a prominent place in the box storage area.

FITTING SPACE

A costume fitting area should be part of the permanent arrangement of the costume shop. Fittings cannot be properly carried out in the open shop. There are too many distractions; and the actor, if he or she does not actively protest the lack of privacy, will find it impossible to relax when the entire staff is looking on. If a separate room is not available for fittings, construct a fitting space with curtains or old flats.

The ideal costume fitting requires three people from the costume staff: the designer; the cutter or costume supervisor, who marks the alterations on the garment; and another technician who records fitting notes. Even if the staff is too small for the ideal, always try to have somebody on hand at fittings to take notes. It is easy to forget details if they are not written down immediately.

The fitting area, therefore, must be large enough for several people to work in comfortably. There must be a full-length mirror, preferably three-way; one or two chairs; and a small dressing table or cupboard for pins, marking chalk, tape measures, scissors, hairpins, wig caps, and other small items necessary for fittings. A rail of some kind should be provided both for hanging the costumes which are to be fitted and for the actor's own clothing.

BULLETIN BOARDS

It is virtually impossible to have too many bulletin boards in a costume shop. Everything from designers' sketches to pattern pieces can be tacked to these boards, as well as work schedules, machine threading diagrams, procedural instructions, and the film program from the local movie house. The life and work in a costume shop is reflected in what hangs on its walls. Sheets of fiberboard make inexpensive bulletin boards which can be glued to almost any surface, even cinder block, with contact cement.

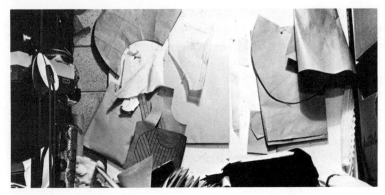 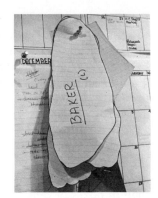

FIGURE 1.8(a) & 1.8(b)   *Costume shop bulletin boards. (Photographs by Jo Brezna.)*

SHOP ARRANGEMENT AND ATMOSPHERE

A costume shop must be in actual operation before the real efficiency of its arrangement can be assessed. During a typical production period, note the normal traffic patterns between the cutting area, the machines, and the ironing board. If necessary, rearrange the machines and tables in such a way that people are not constantly colliding with each other. Conversation between technicians should be possible, and the shop manager or supervisor should be able to observe the whole range of shop operations. Don't hesitate to change the shop arrangement whenever improvements appear possible. The beginning of a season or of a particularly demanding production period is a good time to institute a new layout.

Any place where costumes are being built is a busy place. Technicians—professional, student, or amateur—spend long hours at their various tasks. It is important to make every costume construction space as comfortable as possible. Coffee and tea should be available. A wise supervisor will occasionally bring treats for the staff. These are not insignificant amenities. Good work can always be better and more efficiently produced in pleasant surroundings and with contented companions.

FIGURE 1.9   *A view of the costume shop and staff at the Milwaukee Repertory Theater. (Photograph by Mark Avery.)*

LOCK STITCH SEWING MACHINES, INDUSTRIAL AND DOMESTIC

The first sewing machine was patented in 1790 by Thomas Saint, an Englishman. The machine was wood, made a single thread chain stitch, and was designed to sew leather. It never worked very well. In 1830, Barthelemy Thimonnier of France devised a machine for making soldiers' uniforms. It also carried a single thread which was formed into a stitch by the backward and forward movement of a hooked needle. At one time the French government had eighty of these machines in use. Inventor Thimonnier was almost killed when a mob of angry garment workers attacked him for inventing a machine that put men out of work.

Elias Howe invented the modern sewing machine. His model, patented in 1846, was the first practical sewing machine which could be manufactured and sold to users. Howe's machine had a needle with an eye near the point. A shuttle carried thread below the cloth on a small bobbin and the needle, carrying an upper thread, was fastened to an arm that vibrated on a pivot. The movement of the arm forced the needle through the cloth. The shuttle carried the under thread through the loop of the upper thread, forming a lock stitch.

All the domestic sewing machines sold today are of the lock stitch type. Industrial sewing machines may be either of the lock stitch or the chain stitch variety. Lock stitch industrials, however, are the ones most commonly found in costume shops.

The Singer Sewing Machine Company was the first manufacturer to put an electric motor on a sewing machine. This was in 1889. In 1851 Singer had developed the foot treadle machine. By the turn of the century, Singer Company mechanics were busy converting old Singer treadle machines into electric powered machines. Many of these "converted" Singers are still going strong today.

Few people enter the field of theatrical costuming without some sewing experience. Many costume designers and technicians develop an early interest in making or restyling clothes, either for themselves or, as children, for their dolls and puppets. Since many homes have some sort of domestic sewing machine tucked away somewhere, the child with an interest in creating costumes usually learns to operate it well enough to carry out the task at hand. Sewing classes in elementary and secondary school help develop sewing skills even further.

Because of such home and school sewing experiences, the novice costume technician coming into a costume shop for the first time will certainly find at least one or two familiar domestic sewing machine models. Many shops, however, also use industrial equipment that looks quite strange to the beginner. Although it takes a bit of practice to operate an industrial machine smoothly, industrials function on the same principle as domestic machines and are no more difficult to run.

Industrial sewing machines should be standard equipment in busy professional and educational theatre costume shops. Industrial machines are built for hard, constant use. They stitch faster and will not overheat as readily as domestic machines, which are designed for the home sewer to use only a few hours a week. They perform the operation for which they were designed with great precision. Industrial machines are equipped with knee controls to raise and lower the presser foot, thus saving the operator many hand movements, and with a bobbin-winding device that winds a bobbin while the machine is in normal operation. A few top quality domestic models also offer these last two functions.

The ideal costume shop would probably have several industrial machines, supplemented by automatic stitch domestic machines. That is, if the shop has five machines, three of these would be industrials and two would be automatic stitch domestics. The industrials can handle all the basic seaming and straight stitch hemming operations, while the domestics are reserved for the specialized work that requires a zigzag stitch, a decorative stitch, or stitching on a small area that will only fit onto the domestic machine free arm. By using the equipment in this way, each type of machine will be used to its best advantage. All domestic machines will overheat if used for twelve straight hours to seam floor length capes. Industrial machines will breeze through the same task in half the time, remaining cool throughout.

What kind of industrial sewing machine should a costume shop have? If you look at the catalogue from a large garment industry supplier, such as Cutter's Exchange, you will be met with a bewildering array of industrial equipment, all of which looks, and usually is, terribly expensive. Many of the models in the catalogue will prove to be too specialized for a costume shop.

Purchasing secondhand industrial equipment is the obvious answer for keeping down the cost. Manufacturers of industrial equipment are constantly improving their machines; and the garment factories, always anxious to increase their efficiency, buy improved models and often sell their old models at a fraction of their original cost. Also, because the garment industry is so competitive, firms go out of business with some frequency, putting scores of used machines on the market. Many secondhand industrial machines have found useful, permanent homes in theatrical costume shops.

The issue, however, remains complicated: If it is difficult to sort through the maze of new equipment in an industrial supply catalogue, how can costume shop personnel know what to look for when purchasing used equipment?

An initial step could be to locate and befriend an industrial sewing machine repair person before purchasing industrial equipment. It is quite possible that the repair person's business might include the sale of used equipment; if so, the entire problem is solved without further ado. Certainly, any dealer/repair person who sells a used machine directly, knowing that he will be responsible for servicing that machine, will find it to his own best interests to sell a good machine. By the way, most domestic sewing machine repair persons are not trained to work on industrial equipment and should not be expected to do so.

If there is no industrial repair person available for consultation, contact a garment factory and ask for the staff member who is responsible for equipment maintenance. That person should be able to discuss specific machine brands and models with you and may even recommend a qualified repair shop. If there is no garment factory close by, try contacting the alteration departments of department stores, dress shops, or tailor shops. These shops will have industrial equipment and can recommend specific models and repair people.

Never hesitate to ask advice from people in allied fields. You certainly will not take all the advice that will be offered, but surprising benefits can be derived from such contacts. There have been instances when a garment factory has loaned spare industrial machines to a theatrical costume shop for extended, sometimes indefinite, periods of time. If the theatre is a nonprofit corporation—and most are—the factory can declare the equipment loan as a tax-deductible contribution. Many, many times, contacts made by costume shop personnel with local businesses result in new audience members for the theatre, an extra dividend much to be desired.

Industrial Machine Brands and Models

Singer, Union Special, and Pfaff appear to be the most common industrial machine

FIGURE 1.10   *Union Special, model #63400. (Photograph by Susan Perkins.)*

brands in costume shops around the country. Singer models 241, 251, and 281 are all excellent costume shop choices; so is the Union Special model 63400. Bernina also manufactures high quality industrial machines, much praised by costumers who use them. Less familiar brands are Durkopp, whose model 211–15000 is a good, all-purpose machine; Cut-Line with its model C–211; and the Japanese-made Juki. Before purchasing the lesser known brands, it is a good idea to make certain that parts and service for those brands are available in your community.

The model numbers given above refer only to the machine head. Motors to power these machines can be of different sizes and makes. A one-half horsepower machine motor is recommended. Adjustments to the motor pulley can regulate the speed of the machine, faster or slower, as desired by the operator. When a secondhand industrial machine is purchased, it often comes complete with motor and with a table.

Domestic Machines

Every costume shop should have at least one domestic automatic stitch machine capable of executing a variety of operations: the zig-zag, the hemstitch, the satin stitch, and assorted decorative stitches. These machines will also make buttonholes without a special attachment, although it takes more time to make buttonholes on an automatic stitch machine than with a buttonhole attachment on an industrial or a straight stitch domestic machine. Almost as useful as the flexible stitching on a good automatic stitch machine is the free arm (see Figure 1.11) on which a cuff, a boot top, a glove, or a drawstring purse may be slipped for smooth stitching.

Bernina, Viking, and Pfaff manufacture top quality automatic stitch machines, widely used in theatrical costume shops. The Bernina model 830 is a particularly popular machine with costumers. Most of the parts are metal, and it will take a great deal of heavy use

FIGURE 1.11 *Domestic sewing machine with a free arm. (Photograph by Susan Perkins.)*

without faltering. The thread tension is quite stable, and the machine is easy to clean and oil and simple to thread and operate. In recent years the Viking top-of-the-line model has been a self-oiling machine that requires a thorough maintenance check by a Viking repairperson once a year. The models that preceded the self-oiling machine are said to be more reliable and to require fewer repairs. The Viking performs one stitch that is not included in the stitch repertoire of either the Bernina or the Pfaff: a type of stretch stitch composed of two forward stitches and one backward stitch. This stitch is extremely elastic and very strong, particularly suitable for crotch seams in tight trousers. The Pfaff 360 is slightly more temperamental than the other two machine brands, particularly with regard to frequent thread tension adjustment. Yet it is a sturdy piece of equipment and well suited to costume shop use.

Recent Singer domestic equipment is not widely recommended by costumers. The Touch and Sew line is said to require an inordinate amount of maintenance in costume shops that operate constantly. A Singer Touch and Sew, however, might be completely adequate for a theatre that does not produce plays on a regular basis. One of the most annoying features on the Touch and Sew is the flat, plastic bobbin that refills inside the machine. These bobbins hold far too little thread for the business of constructing costumes, and once the plastic bobbin is nicked—which seems to happen far too readily—the bobbin thread becomes tangled and the bobbin must be discarded. The Singer "electronic" model is much too expensive and too fanciful for a costume shop.

If no industrial straight stitch machine is available for the bulk of the construction seaming, that function can be accomplished on an older model straight stitch or zigzag stitch domestic machine. Singer, Kenmore, and White are all familiar brand names. Some technicians prefer these sturdy, work-horse machines over all others. The engineering of these older models is simple: They are belt-driven and have either foot or knee controls. They are particularly easy for the inexperienced costume technician to operate. They are easy to maintain and to repair; and, except for the slow speed at which they operate, they are very desirable pieces of costume shop equipment.

Although many costume shops depend heavily on secondhand equipment, it is always a good idea to purchase a new automatic stitch machine. They receive heavy use and it is advantageous to have these rather complex machines covered by the factory warranty during the early months of their use. Because of most theatres' nonprofit status, dealers are usually able to give a discount on new machines. If several new machines are purchased at the same time, the discount is often quite significant.

Older model straight stitch machines must be purchased secondhand since many of the most desirable models are no longer being manufactured. Because they are no longer particularly popular with home sewers, it is not unusual to find a machine for less than $100 which will run for years.

Machine Maintenance

Once an industrial machine is properly installed and adjusted, it is easy to maintain. Most are self-oiling, that is to say, there is an enclosed oil reserve and a lubricating system that puts oil where it belongs and keeps it there. The hook is usually oiled only when the machine is in operation. Some sort of gauge will tell you when the oil needs to be replenished. Older model industrials, such as the Singer 400W, will need to be oiled manually in the same way that you oil your domestic machines.

In a garment factory where the machine operator is working on a piece work rate, being paid for the number of operations he or she performs in each work period, it is to the operator's advantage to maintain the machine carefully so as not to lose valuable work time with adjustments and repairs. Each factory operator is responsible for all routine cleaning of the machine on which he or she works. Costume shop technicians must develop similar work habits, even without the piece work rate incentive.

Except for oiling, machine maintenance follows the same routine on both domestic and industrial machines in a costume shop. There is certainly nothing more infuriating than to be pushing toward a deadline and to have a machine break down because of poor maintenance. *The majority of sewing machine breakdowns can be prevented by routine maintenance and good operator habits.* Lint should be brushed away from the feed dog and bobbin areas *at least* once a day—two or three times a day if the machine is running steadily or if the material being used is especially linty. Non-self-oiling machines should be completely cleaned and oiled (top and bottom) once a week when in normal use and more if the use is especially heavy. A drop of oil should be put on the bobbin casing at the end of each five continuous hours of sewing.

Costumers must never be too busy to clean and oil their machines. When stitching is done on a poorly functioning machine, the quality of the garment, as well as the disposition of the costumer and the life expectancy of the machine, will suffer. Rotate the weekly cleaning and oiling among the costume shop staff so that everyone will become familiar with all the equipment. On a daily basis, the person who spends the most time at any one machine should be responsible for brushing away the lint and oiling the bobbin. In every shop there will always be one staff member who has a special knack for dealing with machinery. Encourage this person to learn more about the equipment, to watch when the repair person is in the shop, and to perform adjustment and repairs to machinery as he or she feels capable of doing so.

Machine Needles

No part of the sewing machine takes greater punishment than the needle. So many stitching malfunctions are caused by bent or blunted needles that the first response to any stitching problem should be to change the needle.

A needle that is not suitable for the size of thread being used or for the type of cloth being stitched can also cause problems. The correct needle size and point form (ball point or sharp) must be arrived at by experiment. Keep a variety of needle sizes and types on hand and change the needle whenever you feel it may be slightly damaged or may be the wrong sort for the sewing situation. Purchase sewing machine needles in bulk from an industrial supply company. Schmetz needles are among the finest needles manufactured. There are cheaper brands, but you will probably use more of the less expensive ones. Industrial machines take different needles from domestic machines.

One of the most serious results of stitching with a bent needle is that it may scratch the machine plate, which will then cause fabrics to snag. Pulling heavy fabrics through the sewing machine can cause the needle to bend. Hitting pins or zipper teeth may also bend needles.

Overlock Machines

Any costumer who works in a shop equipped with an overlock machine, or serger, considers that small, odd-looking piece of machinery an absolute necessity. The serger performs a single operation: the overcasting stitch found on the seam edges of most factory-made clothing. The stitch is formed with two, three, or four threads, each coming off a separate spool. There is no bobbin. Most sergers are equipped with a knife that trims the seam as it overcasts; the two-thread serger doesn't always have a knife. The four-thread variety performs a straight "safety stitch" as well as the overlock, seaming and overcasting in a single operation. The serger with a safety stitch is ideal for seaming knits.

Secondhand industrial sergers are usually available for a moderate price from large factory suppliers such as Cutters Exchange. The most common brand name in sergers is Merrow. Many people refer to the serger as the "merrowing machine" in the same way that our grandmothers called their refrigerator the "frigidaire." Union Special, Remaldi, Yamato, and other manufacturers of industrial equipment also makes sergers. For only a bit more than the price of a secondhand industrial serger, you can purchase a Rex portable "baby" overlock machine that uses two threads and has a knife. It is not as sturdy as the larger industrial models, but it is quite serviceable for most small- and medium-sized costume shops.

Because of the hard wear given to stage costumes, it is almost always advisable to finish seams. When a serger is not available, seam finishing is usually done with a zigzag stitch. This is time consuming and very wearing on a domestic machine over a sustained period of time. It is possible to obtain an industrial zigzag machine for seam finishing, but the serger is better for the job and is also less expensive. An overlocked seam edge is softer and more pliable than a zigzagged edge.

Sergers are somewhat complicated to thread, and each brand and model will differ slightly. It is the goal in most costume shops to rethread the serger as little as possible. When it is necessary to change the thread color, cut each thread well above the machine and tie on the new spools with square knots. Trim the thread ends fairly close. Run the machine and the new threads will move through the threading positions.

FIGURE 1.12   *An overlock or serger. (Photograph by Susan Perkins.)*

Blindstitch Machines

The blindstitch machine also performs one function: it makes a single-thread chain stitch

FIGURE 1.13 *A small, portable blindstitch machine. (Photograph by Susan Perkins.)*

of these machines in operation, visit a garment factory or a tailoring shop in order to do so.

The most common large industrial blindstitch machine is made by U.S. Blindstitch. Secondhand blindstitch machines do not seem to be as plentiful as secondhand sergers, and they tend to be expensive. The Rex Company also manufactures a small, portable blindstitch machine, including motor, which sells for about the same price as or less than a secondhand U.S. Blindstitch. It is an excellent choice for costume shops of any size.

Thread Stands

It is much more economical to purchase thread on cardboard spools or cones than on small wooden or plastic spools from retail fabric shops. Cardboard spools and cones of thread can be ordered from many garment industry suppliers; several are included in the Source List at the end of this book. When you use cardboard spools or cones, it is best to place them on thread stands. (See Figure 1.4 for a photograph of a thread stand.) The thread moves smoothly off the stand and through the machine without any tugging to ensure even stitches. Thread stands can be ordered quite inexpensively from a supplier such as Cutters Exchange, and they can be installed on a wooden sewing table in minutes.

that tacks a hem visibly on the inside of the garment and almost invisibly on the outside. The machine operates much faster than the blindstitch available on automatic stitch domestic machines, and it is made with a free arm that allows you to machine-hem cuffs and pants legs. If you have never seen one

LAUNDRY MACHINES

Most medium-sized and large costume shops will want to have a washing machine and dryer as part of the standard shop equipment. Small shops and part-time producing organizations may rely on coin-operated laundromats. Maytag, Speed Queen, General Electric, and Kenmore equipment appear to be the machines most commonly in use, although most costumers who have recently purchased laundry machines admit that they were more

influenced by price than by brand name. It is convenient to have a machine that will wash a small load as well as a full-sized load, particularly since much costume shop laundry involves only a small piece of material or a couple of pairs of tights. The machine should also offer different water temperatures: cold, warm, or hot. However, if the machine does not automatically control water temperature, this can be controlled by allowing the machine to fill with only hot water, only cold water, or with a suitable mixture. It is not necessary for a costume shop washing machine to have two different washing speeds. Single speed cycle washing machines usually require less repairs than multiple speed cycle machines.

Costume shop dryers should have regular, permanent press, and air fluff cycles. Fabrics should be placed in the machine at the correct setting and left for a period of time no longer than it takes to dry them. Excessive heat shortens the life of any fabric, and sewing threads are particularly susceptible to the weakening effects of heat. Dryers are also expensive to operate. Acquire a dryer with an automatic timer if at all possible.

Household laundry equipment is quite satisfactory for most costume shops. Some shops do choose to purchase the heavy duty commercial models, such as those often found in laundromats. They are, however, more expensive than household models, are sometimes less flexible, and seem to require just as many repairs.

Small costume shops without the necessary plumbing facilities for installing automatic machines find the portable washing machines very handy. Excellent models are made by both Maytag and Hoover. These machines might be particularly suitable for a summer stock company that operates only three months out of the year and must keep its equipment in storage the rest of the time.

The Easy washing machine is another useful piece of equipment to consider. This machine was a transition between the wringer washing machine and today's automatics. It has a washing tub and a small spinning tub and it can be hooked up to an ordinary sink. The spinner is quite efficient. The Easy is no longer being manufactured, although many laundry machine shops carry reconditioned models. Parts are still available. The Easy is an excellent machine to use for tinting fabrics.

Very few costume shops will ever want to invest in commercial dry cleaning equipment, although large rental houses find it a money-saving practice. The fluids used in the dry cleaning process are highly volatile, and stringent safety codes must be observed to the letter. The space required to install a dry cleaning machine is often far greater than that which is available. The cost is high. Resort to coin-operated dry cleaning establishments if you must; or, better still, make a deal with a local dry cleaning company to send in all your soiled garments in exchange for a discount.

STEAM IRONS

An industrial steam iron is a necessity in a costume shop which has a heavy building schedule and the desire to turn out high quality garments. Home-style irons do not provide enough steam pressure to shape heavy fabrics and they are not built to withstand the heavy use demanded by costume construction. Over the long run, the cost of an industrial steam iron will probably equal the combined cost of the several home-style irons that you would have to buy during the industrial steam iron's lifetime.

The most common industrial steam iron in costume shops in this country today is manufactured by Sussman. The iron itself comes in five and one-half and seven pound weights; the lighter weight iron is less expensive and is quite suitable for costume shops. The industrial steam iron system is composed of the iron itself, a pump, and a water source. The least expensive, and probably most reliable, system is a combined pump and water tank which must be pumped up manually each time the iron is turned on. Slightly more

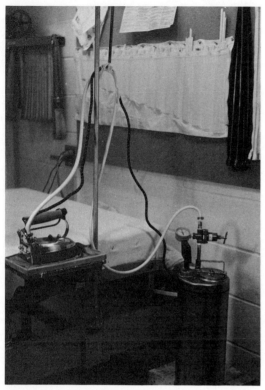

FIGURE 1.14   *An industrial steam iron with pump and water tank. (Photograph by Frances Aronson.)*

as a gallon jug of water on the floor beneath the ironing board.

All steam irons (industrial and home-style) operate better and have a longer life span if distilled water is used to create the steam. A build-up of mineral deposits inside the iron is the most common reason for iron malfunction. There are various mineral dissolving chemicals sold commercially for cleaning out home-style steam irons. None of these are particularly effective for cleaning industrial steam irons. It is always better to try to prevent mineral deposits than to have to remove them.

The Cissell company also manufactures excellent industrial steam iron equipment, but they do not make a small, portable system that is particularly suitable for costume shops.

If you must have a home-style iron instead of or in addition to an industrial steam iron, purchase a well-known brand, such as General Electric or Sunbeam, and choose the heaviest model on the shelf. Many home-style irons bite the dust after one, or several, falls on the floor of the costume shop. The lighter the iron, the more apt it is to fall.

A portable steamer, such as the Jiffy, is a useful piece of equipment for touch-up pressing. It can also be used to steam and shape hats and to aid in "distressing" woolen jackets and pants.

complicated, and a bit more apt to develop mechanical problems, is the Aquamatic II pump unit which operates without manual pumping. A water source must be provided for the Aquamatic II, but this can be as simple

DYE MACHINES

Although most costume shops still do fabric tinting and dyeing in automatic washing machines, in older wringer type or Easy washing machines, or in kettles heated on stoves or hot plates, more and more shops are investing in equipment that operates with steam pressure. Fabrics cannot be properly dyed at temperatures under boiling; the process of coloring fabrics in washing machines should be referred to as tinting. The colors that are

achieved in the washing machine process will always fade when the garment is washed or dry cleaned. Some colors can be permanently fixed—that is to say, the fabric can be dyed—by boiling the fabric in the dye solution, but some require even higher temperatures, which can only be achieved in a sealed vat with steam pressure.

Commercial dye vats are usually too large for costume shops. The common alternative is the commercial steam-jacketed soup kettle. The kettles most often purchased have a thirty or forty gallon capacity. They may generate their own steam, or they may be hooked up to an existing steam pipe if one is available.

The Legion Equipment Company and the Groen Corporation are two manufacturers to consider when you are shopping for soup kettle dye vats. A restaurant supply company will be able to answer most of your questions about this equipment, and they can also install it for you.

FIGURE 1.15   *A commercial soup kettle used for fabric dyeing in the costume shop at the University of Wisconsin-Milwaukee. (Photograph by Richard Bryant.)*

SHEARS AND SCISSORS

Sharp shears and scissors are almost as important to costumers as smoothly functioning sewing machines. Good shears and scissors are expensive and should be treated with care. With proper care, they will have a long life.

Cutting shears generally measure seven inches or more in length. The handle is bent and the two blades are hinged with a screw. The bottom blade has a large handle which will accommodate two or three fingers for better control and leverage. Because of the bent handle, the fabric can remain flat on the cutting surface when it is being cut. Left-handed shears are available and are much more comfortable for the left-handed costumer. It is good to have one pair of extra large shears, twelve to fourteen inches in length, for cutting especially heavy fabrics, felt, and other thick materials. Leather shears

with serrated edges for gripping the leather are quite useful.

Scissors are six or less inches in length. They have small, round handles and are used for delicate cutting and trimming. Small scissors should not be used for cutting extremely thick materials. If you have to force a pair of scissors to cut, the fabric is too heavy and the scissors are in danger of being damaged.

Pinking and scalloping shears are intended to finish the raw seam edges of fabrics which do not ravel easily. Since most costume seam edges are serged or zigzagged, these specialty shears are not widely used. Pinking shears, however, are a must for trimming wig lace.

Home-style electric scissors are not particularly popular with costumers. The common models are clumsy to handle and it is difficult to cut as precisely with them as with hand-operated shears. Some shops use a small, electrically powered industrial cutter, such as the Chickadee, when there is a large amount of relatively straight cutting to be done. The Chickadee is moderately expensive and takes some practice to operate.

Sharpen shears and scissors at regular intervals. Some fabrics, especially those with metallic threads, are especially hard on blades. It helps to rub the blades of shears or scissors on the palm of the hand every now and then; oil present on the skin will help protect the sharp blade. Even when care is taken, cutting shears in a busy shop will need resharpening every two or three months. Take them to a good professional blade sharpener. Do not try to sharpen scissor blades yourself. Because scissors are assembled with great precision to make smooth, clean cuts, a fall on the floor can permanently damage them, particularly if the floor is concrete.

Always buy good shears and scissors. Never buy a pair that has a rivet rather than a screw attaching the blades; there is no way to adjust riveted blades. Wiss is probably the most widely used brand of shears and scissors in costume shops. Singer and Dritz also make good products. One of the best brands, Stille, is imported from Germany; and although these are the most expensive shears, they are an excellent investment. Always shy away from unfamiliar brand names in shears and scissors.

Keep a pair of scissors designated for paper cutting in the shop; never let anyone cut paper with the fine quality shears used for fabric. The stainless steel bladed Fiskar scissors are excellent for paper cutting and are also quite adequate for trimming fabric. They seem able to go from paper to fabric without apparent damage to the blades. Fiskars can be resharpened as necessary.

FIGURE 1.16   *Nippers, scissors, and shears. (Photograph by Susan Perkins.)*

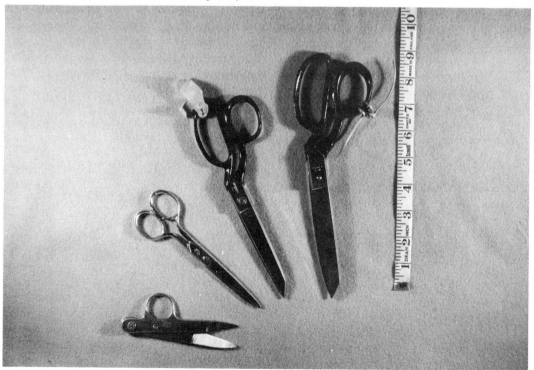

Virtually every costume shop needs equipment for setting grommets, the metal reinforcement for functional or decorative holes punched into fabric or leather. Grommets come in a wide variety of sizes and may be purchased at craft shops. Large-sized grommets are usually available from sailmakers and from companies that make awnings. Grommets come in two pieces. Each size grommet must be inserted with a die setter of the corresponding size. Die setters may be either a simple, two-piece device that holds the two grommet pieces in place while they are pounded into the cloth or leather with a hammer or a more elaborate lever-operated type. When you are pounding grommets into place with a hammer, it is best to work on a very hard surface such as concrete. Holes for inserting grommets can be punched in most materials with a leather punch.

Eyelets serve essentially the same purpose as grommets, but they are always small and are usually made in one piece. A hand-operated tool is used to squeeze the eyelet into the cloth. Eyelets do not hold up as well as grommets and should be used only in places where there will be no great stress. Corset lacing holes, for example, should always be reinforced with grommets.

Pop rivets are exceptionally useful for fastening thick costuming materials together, such as leather straps to vacu-form or sized felt armor; metal or plastic decorations to cloth, felt, or leather; elastic headbands to celastic masks. Although pop rivets are not new, they have only recently been discovered by costumers, who find new uses for them every few days. Except for a drill, which is necessary to make the correct size hole in the materials being fastened together, the only tool required to set pop rivets is an inexpensive pop rivet gun which looks a bit like a large pair of pliers. The rivets themselves are sold in boxes or in plastic packets and are quite cheap.

The rivet consists of two parts: a mandrel, which looks like a blunt nail, and the rivet body through which the mandrel passes. The mandrel serves as the means for pulling or compressing the rivet body; it is the rivet body which actually does the gripping after the mandrel has forced it into place and broken away.

Pop rivets come in three diameters: $\frac{1}{8}$-inch, $\frac{5}{32}$-inch, and $\frac{3}{16}$-inch. The thinner rivets are most generally used for costume shop projects. The rivets also come in different lengths for materials of different thicknesses. Short rivets are suitable for materials up to $\frac{1}{8}$-inch in thickness, medium for up to $\frac{1}{4}$-inch and long for up to $\frac{1}{2}$-inch.

Pop rivet guns and pop rivets are available at most hardware stores.

THE HOT MELT GLUE GUN

Another very useful and inexpensive piece of costume shop equipment is the hot melt glue gun. This handy tool dispenses hot glue, which can be used either for binding materials together or for creating dimensional designs on armor, helmets, jewelry, and so forth. The glue itself comes in pellets about the size of a fat crayon which feed into the hot gun. Liquid glue comes out of a small tip. In the most simple guns, the glue is pushed through the gun manually; others are equipped with triggers which release liquid glue when they are pulled or depressed. When you use hot glue for binding materials together, you can also unbind them by applying the heated tip of the gun to the glue that is already set. The glue will soften up immediately, and whatever you have bound together will come apart. Hot glue is not water-proof.

Many of the machines and tools that have been introduced in this chapter will be referred to again in later chapters, often in greater detail and with more precise instructions for use. The shop machinery, tools, and equipment lists which follow for different sized costume shops include only very basic equipment. Specialized equipment for constructing costume properties, hats, shoes, and so forth will be discussed in the chapters devoted to individual processes.

THE LARGE, FULLY EQUIPPED COSTUME SHOP

With:

a staff of more than six persons
permanent quarters
a preplanned schedule of several productions

Few costume shops start out "fully equipped." Equipment is added over the years as it is needed and as the money becomes available to invest in equipment. It is always preferable, however, to grow with a plan. Assess shop needs at regular intervals, giving priority to machines and tools that directly affect production costs, labor time, and costume quality. Be both patient and persistent. Purchase carefully and care for what you have.

Considerations for Designing and Remodeling Costume Shops

- windows if at all possible
- wood or asphalt tile floor (concrete floors are the worst)
- adequate ventilation
- incandescent lighting with provision for additional clip-on lights
- adequate wiring
  plugging strip electrical outlets
  grounded outlets
  twist lock outlets for industrial equipment
  220 line for electric dryer and stove

several *heavy-duty* extension cords for special uses
- venting system for clothes dryer
- plumbing for automatic washer, including drainage pipe
- stationary laundry tubs
- counter space near laundry machines
- built-in shelving and cabinets throughout
- bulletin boards

The following equipment and supply list is organized to reflect the various phases of costume production:

Planning

- desk and desk chair*
- file cabinet*
- typewriter
- costume books, catalogues, and source materials*
- paper, pens, pencils*
- telephone*
- telephone directories and telephone number file*
- telephone message pads*

Cutting

- cutting table* (the fully equipped shop will have two or more)
- floor pad

---

* Asterisks refer to supplies and equipment necessary for a medium-sized shop. See the next section.

FIGURE 1.17 *An assortment of tailors' dummies. (Photograph by Jo Brenza.)*

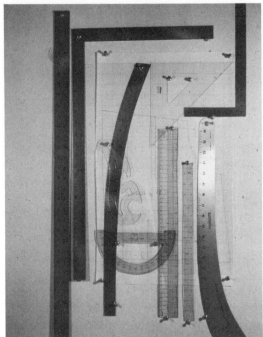

FIGURE 1.18 *Pattern drafting tools. (Photograph by Susan Perkins.)*

- high stool
- dummies; male and female in a variety of sizes*
- roll of brown paper*
- supply of pattern paper, squared
- drafting tools*
  metal yardstick
  tailor's square
  tailor's curve
  French curve
  six-inch ruler or gauge
- indelible markers
- tracing paper in large sheets (red, yellow, blue, white)*
- tracing wheels (needle point, dull point, smooth)*
- push pins*
- T-pins*
- chalk (stone and wax in a variety of colors)*

- chalk pencils*
- tape measure*
- cutting shears*
- paper cutting shears*
- manila envelopes for storing patterns
- file cabinet or cupboard for storing pattern envelopes

FIGURE 1.19 *Tracing wheels. (Photograph by Frances Aronson.)*

* Asterisks refer to supplies and equipment necessary for a medium-sized shop. See the next section.

Machine Stitching

- industrial lock stitch machines*
- automatic stitch machines*
- straight stitch or zigzag machines
- machine attachments*
    zipper feet
    hemmers
    gatherers
    buttonhole attachments
- overlock machine (serger)
- blind hemmer
- stout sewing tables
- sturdy chairs with good back support
- thread stands for all machines
- thread nippers for all machines
- pin boxes for all machines
- bobbins for all machines
- machine needles in adequate sizes and point styles for all machines
- cleaning equipment*
    machine oil (follow each manufacturer's suggestion for preferred oil weight)
    ¾-inch nylon bristle paint brushes for cleaning out lint
    toothpicks for cleaning feed dog and bobbin casing
    screwdrivers, large and small

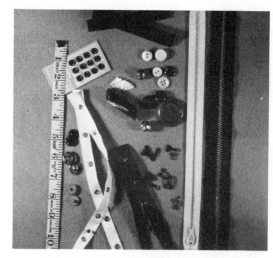

FIGURE 1.21   *Assorted fastenings. (Photograph by Susan Perkins.)*

- muslin or plastic covers for all machines*
- thread on cardboard spools or cones (cotton, cotton-covered polyester, nylon)*
- silk pins, sizes 18 and 20*

Hand Stitching

- table
- comfortable chairs
- hand-sewing needles of various sizes and types*
- thimbles in several sizes*
- seam gauges*
- beeswax*

Assorted Fastenings

- snap fasteners and hook and eye fasteners, black and silver, sizes 4 through 10
- skirt and trouser hooks and eyes
- hook and eye tape
- snap tape
- zippers
- zipper tape, stops, and sliders
- Velcro
- buttons

FIGURE 1.20   *Hand sewing equipment. (Photograph by Susan Perkins.)*

* Asterisks refer to supplies and equipment necessary for a medium-sized shop. See the next section.

- seam rippers*
- razor blades
- scissors*
- pincushions and containers for supplies
- heavy-duty thread*
- nylon slipstitch thread*

Fitting

- three-way mirror
- clip-on lights if necessary
- chair
- rack for hanging
- supply cupboard with*
  safety pins in various sizes
  indelible marker
  chalk
  tape measure
  scissors
  wig cap
  bobby pins
  shoe horn
  glove sizer
  ring sizer

FIGURE 1.22 *Assorted pins. (Photograph by Susan Perkins.)*

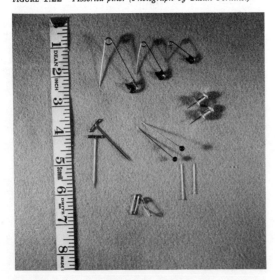

Pressing

- industrial ironing board and/or ironing table
- industrial steam iron, pump, and water source
- portable steamer, such as the Jiffy
- iron rest
- sleeve board*
- press mitts
- tailor's hams*
- point presser
- needle board for velvet
- pressing cloths*
- spray starch and spray sizing
- clothes brushes*
- iron cleaner*

Dyeing

- steam-jacketed soup kettle dye vat
- washing machine and dryer
- hot plate
- stainless steel or enamelware kettles and buckets
- long-handled stirring spoons
- assorted glass jars and covered plastic containers
- bulk dye pigments
- fixing chemicals
- stainless steel or glass measuring cups
- measuring spoons
- gram scale
- fabric scale (baby scale)

Crafts

This list includes basic items only; a detailed list of craft equipment and supplies is in Chapter 11.

- work table
- high stool
- electric drill
- Dremyl with various bits

* Asterisks refer to supplies and equipment necessary for a medium-sized shop. See the next section.

- grommet setters and grommets
- eyelet setter*
- pop rivet gun and a supply of rivets
- staple gun
- hammer
- screwdrivers, regular and Phillips
- large pliers
- jewelry and needle-nose pliers*
- file
- leather tools
    awl*
    leather punch*
    thong stripper
    leather knife

Storage

- racks, permanent and rolling*
- shelving, various widths and depths
- boxes (preferably with tops)*

- supply drawers, various sizes*
- ladders, tall and two-step

Maintenance

- washing machine
- dryer

} not the same machines as those used for dyeing

- detergent, softener, and stain remover*
- enamelware pans for hand washing
- lines or racks for drying hand washables*
- tackle box with emergency stitching supplies for backstage
- shoe polish, applicators, and brushes*
- antistatic spray
- spray Lysol
- industrial vacuum cleaner
- broom and dustpan*
- garbage cans*

THE MEDIUM-SIZED COSTUME SHOP

The medium-sized shop will probably have a staff of from three to six persons, permanent quarters, and a preplanned schedule of productions to build. The shop will execute costumes for fewer productions than the large shop, and the work will tend to be less elaborate and detailed. Costume budgets will be moderate to small.

The major difference between equipment in the large and medium-sized costume shops is in number of machines, since the same basic machinery is necessary in both. Specialty machines, such as the serger and the blindstitcher, are not usually found in medium-sized shops.

Bulk supply purchasing is often not possible in medium-sized shops because costume expenditures are tied directly to current income and large sums are not available for advance buying. The modest-budget shop must be particularly attentive to supply purchases, however, since buying certain items in small quantities can, over a season, prove exorbitantly expensive. Pins bought in small plastic containers rather than in one pound boxes cost several times as much; small spools of thread are comparably more expensive. Muslin is another item that can be purchased far more cheaply in 100-yard lots than per yard at the local fabric shop. It is always economical to try to adjust even the lowest budget to include some bulk buying.

The starred items in the preceding list of equipment and supplies for the large, fully equipped shop are essential for the medium-sized shop that expects to execute high quality costumes.

---

* Asterisks refer to supplies and equipment necessary for a medium-sized shop. See the next section.

THE SMALL COSTUME SHOP

The small costume shop is staffed with from one to three persons. It is set up in a nonpermanent location and often just for the purpose of creating costumes for a single production. The items in the following list can easily be borrowed. They are absolutely the minimum requirements for constructing stage costumes.

- automatic stitch machine
- straight stitch or zigzag stitch machine
- domestic steam iron
- ironing board
- cutting shears
- scissors
- paper shears
- cutting table (banquet table or pool table set up on cinder blocks)
- brown paper for patterns
- yard stick
- square
- tailor's curve
- pencils
- muslin for mock-ups
- indelible marker
- pins
- tape measures
- gauges
- thimbles
- hand-sewing needles
- thread
- beeswax
- heavy-duty extension cord

2

Fabrics

Before the 1940s, any discussion of clothing fabrics was a great deal simpler than it is today. With the exception of rayon, the first synthetic textile fiber to be produced, in 1884, the only fabrics available were those derived from natural sources: chiefly cotton, linen, silk, and wool. Variations in the spinning process and in the methods of weaving and knitting these natural materials resulted in a great many different fabrics. However, no matter what kind or quality of fabric was produced, the natural fibers exhibited certain inescapable properties with which everyone was familiar. Wool was warm, yet it "breathed" and was excellent for winter work clothes. Cotton was cool, usually soft, and required a lot of ironing. Linen was very durable, had a natural luster, and required even more ironing. Silk was both warm and soft, draped superbly, and had to be laundered with care.

During the past thirty to forty years this situation has changed radically. There are now dozens of synthetic fabrics, occurring in a bewildering array of mixtures and blends, under a sea of names, some generic and some trademark. Each of these new fabrics has a life of its own, and each reacts differently to heat, water, dyes, and sunlight. Each has a different "hand" (the technical term for the way a fabric feels), and each drapes in its own way. Indeed, it has become so necessary to be aware of the properties of so many different fabrics that every garment sold today must include, by law, a set of instructions for its care.

These new fabrics have had a tremendous effect on the garment industry, and modern clothes are designed to take full advantage of the properties of the various synthetics. Skin-tight, knit garments that never sag simply weren't possible a few years ago. There are wrinkle-proof shirts, skirts, and trousers, as well as wool-like sweaters we can toss into the washing machine.

Unfortunately, although the synthetics are a blessing to the busy modern housewife, who has cut her ironing by half at least, they are a mixed blessing to the costumer. About 80 percent of the garments made in a theatrical costume shop are intended to dress dramatic characters who lived before the invention and wide use of the synthetics. Just as modern clothing is designed to be made up in modern fabrics, clothing of any other time was designed to be executed in the fabrics then in use.

In most instances, a successful stage costume tries to achieve a feeling of authenticity. Even if the costume isn't an exact copy of the period garment, much of this authenticity, or sense of "realness," is derived from the fabric out of which it's made.

It is impractical, however, to advise against the use of synthetics when building period garments. Woolens and silks are often prohibitively expensive, and cotton prices will never be as low as they once were. At the same time, the synthetics become less and less expensive to produce. Furthermore, it's growing difficult to purchase a wide range of natural fabrics, particularly if you happen to live some distance from a large city. Because costumers are ever slaves to their budgets, most costume shops will have to use some synthetic fabrics in their period costumes. Therefore, it is imperative to understand the basic properties of the most common man-made fabrics in order to know what may be expected of them and, perhaps even more important, what may not be expected. (Because the bulk of our work involves period dress, we make no claim to fairness in our discussion of fabrics; our bias lies strongly in favor of the natural.)

In order to understand the characteristics of the fabrics most commonly used in constructing theatrical costumes, it may be helpful to examine, briefly, the processes through which textile fibers become fabrics. It is important that costumers develop a real respect for the basic steps that go into the production of the yards of cloth that pass through our hands day after day. Out of this respect one can fully develop a sense of feel for different fabrics. When working with cloth, knowledge and a keen sense of touch are equally important.

FIBERS AND FILAMENTS

All fabrics begin with fibers or filaments. Cotton, linen, and wool begin as fibers; silk begins as a filament. The fibers that are processed into cotton cloth grow in a white, fluffy mass from the seed of the cotton plant. The flax plant provides fiber for linen. Wool is normally produced from the fleece of sheep, but it can also come from, or include, the hairs of goats, camels, horses, or rabbits. These natural fabric fibers range from approximately one to ten inches in length and must be spun (twisted) into yarn before they can be woven or knitted into cloth.

The formation of yarn from fibers is possible because the fibers have uneven surfaces capable of adhering to one another. The elasticity or flexibility of the fibers permits them to be twisted together. The natural adherence property plus the "twistability" of cotton, flax, and wool fibers make it possible to produce many different types of yarn, some very strong indeed.

A filament is a continuous strand that need not be spun before it is made into cloth. Silk is the only natural filament used in fabric manufacture. The strands are wound by the silkworm in two continuous filaments, each some two miles in length, around its cocoon.

The filaments spun by silkworms raised especially for the silk industry are quite smooth and very lustrous. Some wild, or Tussah, silk is available from a wild silkworm that eats an uncontrolled diet and produces a more irregular, coarse filament. Wild silk is usually left its natural tan color and woven into textured fabrics like shantung or pongee. Wild silk is less lustrous than natural silk, very durable, and somewhat less expensive than cultivated silk.

The original impetus for the development of synthetic filaments for fabric production was the desire to produce a low cost, imitation silk. For centuries silk has been the reigning queen of fabrics, unequaled in luster and draping qualities. Unfortunately, because of the limited supply and the high production costs, silk has also always been the most expensive fabric made. The synthetics, it was hoped, would produce silk-like fabric at a price everyone could afford.

The synthetics all begin as continuous filaments which can be hundreds of miles long, but which may be cut into fibers of any desirable length before being fashioned into yarn. In their original state, synthetic filaments are much smoother than natural silk filaments, and, therefore, they are much more lustrous because there is more unbroken surface off which light can reflect. All of the early synthetic yarns were very shiny and tended to look artificial. This glassy quality can be particularly unpleasant on the stage where high-powered stage lighting instruments cause the fabrics to reflect even more light than they would under normal conditions. Many of the subsequent advances in the synthetic fabric industry have attempted to reduce this lustrousness. At this time, however, there are very few synthetic fabrics that feel or look like natural silk, and those that do are as expensive as silk.

In the preparation of filament yarn, the required number of filaments are merely laid parallel to each other, sometimes lightly twisted and sometimes not. The only common use of a single filament yarn is in women's nylon stockings.

YARN COUNT

Those who work in theatrical costuming know that sewing cotton is identified by a number; for example, #50 or #60 is the thread most commonly used. These numbers indicate a specific method of calculating yarn thickness, originally applied only to cotton yarn but also now used for cotton-like spun yarn.

Yarn count is determined by the relationship between the weight of the original quantity of fiber and the length of the yarn produced from that fiber. The standard is: one pound of cotton fiber drawn out to make 840 yards of yarn = #1. (A #10 yarn count would tell us that one pound of cotton fiber has been drawn out 10 × 840). The yarn becomes thinner as the numbers rise. Yarns with a count of from #1–#20 are considered coarse; those from #20–#60 are medium; those above #60 are fine. The finest cotton yarn ever made in the United States was #160: one pound of cotton drawn out to a strand 134,000 yards long (over 76 miles!). The very finest yarns spun in England have been as high in count as #400.

One should avoid using material woven from the very fine cotton yarns because, although soft and drapable, it lacks strength. A medium-quality, bleached muslin, once it has been treated to a half-dozen washings, will read beautifully from the stage, and can be counted on to last the run. Besides, the finer the yarn, the more expensive is its manufacture because a greater amount of care must be taken to draw out the fibers and put in the additional twists.

The yarn count of reeled silk thread is based on weight, or denier, and has little practical application in a costume shop. The 13/15 denier count of most common silk from Japan is roughly equal to a #350 cotton yarn—and there might be eight to fourteen filaments in it! We do sometimes use spun silk thread. The short, inferior, waste silk filament pieces are used to make this thread and they are spun in much the same way as cotton. The resulting thread isn't as lustrous as first quality reeled silk, yet it is very nice for top-stitching. The yarn count of spun silk thread is similar to that used for cotton yarn, but with an important difference: In cotton, the term 2/60 signifies a two-ply yarn (see ply yarns), each strand having a yarn count of 60. In spun silk, 60/2 means that two yarns, each with a separate count of 120, have been twisted together, producing a ply yarn with a new count of 60. In either case, the number 60 identifies a specific kind of yarn.

Novelty Yarns

Novelty yarns are often fashioned by odd and uneven twisting. So-called slub yarns have areas which are completely untwisted. Although materials woven from these yarns have a very desirable texture for use in stage costumes, care should be taken in their purchase. A very loose fabric woven from unevenly twisted yarns won't wear well and should certainly be avoided when a costume is being built that must go on an eight-month, cross-country tour.

Ply Yarns

When two strands of prepared yarn are twisted together, the result is a ply yarn. Sometimes a ply yarn is created for color or texture interest. However, if a two-ply yarn is made up of two identically twisted strands of yarn from the same fiber, the ply yarn is double the strength of the single. An example of the labeling of a cotton ply yarn is 3/30; this indicates a yarn consisting of three strands of #30 count yarn. All sewing threads are ply yarns.

YARN TWIST

Yarn may be twisted from the right to the left or from the left to the right. The former is referred to as the Z twist, the latter as the S twist. This is not a fact that need concern costumers greatly, although it's interesting to know that authentic crepe effects are done by alternating yarns with opposing twists so the resulting fabric will come out crinkly. A great deal of frustration may be avoided, however, if the direction of the twist in reels of sewing thread is noted and if machines are threaded with the twist rather than against it. One should thread hand-sewing needles with the thread as it comes off the

FIGURE 2.1   *S and Z yarn twist.*

reel and cut the thread only after the needle is threaded. Needles thread more easily and you are far less likely to be troubled with tangles or knots if you go with the twist.

YARN TO FABRIC

Fabric weaving is an interlacing of yarns accomplished on a loom. At one time or another, most costumers have probably done some simple form of weaving: perhaps in a primary art class or in the Scouts, where one wove a potholder for one's mother. Or one might have received a weaving kit for Christmas, containing a small frame loom and a quantity of colored yarns. Primitive peoples discovered weaving at the very dawn of civilization, and even today the most powerful industrial looms contain essentially the same parts and perform the same operations as the crude, hand-operated looms of the past.

The original purpose of the loom, which began as a simple frame, was to hold the warp threads in position so that the filling threads (also called the woof or weft) might be passed from one side to the other, over one warp thread, under the next, and so on. At first the warp threads were picked up manually; later they were separated by a stick or bar. The development of the harness of heddles (or heddle-frame) paved the way for a much more rapid cloth production. The harness remains a major part of modern looms. The heddle is a wire with a hole in the middle, through which the yarn is threaded. All of the heddles attached to one harness may be raised simultaneously with a single motion. The plain, over-and-under weave may be carried out on a loom with only two harnesses, each harness raising an alternating set of warp threads. By using additional harnesses, very intricate weaving patterns can be carried out.

There are three distinct steps in the weaving process. *Shedding* is the formation of an opening, or shed, between the warp threads in which the filling thread can be inserted. It is performed by raising a harness. When the shed is formed, the filling thread is carried across the warp threads by a shuttle. One pass of the shuttle is called a *pick,* and the process is called *picking. Battening* is the operation by which the pick is beaten into the cloth by a batten, or reed, so that the weave will be close and firm.

Accompanying the shedding, picking, and battening processes are the *taking up* and *letting off* processes in which the newly woven cloth is rolled up on the cloth beam and the warp threads released from the warp beam.

Fabric Width

The width of any piece of fabric is determined by the width of the loom on which it was woven. Before the 1950s, most fabrics were 36 inches wide. Since then, there has been a move to weave wider fabrics so the garment cutters can lay out their patterns to better advantage. Nowadays, cotton is usually 45 inches wide, wool fabrics are from 54 to 60 inches wide, and silk and silk-type synthetics are from 40 to 45 inches wide. Fabrics made expressly for draperies are wider than dress goods—at least 45 inches wide and often more. These widths, however, are only the general rule and it is always best to measure the width of any piece of cloth before you make a purchase.

Fabric Grain

Warp and filling yarns are always at right angles to each other and differ from each other because of their performance on the loom and their function in the fabric. Warp yarns usually have more twist and are of a higher quality than filling yarns; this is so they can withstand the tension under which they operate on the loom. Filling yarns might be unevenly twisted in order to provide a texture to the cloth and they can be of a lesser quality because they do not exist under tension in the weaving process.

The differences between the warp and filling yarns make the determination of fabric grain important. *Lengthwise grain* indicates the direction in which the warp threads run. *Crosswise grain* is the direction of the filling yarn. In a newly purchased piece of fabric, the warp yarns will run parallel to the selvedges, which are the outer borders of a length of woven fabric where the filling yarn is turned for the next pick. Selvedges are generally more tightly woven then the rest of the fabric. In a piece of fabric without selvedges, the warp yarns may be recognized because they are more regular and because they stretch less than the filling yarns; in a textured or decorative fabric, the warp yarns are the most ordinary in appearance.

There are three reasons why it is important to recognize the lengthwise grain of a piece of fabric before we cut a garment from it. (1) The fabric is stronger in the warp direction and usually stretches least. (2) Fabrics are often stiffer in the warp direction because the warp yarns have more twist and, therefore, the fabric will drape very differently on the lengthwise grain than on the crosswise grain. (3) Almost all fabrics will shrink more in the warp direction.

Inexperienced costume cutters will often make the mistake of fitting a piece or two of a pattern on the crosswise rather than the lengthwise grain in a misguided attempt to save fabric. As can be seen from the preceding discussion this sort of off-grain cutting will almost certainly result in problems with drape, shrinkage, and uneven wearing. Countless garments have been spoiled in the cutting because the person wielding the scissors misunderstood the importance of using fabric grain determinations.

The diagonal direction of a piece of fabric is referred to as the *true bias*. This is the direction in which the fabric will have the most give, and from which it achieves the deepest drape. Women's garments are sometimes designed in which the true bias is substituted for the usual lengthwise grain of the fabric. These garments have a figure-moulding drape and uneven hems; they were particularly popular in the 1920s and the 1930s, but they also crop up in other periods as elegant, aberrant styles or fads.

Any other position on a piece of cloth between true bias and either lengthwise or crosswise grain is called the *garment bias*. A garment bias edge ravels more than a bias cut edge or than either grain edge. Most seams in any garment will be cut along a garment bias. The greater tendency for these edges to ravel makes some sort of seam finishing necessary in garments that are expected to wear well. The most common seam finishing in costume shops is a simple overcast with a zigzag stitch, although a much faster and more satisfactory method is serging, using the specialized industrial machine discussed in Chapter 1.

Thread Count

The thread count of a fabric is the number of warp and filling threads per square inch when it is taken from the loom, that is, before any finishing processes are applied. The count may be written with the warp count first, such as 80 × 76, or as a total of the two, such as 156. (The warp count is almost always slightly higher than the filling count.) The understanding of thread count is important in buying muslin, a fabric used in quantity in the construction of stage costumes.

The higher the thread count, the better the quality of the muslin. A muslin with a high thread count will not shrink so much as one with a low thread count; it will be more durable and will ravel less. Also, a muslin with a low thread count is likely to be impregnated with starch to fill up the spaces left by the loose weave; and, if the fabric is used before washing, as is most often the case when constructing muslin pattern garments, the material will become a sticky and unpleasant mess with which to work.

MUSLIN THREAD COUNT CHART

Grade	Thread Count	Properties & Uses
Back-filled muslin	Less than 112 threads to the square inch	Very loosely woven; contains excess starch; when washed it is too limp for most uses
Light-weight muslin	Not less than 112 threads to the square inch	Too much starch to be used without washing; loose, soft drape when washed; wears moderately well; good for soft undergarments, peasant blouses, and the like
Medium-weight muslin	Not less than 128 threads to the square inch	Strong, with very little filling; unwashed it is excellent for draping bodices, coats, and so forth; washed it makes nice petticoats; widely used for costume underlining
Heavy-weight muslin	Not less than 140 threads to the square inch	Sturdiest, longest wearing muslin; used largely in hospitals where durability is important; generally too expensive for costume shops

Fabric Weaves

There are three basic fabric weaves that can be accomplished on an ordinary loom, and there are a number of variations upon these. Since each weave results in a fabric with its own individual pattern of behavior, garments are designed for specific fabrics. Every care should be taken to execute a design in the fabric indicated by the designer and no substitutions should be made without consulting the designer.

PLAIN WEAVE We have already referred to the plain weave wherein each filling yarn interlaces with each warp yarn in an alternating pattern. This arrangement effects the maximum number of interlacings. Plain weave produces the strongest fabrics and, because of its simplicity (requiring only a two-harness loom), is the least expensive of the weaving processes. Unless there is a printed or em-

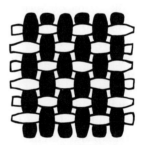

FIGURE 2.2 *Plain weave.*

bossed surface finish or design, plain weave fabrics have no right or wrong side.

Since there is minimum of surface texture in plain weave fabrics, printed designs are often added. When purchasing a plain weave printed fabric, it is always a good idea to check the relationship of the fabric grain to the printed design, especially when the fabric has a low thread count. The more loosely woven the fabric, the more apt it will be to slip around in the printing process, thus throwing the design off grain. Off-grain prints are, of course, most serious in stripes or plaids. Never buy a plaid that has been printed off grain. A costume constructed from such a fabric will either be an off-grain garment or one in which the plaid runs in odd angles. Either will be a disaster that stage lights will only magnify.

Plain weave fabrics may also have a woven-in design. Because of the complexity of threading the loom with different color yarns, woven patterns result in a more expensive fabric than printed patterns. In a woven patterned fabric, check to see that the weave is tight and that the fabric does not contain excess amounts of starch. In a loose weave, the threads can slip enough to shift the whole piece of fabric off grain. Because the filling yarns are the loosest in any weave, the crosswise grain will be more adversely affected than will the lengthwise grain. Can you see how a bold, horizontal stripe could be harmed by such slippage?

Plain weave fabrics may be light-weight, medium-weight, or heavy-weight. The fabrics may be woven from already dyed yarns, or the fabrics may be dyed after weaving. They may be woven of any yarn, natural or synthetic. Some of the more commonly used plain weave fabrics are: batiste, cheesecloth, muslin, organdy, chiffon, voile, gingham, taffetas, cotton suiting (Indian Head is a familiar trade name), and butcher linen. Tweed is a plain weave that is always characterized by the presence of different color nubs.

When the number of warp yarns is increased until there are almost twice as many warp yarns as filler yarns, the weave is called an unbalanced plain weave and the fabric has a crosswise ridge. If the filling yarns are larger than the warp yarns, the ridges are more pronounced. Broadcloth has a very slight ridge; faille, bengaline, and grosgrain all have prominent ridges. These unbalanced weaves wear less well than balanced weaves. Wear occurs on top of the warp threads and

splits will appear in the fabric. Because of this problem with wear, it would be best, for example, not to choose an unbalanced plain weave to construct men's eighteenth-century knee breeches. On the other hand, a fabric such as faille is a particularly good choice for certain period garments such as waistcoats, capes, and simple bodices, because the ridges give the fabric a pleasant depth and excellent body.

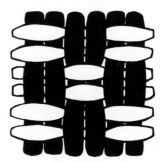

FIGURE 2.3   *2/2 Hopsack or basket weave.*

The basket weave is a variation of the plain weave in which two or more filling yarns are interlaced with a corresponding number of warp yarns or in which a filling yarn is used that is equivalent to two warp yarns. The resulting weaves are loose and hang well. They make excellent draperies.

Cotton monk's cloth, woven with four yarns interlacing four yarns, is a very well known basket weave. Other fabrics similar to monk's cloth are: friar's cloth, bishop's cloth, druid's cloth, and mission cloth. All of these are generally a brownish white or oatmeal in color.

Monk's cloth is widely used in costume construction, particularly for peasant wear from the middle ages and for long medieval robes. Monk's cloth is relatively inexpensive and it does drape beautifully. However, monk's cloth has its disadvantages. The loosely woven cloth is likely to slip at the seams of a garment. The long yarns snag easily and are apt to pill. Pressing will flatten the weave and decrease the texture. Indeed, monk's cloth can be a mixed blessing for costumers; it seldom looks as wonderful made up as it did on the bolt. Approach it with caution.

TWILL WEAVE In the twill weave the filling yarn interlaces or "floats" over more than one warp yarn but seldom over more than four. On each successive line of the weave, or pick, the design is moved one step to the right or the left, forming diagonal wales which may vary in prominence, direction, and degree of angle, but which are always present in the twill weaves.

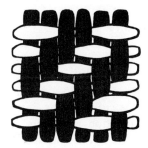

FIGURE 2.4 *2/2 Twill weave.*

A twill weave fabric, such as gabardine, has prominent wales and may become shiny due to the pressure it receives in everyday wear. Steaming may help to raise the wales and reduce the shine. It is also helpful to dip a piece of soft fabric into pure white vinegar and rub briskly in both directions on the shiny area. Shiny spots are a common problem on gabardine suits, occurring most often at the elbows, the knees, and on the trouser seat.

The twill wale usually goes from the lower left of the fabric to the upper right in a wool and in the opposite direction in cotton or cotton-like fabrics. This is only important in that it might help in determining the right or wrong side of a fabric. With fabrics that have a very prominent wale, or with those that

are made from two different colors of yarn, the two lapels of a suit or coat cannot be made to look the same. If this is sufficiently disturbing to the eye, the fabric should be avoided for that use.

FIGURE 2.5 *2/2 Twill–herringbone weave.*

Twill weave fabrics all have right and wrong sides and, because of the interesting surface pattern provided by the weave, twills are seldom printed with additional designs.

Common twill fabrics are: serge, twill flannel, drill, denim, and gabardine. Herringbone fabrics are twills in which the twill line is reversed at regular intervals in order to create a design that resembles a fish backbone.

FIGURE 2.6 *5 Thread satin weave.*

SATIN WEAVE In the satin weave, either warp or filling yarns are passed across several yarns and then beneath a single yarn. These long stretches of yarn are called floats and they produce a fabric surface that appears to be unbroken. These floats reflect light, produce a rich luster, and give the fabric a smooth, almost slippery feel. When it is the warp yarns that form the surface floats, the fabric is called a true satin and is usually woven from a filament fiber such as silk, acetate, or nylon. If the surface is made up of filling floats, the fabric is called sateen and is usually made of cotton.

FIGURE 2.7   *5 Thread sateen weave.*

All satin weave fabrics have a right and a wrong side. If the yarn count is high, that is, if the weave is firm and tight, the fabric will be durable. A lower yarn count will produce a looser fabric that ravels easily and is apt to snag because of the presence of the long, loose floats.

Satin weave coat linings are desirable because the satin weave produces a fabric that slips easily on top of other fabrics. Compared to taffeta linings, satin is more pliable and therefore not so apt to split at hemlines and other "folded" points. However, high quality in satin linings is important. Low-count satin linings will tend to slip in the seams and the long, loose floats will shift out of shape to produce wrinkled or bubbly areas.

Firm, drapery-weight, cotton-backed satins are excellent choices for period garments. Crepe-backed satins, in which crepe yarns are used as filling yarns and low twist filament yarns for the warp, have a particularly smooth and lustrous surface, and the crepe yarns add softness and durability. They are excellent for more contemporary gowns but are often too shiny for the earlier periods.

Pile Fabrics

Pile fabrics have loops or tufts standing up from the base cloth. These stand-up yarns are formed from an additional set of warp or filling yarns which are raised by short wires in the weaving process. The pile may be cut or left uncut.

The quality of pile fabrics is related to thread count. The higher the count, the denser the pile and the stronger the base cloth. The closer the weave, the less likely the pile will be to snag or to pull out. Before you purchase a piece of pile fabric, hold it up to a light to examine the compactness of the weave. Many cheap, skimpy velvets are on the market, some with such a scant pile that the base cloth is clearly visible. These fabrics should be avoided.

Pile fabrics usually have an up and down direction which we call nap. Light reflects differently on a piece of fabric depending upon whether the nap goes down or up. Garments must be cut with the nap all running in the same direction. Otherwise the garment will look as though it was made from two different colored materials.

Common pile fabrics are: terry cloth, velveteen, corduroy, velvet, velour, plush, and fake furs.

Felt

Felt is a fabric, commonly used in costume shops, that is neither woven nor knitted. The preparation of felt depends upon a unique property of wool fibers called felting. These fibers, because they are so springy and kinky, have a tendency to mat together in the presence of pressure, moisture, and heat. You may have experienced the felting property of wool in the underarm areas of woolen sweaters where heat and perspiration have stiffened and matted the yarns, or when you accidentally put a wool garment in the washing machine and have had it come out a small, much more compact version of its original shape. When controlled pressure, moisture, and heat are deliberately applied to wool fibers, the result is a material we call felt, in which the fibers have, in effect, been jammed together.

The best felt is made of all wool fibers, but it is expensive and not always available. The thin, colored felt that is commonly sold in handcraft shops contains only just enough wool fiber for the felting effect to take place. Short, cotton fibers predominate, although this sort of felt may also contain assorted rayon and/or synthetic fibers. This felt may be readily pulled apart and will not withstand any abrasion at all.

Heavily sized felt is important for making hat forms. These forms are used to make a wide variety of men's and women's contemporary hats. Costumers use these forms to shape hats from many periods.

Although light-weight felt is sometimes used to underline very heavy robes, gowns, or capes, its most common use by far in costume construction is for accessories such as armor, crowns, large pieces of jewelry, belts, and so forth. The felt used for this purpose is called industrial felt and cannot be purchased at ordinary fabric stores. (See the shopping guide for sources of industrial felt.) Industrial felt will come in thicknesses from one-eighth- to better than one-half-inch. An especially good felt for costume accessories is called orthopedic felt; it is 100% wool and is between one-eighth and one-quarter-inch thick.

Although felt has definite specialized uses, it is not generally suitable for garment construction. Because of its "pressed-together" nature, felt will disintegrate in water or if it is subjected to agitation or abrasion. It also tends to come apart on a fold or a stitching line.

Knitted Fabrics

Knitted fabrics have been increasingly in demand over the last ten years. New technical advances in the knitting industry, and in the production of synthetic fiber, have made a still growing number of new knit fabrics available. These fabrics give readily with body movement and, if the fabric is of good quality, return smartly to their original shape. Most are machine washable and require little or no ironing. Some people find knit fabrics uncomfortably warm, especially if they are constructed from synthetic fiber yarns; but despite this drawback, they are widely worn and appreciated.

Because there has been such a tremendous increase in the use of knit fabrics in recent years, one may forget that industrial knitting has been around for a long time. Indeed, the first knitting machine was invented by the Reverend William Lee in 1589. However, until recently, the knitting industry was primarily engaged in knitting hosiery. Knitted yard goods, with some exceptions such as wool and cotton jersey, did not come into their own until the development of synthetic yarns.

There are two types of industrial knitting. The first, *filling knit,* is accomplished with one continuous yarn. The fabric is tubular and it is quite like hand knitting in construction. A plain stitch, a purl stitch, and a ribbed stitch are all possible. Filling knit fabric will go into ladder-like runs if a thread is snipped.

Warp knitting is done with a series of yarns working side by side. Loops are made simul-

FIGURE 2.8 *Plain knit—face side.*

FIGURE 2.9   *Plain knit—reverse side.*

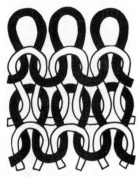

FIGURE 2.10   *Pearl knit—reverse and face sides are the same.*

FIGURE 2.11   *1/1 Rib knit.*

taneously by interlooping individual warp yarns into the loops of adjacent warp yarns. Warp knitting is the fastest method of cloth production. A warp knitting machine can accomplish 4,700,000 stitches per minute. Warp knit fabrics are less elastic than filling knit. They are stronger, firmer, and do not snag so easily; they will not run if a single thread is snagged.

In *Designing and Making Stage Costumes,* Motley states: "In period costume, wool jersey is indeed the boon and solace of the harassed designer, the very *beau ideal* of fabrics." This is extravagant praise, but quite warranted. Knitted wool jersey is strong yet light in weight, it comes in a wide variety of colors, it has an elegant feel, and it drapes beautifully. Unfortunately, wool jersey is prohibitively expensive for most modest budget productions and the synthetic jerseys invariably lack weight and authority. Use wool jersey whenever it is suitable to your needs and you are able to afford it. Working with wool jersey can be a real joy.

Modern knitted dance tights have put an end to the baggy-kneed look that once characterized Shakespearean actors. Cotton or wool knit tights will invariably bag. Underhanded wardrobe personnel used to coax actors into damp cotton tights in an effort to prevent bagging; the tights would dry stuck to the actor's legs and, it was hoped, would stay there. Not only did this practice encourage pneumonia, it was ineffective in the long run. It took nylon to remove the bags beneath the knees; and today's actors can present as firm and trim a leg as Shakespeare ever praised.

Knitted nylon hosiery might be a boon to the modern woman, but the costumer often bemoans the scarcity of old-fashioned silk stockings. Silk stockings are still made, in very limited quantities, and can be purchased (see shopping guide), but they are a speciality item—very expensive and quite fragile. People often find old silk stockings tucked away in attics and seldom-used bureaus, which they then donate to costume shops. Unless they have been subjected to moisture and mildew, these old silk stockings are apt to wear just as well as new ones. It's always well to let your community know that you would be interested in receiving any silk stockings that are turned out in attic cleanups.

Most cloth, when it comes directly off the loom or the knitting machine, is dull, limp, rough, and marred with blemishes. At this stage it is called "gray cloth." A series of finishing processes are usually required to produce the bolts of widely different fabrics found on piece good shelves or made up in ready-to-wear garments.

There are many more fabric finishes than will be discussed here; it's estimated that approximately 200 possible finishes exist. This discussion is limited to those processes that may be most pertinent to costumers. Those of you who are interested in looking more fully into the subject of fabric finishes may take a look, as a starting place, at the list of commonly used finishes with brief explanations in George E. Linton's *Applied Basic Textiles,* beginning on page 231.

Fabric dyeing and printing are important finishing processes that we will save for a separate chapter (see Chapter 6). It is a large topic, one of special interest to costumers, and deserves a chapter of its own.

All fabric finishes are applied in order to make cloth look better, feel better, and give better service. Some finishes are permanent and some are not. Some involve recent industrial techniques and were not possible twenty or thirty years ago. As costumers concerned with constructing period costumes with an authentic feel, you should be aware that certain fabric finishes, particularly those that give the fabric drip-dry properties, will work against the period look and should be avoided.

Finishes for Luster

There are four major industrial finishing processes that create added luster on fabric surfaces. In *mercerization* the cotton fibers are treated with caustic soda, which causes the fibers to swell and straighten and present a smoother surface for light reflection. Cotton sewing threads are almost always mercerized for uniformity and strength, as well as for appearance. Linen and cotton fabrics are sometimes *beetled,* which means that the fibers are pounded and flattened out to reflect more light. In the process of *calendering,* fabric is run between rollers which are polished and heated and under pressure. Like beetling, this will produce a flatter, smoother fabric surface. Polished cottons and chintzes are produced by *glazing,* in which the shiny surface is caused by the addition of resins or gums, starches, or sugars. These fabrics hold their glaze for a long time but are not permanent.

3–D Effects

The *moiré* effect is achieved by running fabric between rollers that have been engraved with wavy, irregular designs. Heat and pressure transfer the design onto the fabric; the process is a variation of the calendering process. Silk moiré isn't permanent; the design will disappear if the fabric is washed and will even eventually disappear with wear. If the fabric is woven from heat-sensitive synthetic fibers, such as acetate or nylon, the pattern is actually melted into the surface of the fabric. The design becomes a part of the fabric and is absolutely permanent.

Crinkle effects are sometimes woven into fabric—as in seersucker—but often these puckers are added after weaving, as a finish. Chemicals are applied in stripes to plain weave fabrics. The fabric is then given an overall chemical application which causes the stripes to shrink and the untreated portions to crinkle. Chemically crinkled fabrics should be ironed lightly with a cool iron so the finish will not be harmed.

Embossed designs are raised from the fabric. They are achieved by sending the fabric through rollers on which a design has been carved. Since heat and pressure are used, the embossing will be quite permanent on the heat-sensitive synthetics and not quite so permanent on natural fabrics. Embossed fabrics should be laundered with care. It helps the life of the embossing to iron these fabrics on a thick pile towel, using more steam than pressure.

Flocking is achieved by painting designs on fabric with adhesive and then dusting short, fibrous particles over them. Flocked designs stand out from the fabric and are more or less permanent, depending on the kind and quality of the adhesive used.

Sizing

We generally assoicate the addition of sizing to fabric with a way of making inexpensive, loosely woven material temporarily appear to be smoother and have a higher thread count than it actually does. Additions of starch, gum, and resin sizings fill in the open spaces in the weave and stiffen the fabric. Most of these sizings will wash out; indeed, much will be lost through normal wear before washing. Permanent sizing is, however, possible and, in some cases, desirable. Organdy, for instance, can be made permanently crisp by an acid treatment. Organdy so treated may be expected to retain its body for the life of the garment into which it was placed, saving wardrobe personnel hours of starching.

Improving Performance

Shrinkage control is an important performance finish. There are many factors that affect shrinkage in fabrics: the original stability of the fiber, the amount of twist in the yarn, the type of weave, the yarn count, the other finishes that the fabric has undergone. Shrinkage control processes come under various trade names and are variously effective. Since it is almost impossible to prevent some additional shrinkage in preshrunk cottons and cotton blends, we have found the most trustworthy shrinkage control under labels that promise the fabric will not shrink more than another 1 percent. A 1 percent shrinkage will not affect the fit of most garments. Labels that merely read "preshrunk" promise nothing with regard to the fabric's future behavior in the wash tub.

Some fabrics that have a crease-resistant finish will not shrink noticeably until that finish has been damaged by wash water that is too hot, or by too vigorous agitation. Once the finish has broken down, the fabric will shrink "overnight."

By now you are beginning to see how many interrelated steps are involved in producing a length of fabric. Only if you understand something about these steps can you predict the fabric's behavior. Then, having purchased the fabric and constructed a costume from it, you must care for it in such a way that the fabric's behavior remains predictable.

Crease-resistant and Drip-dry Finishes

Chemical crease-resistant finishes may be given to linen, cotton, or rayon fabrics in order to increase the elasticity of the fibers, thus discouraging wrinkles. Either the yarns or the woven fabric may be impregnated with synthetic resins and gums. Most commonly used are phenol formaldehyde, urea formaldehyde, and acrylic resins. These chemicals give the fabric an elasticity that remains after washing and dry cleaning, if care is taken not to use excessively hot water or vigorous agitation. Fabrics treated with crease-resistant chemicals do have a smoother, shinier surface and, sometimes, a plastic-like sheen under stage lights. It is usually better to use fabrics that have not been treated with these chemicals, but there are occasions, such as touring, when the easy-care properties outweigh purely aesthetic considerations.

Knowing that these chemical crease-resistant finishes can, theoretically, be removed from a fabric by very hot water and vigorous agitation, you may be tempted to try to remove them on purpose. The results are not likely to be good. Either the chemical finish will prove to be impervious to your efforts, or you will be left with a limp, frizzy piece of fabric that has no body at all. Today's fabrics are the result of complex processes that impart properties one cannot easily, or predictably, alter.

Drip-dry, or permanent press finishes are much more permanent than crease-resistant finishes because the fabric or the ready-made garment is subjected to a heat curing process after being treated with chemicals. During this heat curing, trouser creases or skirt pleats are set permanently. Permanent press garments are simple to launder and, if properly dried, never need ironing. Puckering in the seams is generally from a fault in thread tension when the seam was sewn.

Some of the prominent permanent press trademarks are: Dan-Press, Koratron, Never-Press, Penn-Prest, and Primatized. Only cotton and some cotton and polyester blend fabrics are given permanent press finishes. Synthetic drip-dry or wash-and-wear fabrics have these properties because of the nature of the synthetic fiber involved.

Once permanent press, always permanent press seems to be a good dictum to remember. There is no use trying to iron a sharp crease into permanent press fabric and absolutely no way of removing one once it's there—at least not with the equipment normally found in costume shops. (We are reminded of a friend who purchased several pairs of permanent press men's work pants which she wished to turn into ragged cut-offs for a group of actors playing Mexican peasants. The pants were subjected to strenuous distressing; they were beaten, torn, and washed innumerable times. The final product was mottled in color, ragged at the leg, baggy and ripped in the pocket, but each pair of pants still retained its knife-sharp permanent press crease.)

It is difficult to remove stains from fabrics that have been treated with either crease-resistant or permanent press finishes. Oily stains are the most stubborn.

These finishes also tend to weaken cotton cloth noticeably. Polyester yarns are frequently mixed with cotton yarns in shirting-type fabrics in order to strengthen the cloth.

Napping

Napping is a finish that affects both appearance and performance. Little wire brushes are used to pull up fibers on one or both sides of a napped fabric. These raised fibers form a downy surface, changing both the look and the hand of the cloth. Napped fabrics are more crease resistant because the napping process increases fiber elasticity. Pile and napped fabrics are sometimes confused and it may be difficult to tell them apart without close examination.

Napping is only possible when some loosely twisted yarns are included in the weave. These loose yarns may weaken the fabric and the napped surface hides the original yarns so well that it's often difficult to determine quality. Most napping will wear down eventually, but low quality napped fabric will wear quickly, particularly if the material is subjected to abrasion. Of the two similar appearing fabrics, pile and nap, pile fabrics are the most durable.

Flameproofing

Costumers are often called upon to flameproof costumes. Each state in the United States has laws stating what must be flameproofed in public theatres. Stage scenery is usually required to be flameproof, but, except in extraordinary circumstances, costumes are not. Flameproofing costumes is usually a matter of common sense safety. If, for example, an actor in a flowing garment must pass close to a torch or a candle, the costumer should be requested to flameproof the garment.

Most dry cleaners can apply a flame-retardant finish to garments, but this is expensive and it is possible to accomplish it yourself, at least with washable fabrics. Following directions issued by the United States Department of Agriculture, purchase three ounces of boric acid and seven ounces of borax from a drugstore. Dissolve these in two quarts of warm water. The fabric must be completely soaked in this solution; when it is thoroughly dry, it will not support flames. This finish has to be reapplied after each laundering or dry cleaning. The solution can be applied with a spray gun if the garment cannot be laid in it, but it must be sprayed until the fabric is saturated.

Some high luster fabrics will be somewhat dulled by a flameproofing finish and some very light fabrics will be stiffened. Nevertheless, safety is paramount in instances where fireproofing is called for. Furs and fabrics that will be harmed by water must be sent to a professional for flameproofing.

MAN-MADE AND SYNTHETIC FABRICS

So far, it may seem that little more has been said about the man-made and synthetic fabrics than a warning against them. However, you cannot avoid using them altogether, so you should use them as creatively as possible. The key is knowing enough about the fabric to make the best choice. Any fabric may be unsatisfactory when put to the wrong use.

The term "man-made" refers to those cellulose fibers made from a natural base: sea weed, wood pulp, end pickings of cotton, wood, or milk. Those fibers that are produced from chemical combinations of hydrogen, nitrogen, oxygen, and carbon are called synthetic. Only the most commonly used synthetic and man-made fibers will be discussed here. Many of the others have very specialized uses that don't relate to costuming; more are being developed every day.

Rayon, Acetate, and Triacetate

Rayon, acetate, and triacetate are familiar man-made fabrics. Rayon was first produced in 1884 by Count Hilaire de Chardonnet and was referred to, for about fifty years, as artificial silk. In the years after it went on the market, rayon was widely used as linings, ribbons, lingerie, and rather limp, sometimes sleazy, yardgoods. Rayon was not important in good quality dressmaking until the late 1930s after the discovery of wrinkle-resistant resins.

Rayon yarns may be either filament or spun. Spun rayon yarns can be made to resemble cotton, linen, or wool; filament yarns can resemble silk.

Rayon fibers are weaker than cotton, linen, or silk. They are extremely absorbent, but the cloth loses seventy percent of its strength when wet. Wet rayon must be handled carefully so as not to damage the fabric. Shrinkage is approximately the same as cotton. Rayon has very little elasticity and creases readily. The fabric does drape nicely and takes dyes, especially the brighter colors, very well.

Wool and rayon blend fabrics can be good choices for costumes. They have the look of wool and are much less expensive. This is a case where one may weigh economy against durability, sacrifice a measure of durability, and still be satisfied with the economical choice. Rayon and silk blends are also satisfactory money-saving purchases. Fine quality rayon linings are preferred for tailored suits and wool dresses.

Acetate is made from the same raw materials as rayon, but the chemical process is entirely different. It was developed in England, in 1918, by Henri and Camille Dreyfus. Some American trade names are: Acele, Celacloud, Celacrimp, Celafil, Celaloft (and several other sound-alike names from Celanese Corporation of America), Estron, and Loftura.

Unlike rayon, acetate is thermoplastic, a property it shares with most of the synthetics. Thermoplastic fabrics are softened by the application of heat and can be pressed into particular shapes. This property permits permanent embossing or moiréing. Creases and pleats may be heat set into the fabric.

Acetate fabrics are more elastic than rayon and therefore wrinkles hang out. Unfortunately, the fabrics are weak and have especially poor abrasion resistance. Although many popular linings are woven from acetate yarns, rayon linings are usually more satisfactory.

Triacetate is related to acetate and is produced by the Celanese Corporation of America under the trade name Arnel. Triacetate is stronger than acetate, although it is still a relatively weak fiber. At one time sharkskin made from triacetate was very popular for tennis dresses; it has current wide use in knit fabrics.

Nylon

Nylon was discovered by Du Pont chemists in 1935. It was first announced in 1938, and on May 15, 1940, nylon hosiery went on sale in the United States. Nylon was the first synthetic fiber and its development marked the beginning of a fabric revolution.

Nylon fibers are transparent, and early nylon fabric was glassy in appearance. Delustering processes have permitted the nylon fiber to become more opaque and silk-like. Nylon is the leading yarn for lingerie and hosiery. It is strong and sheer; it stretches and returns to shape; it dries easily. Next to fiberglas, nylon is the strongest of all fibers. Costume shops depend on nylon net for stiffening, on nylon slipstitch thread, and on "horsehair"

made from nylon, as well as on nylon tights, stockings, and underwear.

Sweaters knitted from nylon yarn are not recommended. Besides causing the actor to feel hot and steamy when under stage lights, nylon sweaters pill badly. Suiting that is blended from 10% to 15% nylon yarn and the remainder from wool will be stronger than 100% wool and much lighter. This is a satisfactory fabric for the stage.

Polyester

The polyester fiber was developed in England between 1939 and 1942; it was marketed under the trade name Terylene. Du Pont introduced polyester into this country, calling it Dacron. Other American trade names include: Avlin, Fortrel, Kodel, Trevira, and Vycron.

Polyesters have excellent wrinkle resistance. Essentially permanent creases may be ironed in but, except in instances when a baked-in, drip-dry finish has been added, these creases may be removed by home or industrial steam irons. Polyester fibers are very strong and retain their strength, as well as their wrinkle-resistant properties, even when wet.

Polyester fabrics breathe somewhat better than the other synthetics, although they have very poor absorbency. The common cotton/polyester blend of 65% polyester and 35% cotton that is used for a wide variety of shirt fabrics is relatively pleasant to wear. The polyester gives the fabric easy-care properties and the cotton provides absorbency. When there is much less polyester than cotton in the fabric, a drip-dry finish is often added, causing the surface to be somewhat shiny and less desirable for the stage.

A wool and polyester suit fabric will have outstanding wrinkle resistance and crease retention. It is about the same price as 100% wool.

Acrylic

Du Pont perfected acrylic fiber in 1944 and, in May, 1950, began production of Orlon. Other trade names for acrylics are Acrilan, Dynel, Creslan, and Verel.

The thermoplastic properties of acrylic fibers have brought the process of heat setting to perfection. Once a garment made from knitted acrylic yarns is set into shape, it is virtually impossible to alter that shape.

The acrylic fiber is very bulky and can be spun into remarkably wool-like yarn. You may be fooled by the appearance of acrylic sweaters, mistaking them for wool—that is, until you feel them. Acrylic sweaters may look like wool and may hold their shape better than wool, but they do not breathe and they are not absorbent. (We once put an actor in a long tunic constructed from an acrylic knit. The knit had been chosen because it was a stunning color. The actor remained less than pleased about his costume as he left the stage after each performance, soaking wet beneath it, red-faced, and puffing.) The insulation provided by acrylic fibers might be nice for ski wear but it's not pleasant on stage.

The acrylics find their way into costume shops most often in the form of fake furs. It is extraordinary to go into a shop where fake furs are sold today. The variety is remarkable and the quality is getting better all the time. Realistic fake furs are quite expensive, however, and the cheaper ones do tend to have a skimpy pile and look rather plastic. Often, when you are searching for a relatively rare fur—ocelot, for example—you will. be able to find a perfectly suitable fake. Fake furs are made from other synthetic fibers, but acrylics are most often used for this purpose.

SOME GENERAL DISADVANTAGES OF SYNTHETIC FABRICS

Absorbency

None of the synthetic fabrics absorb moisture well. Since most of them are not good conductors of heat either, the fabrics are generally uncomfortable to wear under powerful theatrical lights. Wool, although very warm, does breathe and absorb moisture, thus allowing the actor's perspiration to evaporate rather than being trapped on the skin. Some blends of synthetic and natural fibers will result in fabrics that are both handsome and cool to wear on stage, but the general lack of absorbency of the synthetics is a factor that should be considered when you are purchasing fabrics.

Static Electricity

Static electricity builds up in all the synthetic fabrics, but especially in polyester. The presence of static electricity causes the fabric to cling to the body and disturbs the hang of the garment. A static-free finish is sometimes applied at the factory. Ordinary fabric softener in the washing machine or dryer can help if the fabric is washable, but neither of these methods is foolproof. (We recall seeing a production in which men's suits from the 1930s had been built from a fabric that contained synthetic fibers. The trouser legs clung to the actor's socks most unbecomingly and absolutely shattered the scene's authenticity.)

Pilling

All synthetic fabrics have a tendency to pill, that is, for little balls of fiber ends to collect on the fabric's surface. This is more pronounced in the wool-like fabrics but is common to all. Natural fabrics also pill, but the fiber balls break off and are brushed away;

the synthetic fibers are so strong and dense that the balls remain on the fabric surface.

Stains

Waterborne stains wash easily out of synthetic fabrics because they do not penetrate the fibers but lie on top of the fabric. These fabrics do pick up oily stains, which are difficult to remove because the fabrics' lack of absorbency keeps waterborne detergents from getting at the soil to emulsify it and take it away. Dry-cleaning solvents remove oily stains sometimes but not always. A "cold-spotting" treatment may be effective: Work a *strong* solution of detergent into the spot with a sponge or brush. Rinse in cold water. Be sure to manipulate the spotted area thoroughly or until the water is clear. Then wash in the regular manner.

BURN-TESTING FOR FIBER IDENTIFICATION

It is possible to identify the natural, manmade, and synthetic fibers in a fairly reliable manner by burning a snip of fabric and observing the behavior of the flame and the character of the residue. This test doesn't work for blends and mixtures, although it's always possible to determine if synthetic fibers are present, even if you can't identify the particular kind. In addition to the burn test, one can test for acetate by placing a piece of fabric in a dish of acetone (nail polish remover). Acetate fibers will disintegrate.

FIBER BURN-TESTING CHART

Fiber	Reaction to Flame
Cellulose fibers cotton, linen, rayon	Burns quickly with a bright flame Continues to glow after flame is removed Smells like burning paper Leaves a soft, gray ash
Protein fibers silk, wool	Burns slowly, sizzles Curls away from the flame Self-extinguishing after flame is removed Smells like burning hair or feathers Leaves a crushable, gray ash
Acetate	Burns and melts in flame Burns and melts after flame is removed May smell like vinegar when burning Leaves a hard, brittle, black bead
Nylon	Shrinks away from flame Burns slowly and melts Self-extinguishing when removed from flame Smells like celery when burning Leaves a hard, gray bead
Polyester	Shrinks away from flame Burns slowly

Fiber	Reaction to Flame
Polyester (cont.)	Gives off black smoke Usually self-extinguishing when removed from flame Smells slightly sweet when burning Leaves a hard, black bead
Acrylics	Burns and melts in flame Burns and melts after flame is removed Leaves a hard, brittle, black bead

FIBERGLAS—A WARNING

Fiberglas is the trade name for a synthetic fiber used, among other things, to make drapery fabric. Under no circumstances should Fiberglas fabric be used in a costume that will come in touch with an actor's skin. It is very irritating and many people develop violent allergic reactions to Fiberglas.

COMMON COSTUME FABRICS

Bedford Cloth or Bedford Cord

Bedford cloth is a special weave with prominent vertical cords. It is a firmly woven, hard-wearing fabric, used extensively for riding breeches and also suitable for suits and skirts. Traditionally, it is woven from wool, cotton, or wool and cotton yarns; it is also now woven from man-made spun yarns.

Calico

Calico is a plain weave, smooth surface, cotton cloth. The name once referred to a wide assortment of basic cotton fabrics in bleached white, plain colors, stripes, or printed styles. Now the term usually means a cotton fabric with a bright, sharply contrasting, usually small print design of the sort that is popular for patchwork. Remember the different appearances of calico when you encounter the word in period costume sources.

Canvas (duck, sailcloth)

Canvas is a strong, heavy, usually plain weave fabric. Ordinarily it is made of cotton but sometimes it has synthetic yarns mixed in. Canvas is heavier than duck or sailcloth, although these three names are often used interchangeably. Duck, sailcloth, or light-weight canvas make excellent interlinings for stout, period bodices.

Challis

Challis is a soft, light-weight, plain weave fabric, traditionally printed with vivid floral patterns on a dark background or with a paisley design. The loveliest challis is woven from wool; it may also be made from cotton or rayon. Wool challis is quite expensive.

Chiffon

Chiffon is a soft, flimsy, very light-weight, plain weave fabric. Silk chiffon moves, drapes, and flows exquisitely and is expensive. Nylon and polyester chiffons are cheaper, stiffer, and much less flexible. If budgetary pressures force one to use synthetic chiffon, soaking the fabric in a strong solution of fabric softener will enhance its draping qualities. This finish is, of course, only temporary.

Corduroy

Corduroy is a familiar ribbed pile fabric made of cotton or of polyester and cotton. Originally made as a very tough, durable fabric for work clothes, it is now produced in medium and light weights for fashion wear. Corduroy is inexpensive and widely used in costume construction. We aren't enchanted with corduroy in most period costumes. No matter what you do to corduroy, it still looks like corduroy; and before the turn of the century, that's the wrong look.

Crepe

Crepe is the term used to describe the crinkled surface given to certain dress fabrics. The effect may be achieved by using high-twist creped yarns, by a special weaving process, by a chemical process, or, on thermoplastic fabrics, by embossing. The surface of a crepe fabric has depth and interest. Wool crepe is magnificent and rayon crepe is highly satisfactory, particularly for bias-cut dresses.

Crêpe de Chine

Originally, crêpe de Chine referred to a fine silk woven in a plain weave with a soft twisted warp and a tightly twisted filling where the yarns alternate between the S and the Z twist. The tight filling yarns cause the crinkle. A cheaper blend of crêpe de Chine with rayon filling yarns and acetate warp was widely used for lingerie before the widespread use of nylon tricot. This fabric is still produced for linings.

Denim

Denim is a twill weave fabric that always used to be woven with a dark-colored warp and a white filling. The normal warp color was dark blue and the fabric was used for heavy duty work clothes. Now denim has become widely accepted for fashion garments and is produced in a wide variety of weights and colors. It is made of cotton or a cotton and polyester blend. The blends are quite stiff, whereas cotton denim, once it is well washed, has a nice drape.

Drill

Drill is a handsome, strong, hardwearing fabric that is similar to denim but better in quality and smoother in appearance. It is made in a twill weave or a satin weave. In white or khaki, it is used for uniforms and tropical wear. Bush jackets, for example, are usually made from drill. The best drill is made from cotton, but it is also woven in synthetic blends.

Faille

Faille is a semi-lustrous, plain weave fabric with a pronounced crosswise rib. Originally, it was made from silk but it is now made from rayon and acetate as well. Ottoman is a smiliar fabric in which the ribs are wider. Faille is used as a dress fabric, in linings, and to face lapels in dress suits. A good faille has excellent weight and drapes beautifully.

Flannel

Flannel is a soft, plain weave fabric with a napped surface. Wool flannel is soft and full to the touch and drapes well. It is traditional for men's casual trousers.

Flannelette

Flannelette is a thin cotton version of flannel, napped on both sides and widely used in making sleepwear. It may also be woven in a cotton and synthetic blend.

Gabardine

Gabardine is a twill weave fabric with a tight, hard surface that may come in light, medium, or heavy weights. Traditionally made of wool, it is now made from nearly every fiber. It is very popular for rainwear. Drill and gabardine are often difficult to distinguish from each other.

Gingham

Gingham is a traditional cotton fabric woven in a plain weave with yarn-dyed checks, stripes, or plaids. Some people use the name gingham to refer only to the checked variety. Today, ginghams are woven from a variety of cotton and synthetic blends and some may have printed rather than woven patterns.

Grosgrain

Grosgrain is a wonderful plain weave fabric with prominent, rounded ribs. It is most familiar in ribbons but is also available in wider fabrics, although these are seldom wider than 36 inches. A variety of grosgrain with larger ribs is used for academic gowns. Grosgrain was once made entirely of silk but it is exceptionally expensive in this form. A satisfactory sort is made from a rayon or acetate warp and a cotton filling. Although it can be difficult to find, except in large cities, grosgrain is an excellent fabric for period costumes.

Jersey

The proper definition of jersey is a single knit fabric with plain stitches on the right side and purl stitches on the wrong side. The term is often wrongly used to mean any knitted fabric. Wool jerseys are the fabric of choice for Greek and Roman costumes, with the less expensive rayon jersey a not-so-satisfactory second choice.

Linen

Linen is the name of a fabric as well as a fiber. Linen fabric was once made exclusively from fibers derived from the flax plant, but now linen is combined with a variety of man-made and synthetic fibers to improve its wrinkle resistance. Linen yarns may be somewhat irregular, giving interest to the fabric surface. Linen can be woven in a variety of weights. It is a virtual necessity for garments from the late nineteenth- and early twentieth-century periods: motoring coats, skirts, men's summer jackets, and so forth.

Melton Cloth

Melton cloth is a woolen coating fabric with a soft, nondirectional nap. Usually it has a twill weave, although the weave is hidden by the nap. Originally, it was made from wool or wool and cotton but nowadays, man-made and synthetic fibers may be added. The lighter weights are excellent for uniforms.

Organdy

Organdy is a thin, translucent, originally all-cotton fabric, woven in a plain weave and treated to a special finish that gives it the characteristic stiff finish. The addition of permanent press finishes and synthetic yarns has removed the basic objection to organdy: its tendency to crease and wrinkle. This is an instance where the wrinkle-resistant version is preferable to the all-cotton original.

Poplin

Poplin is a very closely woven fabric with a fine horizontal rib. Most poplin is made from cotton but some are woven from cotton and synthetic blends. It has a crisp feel and a somewhat lustrous look and is an important fabric for nineteenth-century women's skirts and suits.

Sateen

Sateen is a strong, lustrous, satin weave fabric made of cotton. The weave is a filling-faced version of satin—that is, the filling yarns are on the right side, whereas in the satin weave the warp threads are on the right side. Sateen is most commonly used as a lining fabric and is excellent for this purpose.

Satin

The term refers both to the basic weave and to a group of fabrics woven in that manner. There are several important types of satin:

Antique satin—a satin weave fabric that can be used on either side. The right side is a smooth, lustrous surface; the wrong side looks a bit like shantung. Antique satin is usually purchased in a drapery shop and is good for period costumes.

Crepe-backed satin—a fabric that has a smooth, satin side and a crepe side. Lighter weight than antique satin. Excellent fabric for coat and jacket linings.

Double-faced satin—a satin fabric that has the satin appearance on both sides. Dress-weight fabric.

Duchesse satin—one of the heaviest and richest looking satins. Widely used for wedding gowns.

Slipper satin—an exceptionally tightly woven satin, lighter in weight than duchesse satin. Used, among other things, for evening shoes and slippers.

Serge

Serge is one of the basic suiting fabrics. It has a firm, compact twill weave. Tradition-ally, it was a hard-wearing woolen, but today the wool is often blended with synthetic fibers.

Shantung

Shantung is a plain weave fabric with a rough texture caused by irregularities in the yarn. Originally, it was made from silk, but it is terribly expensive in this form. Moderately priced shantung is made from synthetic yarns which have been deliberately made irregular. Shantung is a texturally interesting fabric on stage, but it does not wear well.

Silk

There are several silk fabrics which should be identified:

China silk—a lightweight, relatively inexpensive silk fabric used chiefly for linings.

Pongee—a fairly light-weight silk fabric with a slight irregularity in the yarns.

Raw silk—a term incorrectly used to mean wild silk. Raw silk is covered with a glue-like substance which must be removed before the filaments can be woven.

Shantung (see section above)

Surah—a silk fabric that can be recognized by its twill weave and high sheen.

Thai silk—silk made in Thailand. Of fairly heavy weight, often slubbed, and woven in brilliant colors which are iridescent.

Tie silk—silk fabric used for making men's neckties.

Tussah—silk fabric woven from silk made by wild, uncultivated silkworms. Naturally tan in color, it cannot be bleached and it has a rougher texture than cultivated silk. The best possible fabric for constructing all sorts of peasant or beggar rags. There is no other cloth that ages so well or so convincingly. (Even though it is technically incorrect to do so, this fabric is called raw silk.)

Taffeta

Originally, a taffeta was a plain weave, silk fabric with a stiff feel; it produced a rustling noise (called scroop) when worn as a skirt or petticoat. Now it is more commonly woven from rayon or acetate. There are several common sorts of taffeta:

Antique taffeta—a stiff fabric made to resemble eighteenth-century fabrics. It is often iridescent.

Faille taffeta—taffeta woven with a prominent crosswise rib, as in faille.

Moiré taffeta—this is the most common moiré fabric. The moiré design is produced by passing the fabric through engraved rollers. If the fabric is thermoplastic, the design is permanent; if not, it will wash out or wear out.

Paper taffeta—a very light in weight, very crisp taffeta that makes a sound like rustling paper.

Velvet

Velvet is a fabric with a short, closely woven pile. Velvet can be woven perfectly plain or a figured design can be produced by weaving pile patterns or by cutting or shearing some of the pile into designs. Panne velvet is produced by crushing part of the pile in different directions.

Velvet comes in different qualities. Silk velvet is the finest but it is terrifically expensive; high quality rayon velvet may be beautifully dense and lustrous; nylon velvet is generally a bit skimpy and looks fake. It is well to check the base cloth beneath the pile before you purchase a piece of velvet. If it is inferior, the fabric may hang poorly, slip at the seams, or wear out before it should.

Velveteen

Velveteen is a term that once differentiated between velvet, in which the pile was made with the warp threads, and a similar fabric with its pile formed from filling threads. Today, velveteen refers almost exclusively to a cotton pile fabric which, for the purposes of costuming, can be an entirely satisfactory substitute for velvet. The single exception to this is the color black. Black velveteen is never rich enough nor black enough to read properly from the stage.

Velour

Velour is a knit or woven fabric with a thick, short pile. Velours have a rich look and may be substituted for velvet or velveteen.

Whipcord

Whipcord is a strong, twill weave fabric usually made from cotton or wool worsted. Whipcord is heavier than gabardine, which it resembles. It is used for uniforms and riding clothes or wherever a sturdy fabric is desired.

3

Pattern Development

There is nothing unusually difficult or unduly mysterious about learning to develop a garment pattern or to cut out fabric pattern pieces. Yet many costume technicians feel uncertain about their cutting and patterning skills. Student costumers complain that their training in cutting and pattern development is slighted. Many feel that the ability to cut well is an innate talent which one is either born with or must live without. Although it is true that some people do have a natural ability to develop garment patterns and that some technicians will always be better cutters than others, the basic drafting and draping skills can be learned by every serious student of costuming. Each costume technician ought to be secure in his or her own ability to draft and drape slopers (basic pattern blocks) and to shape them into patterns for any garments costume designers might conceive.

Fine patterning requires the costume technician to have a combination of technical skills, craftsmanship, and artistry. The technical aspects of drafting and draping must be thoroughly learned and rigorously practiced. The craftsmanship necessary to carry out each drafting or draping project is largely a matter of using the hands well. Some people are naturally skillful with their hands; others may have to cultivate craftsmanship. The artistry is revealed in the ability to render the design pattern with precise attention to proportion, seam placement, and dart placement, translating the small drawing into a vibrant, life-size version. Artistry, like craftsmanship, comes more naturally to some people than to others, yet it can be developed in everyone.

The primary goals of garment patterning are to manipulate a flat piece of cloth in such a way that it conforms to the curves of the human body, allows for adequate body movements, and meets with contemporary style requirements. To achieve these ends, the cloth may be cut, draped, seamed, or shaped with steam. No matter what fashion silhouette is required, the basic goals remain constant; only the means of reaching these goals differ, resulting in what is called the "period look." For example, many methods of fabric manipulation have been employed to shape a garment over the female bust: Darts, gathers, curved seams, tucks, shirring, drawstrings, and elastic, occurring singly or in combination, can create the necessary fullness. Style dictates the method. Once the pattern cutter learns how to manipulate one basic solution to the bust-shaping problem, however, all the other methods become variations on the original solution, not singular, unrelated problems. That is to say, if you can execute a pattern for a bodice front with conventional waist and bust darts, you can then use that basic bodice solution to accomplish any of the others.

Because a great many costume shops (both academic and professional) depend on commercial paper patterns, either in their entirety or as a starting point, for period costumes, technicians often do not have the opportunity to develop their own patterning skills. Whereas commercial paper patterns can be valuable time savers in certain situations, which will be mentioned later, their general use in a costume shop is not recommended. The costumer who relies on commercial paper patterns for most shapes will always be limited in what he or she can cut.

There are a few costume books on the market making the claim that theatrical costumes from all periods can be successfully cut from a small selection of basic pattern shapes. If the costumer's goal is the creation of a specific design for a specific actor, such a simplified approach will not be suitable. Clothing shapes change constantly in the busy history of fashion, and no two human bodies are identical. Basic patterns cannot incorporate the subtleties of shape and fit that distinguish a fine stage costume.

WHERE TO BEGIN

There are two approaches to developing period costume patterns. One approach begins with the garment, the other with the actor's body. A widely used example of the first approach is the practice of selecting period patterns from pattern research books, drawing them out on muslin or on brown paper (often using an opaque projector to enlarge the pattern onto a piece of paper or cloth), and then grading the pattern size up and/or down so that it finally corresponds to the actor's measurements. Very handsome costumes may result from this patterning method, but the process is often accompanied by serious fitting problems. Period patterns that have been taken directly from period garments are not easily adaptable to contemporary bodies that are heavier, taller, broader of shoulder, and longer of limb than bodies used to be.

A few recent period pattern books, principally *The Evolution of Fashion* by Hill and Bucknell, present period patterns that have been adapted to modern bodies, incorporating standard sizes. These patterns may be drafted up in the size given and graded up or down for the individual actor. Proper fitting remains the central problem. A standard size 10 dress in a relatively simple, contemporary style will fit a great many women who are all somewhat different in shape. This is not true of a snug, boned, multi-pieced seventeenth-century bodice. And, there is no such thing as a standard size 40-regular Elizabethan doublet. The more complex the fashion shape, the more pronounced will be the individual fitting problems.

When the costume pattern is approached by way of the actor's own body, rather than by beginning with a period pattern, major fitting problems can be solved early in the process. There are costume cutters who have the technical training, the skill, and the native ability to cut a garment pattern—even a very complicated garment pattern—directly from the actor's measurements. Haute couture fashion courses teach this approach to cutting, and some theatrical cutters simply learn to do it after a great deal of experience in cutting many different periods. In most cases, it takes rather a long time and a significant amount of experience to learn to work this way.

The approach described in this chapter begins with a basic body block—either drafted from the actor's measurements or draped on a dummy that is very close to the actor's size. Using period patterns as research tools, the costume cutter can then shift seamlines and fullness, working from the basic block, in order to achieve the period shape required by the design. A correct fit will not be the major problem, and attention can be turned to the fine details of cut that distinguish an outstanding stage costume. Naturally, final fitting adjustments will never be wholly eliminated, but they certainly ought to be minor

ones if the original body block has been properly cut, stitched, and fitted to the actor, and if the pattern construction steps are carried out carefully.

There are only a few hard and fast rules for developing costume patterns. Each cutter has his or her own individual ways of solving patterning problems. Neither the basic approach nor the specific methods that follow are meant to be read as the only, or even the best, ways of working for everyone. Nevertheless, it is necessary to begin somewhere.

The following section contains detailed, illustrated instructions for drafting a male and a female body block and instructions for stitching and fitting muslin slopers. Then there are several examples of ways to move from the basic sloper to the specific garment pattern. The torso is the most difficult portion of the human body to fit; once you have mastered a way of cutting bodices, doublets, and jackets, you will find that sleeves, collars, skirts, and even pants, are simpler problems. The latter portion of this chapter contains a one-piece sleeve block and a two-piece sleeve variation, a discussion of commercial paper patterns, and hints for cutting fabric.

CREATING BASIC SLOPERS

Only six measurements are needed to draft a male body block and eight measurements for the female version. With a little practice, you will be able to compute and draw out the lines in about twenty minutes. In another twenty minutes you can trace the lines onto a piece of muslin and construct the muslin sloper. Twenty minutes worth of fitting and pattern adjustment and you are ready to move on to the garment pattern. If you work in a situation in which you construct many different costumes for the same actor, this hour spent on the body sloper will not have to be repeated, and you will have a basic

form from which much of the cutting for that actor can be done.

The muslin sloper is not in itself a garment; it is a representation of the body constructed with a minimum of garment ease. After doing a half dozen body slopers, you will have grown much more sensitive to body differences and to what changes occur in the pattern shapes to allow for such variations as narrow or sloping shoulders, a large bust, or a curved back. If the cutting problem includes women's bodices that will be worn over a corset, measure the actor in the corset and draft up a sloper to fit the corseted body.

Measurements for the Body Block

To take correct measurements with which to draft the body block, you will need a flexible tape measure and three lengths of narrow ribbon or cording. You may measure an actor who is wearing a lightweight shirt or blouse, although the beginner might find it instructive to have the actor clad only in undergarments or a leotard. Any bulky clothing should be removed and all pockets should be emptied. A small-busted woman can be measured without a brassiere, but a large-busted woman should wear a simple, support bra, not one that gives her an extreme uplift. If the bust is to be uplifted for a particular period garment, such as one from the 1950s, this adjustment can be made in the garment pattern. Make sure the actor is standing firmly on both feet, head erect, arms hanging loosely to each side, and abdominal muscles relaxed.

Tie one piece of the ribbon or cording firmly around the natural waist. The natural waistline lies approximately midway between the bottom of the ribcage and the top of the hipbone. Pass another piece of ribbon or cording under each arm and tie on top of the shoulder. (See Figure 3.1 for correct placement of these markers.)

Take snug measurements but do not draw the tape measure too tight. The chest or bust measurement should come straight around the back and across the most prominent portion of the chest or bust. The waist measurement should follow the position of the waist

FIGURE 3.1   *Body block measurements: (a) ribbons tied around armscye and waist; (b) bust/chest; (c) waist; (d) back nape to waist; (e) neck to shoulder; (f) center of shoulder to bust point; (g) bust point to bust point; (h) front width; (i) back width.*

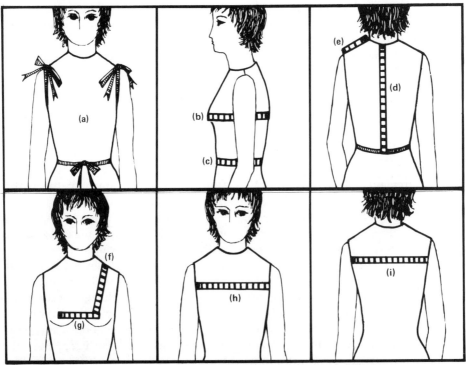

(a) Ribbons tied around armscye and waist	(b) Bust/chest	(d) Back nape to waist
(f) Center of shoulder to bust point	(c) Waist	(e) Neck to shoulder
(g) Bust point to bust point	(h) Front width	(i) Back width

tape. Begin the nape to waist measurement at the top of the most prominent cervical vertebra. The neck to shoulder measurement should begin just at the base of the neck and continue out to the armscye marker. Begin the shoulder to bust point measurement at the exact center of the neck to shoulder measurement. The front width should extend across the upper chest, approximately halfway between the base of the armscye and the top of the shoulder; the back width at the same place across the back. The front bust point to bust point measurement (which, along with the shoulder to bust point measurement, are not taken on men) is self-explanatory.

Never rush when taking measurements. These measurements must be taken accurately in order for the sloper to fit.

Drawing the Body Block

Read through all the directions for drafting the body block before beginning. Note carefully the two charts which you will use to determine the depth of the bust dart and the width of the waist dart.

Use heavy brown wrapping paper or squared pattern drafting paper for drawing the block. The first time you draw a body block, proceed slowly, checking each measurement. As the steps become familiar to you, your speed will pick up considerably. The neckline and the bottom half of the armscye will be "eyeballed," that is, drawn in freehand. Refer to the illustrations for the shapes of these curves. Until you have more experience drawing the shape of these curves, draw them too shallow rather than too deep. It's easy to trim excess fabric away in the fitting and not so easy to replace it.

The paper block will constitute a permanent record, once it has been adjusted from fitting the muslin sloper. In a shop where many costumes will be cut for the same actor, it is advantageous to transfer the altered paper shape to a more durable cardboard or tagboard.

DRAFTING A FEMALE BODY BLOCK FROM INDIVIDUAL MEASUREMENTS

Tools Needed

24" ruler or yardstick
12" ruler
right angle
pencil
heavy paper or cardboard

Measurements Required*

1. bust
2. waist
3. back nape to waist
4. neck to shoulder

SCALES FOR DETERMINING SIZES OF BODY DARTS

Depth of Bust Dart[a]	Width of Waist Dart[b]
30½–32" bust = ½"	4– 5½" difference = ½"
32½–34" bust = ¾"	6– 7½" difference = ¾"
34½–36" bust = 1"	8– 9½" difference = 1"
36½–38" bust = 1½"	10–11½" difference = 1¼"
38½–40" bust = 1¾"	12–13½" difference = 1½"
40½–42" bust = 2"	14–15½" difference = 1¾"
42½–44" bust = 2½"	
And so on!*	

[a] If the person is especially heavy busted, make dart deeper by ½"; further adjustments to be made in fitting.
[b] Waist dart sizes are determined by the difference between bust and waist measurements.

* Expand fractional measurements to the next ½" measurement; for example, 33¼" becomes 33½" and 18¾" becomes 19".

5. center of shoulder to bust point
6. front width
7. back width
8. bust point to bust point

Measurements used for the female body block sample drafted in Figures 3.2(a)–3.2(n) are as follows:

1. bust—36"
2. waist—24"
3. back nape to waist—16"
4. neck to shoulder—4½"
5. center of shoulder to bust point—9"
6. front width—12"
7. back width—13"
8. bust point to bust point—7½"

   bust dart = 1"
   waist darts = 1½"
   scale: one square = 1"

Draw a Rectangle

The length of A–B and C–D is the back nape to waist measurement, *plus* the *depth* of the bust dart. Example:

nape to waist	16"
36" bust requires a 1" deep bust dart	1"
length of A–B and C–D	17"

The length of A–C and B–D is one-half the total bust measurement, *plus* ½". Example:

The bust measurement is 36".

The length of A–C and B–D is *18½"*.

Add Construction Lines

• Divide A–C and B–D in half and draw a vertical line E–F.

• From points A and C, measure down one-quarter of the back nape to waist measurement. Connect these two points, forming a horizontal line, G–H. G–H is the front and back width line.

• From points G and H, measure down the same distance again (one-quarter of the back nape to waist measurement). Con-

FIGURE 3.2a   *Drafting a female body block.*

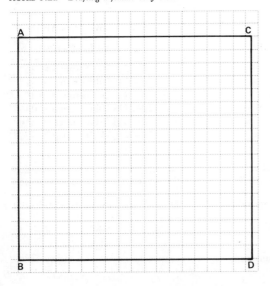

FIGURE 3.2b   *Drafting a female body block (cont.).*

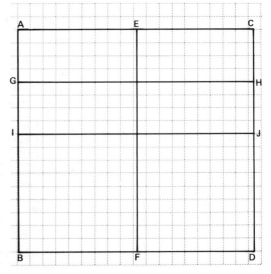

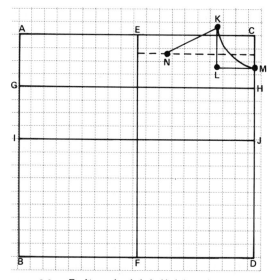

FIGURE 3.2c *Drafting a female body block* (cont.).

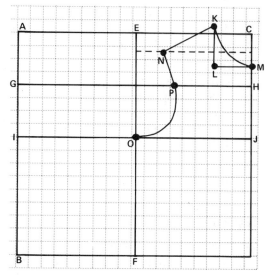

FIGURE 3.2d *Drafting a female body block* (cont.).

nect these two points, forming a horizontal line, I–J. I–J is the chest line.

Now the front and back of the female body block can be drafted. You *must* begin with the front section.

FRONT SECTION

Neck and Shoulder

- 3" to the left, and ½" up from C, mark K.
- 3" down from K, mark L.
- 2½" down from C, mark M.
- Connect K to L and L to M with straight lines; then draw in the neck curve from K to M.
- 1⅜" below the E–C line, draw a horizontal dotted line.
- Draw front shoulder line by placing a ruler with one end on K and angling it to hit the dotted line at exactly the neck to shoulder measurement.

- Mark N at this point and join K to N with a straight line.

Armhole

- Mark O on the I–J line at the point where it *crosses* the E–F line. O is the base of the armhole. To the left of H, measure half the front width measurement and mark P. Connect N to P with a straight line, and P to O with a curve to complete the armhole.*

Waist

- To the left of D, measure one quarter

* Refer to the accompanying illustration for the general shape of the armhole curve. Do not make the curve too deep. Final adjustments will be made in the muslin fitting.

of the total waist measurement, *plus* ¼",
plus the width of the front waist dart,
and mark Q. Example:

The waist measurement is 24"; the bust
  measurement is 36".
¼ the waist measurement   6"
plus width of waist dart cal-
  culated from preceding chart   1½"
plus   ¼"
                              D–Q = 7¾"

- Q is the base point for the side seam.

Bust Point Line

- To the left of D, measure in half the
  total bust point to bust point measurement and draw a vertical line up to
  the O–J line. This line will be the center
  of the front waist dart.
- Find the center of the shoulder line (K–
  N) and mark R.
- Place a ruler with one end on R and angle
  it so that it hits the line just drawn at
  exactly the shoulder to bust point measurement. This is S, the bust point.

- Draw a dotted line, horizontal to O–J,
  out to lines E–F and C–D. This is the
  bust point line.

Bust Dart

- To the left of the bust point, toward the
  E–F line, measure ½" from the bust
  point and mark T for the point of the
  bust dart.
- On the E–F line, measure down from the
  bust point line the *total* depth of the bust
  dart and mark it U.
- Connect T and U with a straight line.
  This is the center line of the bust dart.
- On the E–F line, measure out one-half
  the total bust dart depth on each side
  of U.
- Connect each of these marks with the
  bust dart point to complete the dart.

Side Seam

- Measure the length of the top line of
  the bust dart.

FIGURE 3.2e   *Drafting a female body block (cont.).*

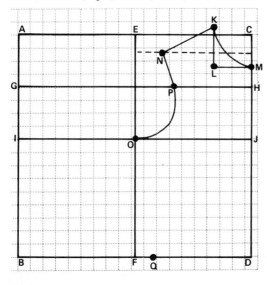

FIGURE 3.2f   *Drafting a female body block (cont.).*

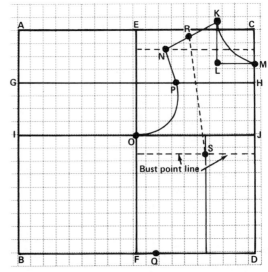

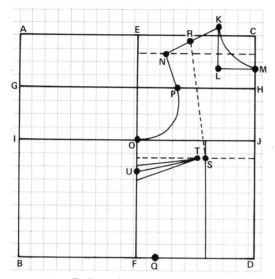

FIGURE 3.2g *Drafting a female body block* (cont.).

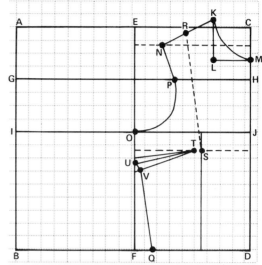

FIGURE 3.2h *Drafting a female body block* (cont.).

- Measure the same length on the bottom line of the bust dart, and mark V.
- Connect V and Q with a straight line, completing the side seam.
- Connect V to U.

Waist Dart

- The center line for the waist dart has already been determined.
- On this line, measure down 1" from bust point, S, toward B–D line and mark W for the point of the waist dart.

FIGURE 3.2i *Drafting a female body block* (cont.).

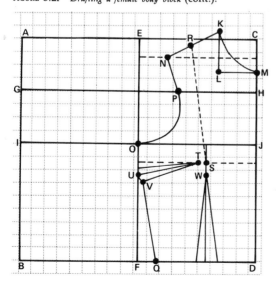

FIGURE 3.2j *Drafting a female body block* (cont.).

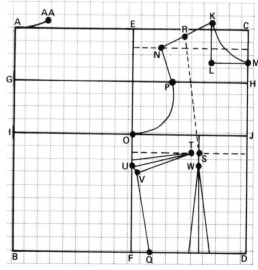

- On the B–D line, on either side of the place where the waist dart center line falls, mark half the total dart width.

- Connect these marks with W, completing the waist dart.

BACK SECTION

Neck

- 2½" to the right of A, and ½" up, mark AA.
- Connect A to AA with a slight curve. This is the back neck.

Shoulder

- To the right of G, measure half the total back width and mark BB.

- 3" up from BB, mark CC.
- Place one end of the ruler on AA and angle it so that it passes through CC.
- Draw a straight line from AA toward CC that is the length of the neck to shoulder measurement, *plus* ½". Mark DD. (AA–DD may be longer or shorter than the distance from AA–CC, depending on the neck-to-shoulder measurement.)*

FIGURE 3.2k   *Drafting a female body block* (cont.).

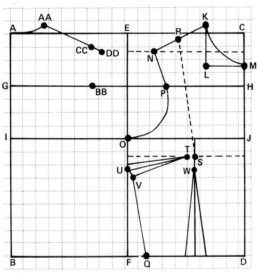

FIGURE 3.2l   *Drafting a female body block* (cont.).

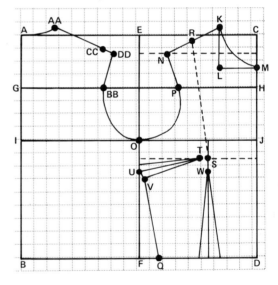

* The back shoulder is ½" longer than the front shoulder. This ½" must be eased into the seam when the body block is constructed from fabric in order to allow for shoulder movement.

** Refer to Figure 3.2l for the general shape of the armhole curve. Note that the back armhole is not as deep a curve as the front armhole. Final adjustments will be made in the muslin fitting.

Armhole

- Connect DD to BB with a straight line.
- Connect BB to O with a slight curve to complete the armhole. (See ** page 60.)

Side Seam

- To the right of B, measure ¼ of the total waist measurement, *plus* the width of the waist dart, *minus* ¼". Mark EE.
- Draw a vertical dotted line up from EE to the I–J line.
- Measure the length of the V–Q line on the front section of the block.
- Place the ruler with one end on the *top* of the bust dart where it meets the E–F line.
- Angle the ruler toward the vertical dotted line just drawn on the back section.
- Where the V–Q measurement crosses the dotted line, mark FF.

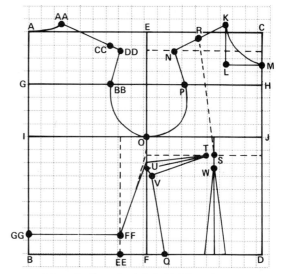

FIGURE 3.2n *Drafting a female body block* (cont.).

- Draw a straight line from the *top* of the bust dart where it meets the E–F line to FF. This is the side seam.

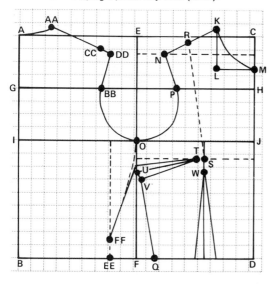

FIGURE 3.2m *Drafting a female body block* (cont.).

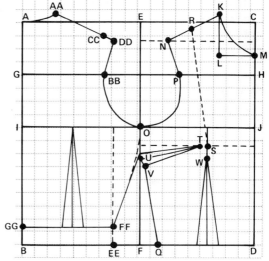

FIGURE 3.2o *Drafting a female body block* (cont.).

- Curve slightly as shown in Figure 3.2m.

Waist

- Measure the distance from EE to FF.
- Measure this same distance up from B on the A–B line. Mark GG.
- Connect GG to FF for waist line.

Waist Dart

- To the left of FF, measure in half the distance between FF and GG, *plus* ¾". Mark.
- Draw a vertical line from this mark to the I–J line. This is the center line of the back waist dart.
- To each side of the center line of the back waist dart, measure out half the width of the dart and mark.
- Connect these marks with straight lines to the point of the waist dart, which rests on the I–J line.

DRAFTING A MALE BODY BLOCK FROM INDIVIDUAL MEASUREMENTS

The male body block is considerably simpler to draft than the female block because of the absence of the bust dart. All the other steps are very similar to constructing the female block. Therefore, only one illustration, that of the completed male body block, is included in the following instructions.

Tools Needed

24" ruler or yardstick
12" ruler
right angle
pencil
heavy paper or cardboard

Measurements Required*

Measurements used for the male body block sample drafted in Figure 3.3:

1. chest—38"
2. waist—31"
3. back nape to waist—17"
4. neck to shoulder—5½"
5. front width—15"
6. back width—16"

waist darts—1"
scale: one square = 1"

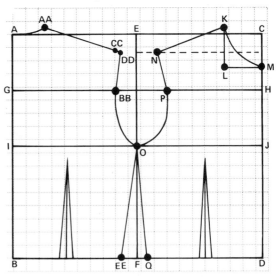

FIGURE 3.3 *Male body block.*

---

* Expand fractional measurements to the next ½" measurement; for example, 33¼" becomes 33½" and 18¾" becomes 19".

Determining Width of Waist Dart

(Waist dart widths are determined by the difference between chest and waist measurements.)

4–5½" difference equals ½"
6–7½" difference equals ¾"
8–9½" difference equals 1"
10–11½" difference equals 1¼"

Draw a Rectangle

The length of A–B and C–D is the back nape to waist measurement. The length of A–C and B–D is one-half of the total chest measurement, *plus* ½".

Add Construction Lines

- Divide A–C and B–D in half and draw a vertical line E–F.
- From points A and C, measure down one-quarter of the back nape to waist measurement. Connect these two points, forming a horizontal line, G–H. G–H is the front and back width line.
- From points G and H, measure down the same distance again (one-quarter of the back nape to waist measurement). Connect these two points, forming a horizontal line, I–J. I–J is the chest line.

Now the front and back of the male body block can be drafted.

FRONT SECTION

Neck and Shoulder

- 3" to the left, and ½" up from C, mark K.
- 3" down from K, mark L.
- 2½" down from C, mark M.
- Connect K to L and L to M with straight lines, then draw in the neck curve from K to M.
- 1⅜" below the E–C line, draw a horizontal dotted line.
- Draw front shoulder line by placing a ruler with one end on K and angling it to hit the dotted line at exactly the neck to shoulder measurement.
- Mark N at this point and join K to N with a straight line.

Armhole

- Mark O on the I–J line, at the point where it *crosses* the E–F line. O is the base of the armhole. To the left of H, measure in half the front width measurement and mark P. Connect N to P with a straight line, and P to O with a curve to complete the armhole.*

Side Seam

- To the left of D, measure one-quarter of the total waist measurement, *plus* ¼", *plus* the width of the front waist dart, and mark Q. Example: The waist measurement is 31"; the chest measurement is 38". The distance from D to Q will be 8" (one-quarter of the waist measurement), *plus* ¼", *plus* ¾" (the width of the waist dart, calculated from the difference between the chest and waist measurements: 7"). The distance from D to Q is 9".

---

* Refer to Figure 3.3 for the general shape of the armhole curve. Do not make the curve too deep. Final adjustments will be made in the muslin fitting.

- Connect O and Q with a straight line, completing the side seam.

Waist Dart

- From a point halfway between Q and D, draw a perpendicular line to a point 1" below the chest line. This is the center line for the waist dart.

BACK SECTION

Neck

- 2½" to the right of A, and ½" up, mark AA.
- Connect A to AA with a slight curve. This is the back neck.

Shoulder

- To the right of G, measure half the total back width and mark BB. 3" up from BB, mark CC.
- Place one end of the ruler on AA and angle it so that it passes through CC. Draw a straight line from AA toward CC that is the length of the neck to shoulder measurement, *plus* ½". Mark DD. (AA–DD may be longer or shorter than the distance from AA–CC, depending on the neck to shoulder measurement.)*

Armhole

- Connect DD to BB with a straight line.

- On the B–D line, on either side of the place where the waist dart center line falls, mark half the total dart width.
- Connect these marks with the top of the waist dart center line, completing the waist dart.

- Connect BB to O with a slight curve to complete the armhole.**

Side Seam

- To the right of B, measure ¼ of the total waist measurement, *plus* the width of the waist dart, *minus* ¼". Mark EE.
- Connect O and EE with a straight line, completing the side seam.

Waist Dart

- From a point halfway between B and EE, draw a perpendicular line to a point 1" below the chest line. This is the center line for the waist dart.
- On the B–D line, on either side of the place where the waist dart center line falls, mark half the total dart width.
- Connect these marks with the top of the waist dart center line, completing the waist dart.

* The back shoulder is ½" longer than the front shoulder. This ½" must be eased into the seam when the body block is constructed from fabric in order to allow for shoulder movement.

** Refer to Figure 3.3 for the general shape of the armhole curve. Note that the back armhole is not as deep a curve as the front armhole. Final adjustments will be made in the muslin fitting.

Transferring the Body Block from Paper to Muslin

Do not cut out the paper body pieces at this point. This is so you will be able to make adjustments to the pieces after fitting the muslin sloper.

Use a large piece of tracing paper to transfer the lines from the paper to a length of un-washed, medium-weight muslin, pressed and folded double. Make sure the muslin is folded on the straight grain of the fabric and that the pattern is laid on with the back and front center lines on the straight grain. Secure the muslin and the brown paper pattern to the cutting table with T-pins or push pins so they cannot slip while you are tracing. After tracing the front section, move the paper pattern in order to leave space for seam allowances around both pieces. Trace only the outer lines and the dart lines; you need not trace any construction lines on the muslin.

Do not cut either the center front or the center back on the fold of the fabric. It is preferable, especially for women, to leave the center back seam open.

Determining Seam Allowance

Determining the amount of the seam allow-ance to be left around the outside of the pieces is a matter of individual preference. In some shops the stitching lines are traced on each piece of fabric cut and the seam al-lowance "eyeballed," that is, cut freehand without measuring. When this method is used, the person who sews the seams must do a very careful job of pinning before stitch-ing since the edge of the cloth cannot be re-lied on at all for alignment, and the stitching lines must be matched exactly.

Whereas it is always a good idea to trace the actual stitching lines on all fabric pieces as an accuracy check, it is also helpful to measure the seam allowance as well so that the edges of the cloth can be aligned. In shops that measure seam allowances, the width may vary from one-half-inch to one-inch in width. Commercial patterns are all drafted with a five-eighths-inch seam allowance, a width chosen both because it is sufficiently wide to allow room for adjustments, and not so wide that it becomes difficult to fit a curved seam. If you choose to measure seam allow-ances, this can be accomplished with a small seam measurement guide or gauge. Simply move the guide around the outside of the pattern line, marking the allowance with a pencil dot every two or three inches. Follow the dots as you cut. In some shops the mea-sured seam allowances will remain a constant width and in others they will change for dif-ferent garments. Always make sure the per-son stitching up the garment knows what seam allowance has been measured.

CONSTRUCTING THE MUSLIN SLOPER

Stitch the pieces of the muslin sloper together with a long machine basting stitch. Follow the stitching lines precisely. Notice that the back shoulder piece is one-half-inch longer than the front; this extra one-half-inch must be eased into the front shoulder piece. This ease is supplied to allow for normal shoulder movement and is standard on most patterns. In order to distribute this ease, pin each edge of the seam together. With the back piece up, stretch both pieces slightly over your knee, or over a tailor's ham. Place a pin in the center of the seam, then two or three in each half, distributing the extra back full-ness evenly. Machine-stitch the seam with the back piece up. If you end up with a tuck in the seam, you have not distributed the fullness evenly.

The muslin sloper should be tried on over undergarments only. Before putting it on the actor, slash the under part of the armhole and the neck edge in several places to within one-eighth-inch of the stitching line. Put the muslin sloper on the actor with the seams to the outside. Fasten the center back seam with safety pins exactly on the stitching lines. Even if the sloper is too big around the body, you will not want to take in all the excess in the center back seam, or closing. Pull the sloper snugly down onto the body. It is helpful to tie a ribbon or tape around the waist to hold the sloper down during the fitting. Stand away from the actor for a moment and observe the sloper muslin on the body. Don't start making adjustments until you have looked at it from every angle.

If the muslin sloper is more than an inch too big around the fullest part of the chest or bust or across the front or back width, check the original measurements and the drafted pattern pieces for mistakes. These areas should be nearly correct in all body slopers. In a woman's sloper the bust dart point and the waist dart point should lie in the correct relationship to the individual woman's bust apex. These points should be neither too close to the apex nor too far from it so that the sloper fits smoothly over the bust without strain or puckers. If this is not the case, you will want to return to the drawing board. These are the crucial fitting areas in any garment that is cut for the torso and it is vital that the sloper fit these areas with only minor alterations.

Once you have seen that the upper chest area fits nicely, turn your attention to the areas where alterations will be common. The front waist darts on the woman's sloper nearly always need to be nipped in, usually on a slight curve so that the sloper will fit snugly beneath the bust. Each body is differ-ent and this is an easy adjustment to make in fitting.

The neck curve will almost always need redrawing. We have deliberately indicated a smallish, high neckline since, when fitting the sloper on the actor, it's far easier to establish a new lower neckline than to raise a neckline that has already been cut too low. When redrawing a neckline on a tall actor, it is helpful to have him or her sit down on a chair. When you are looking up, it is easy to distort the proper shape of the neckline. Draw the neckline right at the base of the neck so it is in the optimum position for attaching a collar. Use a pencil, a marker, or a piece of sharp colored chalk for drawing the neckline. When the muslin has been removed from the actor, the curve can be made true with the help of a French curve and the new line transferred to the paper block pattern.

The lower armhole curves, both front and back, may also need adjustment. Be sure to keep the armhole close and snug to the body, but not binding.

Check the position of the waistline on the body. Often the back waistline will ride too low. Redraw the correct line on the muslin.

Some adjustment is often needed in the shoulder seams to account for the different shapes and slants of human shoulders. The side seams may also need to be either nipped in or let out. Pin these adjustments carefully with safety pins.

The muslin sloper should fit the body closely but it should never be skin tight; it should not have any bulgy or wrinkled areas. If the actor carries his or her shoulders especially erect, there may be some fullness at the front of the armhole; this fullness will usually disappear when sleeves are set in to whatever garment pattern is created from the sloper.

If there is a large discrepancy between the

two halves of an actor's body, it is best to mark the adjustments carefully on the muslin, indicating which half is the right side and which is the left. Keep the muslin sloper attached to the paper pattern. In most instances you will not cut a garment pattern to conform to the uneven body, but will add padding to the lower, or smaller, side so the body will appear to be balanced. It is necessary, however, to have a record of the actual body shape in order to plan the adjustment. (The most common torso discrepancy is one shoulder lower than the other. A low shoulder is easy to pad.)

Marking Adjustments on the Paper Body Block

When the muslin sloper has been removed from the actor, lay it out on the cutting table

and mark all the new stitching lines that have been pinned in. Make sure to mark both sides of each seam. Remove the pins and take the muslin pieces apart. Press the pieces to remove wrinkles that occurred in the fitting. Spread the pieces on the table and draw in the new stitching lines carefully. In most cases you need only make these final adjustments on the sloper.

Now lay the corrected muslin pieces exactly over the paper body block and pin down with push pins. Using tracing paper, transfer the corrections to the paper pattern. After the corrections are all transferred, cut out the paper pieces. Place the actor's name on each pattern piece. Store the paper pattern and the muslin pieces in a large envelope with the actor's name on it. If the paper pattern is transferred to cardboard or tagboard, punch a hole in the board and hang the pieces on a nail.

DRAPING A BODY SLOPER

If you have a clothing dummy that is quite close to the same size as the actor for whom a sloper is being constructed, a sloper can be draped directly on the dummy. The important measurements that should, as nearly as possible, correspond to the actor are: across front, across back, nape to waist, bust, and waist. If the bust and waist of the clothing dummy are smaller than those of the actor, these areas can be padded with polyester or cotton batting and covered with muslin to make the padding secure. Figures 3.4a–n illustrate the steps in draping a sloper on a female clothing dummy. Once a costumer has practiced both drafting and draping slopers, each method should take about the same length of time. Some costume technicians prefer one method over the other, but each produces essentially the same outcome. You cannot, however, drape a body sloper adequately if you do not have a clothing dummy that is the correct size.

Three views of a clothing dummy with tapes marking the neckline, shoulder seam line, center front, center back and side seam lines, and bustline position (Figures 3.4a–c).

The costume technician secures a muslin rectangle to the center front of the clothing dummy, making certain that the straight grain of the fabric follows the tape marking the center front (Figure 3–4d).

The fabric is clipped to the neckline tape so it can be curved around the neck.

Taking care to maintain the fabric crossgrain directly across the front, the bust dart is pinned into place.

The waistline is secured at the base of the side seam. Notice the grainline marking on the muslin.

The side seamline is drawn onto the muslin with a felt-tipped marker.

The fabric below the waistline has been trimmed and slashed to the waist tape, and the waist dart is being pinned in place. Note:

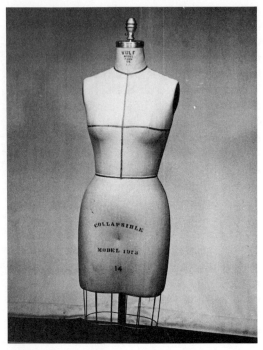

FIGURE 3.4a   *Draping a body sloper. (Photographs by Richard Bryant.)*

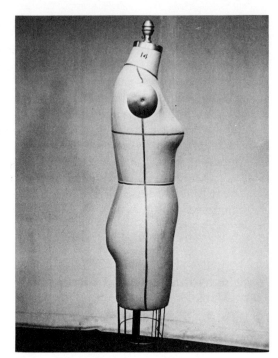

FIGURE 3.4b   *Draping a body sloper* (cont.).

FIGURE 3.4e   *Draping a body sloper* (cont.).

FIGURE 3.4f   *Draping a body sloper* (cont.).

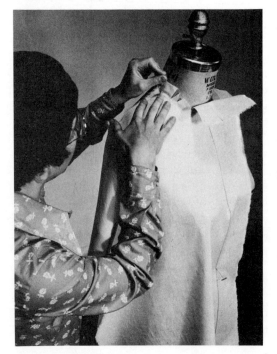

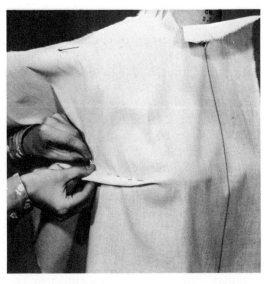

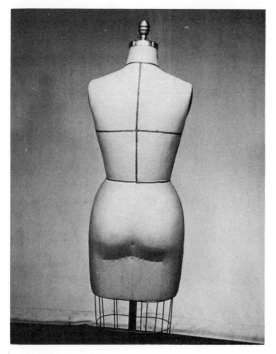

FIGURE 3.4c   *Draping a body sloper* (cont.).

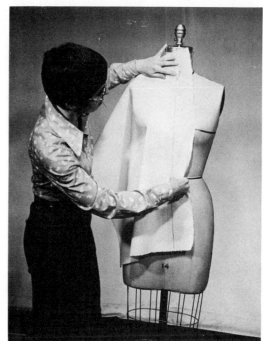

FIGURE 3.4d   *Draping a body sloper* (cont.).

FIGURE 3.4g   *Draping a body sloper* (cont.).

FIGURE 3.4h   *Draping a body sloper* (cont.).

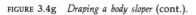

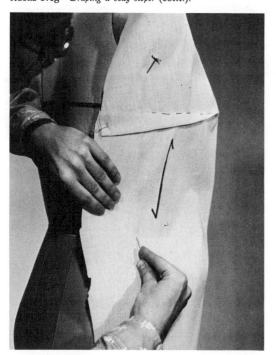

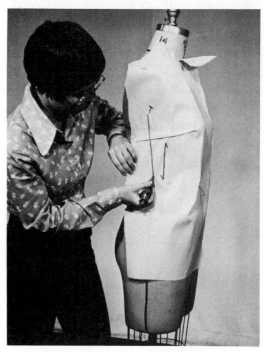

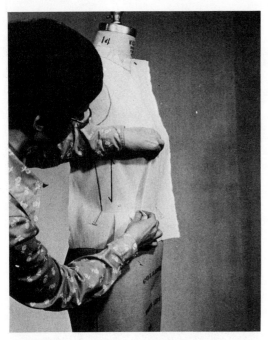

FIGURE 3.4i *Draping a body sloper* (cont.).

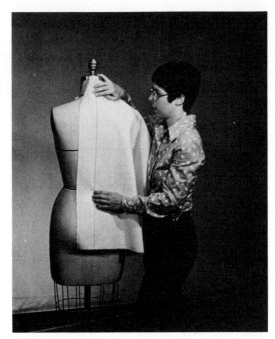

FIGURE 3.4j *Draping a body sloper* (cont.).

FIGURE 3.4m *Draping a body sloper* (cont.).

FIGURE 3.4n *Draping a body sloper* (cont.).

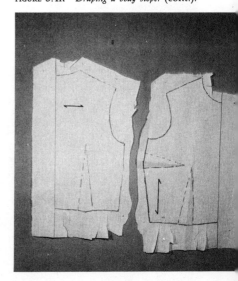

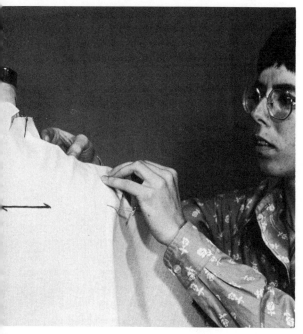

FIGURE 3.4k *Draping a body sloper* (cont.).

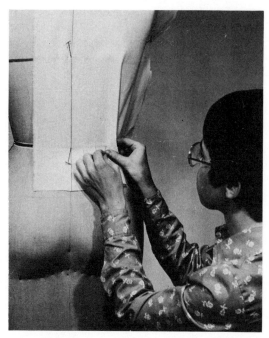

FIGURE 3.4l *Draping a body sloper* (cont.).

Neither the bust dart point nor the waist dart point should extend all the way to the bust point. All the remaining seamlines—center front, shoulder, armhole, and waist—may be drawn in now.

Another rectangle of muslin is secured to the center back of the clothing dummy. The center back must also lie on the straight grain of the fabric.

The neckline and shoulder seam are molded into place. As on the drafted sloper, the back shoulder seam should be ½ inch

longer than the front shoulder seam. Notice the arrow marking the fabric crossgrain which runs straight across the back.

The back waist dart is pinned in place.

A side view of the muslin pieces draped on the clothing dummy with seamlines drawn in.

The finished sloper pattern with darts and seamlines shown.

The pattern can now be transferred to muslin and constructed; steps are identical to those outlined for the drafted sloper pattern.

THE COMPLETE MEASUREMENT BLANK

When you begin to create garment patterns for individual designs, you will need a great many more measurements than you needed for the body block. Figures 3.5a and 3.5b are examples of measurement blanks. Each costume shop will inevitably devise its own

measurement blank and individual cutters will have their own sets of measurements. Some will put the completed blanks in a loose-leaf notebook; others will use large cards in a file box. The best system is the system that works best for your own situation. Do check over these sample blanks for the measurements most often taken. Always take too many measurements rather than too few so you will have them on hand should you need them.

It is always a good idea to have two people taking measurements: one to measure the actor and the other to record the measurements. Create a situation in which the actor is comfortable and can relax. Initiating a conversa-tion with the actor will prevent him or her from tensing the abdomen or shoulders in such a way that the measurements taken are inaccurate. Always refrain from commenting on the actor's measurements. There are very few other professions that cause a person to be more self-conscious about physical size and shape than acting.

The information on the first part of the sample measurement blanks can be gotten

FIGURE 3.5a   *Sample measurement sheet.*

	Season _____
Name _____	Role(s) _____
_____	_____

Height _____ Weight _____ Shoe size _____ Glove size _____
Ring size _____ Dress size (women) or Suit size (men) _____

Men only: Shirt size: Neck _____ Sleeve length _____
             Trousers size: Waist _____ Inseam _____

Women only: Bra size _____   Stocking size _____ Underpants size _____
               Ribcage _____   Neck to floor: _____ Front _____
                                                            Back _____

Bust or chest _____ Waist _____   Outseam _____ Inseam _____

Hips: 5" down _____ Around: Thigh _____   Above knee _____
      7" down _____   Calf _____   Below knee _____
      9" down _____   Ankle _____   Armscye _____

Shoulder to shoulder (back) _____   Shoulder to elbow (bent arm) _____
Back width _____ Front width _____   to wrist (bent arm) _____
                                                    to wrist (straight arm) _____
Shoulder to bust point (women only) _____   Inner arm to elbow (straight arm) _____
Bust point to bust point (women only) _____   to wrist _____

Neck to shoulder _____   Around:
      to waist: Front _____ Back _____   Biceps _____ Forearm _____
Underarm to waist _____   Wrist _____ Hand _____

Waist to knee: Around head _____ Hat size _____
    Front _____ Side _____ Back _____ Hairline circumference _____
Waist to floor: Ear to ear, front _____
    Front _____ Back _____   Eartop to eartop _____
                                            Forehead to nape _____
                                            Rise _____

Around neck _____   Around base of neck _____

Comments: Note significant differences between sides of
the body, unusual posture, fabric allergies, etc.

TRACE FOOT ON BACK

Date_____   Dept._____

Name_____Home Tel._____Sex_____

Address_____

Height _____   Shirt/Blouse _____   Glove _____

Weight _____   Bra _____ _____   Ring _____

Shoe _____   Tights/P. Hose_____   Lft/Rt. Handed _____

Ballet Shoe _____   Hose _____   Pierced Ears _____

Suit/Dress_____   Hat _____   Allergies _____

Pants W._____Ins._____   Remarks_____

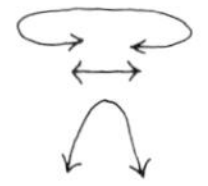

Mid. Neck_____

Base Neck_____

Across Front _____

Over Bust_____

Bust/Chest_____   Armscye_____

       Ex._____   Throat Base to Waist _____

Under Bust/Ribcage_____   Armpit to Waist _____

       Ex. _____   Nape to Waist _____

Waist _____   to Floor _____

Hip: Upper _____   F. Waist to Below Knee _____

     Lower_____   to Floor_____

Neck to Shoulder_____   Outseam to Ankle _____

Across Back _____   to Floor _____

With Arm Bent: Inseam to Ankle_____

Nape to Shoulder _____   to Floor _____

To Elbow_____To Wrist_____   Girth: W. Front to Back _____

With Arm Straight: Shldr. to (same) Shldr. _____

Inseam to Elbow_____To Wrist_____   Crotch Depth_____

Bicep_____   Elbow_____   Forearm_____   Wrist_____   High Thigh_____

Low Thigh_____   Above knee_____   Bel. Knee_____   Calf_____   Ankle_____

Wig Measurements: Hair Col._____

(1) Head Circumference _____

(2) Forehead to Poll_____

(3) Ear to Ear Across Top_____

(4) Hairline Circumference _____

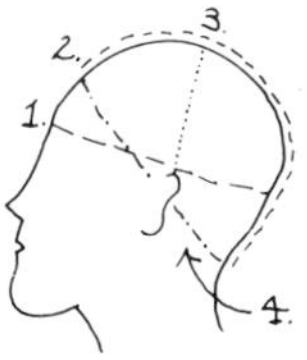

Trace Foot On Back

(1)_____
(2)_____
(3)_____

FIGURE 3.5b   *Sample measurement sheet.*

from the actor. Mark any size the actor is not certain of with a question mark until you have an opportunity to check the size against a purchased garment.

Unless there is a marked discrepancy between the two sides of the body, measure the right side. In cases of a significant, visible difference, you may want to take certain measurements on both sides, for example, neck to shoulder, shoulder to bust point, underarm to waist, and the arm length measurements. Some costumers measure the actor's dominant side, the right if the actor is righthanded and the left if he is lefthanded. There is often a bit more muscle development on the dominant side, but the difference will not usually be great enough to warrant interrupting the rhythm of always measuring the same side.

Be sure to tie waist and armhole tapes as described and illustrated earlier in this chapter. If the armhole tapes have a tendency to slide down onto the arm, pin them to the actor's clothing or, if the measurements are being taken in underwear, secure them with a bit of plastic tape.

Most of the measurements called for on the sample blank are self-explanatory, but a few notes may prove helpful. To measure the chest expanded or relaxed is a matter of choice. If a relaxed chest is measured, sufficient room for chest expansion must be allowed for when the garment is cut. The female ribcage (just under the bust) is always measured expanded. It is common to take the inseam and outseam measurements all the way to the floor to assure that when pants are cut there will be sufficient length for an adequate hem. The hairline circumference, ear to ear front, eartop to eartop, and forehead to nape measurements are useful for wig and mask work.

With the exception of corsets and tightly laced bodices or doublets, most clothing rides on the body with room for movement. Take measurements snugly but never pull the tape so tight that it indents the flesh. It is particularly important that the back width, front width, and neck to shoulder measurements be accurate.

FROM BODY BLOCK TO GARMENT PATTERN

The basic female body block in this book is drafted with both waist and bust darts. You will find other versions of the basic female block in other books that call for only one dart, usually the waist dart, to control fullness. It is difficult to achieve a fine fit, particularly on a woman with a large bust, when the fullness is controlled by only one dart. The success of later garment patterns will depend upon achieving a sloper that conforms to the body's curves, and this can be best achieved in the beginning by controlling fabric fullness in two places rather than in only one.

Very few costume designs, however, will call for the arrangement of darts found on the basic body block. The fabric fullness which is controlled by the waist and bust darts in the sloper can be controlled in other areas, and in other ways, although not every arrangement of fullness control will result in a smooth form-fitting garment. In addition to the waist and bust dart combination, you may expect a close fit from combining the waist and shoulder darts and from the curved body seam (the "princess-line"). Other arrangements of fullness will provide adequate fabric to shape the garment over the bust but will be less form fitting. Learning to shift fabric fullness control points is the key to developing patterns. It is not a difficult process and several examples follow.

Swinging Bust Dart Control into a Shoulder Dart

The first step in shifting, or swinging, the position of one or both of the standard sloper darts is to trace the adjusted front block piece onto another piece of brown or pattern paper. Trace dart lines, including the center line of each dart. This will become the *construction pattern.* Cut out the construction pattern.

Lay the construction pattern on the cutting table and pin the bust dart closed. A bulge will appear at the bust. Place the construction pattern on a dummy of an approximately corresponding size and sketch in a dart center line that runs from the middle of the shoulder seam to a point one-half inch above the bust point. This step can be eliminated if a clothing dummy is not available, but its use helps to reinforce the dimensional shape of the pattern and to locate the new control point in direct association with the body. Without a clothing dummy, the center line of the new shoulder dart may be taken from the shoulder to bust point construction line on the original body block pattern. Place the construction pattern back on the cutting table and slash the shoulder dart center line. The slashed area will open up to create the new dart position.

Swinging Darts to Other Positions

Using this same method, dart control can be shifted to several different places on the pattern front. Figure 3.6 shows the normal dart positions on the female bodice or blouse front. Fullness can be controlled by a single dart, if the bust is not exceptionally full, or by an assortment of darts. Shifting dart control changes the fashion line of the body garment but should not alter the basic fit. Minor fitting adjustments can be made on the muslin mock-up which should be constructed from each garment pattern developed from the basic sloper.

FIGURE 3.6   *Normal dart positions on female bodice (front).*

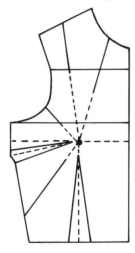

There is much less fullness to be controlled in the back of a bodice or blouse. In the sloper this fullness is controlled by waist darts. Back control can be shifted in the manner described above. Figure 3.7 shows normal dart positions on the female bodice or blouse back.

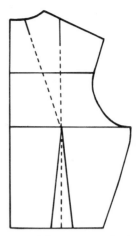

FIGURE 3.7   *Normal dart positions on female bodice (back).*

Fabric fullness that allows cloth to curve over the female bust can be controlled by tucks, gathers, and seaming, as well as by darts. An example of each alternative follows. Once you understand the theory of fabric fullness control and are familiar with the steps involved in swinging it from place to place, you will be able to apply this knowledge to the creation of many different garment patterns. From that point on, experience will be your best teacher.

When the problem of swinging dart control is as simple as shifting it from the bust dart into a shoulder dart, it is only necessary to make one construction pattern which can then be used directly to cut and construct a muslin mock-up of the garment pattern. Other problems, however, will require that the construction pattern be pinned or taped and slashed more than once, and in these instances you may make two or even three construction patterns. Each time you prepare a new construction pattern, use the original body block pattern for the outline. The construction pattern piece, on which slashing, pinning, and taping is done, will never lie completely flat on the table. There will always be a small bulge in the area of the bust point; the larger the bust, the larger the bulge will be. Do not slash further into the pattern than one-quarter-inch away from the bust point. Smooth down the bulge as neatly as possible and trace the pattern outline accurately, adding the new dart positions or other fullness control designations from the construction pattern piece onto a clean sheet of paper. On the final construction pattern it is also a good idea to add grain line markings and any other pattern notations that are pertinent to that particular piece. Be sure to mark the center front or center back and to indicate if either is to be cut on the fold of the fabric. Finally, put the actor's name and probably the name of the play and the character for which the costume is being constructed on each pattern piece.

Controlling Front Bodice Fullness in Multiple Waistline Tucks

Trace a construction pattern from the adjusted body sloper pattern.

Swing all the fullness controlled by the waistline dart into the bust dart. Do this by taping or pinning the waistline dart closed and slashing the bust dart down the dart center line (see Figure 3.8a).

Prepare a new construction pattern with

the enlarged bust dart. Establish a line on this construction pattern which will mark the upper end of the tucks and draw in slashing lines for three evenly spaced tucks. Extend these lines up above the horizontal line just drawn so they will converge at a single point one-half-inch below the bust point (see Figure 3.8b).

Pin or tape the enlarged bust dart closed. Slash the three tuck lines to within one-eighth-inch of the point where they converge. Lay the construction pattern flat on

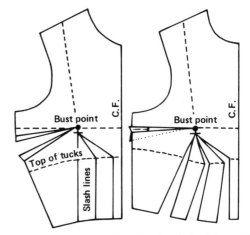

FIGURES 3.8b and 3.8c   *Controlling front bodice fullness with waistline tucks (cont.).*

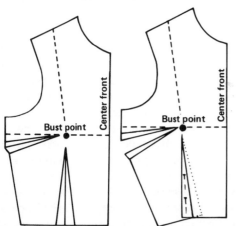

FIGURE 3.8a   *Controlling front bodice fullness with waistline tucks.*

FIGURE 3.8d   *Controlling front bodice fullness with waistline tucks (cont.).*

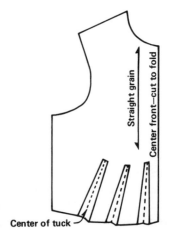

the cutting table. The tuck slashes will spread to the widths that are necessary to provide adequate fullness for the bust (see Figure 3.8c).

Prepare the final construction pattern, which will look like the one in Figure 3.8d.

Fine Adjustments of Multiple Waistline Tucks

A bodice front in which fabric fullness is controlled by multiple waist tucks is most successful on a youthful, small-busted figure. If the actor has a large bust, it is often best to choose gathers rather than tucks in order to achieve the necessary fullness.

Spacing between the waist tucks, and the angle at which they lie, can create different illusions in the fashion line. If the darts are situated as they were in the previous example, parallel to the center front and to each other, they will create the illusion of a larger waistline. But if the first line is drawn parallel to the center front and the next two are fanned out slightly, the illusion of a tapering waistline will result. See Figure 3.9 for the shapes of these tucks.

A variation of this pattern can be adapted

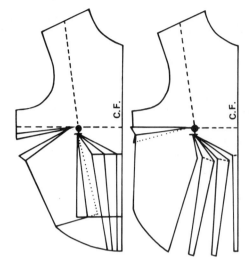

FIGURE 3.10 *Another variation on waistline tucks.*

for cutting simple, turn-of-the-century shirtwaists. Lengthen the center front from the original sloper pattern about three inches, curving the bottom of the bodice gently back up to the natural waistline on the side. Shift the tucks closer to the center front. This variation will achieve the extra fullness and the pouch front effect characteristic of these shirtwaists. The construction pattern will look something like Figure 3.10.

Developing a Bodice Front Pattern with a Yoke and Fabric Fullness Controlled by Gathering

Trace a construction pattern from the adjusted body sloper pattern. Swing all fullness controlled by the waistline dart into the bust dart as described in the last example. Prepare a new construction pattern with the enlarged bust dart.

Place the pattern piece on a clothing dummy if one is available and draw in the yoke as shown in Figure 3.11a. Put in matching notches.

Draw construction lines for slashing and spreading from the bottom of the yoke to the bottom of the bodice (see Figure 3.11b).

FIGURE 3.9 *A variation on waistline tucks.*

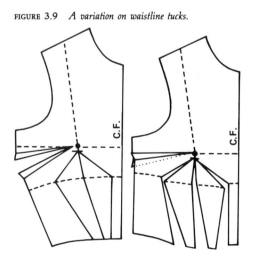

Pin or tape the enlarged bust dart closed. Cut the yoke away from the bottom of the bodice. Slash the construction lines down to within one-quarter-inch from the bottom of the bodice. Lay the piece flat on the table. The slashes will spread out to indicate the amount of gathering necessary to provide sufficient fullness to cover the bust (see Figure 3.11c).

Make the final pattern with relevant markings and add a seam allowance if desired. Figure 3.11d is an example of what this final pattern may look like.

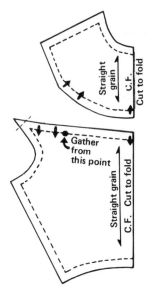

FIGURE 3.11d *Bodice front with yoke and fullness* (cont.).

Developing a Bodice Front Pattern in Which Fabric Fullness is Controlled by a Curved Seam

Trace a construction pattern from the adjusted body sloper pattern. Swing all fullness controlled by the waistline dart into the bust dart as described in the last two examples and prepare a new construction pattern with the enlarged bust dart.

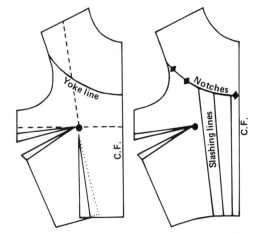

FIGURES 3.11a and 3.11b *Bodice front with yoke and fullness.*

FIGURE 3.11c *Bodice front with yoke and fullness* (cont.).

FIGURE 3.12 *Bodice front with fullness controlled in a curved seam.*

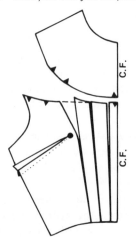

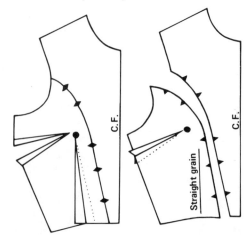

Using a clothing form if one is available, draw in the desired seam line. Draw in straight of grain line parallel to c.f. as shown in Figure 3.12, and add match up notches. Cut the pattern piece in two pieces on the seamline. Pin the enlarged bust dart closed.

Note the change in the curve of the smaller pattern piece. When you stitch the two curves together, match the notches and align the opposing curves carefully.

Make a final pattern with relevant markings, and add a seam allowance if desired.

DEVELOPING PATTERNS FROM THE MALE BODY BLOCK

The male body block is less complicated than the female block because there are fewer curves around which the fabric must go. Waist darts are usually sufficient to control fullness required by the chest bulge. In male garment patterns waistline darts will almost always be replaced by curved seam fabric fullness control.

The male body block will not be used to develop patterns for the majority of garments worn by men since the middle of the nineteenth century. The major clothing styles for men from about 1850 to the present are tailored into shape and hang rather loosely on the body. Patterns for these garments are usually drafted from period tailoring instructions or, in the case of modern suits and shirts, taken from commercial patterns. Men's clothing before 1850 can be patterned from the basic male body block; this includes tunics, jerkins, doublets, and a variety of form-fitting jackets.

the construction pattern pieces. The seamlines will be established either from the design or from period pattern research. Draw match-up notches on each seamline as shown in Figure 3.13.

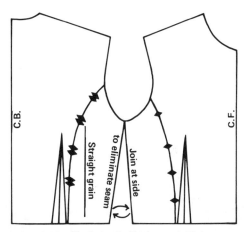

FIGURE 3.13   *Developing doublet from male block.*

Developing a Doublet Shape from the Male Body Block

Trace a construction pattern from the adjusted male body sloper. In this instance you will work with both the back and the front pieces. Draw in the necessary seamlines on

Cut out the pattern pieces on the seamlines. Pin or tape both front and back waistline darts closed. Notice the alteration in the curve that is caused by closing the dart. Transfer the construction pattern pieces to a piece of clean pattern paper. Add pattern markings and a seam allowance, if desired.

EXPERIMENTING WITH PATTERN SHAPES

In some fashion periods, clothing fits snugly around the body; in others, the garments fall loosely in tunic shapes or in folds. In still

other periods, some additional artificial shapes are inserted between the body and the clothes, such as a hoop, a bustle, a bum-roll, exaggerated shoulder padding, and so on. Virtually all garments, however, whether snug, loose, or artificially shaped, are suspended from the shoulders or the waist, and the entire fall of the garments depends on a good fit in these areas. All garments that fall from the shoulders (with the exception of tailored suits, mentioned earlier) can be patterned from the body block. A correctly shaped neckline, a good fit across the front and back of the upper chest, and an accurate armhole provide the basis for most garment patterns. Beginning with an accurate body block, slash, spread, add length and width, and position seams wherever necessary. The construction pattern can be turned into an endless number of shapes. Never hesitate to experiment until you have achieved what you want.

THE MUSLIN MOCK-UP

Unless the garment being patterned is extremely simple, a muslin mock-up should be made and fitted before any costume is cut from the intended fabric. This is a way of checking the accuracy of the pattern and it is also an opportunity for the designer to change seam positions, add or subtract fullness, re-establish necklines, and so forth before the actual garment is cut.

Use the clean pattern to cut out muslin pieces and trace those pattern marks that are necessary for construction: darts, tucks, and gathering lines—as well as stitching lines. Notches may be snipped in the fabric for matching up, or match-up marks may be drawn on the muslin.

Construct the muslin mock-up the same way the sloper was constructed. Use a long

FIGURE 3.14   *Costume designer Susan Tsu fitting a muslin mock-up on actress Rose Pickering at the Milwaukee Repertory Theater. (Photograph by Mark Avery.)*

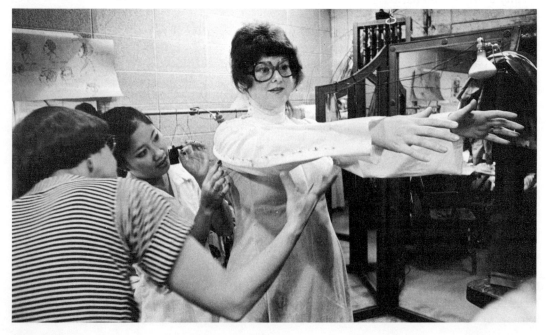

machine stitch so it will not be so difficult to take apart after the fitting. In some costume shops the muslin mock-up itself is used for underlining the fabric. If this procedure is followed, be sure that the muslin used has been washed first to prevent its shrinking.

Follow the fitting procedures discussed in Chapters 4 and 5 and mark alterations clearly on the muslin. If a great many alterations have been made to the muslin mock-up, it is a good idea to prepare a second mock-up. Changes are easy to make in the muslin stage; they are much more difficult to make, and much less apt to be satisfactory, if they occur after the costume has been assembled in fabric.

DRAFTING SLEEVE BLOCKS

The following sleeve blocks may serve as basic starting points for developing many different kinds of sleeves. The one-piece sleeve will fit into the sloper with a smooth cap. It falls straight from the shoulder and rides easily around the arm. The two-piece sleeve that is developed from the one-piece sleeve also has a smooth cap but is considerably fuller around the arm.

When fitting the cap of a sleeve into an armhole, the rule of thumb is that, in order to achieve a smooth cap, the sleeve should be between one and one-half to two inches larger around the top than the circumference of the armhole. More fullness will generally be eased into the back of the armhole than into the front. Note the difference between the back and front curves of the sleeve cap in Figure 3.15.

DRAFTING A SLEEVE BLOCK FROM INDIVIDUAL MEASUREMENTS

Tools Needed

24" ruler or yardstick
right angle
pencil
heavy paper or card

Measurements Required*

1. shoulder to wrist
2. wrist
3. underarm to wrist
4. bicep

Measurements used for sleeve block sample drafted in Figure 3.15 are as follows:

* Taken with arm straight down.

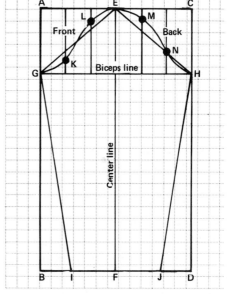

FIGURE 3.15 *Basic sleeve block.*

Shoulder to wrist—22½"
Wrist—6"
Underarm to wrist—17"
Bicep—10½"
Scale—one square = 1"

- Draw a lengthwise rectangle. A–B and C–D equal shoulder to wrist measurement. A–C and B–D equal bicep measurement *plus* 3".

- Add construction lines. Points E and F lie exactly halfway between A–C and B–D. Connect points E and F with a straight line.

- B–G and D–H equal underarm to wrist measurement. Connect G and H with a straight line.

Note: The section to the right of the E–F line is the back of the sleeve and the section to the left of the E–F line is the sleeve front.

Wrist

- From F, measure out on each side half the wrist measurement *plus* 1".
- Mark I and J at these points.

Side Seams

- Connect G to I and H to J for side seams.

Cap

- Divide the distance between A–G and C–H into six *equal* parts.
- Draw vertical construction lines up from the G–H line to the A–C line.
- Connect G to E and E to H.
- Working from left to right, starting on the first vertical construction line:
- Mark K ¾" *below* the G–E line;
- Mark L ¾" *above* the G–E line;

- Mark M 1" *above* the E–H line;
- Mark N where the E–H line intersects with the last vertical construction line.
- Connect G, K, L, E, M, N, and H with curved lines to complete the sleeve block.

Changing Basic Sleeve to a Two-Piece Sleeve

This version of the two-piece sleeve has one seam at the back of the arm and the other approximately 1½ inches forward of the normal inside seam position. The sleeves are curved from the elbow to compensate for the normal angle of the arm as it hangs naturally. The additional measurement required is from the shoulder to the elbow.

Blocking Out Construction Pattern

- Trace individual's sleeve sloper onto another piece of paper. Draw in center line and bicep line. Mark the front and back sections of the sleeve cap.

FIGURE 3.16a   *Two-piece sleeve.*

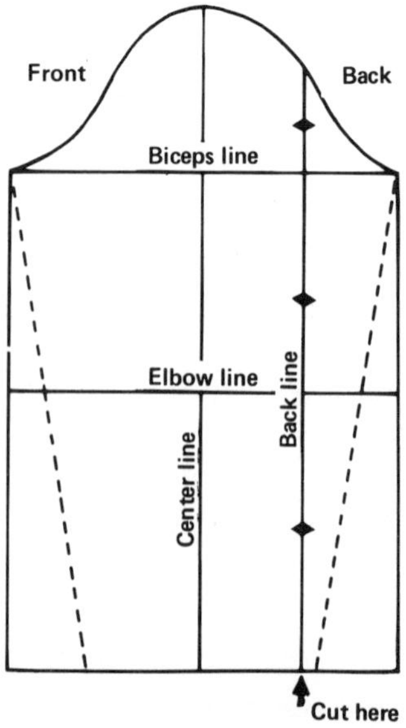

- Construct new side seamlines parallel to sleeve center line.
- Using the shoulder to elbow length measurement, construct the elbow line perpendicular to the center line.

Creating Back of Arm Seam

- Determine the back of arm position on the biceps line at a point halfway between the sleeve centerline and the back edge of the sleeve. Draw a line from this point, parallel to the center line, the full length of the sleeve.
- Mark notches and cut construction pattern along this line.

Creating Front of Arm Seam

- Tape the back section of the sleeve to the front section.
- Measure 1½" to the right of the newly joined edges and construct a line parallel to the center line. Notch and cut.

Shaping Sleeve Sections

- Reverse undersleeve section so the back side of each section is to the right, facing you.
- Curve back seams of both sections from the elbow line to a point 2" to the left of the original back seamline as shown in Figure 3.16c.
- Draw new wrist lines at right angles to the back seam line.
- Curve front seam of undersleeve section slightly as shown in Figure 3.16c.
- Curve front seam of upper sleeve section 1" out from original seamline, starting at the elbow line. Tape on additional paper for this extension.
- Measure the length of the front inside seam and adjust the length of the front outside seam to correspond with it.

These sleeve blocks should always be executed in muslin and fitted before cutting them from costume fabric. Additional shaping is

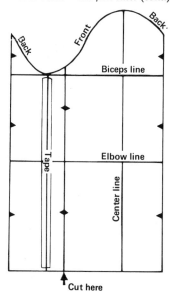

FIGURE 3.16b *Two-piece sleeve* (cont.).

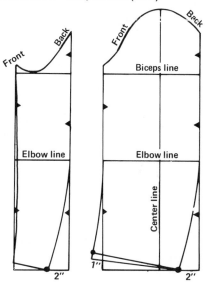

FIGURE 3.16c *Two-piece sleeve* (cont.).

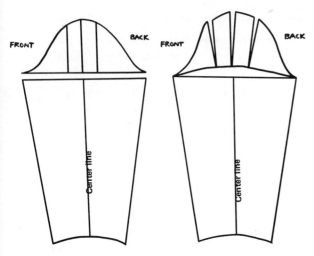

FIGURE 3.17 *Slashing and spreading for a gathered cap.*

A sleeve with a smooth cap and fullness at the bottom can be patterned by slashing and spreading the lower portion of the sleeve. See Figure 3.19 for an example of this technique.

The popular bishop sleeve may be patterned from the two-piece sleeve block as in Figure 3.20. The fullness in the bishop sleeve is contained only in the back, forming a particularly graceful line.

An endless number of sleeves may be developed from the basic blocks. Experiment with shapes until you have executed exactly what the costume design requires.

almost always necessary in order to obtain the most attractive line and shape.

The basic one-piece sleeve may be slashed and spread in order to develop patterns for a variety of sleeve shapes. Slash and spread the cap for a sleeve that is to be gathered into the armhole (see Figures 3.17 and 3.18).

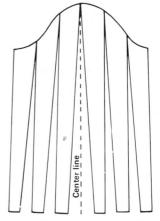

FIGURE 3.19 *Slashing for lower fullness.*

FIGURE 3.18 *A variation on shaping a gathered cap.*

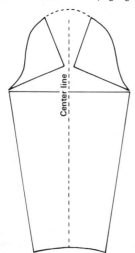

FIGURE 3.20 *Bishop sleeve.*

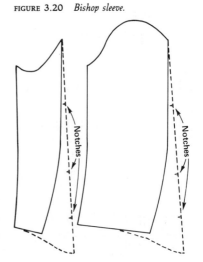

COMMERCIAL PAPER PATTERNS

Pants

It is not common practice in most costume shops to draft individual pants blocks for actors. Pants blocks are complicated to draft and will not be used nearly as often as the male and female body blocks. In recent years, commercial pattern companies have developed excellent, proportioned pants patterns for both men and women, and it is advantageous to the costumer to make use of these patterns to develop specific costume pants.

With the exception of the closure—which can be front, side, or back and executed with a fly or a flap—it is the shape and length of the pants leg that varies the most according to period fashion line. Changing the shape of the pants leg need not effect the basic shape of the crotch to waist portion, which is the area that controls the fit of the pants.

Purchase a commercial pants pattern in a standard, proportioned size, as close to the actor's measurements as possible. Vogue and Butterick patterns are particularly well shaped. Slash and spread the pants leg for additional fullness, adjust length as desired, or shape it according to the actor's leg measurements for a closer fit. Cut and construct a muslin mock-up and fit that on the actor.

In order to develop a sense for the problems of pants pattern drafting, every costumer should be able to draft pants blocks from individual measurements. Consult a good tailoring text for directions on how to draft men's trousers and a book of contemporary women's pattern design for women's pants. In most practical instances, however, the commercial pants pattern will be an adequate starting point.

Tailored Suits

The other main use for commercial paper patterns in a costume shop is for cutting tailored garments. All tailored garments are cut by the flat pattern method, and the most common directions for tailored pattern drafting relate to standard sizes rather than to drafting to individual measurements.

Tailored garments have a shape of their own which is created by the original cut and enforced by shaping: pad stitching and the use of steam. Most tailored garments do not fit the body tightly and therefore a standard size might be quite suitable for many different body shapes. Execute tailored costumes in muslin first in order to make fine style and design changes.

Every costume shop should have a collection of men's and women's suit patterns. Patterns for out-of-date styles can often be bought in resale shops or at rummage sales. Purchase such patterns in a variety of standard sizes so you will have them when you need them.

STORING PATTERNS

You should keep copies of the basic, as well as the interesting and unique, patterns that are developed for specific costumes. Even if they are not used again in their entirety, they will be invaluable in part or for research and pattern development. Store patterns in manila envelopes and file them in an orderly manner in metal drawers, orange crates, or cardboard boxes. Each envelope should contain pertinent information such as: basic measurements of the actor for whom the pattern was developed, historical period, type of garment, name and date of the production, designer, and, perhaps, a simple sketch of the garment.

Once the garment pattern has been developed and adjusted for line and fit, it is ready to be transferred to the fabric chosen by the designer.

Washable fabrics should always be preshrunk before they are cut, and the length of fabric should be pressed carefully with special attention paid to straightening the grain. Woolens may be preshrunk either by pressing with a steam iron and a damp cloth or by leaving the fabric rolled up in a damp sheet for two hours, then removing it and allowing it to dry on a flat surface. Never allow damp wool fabric to hang, for it will stretch.

Lay out the fabric to be cut. If the pattern of the fabric is a plaid or a print that must be matched, the cutting is usually done on a single layer of fabric. Very stretchy or slippery fabrics should also be cut one layer at a time. A firmly woven, solid color or small print fabric can be folded in half and identical fronts, backs, sleeves, and so on can then be cut two at a time. Some shops always insist upon single layer cutting. When cutting on a single layer, it is imperative that identical pairs of pieces be cut. Take great care not to let the pattern piece slip.

It is a good idea to lay out all the pattern pieces for a garment on the fabric before cutting anything. This will help you to make the most economical use of the fabric. If there is a directional nap, such as in corduroy or velvet, make sure that the pattern pieces are all laid on the fabric in the same direction. Check with the designer before determining the direction of the nap. Although most street garments are cut with the nap lying smoothly from top to bottom, many costume garments are cut against the nap. This will cause the fabric to appear deeper and richer under stage lights.

After the pieces have all been positioned on the fabric, check again for correct grain

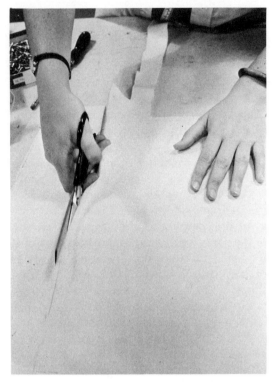

FIGURE 3.21 *Cutting the fabric. (Photograph by Mark Avery.)*

line, nap direction, and spacing. Pin the pieces to the fabric, mark a seam allowance if necessary, and cut around them with shears. Never raise the fabric up in the air to cut it. Always keep the base of the shears on the table. Do not remove the pattern pieces from the fabric until all pertinent markings have been transferred from the pattern to the fabric. This is done with tracing paper and a tracing wheel or, in the case of a soft, thick fabric, with tailors tacks.

It is usually a good idea to cut all the pieces necessary for a single garment at one time. That may include collars, facings, underlining, and lining. The construction process will move much more smoothly if the pieces are all on hand.

4

Theatrical Sewing Techniques

Costume technicians speak of "building" or "constructing" a stage costume while they continue to "make" street clothing for themselves. The choice of words indicates an attitude toward the finished product. Like a building, a costume's foundation is as important as its facade. Its function on the stage often governs its appearance. In short, a stage costume is designed, planned, and built for utility, strength, and beauty with no single aspect slighted in favor of another. It is a true construction process.

Most inexperienced costume technicians are amazed at the wear and tear a costume takes, even in a production that runs for only a few performances. Stage action is not as random as real life action. Playwrights deliberately choose to write the most energetic, rather than the most relaxed, scenes in a character's stage life. Actors on stage engage in much more physical activity during the course of a two and a half hour play than in any comparable time off stage. Even when stage movement is minimal, costumed actors are always in a state of heightened tension; they're turned on, engaged, ready to go. And, unless they are stoutly built, costumes will also go—to pieces.

Costume technicians are responsible for constructing garments that can withstand the rigors of the play and the acting process. This is true even when the garment is made of silk chiffon and must appear to be a fragile bit of nothing. The appearance of fragility may be achieved on stage, but actual fragility in costumes is to be avoided. Sturdy, functional construction comes from the application of good sewing techniques. Because of normal time pressures, a great many sewing short cuts are employed in a costume shop; carelessness and poor sewing techniques are not legitimate short cuts and they waste time rather than conserve it.

This chapter will review some basic sewing

techniques, applying them as precisely as possible to the theatrical situation. There is generally more than one way of performing any sewing task, and in some instances, more than one method is mentioned. It is much more important to have specific procedures for executing individual sewing steps, even if these procedures differ widely, than to become embroiled in arguments about the correctness and incorrectness of a given procedure. The following material is not offered in a dogmatic fashion. It contains a collection of methods and procedures drawn from a variety of costume construction situations.

HAND STITCHING

Despite a heavy reliance on machines in a costume shop, there is a lot of hand stitching to do. Facings must be tacked in place; hems put up; linings attached; buttons, snaps, and hooks and eyes sewn on; pad stitching done; and trim applied. Costume technicians ought to be familiar with the basic hand stitches and which operations they are suitable for. The shop should contain all necessary hand-stitching supplies.

Hand-sewing needles come in a variety of types and sizes. The finer or sheerer the fabric being sewn, the sharper and more slender the needle should be so that needlessly large holes will not be poked into the fabric weave. *Sharps* are medium length needles with small, rounded eyes. *Betweens* are shorter and also have small, rounded eyes. *Milliner's needles* are long with small, rounded eyes. *Embroidery* and *crewel needles* are of medium length and have longer, larger eyes. Each type comes in sizes ranging from 1–24. Sizes 7–10 are the most commonly used, although some larger sizes should be kept on hand for very bulky fabrics. Needles smaller than size 7 will probably sit unused in a drawer. *Glover's needles* are used for sewing on leather. They have three sharp edges as well as the point and should be handled with care. Since technicians vary in the type and size needle they prefer for handwork, it is wise to keep a variety in stock.

Whatever hand-stitching task you are engaged in, use a short length of thread. About twenty inches is good. It takes less time to rethread a needle than to untangle the knots that invariably appear when the thread is too

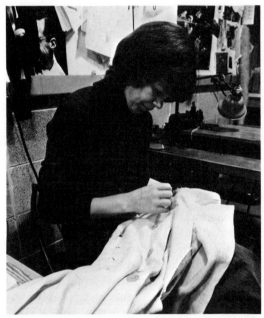

FIGURE 4.1 *Hand stitching in the costume shop at the Milwaukee Repertory Theater. (Photograph by Mark Avery.)*

long. Sewing threads, as stated in Chapter 2, are normally left twist. The thread is wound on the spool with the twist and it is best to thread the needle in the same direction in which the thread comes off the spool. Threading against the twist invites tangles. Rub beeswax on the end of the thread to make needle threading easier. After the needle is threaded, run the beeswax over the thread and smooth it with your fingers before beginning to sew.

Begin and end each row of hand stitching either with several small stitches taken on top of each other or by placing a knot in the thread.

The Running Stitch

This is the most basic of all stitches. It is used for easing, gathering, mending, and basting. With the needle in one hand, take several small bites of the fabric, in and out, until you have from three to six stitches on the needle. Pull the needle through but do not draw the thread too tightly. Repeat this process until you arrive at your destination.

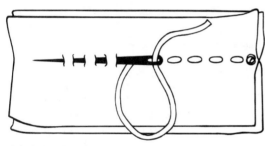

FIGURE 4.2 *Running stitch.*

The Back Stitch

This is the strongest of all the hand stitches. It is especially useful for mending ripped seams that cannot be reached with the sewing machine. It has the appearance of a machine stitch on the right side, but the stitches overlap on the wrong side. Bring the needle through the fabric to the upper side. Then take a stitch back about one-eighth-inch,

FIGURE 4.3 *Back stitch.*

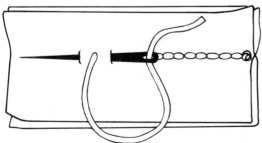

bringing the needle out again about one-eighth-inch beyond the beginning of the stitch. Keep inserting the needle in the end of the last stitch and bringing it out one stitch ahead. The stitches on the underside will be twice as long as the stitches on the upper side.

The Invisible or Prick Stitch

If an almost invisible stitching line is desirable, the prick stitch is a good choice. It is a variation on the back stitch in which the needle is carried back only one or two fabric threads, forming a tiny surface stitch with a reinforced understitch. The prick stitch is often used for putting in zippers by hand.

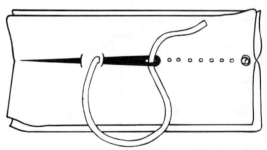

FIGURE 4.4 *Prick stitch.*

The Slip Stitch

The slip stitch is used to hem, to attach linings and to hold pockets and trims in place and is almost entirely invisible. Slide the needle through a thread or two of the under

FIGURE 4.5 *Slip stitch.*

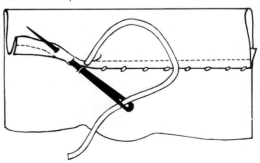

fabric, then up through the folded edge of the upper fabric. Repeat, spacing the stitches evenly about one-quarter-inch apart. Do not pull the thread too tight.

The Hemming Stitch

This stitch can be used for all types of hemming. Take a tiny stitch in the garment and bring the needle diagonally up through the hem edge. Continue in this manner, spacing stitches about one-quarter-inch apart.

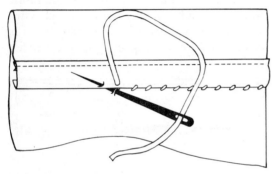

FIGURE 4.6   *Hemming stitch.*

The Locked Hemming Stitch

Use this stitch when you want a particularly stout hem. Take a small stitch in the garment and bring the needle diagonally up through the hem edge. Take another tiny stitch, bringing the needle up through the folded fabric only, on top of the first stitch that was

FIGURE 4.7   *Locked hemming stitch.*

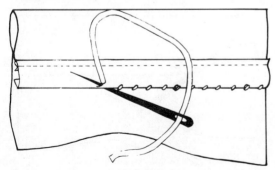

made. Repeat this lock stitch every fourth and sixth stitch. This locks the hemming stitch in place. These stitches may be placed somewhat further apart than unlocked hemming stitches.

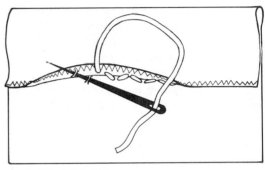

FIGURE 4.8   *Blind stitch.*

The Blind Stitch

This stitch is used for hemming and holding facings in place and is invisible on both sides of the garment. Roll the finished or folded edge of the hem or facing back on the garment about one-quarter-inch; take a small horizontal stitch through one thread of the garment or underlining fabric, then pick up a thread of the hem or facing diagonally above. Do not pull these stitches too tight.

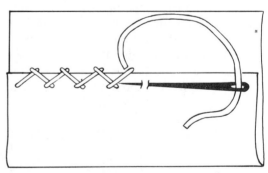

FIGURE 4.9   *Catch stitch, herringbone, or cross stitch.*

The Catch Stitch

The catch stitch (also called herringbone stitch and cross stitch) is used for holding two layers of fabric together in place while still keeping a degree of flexibility. It's commonly used to attach raw edges of facings and interfacings to the wrong sides of garment sections, sewing pleats or tucks in linings, and securing hems in knit fabrics. Work this stitch from left to right. Make a small horizontal stitch in the upper layer of fabric a short distance from the edge. Then make another stitch in the lower layer of fabric, diagonally across from the first stitch. Alternate stitching along the edge in a zigzag fashion, keeping threads loose.

TAILORING HAND STITCHES

Diagonal Tacking

The diagonal tacking stitch is only used to attach an interfacing to an underlining in a coat or jacket front. Diagonal tacking is accomplished by taking a tiny horizontal stitch through the interfacing, catching only a thread or two of the underlining. Repeat this directly below, placing stitches approximately three-quarters to one and one-half inches apart. A diagonal stitch will form on the interfacing side. It doesn't take long to tack an interfacing and it will add significantly to the firm, smooth look of a well-tailored jacket or coat. If there is no underlining, do not tack the facing; it will then be merely machine-basted to the outer fabric along the seam allowance.

In recent years, costume shops have begun to use fusible interfacings, which do save time. If care is taken to choose a fine quality fusible interfacing, suitable in weight for the outer fabric being constructed, and to apply it exactly according to the manufacturer's directions so it will not separate from the garment through wear, fusible interfacings are excellent. No tacking is, of course, necessary.

Pad Stitching

Pad stitching molds undercollars and lapels by actually sewing the shape in place. The stitch is taken through the interfacing and the outer layer of fabric whether or not there is an underlining in between. The stitch is executed exactly like diagonal tacking, catching only a thread or two of the outer fabric

FIGURE 4.11 *Pad stitching on undercollar. (Photograph by Susan Perkins.)*

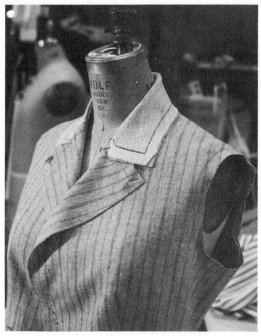

FIGURE 4.10 *Diagonal tacking.*

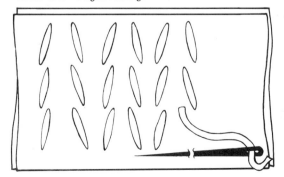

layer. The shape of the undercollar or lapel will already have been set by steaming. Hold in the shape while stitching. An undercollar may be held over the left index finger and a lapel over the knee or over a tailor's ham. Use small stitches on undercollars and larger stitches on lapels. Pad stitching does take time, but it is a necessary step for firm, tailored shapes.

IN DEFENSE OF BASTING

Basting is a temporary stitch that is used in a garment in the early stages of construction and removed after the garment has been permanently stitched. The practice of hand-basting is associated with fine tailoring and dressmaking and is not so often done in a costume shop. Body slopers, muslin proofs, and garments being assembled for first fittings are usually machine-basted, a long machine stitch that is easy to rip out. In many of the instances in which a tailor would baste, the costumer will steam and pin.

There are, however, three specific operations for which hand-basting is recommended. In each instance a regular basting stitch, which is a long version of the running stitch is suitable. Stitches may be from one-quarter-inch to three-quarters of an inch.

1. Whenever velvet is being seamed, especially the more slippery sorts, you will ultimately save time by basting the seams before machine-stitching them. Velvet is particularly difficult to control under the pressure foot. Even with very careful pinning, the top layer of fabric will stretch just enough to throw off the seam. Baste first and avoid frustration. It is sometimes advisable to do a first fitting on a velvet garment when the seams are hand-basted. A line of ripped machine stitching in velvet occasionally leaves a mark that is all but impossible to remove. Use very fine machine and hand needles when working with velvet. A teflon foot will also help to lessen the pressure when machining.

2. Baste up hems for the final fitting and do not press the fold until after the hem is set and stitched. Run the basting line from three-quarters to one-inch up from the bottom edge of the fold.

3. It is often helpful to baste down facings, close to the folded edge, before pressing them. Finger the facing just slightly to the inside of the garment, establishing a clean edge and preventing the facing from being visible on the outside. This treatment is especially good for curved, faced edges such as necklines and for scalloped or dagged edges. Take care not to press over the basting stitches as they may leave an indentation on the fabric, especially on fine woolens.

SEWING ON BUTTONS

Buttons may be sewn on with or without a shank. The shank is an extra thread neck between the button and the garment which permits the overlapping side of the garment with the buttonhole to lay smoothly beneath the button without pulling. A shank is not necessary if the fabric in the garment is quite thin, if the button is not practical, or if the button is made with a shank.

Figure 4.12 illustrates one method of creating a button shank. Bring a double, knotted thread up from the underneath side of the fabric through a hole in the button. Lay a toothpick across the button, between the two holes, and carry the thread across the toothpick and down into the other hole. Take about six or eight stitches, then remove the toothpick and bring the needle up underneath the button. Wind the needle thread firmly around the threads between the button and the garment fabric. Bring the thread to the underside of the fabric, knot and cut.

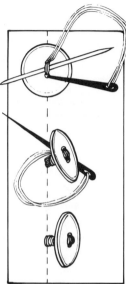

FIGURE 4.12 *Sewing on button with thread shank.*

Another method is to insert the edge of the thumb under the button as it is being stitched on, raising it slightly from the surface of the fabric. Wrap and tie off in the same manner.

When sewing buttons on heavy garments made of loosely woven wools or of leather or suede, it is a good idea to reinforce the button on the underside so it will not tear out. Put a small shirt-size button on the underside, directly beneath the top button; sew both top and bottom buttons on at the same time. Create a button shank as described above.

HOOKS AND EYES

Hooks and eyes may well be the most common costume closings. Extra large sizes are used for heavy skirts and large capes. Medium-sized ones may run the whole back length of a period bodice, with smaller sizes at the collar and cuffs. Sew hooks and eyes on firmly, usually with heavy duty thread. Don't forget to anchor the end of the hook and the outer part of the loop eye, as illustrated in Figure 4.13.

FIGURE 4.13 *Hook and eye correctly anchored.*

SNAP FASTENERS

There are a great many uses for the large-sized snap fasteners called "whopper-poppers." These snaps are extremely strong and are often used for attaching costume props and accessories, such as bandoliers or uniform insignias, as well as for heavy, bulky closures. Whopper-poppers should always be stitched on with heavy-duty thread, making six or eight stitches through each hole.

More normal-sized snap fasteners may be placed at waistline and neck closings, in com-

FIGURE 4.14 *Whopper-popper correctly anchored.*

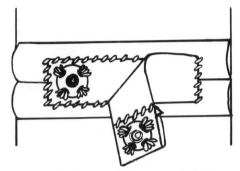

FIGURE 4.15   *Small snap on ribbon sewn inside shoulder seam.*

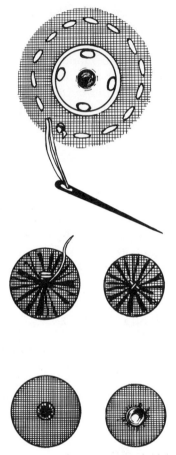

FIGURE 4.16   *Covering a snap with fabric.*

bination with either hooks and eyes or zippers. Many low-necked or sleeveless costumes require holders on the inside of the shoulder seam to secure lingerie straps. They are sometimes made with a bit of chained thread (see Figure 4.66) stitched to the garment on one end and attached to the ball part of a snap fastener on the other. The socket part of the snap fastener is stitched to the garment. They may also be sewn first to narrow ribbon or tape, which is then sewn to the inside shoulder seam of the garment. Lingerie straps can be purchased ready-made at dime stores. In order to completely conceal the shiny metal snap fastener on a sheer costume, cover both parts of the snap with a bit of the costume fabric before stitching the snap to the garment. A sheer covering will not interfere with the snap's performance.

MACHINE STITCHING

All sewing machines have essentially the same working parts, although they may not look the same on different machines. See Figure 4.17 for a diagram of a domestic sewing machine with all parts labeled. When you encounter a machine with which you are not familiar, consult the instruction book in order to familiarize yourself with its working parts. If no instruction book is available, study the machine and practice sewing on a scrap of material; you can usually figure out exactly how it works in a short time by comparing its operation with other machines you have operated.

There are three general types of lock stitch sewing machines manufactured for domestic use. The first is the *straight stitch machine* that will accomplish only a forward and a backward stitch (some older model domestic and many industrial machines do not operate in

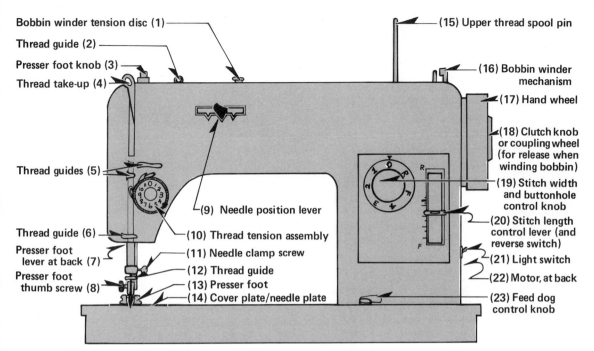

Bobbin winder tension disc (1)
Thread guide (2)
Presser foot knob (3)
Thread take-up (4)
Thread guides (5)
Thread guide (6)
Presser foot lever at back (7)
Presser foot thumb screw (8)
(9) Needle position lever
(10) Thread tension assembly
(11) Needle clamp screw
(12) Thread guide
(13) Presser foot
(14) Cover plate/needle plate
(15) Upper thread spool pin
(16) Bobbin winder mechanism
(17) Hand wheel
(18) Clutch knob or coupling wheel (for release when winding bobbin)
(19) Stitch width and buttonhole control knob
(20) Stitch length control lever (and reverse switch)
(21) Light switch
(22) Motor, at back
(23) Feed dog control knob

FIGURE 4.17 *Parts of a domestic machine.*

reverse). The *zigzag machine* will perform the straight stitch and a zigzag stitch in varying widths. The *automatic stitch machine* will, with certain gear adjustments, perform, in addition to the straight and zigzag stitches, a variety of stretch and decorative stitches. Industrial models that are generally found in costume shops are straight stitch machines, although some shops are fortunate enough to have an industrial zigzag.

Threading the Machine

The upper threading of all domestic sewing machines is similar. Before threading any machine, make sure that the take-up lever is sitting at its highest position. Every machine has a tension device through which the upper thread must be passed. No machine will operate if the thread is put through the needle from the incorrect direction. The final thread guide is usually located on the side of the needle shaft from which the thread should come. In many of the new automatic stitch machines, the needle threads from front to

back rather than from side to side; this is to benefit both right- and left-handed machine operators.

Industrial sewing machines are often slightly more complicated to thread than domestic sewing machines. In many shops, it is common practice to tie on a new thread and pull it through the machine, rather than rethread it each time thread color is changed.

Figures 4.18, 4.19, and 4.20 are threading diagrams for both a domestic and an industrial sewing machine. These are only examples, and each machine you operate will be slightly different.

Most domestic machines have a conventional bobbin winder on the right side of the machine, near the hand wheel. In most instances, wind the bobbin with the same thread used on the top of the machine. For best bobbin tension, never wind one color on top of another. Make sure the thread is wound evenly, in level layers, across the bobbin. Sometimes it is necessary to hold the thread with thumb and forefinger as it is being fed onto the bobbin. This will increase

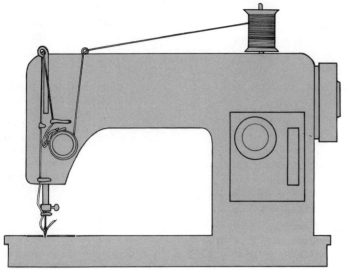

FIGURE 4.19 *Tension threading for domestic machine.*

FIGURE 4.18 *Top threading for domestic machine.*

the tension slightly and a tighter bobbin will result.

Industrial machines have a bobbin-winding mechanism that operates while the machine is stitching. Thread the bobbin from a separate spool of thread. The winding process will stop automatically when the bobbin is full. If you have to thread a bobbin on an industrial machine when you are not sewing, make certain the pressure foot is held up so it won't be scratched by the moving feed dog.

Inside the bobbin case the thread may lead off in either a clockwise or a counterclockwise direction. You may have to experiment. If the bobbin case is improperly threaded, the thread will usually slip out of the threading notches and from under the tension spring. The line of stitching will be out of balance.

Once the upper threading is complete and the bobbin casing inserted, the bobbin thread must be drawn up through the needle hole in the throat plate. To do this, hold the needle thread in the left hand, turn the hand wheel toward you until the needle goes down and up again and the take-up lever is sitting at its highest point. Pull the needle thread; the

bobbin thread will come up through the needle hole in a loop. Pull the loop until the free end appears. Place both needle and bobbin threads under the presser foot and lay them off to the side. Most hand wheels turn towards you; turning them in the wrong direction may cause the top thread to break.

Regulating Pressure

On most sewing machines, the pressure of the presser foot on the fabric can be regulated by a thumb screw or a dial on the top, left-hand part of the machine head. When the pressure is too light, the machine feeds irregularly and the stitching line may be wobbly. If it is too heavy, the stitch length may be uneven and the presser foot can leave marks on soft pile fabrics. Experiment with scraps of the fabric you are using until you no longer see any of the symptoms of incorrect pressure.

Regulating Tension

There are two thread tensions on a lock stitch machine: an upper tension which is exerted

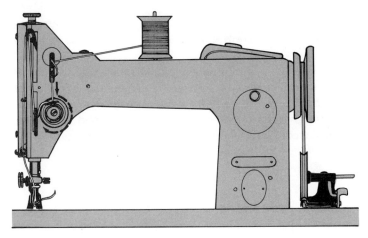

FIGURE 4.20 *Top threading for industrial machine.*

on the top thread and a lower tension which is exerted on the bottom thread. The upper tension is controlled by a dial on the machine face and the lower by a small screw on the bobbin casing.

Thread tension should be perfectly balanced for the fabric on which you are sewing. It will often have to be readjusted for other fabrics. Test for correct tension by threading the machine with two different thread colors: one on the top, the other on the bottom. If the bottom color shows on the top of the stitch, the upper tension is too tight and the lower too loose: if the top color shows on the bottom, the upper tension is too loose and the bottom too tight. Figure 4.21 illustrates greatly enlarged diagrams of balanced, or even, tension and unbalanced tension.

Make tension adjustments gradually, working first with the upper tension. If you must alter the bottom tension—and do this only when absolutely necessary—never make more than a quarter turn of the screw at a time. For a rough tension check as you are adjusting, hold both top and bottom threads between the thumb and index finger and pull them to the back of the machine. If the ten-

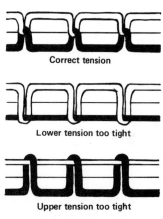

Correct tension

Lower tension too tight

Upper tension too tight

FIGURE 4.21 *Machine stitch tension.*

sion is accurate, each thread should offer equal resistance.

A seam sewn with poorly balanced tension is weak. The tighter thread will pop under stress. Some machines seem to require more patient tension adjustments than others. Take the time, and remain patient; stout seams depend on successful tension adjustments. Sometimes it is helpful to record the top tension settings on individual machines for different fabrics; this list of settings can be referred to when the same material is stitched again.

Regulating Stitch Length

Stitch length depends on the weight and texture of a fabric. Generally, a fine fabric requires a short stitch while a longer stitch is used on heavy fabrics. Stitches should be shorter for a curved seam than for a straight seam. True bias and garment bias seams need a short stitch, and a long stitch is always used to control fullness in a seam that requires easing.

Different sewing machines mark the stitch length in different increments. Experiment with each for the "normal" length (which, on a domestic Singer, is 12) and adjust for longer and shorter stitches from there.

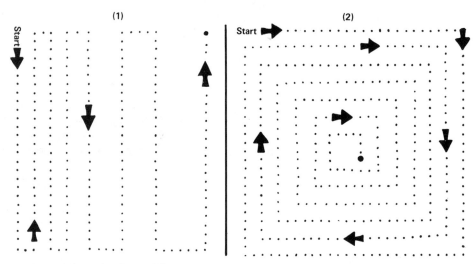

FIGURES 4.22a & 4.22b *Sewing skill exercises.*

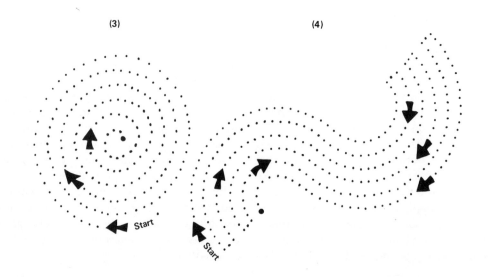

SEWING SKILL EXERCISES

Figures 4.22a and 4.22b contain several diagrams which may be enlarged and drawn on brown paper and used to practice basic machine-sewing skills. They include stitching straight parallel rows, circles, curves, and right angle turns. Stitch directly on the brown paper with an unthreaded machine. Practice on both domestic and industrial machines, gradually increasing sewing speed. As a final test, draw out the diagrams on unbleached muslin cloth and follow the lines, using a bright colored thread.

When you are following an indicated stitching line, do not look at the machine needle, but at a point on the stitching line somewhat ahead of the needle. When the seamline is not indicated, look at the outer edge of the seam allowance.

SEAMS

Whenever two pieces of fabric are stitched together, a seam has been created. Seaming is the most common sewing operation, the foundation of all costume construction. If the machine pressure, tension, and stitch length are properly adjusted for a given piece of fabric, two strips of that fabric can be seamed *on the straight grain,* without pins, and without holding the fabric, and the two pieces of fabric will lie precisely on top of each other for the entire length of the seam, with the edges ending up equal. If the pieces of fabric are cut on the curve or on the bias, and a seam is sewn in the same way, the top fabric will stretch more than the bottom fabric and the pieces will not meet at the end of the seam. The alignment of the entire seam has been thrown off.

Pinning curved or biased seams together at regular intervals is the usual way of maintaining the alignment of two pieces of fabric while the seam is being stitched (very slippery fabrics, such as velvet, may require basting). Some technicians place staying pins vertically on the seam line and remove them as they sew; others place the pins horizontally on the seam line and, if the sewing machine has a hinged foot, sew directly over the pins.

The fastest way of seaming is to manipulate the two pieces of cloth in such a way that the alignment is maintained without the added step of pinning. Rest the left hand firmly on both layers of fabric, to the side and in front of the needle. Separate the two layers with the right hand and exert a slight pressure on the bottom piece as it moves under the presser foot. The amount of pressure will vary according to the stretchability of the fabric. On a long seam, you will want to pause every now and then to check the alignment before proceeding further. Learning to seam without pins takes a bit of practice. Because you will save time in the long run, it is worth the time spent to practice the skill.

If you are stitching a seam permanently, that is, if you are not machine-basting, you should always lock both the beginning and the ending of the seam with a few reversed stitches right on the seamline. When you are using a machine that does not operate in reverse, sew forward a few stitches; then make sure the take-up lever is in its highest position, raise the presser foot, and move the material toward you. Lower the presser foot and resume sewing. Your new stitching will be directly over the first stitches made.

Seam Trimming, Grading, and Clipping

Once a costume garment has been fitted and altered, seams are trimmed in certain areas to reduce fabric bulk. Do not clip seams in costumes unless fit, shape, and hang is adversely affected by the seam width. It is often an advantage to have full width seams for future alterations. Many seams must be trimmed, however, and do not affect future fit.

Facing seams should always be trimmed. Each edge of a facing seam should be trimmed to a different width, which is called *grading*. Trim the garment side of the seam to one-quarter-inch and the facing side of the seam slightly narrower. The wider seam should always lie against the outside surface of the garment.

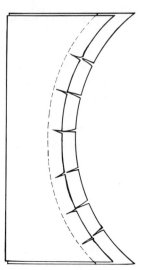

FIGURE 4.24   *Grading and clipping an inside curve.*

eighth-inch from the seamline. These slashes will allow the facing to be turned inside smoothly. On an outside curve, such as a Peter Pan collar, trim and grade the seam as before, then snip small triangular notches out of the seam width to one-eighth-inch from the seamline. The collar will then turn in on itself without puckering.

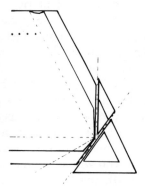

FIGURE 4.23   *Grading and trimming collar point.*

Square corners and points which are to be turned back on each other—collars, pockets, sashes, and the front corners of doublet skirts, for example—should be trimmed and graded in the same manner, with the right side fabric trimmed to one-quarter-inch and the wrong side fabric slightly less. In addition, snip off the point and trim a piece from each side of the point, quite close to the stitching line. Only with careful trimming away of seam allowance will the corner or point be sharp when the fabric is turned.

Curved seams must be notched or slashed, in addition to being trimmed. A neck facing seam is an inside curve. Trim and grade the seam as indicated in the paragraph above and slash the remaining seam width to one-

FIGURE 4.25   *Grading and trimming a Peter Pan collar.*

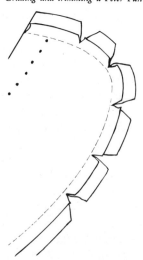

Curved garment construction seams, such as those up the side fronts of a princess line dress, might also have to be slashed and notched so the seam can be pressed open to lie smoothly. It may not be necessary if the curve is slight and if the fabric is a loose weave. Do not slash or notch main construction seams unless the fabric will not lie smooth otherwise, since this also lessens the possibility of future alterations.

Understitching

In order to ensure that the facings inside a garment will not roll back out and be visible, the seam allowances should be stitched to the facing on the underside. Understitching is a finishing step and should not be done until the garment has been fitted and altered, the facing stitched in place, and the seam trimmed and graded. At that point, pull the facing and the seam allowances away from the garment and stitch from the right side, through the facing and the seam allowances, quite close to the seamline. This stitching line will not be visible on the outside of the finished garment. Turn the facing to the inside,

baste down if desired, and secure with a suitable hand stitch. This is an important step for creating a neat garment edge and should not be omitted.

Seam Finishes

Raw seam edges are often given some kind of finish in order to keep them from raveling in the wash or at the dry cleaners. In the costume shop, seam finishes are sometimes applied before the garment is constructed, and sometimes after. It is not necessary to finish facing seams or other seams that will be closely trimmed and covered unless the material is particularly loosely woven.

An overlock stitch, or serge, is the best costume seam finish for all fabrics except extremely light-weight ones such as chiffon. And it is the fastest process. A normal first step for many costume sewing projects is to serge around the edges of each garment piece before stitching the basic construction seams. Always remember to make match-up marks with chalk or tracing paper instead of with notches, which will be hidden by the overlock stitch. Be careful not to cut away any fabric on the serger, unless it is intentional.

In the absence of an overlock machine, the zigzag stitch also makes a fine seam finish. Set it on a wide width setting and a rather long stitch length. A zigzagged edge is not as flexible as a serged edge, nor does it contain an extremely loose weave as efficiently. Nevertheless, it is probably the most common seam finish regularly used in costume shops today.

The seams in a bulky, loose weave wool fabric garment, such as a coat or a cape, will sometimes have to be bound in order to stabilize the seam edges. A bound seam may also be necessary in an unlined garment if the inside will be visible to the audience. Seams are bound after the garment is constructed and before facings are applied. Many domestic sewing machines have a binding attach-

FIGURE 4.26   *Understitching a facing.*

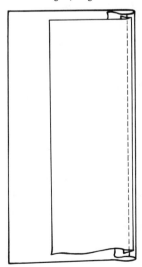

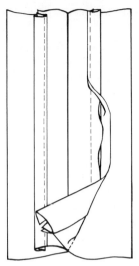

FIGURE 4.27   *Seam finish with bias binding.*

an unlined garment, simply turn under each edge of the seam and sew down with a row of straight stitches close to the edge of the seam. This is a nice, neat finish, but it does not work well if the seams are very curved. In that case, seam binding is better.

Special Seams

Other, more complicated seams may be incorporated into a costume, either for fashion detail or for extra strength. The *single top-stitched seam,* or welt seam, is excellent for

ment that will feed folded bias binding directly onto the seam edge. Stitch it on with a zigzag stitch. If a binding attachment is not available, stitch one edge of the seam binding to the seam edge, then turn the binding, enclosing the edge of the seam, and stitch it down flat.

Rather than binding light- or medium-weight fabrics that fray, or will be seen in

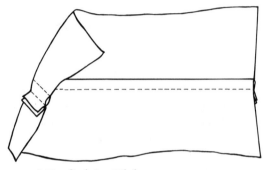

FIGURE 4.29   *Single top-stitched seam.*

places where there will be a great deal of strain on the seam, such as the center back and the crotch. Stitch the seam in the normal fashion. Edges may be serged or zigzagged. Press both edges of the seam to one side and top stitch from the right side of the fabric through all three layers, approximately one-quarter-inch from the seamline. If you are top-stitching both side front or side back seams, make sure the seam edges are both pressed in the same direction in relation to the body; either both toward the center, or both away from the center.

The *double top-stitched seam,* as shown in Figure 4.30, is primarily decorative. Decorative top-stitching is often done on the sewing machine with silk twist thread. When using silk twist for top-stitching, work on the right side of the garment. A long stitch length is usually the most handsome.

FIGURE 4.28   *Seam finish, turned under once and machined.*

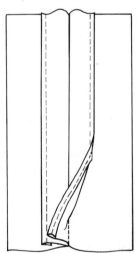

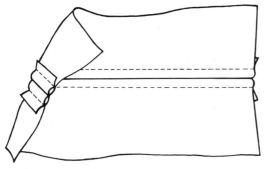

FIGURE 4.30 *Double top-stitched seam.*

Trim the seam close to the stitching line, about one-quarter to one-eighth of an inch. Turn the right sides of the fabric together. Fold and press on the first seamline. Stitch the second seam directly on the seamline.

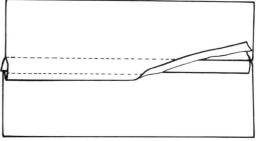

FIGURE 4.32 *Flat-felled seam.*

French seams, as in Figure 4.31, are often chosen for very sheer fabrics and for making lingerie. They do not work well on curved

FIGURE 4.31 *French seam.*

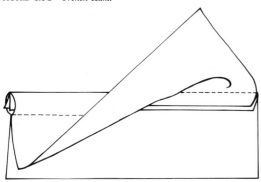

seams. The French seam is accomplished in two steps; actually it is a seam within a seam. Stitch the first seam with the wrong sides of the fabric together, about one-quarter-inch to the outside of the seamline. This seam will appear on the right side of the garment.

The flat-felled seam is appropriate for many men's and boy's costumes. Most shirts and sports garments are made with flat-felled seams. A flat-felled seam is quite stout; it is, however, no stronger than the single top-stitched seam, only more decorative. Place the wrong sides of the fabric together and stitch on the seamline. The seam will be on the outside of the garment. Press both seam edges to one side. Trim the underneath edge. Fold the upper edge under and top-stitch. Only slight curves can be neatly flat-felled. As with single top-stitched seams, make sure seams on both sides of any garment are flat-felled in the same relationship to each other. Flat-felled armhole seams in a man's shirt should always be top-stitched to the body of the shirt rather than to the sleeve.

DARTS

Darts usually occur at the bust, waist, shoulders, and elbows. They are a means of shaping the garment over curves in the body. Darts are always stitched on a garment bias and, therefore, have a tendency to stretch. It is very important to stitch darts properly so they will not stretch out of shape. Darts that occur on each side of a garment must be stitched in exactly the same way so the garment will not be lopsided.

Dart markings are taken from the altered

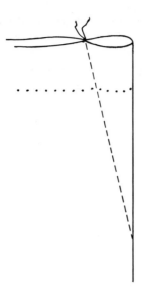

FIGURE 4.33 *Plain dart.*

pattern. Fold the dart and match up the markings. Place a pin at the seam edge of the dart and another at the point. Place several pins along the length of the dart. The heads of the pins should be on the same side as the fold. Begin stitching at the seam edge. Follow the stitching line carefully. The point of the dart should be ended by taking four or five stitches just parallel to the edge of the fold and only a thread's width inside. Continue stitching for about a half an inch below the point of the dart, off the fabric. Do not backstitch the point of a dart, which will tend to create a lump. For extra security, tie off the threads at the dart point. From the right side of the garment, darts should move smoothly into the shape of the garment with no pouches or puckers.

Press darts toward the center of the garment if they are in the skirt back, blouse front and back, and shoulder. Bust and elbow darts are pressed down. Do not press darts on a flat ironing board; their purpose is to follow a curve. Press darts on a tailor's ham. Press from the seam edge toward the point. Some bulky darts should be split down the center, opened, and pressed out to each side.

If the fabric is loosely woven, overlock or zigzag the cut edges.

Contour darts, or fish darts, usually occur at the waist, with the deepest part of the dart at the waistline, tapering to a point above and below. The most precise method of stitching a contour dart is to do it in two separate operations, beginning each time at the waistline and stitching out to each point. If the fabric being darted is quite soft or slippery, this is the preferable method. However, if the fabric is sturdy and tightly woven, a continuous dart line may be stitched in. Start at the upper point and stitch toward the bottom of the garment. Make sure to stitch both contour darts in the same direction. Tie threads at each point; do not backstitch.

In order to have them lie flat, contour darts must be slashed. The deepest slash should be at the waistline and should come to within one-eighth-inch of the stitching line. Do not slash the contour darts until the garment has had a final fitting. You will want to be certain that the garment is not too small before slashing. Some smaller contour darts can be pressed so that half of the dart lies on each side of the center in order to eliminate slashing.

FIGURE 4.34 *Contour dart.*

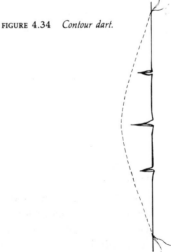

Interfacing darts are traditionally butted rather than folded, in order to eliminate bulk. Cut out the dart section; pull the two edges of the interfacing together and zigzag the dart line together using the widest possible zigzag stitch.

GATHERING

Gathering is such a frequently performed operation in a costume shop, for skirts, petticoats, ruffles, sleeves, and so forth that it is particularly important to adopt simple, efficient ways of doing it. Gathering threads stitched by hand are seldom the best way. Machine-in the gathering threads if at all possible. When running the gathering thread, it is often a good idea to put a heavy duty zigzag over it to attach it to the fabric. Stabilize one end of the nylon thread and pull up the other until the material is gathered in sufficiently.

Many costumes require vast quantities of ruffles. If you are doing more than a yard or two, gather them on the sewing machine rather than by pulling up a gathering thread. Hem first and use the machine ruffler attach-

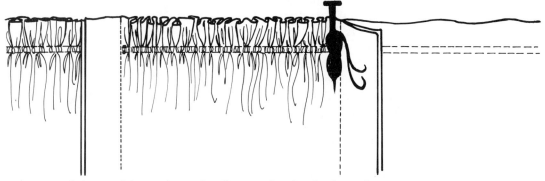

FIGURE 4.35 *Gathering with large machine stitch, pulling up, and winding threads around pin.*

thread on the machine bobbin. Many shops keep a heavy duty, nylon thread just for this purpose, and many also keep a bobbin wound with this thread by each sewing machine. Set the machine for a long stitch length. Two lines of stitching will produce a more even row of gathers than a single line and will also be stronger. When pulling in the gathers by hand, stitch down one end of the gathering threads and pull the bottom threads. Once the fabric has been gathered in the required amount, place a pin across the stitching lines and wrap the pulled threads around the pin, using a figure eight wrap.

Another method of gathering is to lay down a strip of heavy duty nylon thread and

ment on a domestic machine, which is sometimes also called a pleater. The ruffler operates by pushing small pleats into one edge of a strip of cloth. There are normally three settings to determine the distance between the pleats; that is to say, how full the ruffle will be. The tightest pleating, which is usually the right one for costume garments, requires strips of cloth three times the finished length of the ruffle. Most ruffler attachments have a thumb screw in the front that can be tightened to regulate the stitching operation. Ruffler attachments are not particularly sturdy and, if there is a great deal of ruffling to do, it is a good idea to round up at least one spare.

The importance of having a suitable procedure for marking and preparing hems cannot be overstressed. Use a yardstick or a right angle with chalk or pins, or a pin or chalk type skirt marker to mark the skirt an even distance from the floor all the way around. If the skirt has a lining that is attached only to the waistband, mark a hem on the skirt and on the lining in two separate operations. Make chalk marks or insert pins about every two or three inches. Mark a floor length hem by laying the excess fabric on the floor and marking where the skirt hits the floor.

When the garment is off the actor, turn up the hem on the marks. Some irregularities might have to be straightened out, but there should be no radical adjustments. Make sure all vertical seams are pressed open before they are folded in. Baste the hem up about three-quarters of an inch above the bottom fold. Use a long, even running stitch. Lay the skirt on a flat surface with the right side down, and measure the hem width, trimming it so that it is even. Now the hem is ready to be checked and finished.

The edge of the hem may be finished off just like a seam edge: overlocked, zigzagged, or turned under and stitched down. A hem may also be finished by adding straight or bias tape to the top of the raw hem edge and stitching the tape to the garment.

Hems may be stitched down in various ways. The hemming stitch, the locked hemming stitch, and the catch stitch are usually used to put in hems by hand. Be careful not to pull the thread so tightly that the garment will pucker, and don't create any large stitches on the underside that an actor can catch with a shoe heel. The blind hemming stitch on an automatic stitch machine may also be used. Check the instructions for your particular machine to see how this stitch is created. It is a variation on the zigzag stitch. Hems may be put in very easily and rapidly with the blind hemstitch machine that was described in Chapter 1.

Figure 4.36 illustrates a simple method of putting in a curved hem. After the hem is marked and set, a gathering stitch is run along the raw edge. Do not use a heavy duty bobbin thread for this row of gathering. Pull up the gathering thread just slightly, enough so that the hem will lie flat. Maintaining this fullness, stitch on a length of bias tape as indicated in Figure 4.36, fold the tape under, and secure the hem.

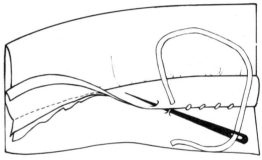

FIGURE 4.36   *Curved hem.*

Some hems, such as those at the bottom of a shirt or blouse, may be simply turned over twice and machine-stitched. This is often referred to as a shirttail hem. A very narrow, rolled under hem can be created with a domestic or an industrial hemming foot. For hemming sheer or loosely woven fabrics, or curved edges with the hemming foot, it is a good idea to run a line of straight machine stitching about one-quarter-inch inside the raw edge before starting the hem. Hemming with the hemming foot is the quickest way to prepare the edges of fabric for ruffling.

Sometimes hems are faced. This may be done where there is not enough material for the necessary hem width. A facing may be created for a scalloped or dagged hem, or for a sharply curved hem such as that on a train.

Gowns that drag on the ground are often faced with a stout, dark-colored material that will not be damaged on the floor.

To face a hem, mark it correctly and trim to within whatever seam width is being used. Hem facings may be shaped or made from bias strips. Stitch the facing or bias strip on to the hem edge, right sides of the fabrics together. Turn over, trim and grade the seam, and understitch the facing. Turn the facing to the inside and secure the hem with any of the methods discussed in the paragraphs above.

If a scalloped or dagged edge is being faced, the facing should have been cut when the garment was cut. The hem on a garment of this sort is usually adjusted by tucks taken above the area of the edging design. Stitch the facing to the garment. Trim and grade the seam; slash and notch as necessary, and turn. Understitching is not usually possible. Press carefully over the tailor's ham.

PRESSING

The proper pressing of costume garments, while they are being constructed, is an integral part of the building process. Each pressing job should be done at the correct stage, not all saved until the end. Seams that are to cross each other should always be pressed open with steam before they are stitched together. Darts should be pressed before garment pieces are assembled.

Pressing is not the same as ironing. Most pressing is accomplished with little movement of the iron. The flat surface of the ironing board is seldom used. Before pressing any fabric of which you are not certain, test a scrap to see how it is going to react to heat and steam. You may have to adjust the iron heat setting for certain fabrics. For others you will always need to have a pressing cloth between the surface of the iron and the surface of the fabric.

Pressing Equipment

The steam iron and ironing board, or ironing table, were discussed in Chapter 1. Several additional pieces of pressing equipment are quite essential. The *sleeveboard* is like a small ironing board which is set on top of the regular ironing board. It is used for pressing sleeves, opening most seams, and pressing fine details. Some shops have two or three sleeveboards of varying sizes. The *seamboard,*

or point presser, is an uncovered wooden board with one pointed end; it is used to press open seams on facings and points. The *tailor's ham* is a fat, stuffed item, shaped rather like a ham. It is very firm and is used to press almost anything that curves. Always press darts on a tailor's ham. Most tailor's hams are covered with wool, and it is quite possible to make one in the shop, filling it with sand or sawdust. The *wooden pounding block,* or clapper, is used in connection with steam to flatten the edges of lapels, collars, hems, pleats, and so forth on tailored garments made of heavy or bulky fabrics. Steam is applied and the pounding block used quickly while the moisture still remains in the wool. Some people call this a *spanking block,* which is quite descriptive of its action. A *pressing pad,* made simply from three or four layers of soft wool flannel interlining attached to a canvas backing, is extremely useful when pressing over a zipper, pockets, bound buttonholes, or any raised detail. For pressing velvet and a few other napped fabrics, a *velvet needleboard* is essential. Needleboards are very expensive, but there is no other way to press velvet without leaving some pressing marks. If a velvet board is not available, use either another piece of velvet or a towel in its place. Make sure to have a supply of clean, size-free *pressing cloths* near the ironing area. Soft, washed muslin is suitable for most things, although wool flannel interfacing is excellent for fabrics that might become shiny when pressed.

Pressing Techniques

Always take out pins and basting stitches before pressing. Both may leave an imprint on the fabric. Open ordinary seams on the sleeveboard. Generally, press from the widest part of the garment to the narrowest (the same way seams should be stitched). Do not put the full weight of the iron down on the seam. Use the tip and steam. Press from the wrong side first, then turn to the right side. Always use a pressing cloth on the right side if there is any danger that the fabric will pick up a shine. Any curved seams must be slashed or notched before they are pressed. Place a curved seam on the tailor's ham for pressing.

Pressing darts has already been mentioned. Press from the largest part of the dart toward the point. Place the dart over the tailor's ham. When pressing a dart, you are molding it into a curve. Use identical motions to press matching darts. Place strips of brown paper between the dart and the outer fabric if the dart is bulky and might make an impression on the garment.

Many costume shops do not press sharp folds into hems. This is to prevent marking the fabric and making it difficult to lower the hem when it might be used by another actor in another production. This is why, in some shops, costume hems are not normally pressed at all until after the final stitching. At that time, use a pressing cloth, press from the underside and never rest the entire weight of the iron on the fabric. In some cases, simply shooting a bit of steam into the fold will be sufficient. When a sharply folded hem is required, such as at the bottom of a man's jacket or doublet, press from the wrong side with moderate iron pressure and lots of steam. Raise the iron and quickly and sharply bang the hem fold with the pounding block. This may be repeated on the right side of the garment. The pounding block will create a firm fold for hems, and for lapel facings, without danger of creating a shine.

MISCELLANEOUS SEWING OPERATIONS

This section is concerned with miscellaneous sewing operations that are frequently performed in the costume shop. Some pertain to the construction of particular period garments, while others have a much broader application. This is by no means an exhaustive list, and the methods described are not the only methods.

Applying Trim

Whenever it is possible to do so, trim should be worked out far enough in advance so it can be stitched on by machine before the final finishing steps are done on the garment. If trim placement has to be left until the garment is completed, it may have to be hand-stitched in place, which is more time consuming. However, it is often difficult for designers to make final trim determinations until after the garment has been assembled and fitted and they have had a chance to judge proportions. Many designers like to put a costume on a dummy and arrange trim pieces, moving and changing until the effect is pleasing. Careful trim placement is often the difference between a successful costume and one that is not quite right. All costume technicians should understand the process of placing trim and be prepared to apply it at whatever construction stage it can be done.

Border trims, such as braids and ribbons, can almost always be machine-stitched just before the facings are attached. They should not be stitched through facings or linings. For most border trims, use a fairly long, straight machine stitch, although some will lie smoother if a zigzag stitch is used. Pin trim on the garment before stitching to avoid both stretching and puckering. Try stitching a piece of the trim on a scrap of fabric to make sure the pressure setting on the machine is correct.

Many types of trim must be hand-stitched in place: appliqués, sequins, beads, and so forth. Set up the trim with pins. If possible, work with the garment on the dummy. Proceed methodically, catching large areas first, filling in small areas last. Use an appropriate stitch and strong, waxed thread; tie off all ends carefully.

In some instances, trim pieces may be adhered to fabric with a bonding adhesive. If used properly, this is a very effective technique; if applied carelessly, the trim will peel off with use and in cleaning. Heat seal bonding #318, made by Beacon Chemical Corporation, is an excellent product. Although it is not sold as a permanent bonding, if it is used correctly, it will endure a long run and many dry cleanings.

Paint a thick, smooth coat of the bonding on the back of the appliqué or braid and allow it to dry completely. Once dry, lay the appliqué on the fabric, cover with a pressing cloth, and iron onto the fabric, using as much steam as possible. It is difficult to perform this operation successfully without an industrial steam iron. The adhering process should continue for about a minute with the iron in constant motion. Take the iron and the pressing cloth away and allow the appliqué to dry completely before removing the garment from the ironing surface. The appliqué and the fabric will be somewhat stiffened by the adhesive.

Bias Strips

To find the true bias of a square of fabric, fold it diagonally so that the lengthwise (warp) threads lie parallel to the crosswise

FIGURE 4.37 *Cutting and joining bias strips.*

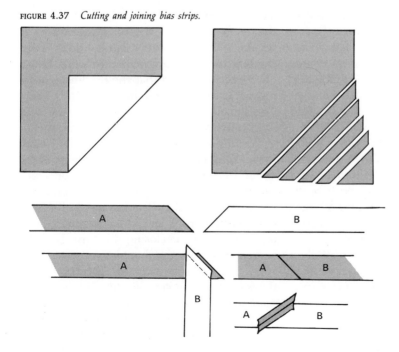

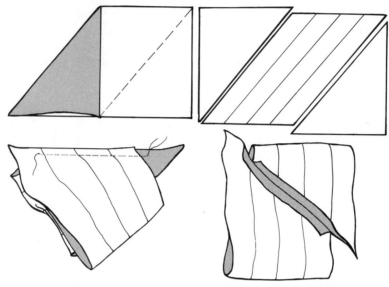

FIGURE 4.38 *Continuous bias strips.*

(filling) threads. Crease or press the fold and cut along the creased or folded line. Determine the width of the bias strip and cut as many strips as needed (see Figure 4.37). To join the strips, place the right sides of the pieces together so the seams match. One strip will be perpendicular to the other. Stitch, then trim off the pointed ends of the seams.

Use the tube method for cutting a large quantity of bias. Begin with a rectangular piece of fabric. Fold it on the true bias at each corner (see Figure 4.38). Using the fold as a guide, mark the desired width of the strips in parallel lines, working from one fold until you reach the other fold. Do not mark beyond the fold lines. Cut off and discard the triangular ends. Join the two shorter ends of the marked strip, which are on the straight grain, with one full bias width extending out at each end of the tube. Pin in place, then machine-stitch. If the piece has been stitched correctly, you can cut along the marked lines and end up with one long, continuous strip of bias.

Costume garment edges are often finished with bias strips. This is a particularly good method when the garment fabric is too rough or bulky to face with itself. Prepare bias strips from a lighter weight fabric that is approximately the same color as the garment. Stitch the bias to the garment edge with the right sides of garment and bias strip together. Trim the seam and slash the seam allowance at regular intervals if it is a curved edge. Turn the bias to the inside, rolling the outer fabric over a bit to ensure that the binding will be inconspicuous. The binding can also be understitched. Turn the raw edge of the bias strip under and hand-stitch down firmly.

Cording is often added to a garment edge for a clean, decorative effect. Cut bias strips about two and one-half inches wide. Fold the bias piece in half, lengthwise, and run the cording down the center, along the fold. Use a zipper foot and stitch through both layers of fabric, enclosing the cord. Lay the corded strip on the right side of the garment edge. Stitch the strip to the garment along the same line that secured the cord. Turn the seam under. Trim the garment seam and slash if necessary. Trim the cording seam that will lie next to the garment. Press and turn the

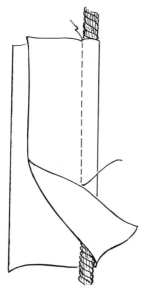

FIGURE 4.39 *Cording with bias strip and piping cord.*

stitch. Trim the seam; grade if necessary. Turn the ruffle down and the bias strip and seam allowances to the inside. Turn the raw edge of the bias strip under and stitch in place.

To construct tubular cording with a bias covering, cut a true bias strip three times the width of the cord, plus one inch. Use a piece of cord twice the length of the finished, covered cording. Enclose the cord in the right side of the bias strip. Use a zipper foot and stitch quite close to the cord. Stretch the bias slightly while stitching, which will prevent

FIGURE 4.41 *Attaching ruffle with bias strip.*

seam allowance to the inside. Turn under the raw edge of the remaining wide seam allowance and catch-stitch to the garment underlining.

Attach ruffles to the edges of sleeves or necklines with a bias strip. Stitch the ruffle to the garment edge, right sides together, seam edges matching. Apply a bias strip and

FIGURE 4.40 *Applying corded strip to garment edge.*

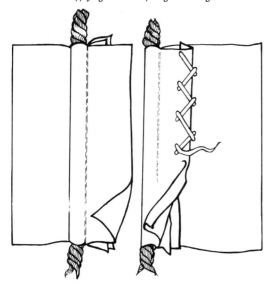

the stitches from breaking when the bias is turned. One-half of the cord will be covered, wrong side out. Trim the seam closely, to about one-eighth-inch. At the point where the bias tube ends, in the middle of the piece of cord, stitch firmly across the fabric and the cord. Carefully work the bias back over the exposed cord, pulling out the cord that was originally encased. Take care not to twist the bias tube.

FIGURE 4.42 *Tubular cording with bias strips.*

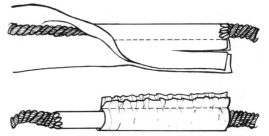

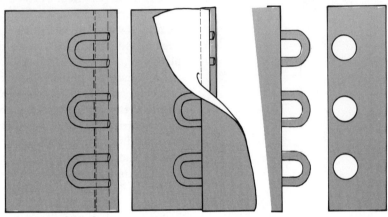

FIGURE 4.43   *Button loops.*

Use tubular cording, or unfilled bias tube, to make button loops for ball-shaped buttons. Stitch on the button loops before the facings. Determine the size of the loop, and the spacing between each one, and mark on the fabric. Lay in the loops and baste them down. Pins are very apt to slip. Stitch the loops in place. Apply facing and turn to the inside. The button loops will extend from the garment edge.

Tubular cording is also used for spaghetti straps, for trim appliqués, and for constructing frogs.

Boning

Boning is no longer made out of bone, and has not been since the middle of the nineteenth century. Prior to that time, most corsets and hoops did derive their superstructure from whalebones, taken either from the whale's fins or from the bony plates that, in a certain species of whale, take the place of teeth. Whalebone was used in women's garments as early as the fifteenth century. Around 1860, the whaling industry finally collapsed, and at the same time, new processes of tempering steel brought about the development of steel "bones" for bustles and corsets. The use of real whalebone disap-

peared completely by the beginning of the twentieth century.

Steel corset stays and continuous steel boning are both used in costume construction. Corset stays come in a variety of widths and lengths. Some are solid blades of steel, shaped rather like tongue depressors or popsicle sticks; others are made from twisted steel wire and are flexible. Corset stays may be purchased from companies that make corsets. If no such company exists in your town, see the Source Guide for purchasing information.

One continuous steel stay must run the length of the boned garment. Do not try to put two short bones together: It won't work. Bones that are too long can be trimmed with tin snips, but the cut end will have to be covered so it will not wear through the cloth, and also through the actor's flesh. A tipping solution for corset stays is available from some corset supply companies. Newly trimmed stays may be dipped into the solution, which is quite thick, and allowed to dry. Drying time may be an hour or two, depending upon the thickness of the solution. Corset stays may also be tipped by wrapping them with adhesive tape.

Continuous steel boning, which is sometimes called crinoline steel, is used in hoops, bustles, and panniers. It can be purchased in large rolls. Again, see the Source List for purchasing information. Lengths of continuous steel boning may be cut with tin snips. Pad the ends with adhesive tape. You may also use steel packaging tape instead of continuous steel boning. Packaging tape is very strong and springy and must be riveted together. It is quite inexpensive but it is not as pleasant to work with as continuous steel boning because the edges are often a bit sharp.

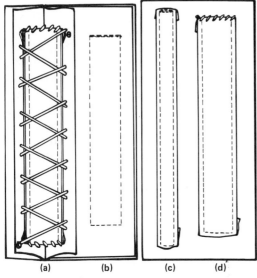

FIGURE 4.44   *Bone casings: (a) Bone encased in two strips of twill tape and cross-stitched over a seam. (b) Bone sandwiched between two layers of fabric. (c) Bone under a single strip of twill tape, which has been stitched directly onto the fabric. (d) Bone slipped inside a special bone-casing tape, which has been stitched directly onto the fabric.*

All boning is attached to garments by being placed inside a sturdy casing. Casing produced for modern corset construction is available from corset or corset supply shops. You may also construct casings from twill tape or grosgrain ribbon, using a double layer. If the garment fabric is light, the casing should enclose the bone on both sides; if the fabric is firm, the casing may be laid on in such a way that the boning will lie between the garment fabric and the casing. Tunnel casings

may also be created in corsets that are made from two layers of fabric.

Continuous steel boning, when it is threaded through the casings on a rounded undergarment such as a hoop skirt or a bustle, always exerts a tension on the casing which holds it in place. This tension causes the casing to wear, particularly at the ends of each strip. Nineteenth-century ladies had to check and mend their crinolines and bustles regularly, and theatrical wardrobe technicians must do the same.

Specific problems of corset construction are too many and too varied to be dealt with fully in this book. The overall problem, however, is to create a garment that will suggest the correct period shape on the body of a modern actor. During most of the periods when corsets were a vital part of the fashion silhouette, corsets were placed upon young girls at a point in their lives when their bones were still soft. The corsets actually reshaped their bodies. It is impossible to reshape the body of a modern, adult actor.

There is a fair amount of material from which period corset shapes can be researched. The most familiar book is *Corsets and Crinolines* by Norah Waugh, originally published by B. T. Batsford, Ltd., London, in 1954, and reprinted by Theatre Arts Books in 1970. Norah Waugh's book includes an assortment of scale patterns for period corsets, hoops, and bustles.

Using the appropriate period seams and shapes in the manner discussed in Chapter 3, develop the corset pattern on a body sloper. Make the corset two inches smaller around than the sloper by subtracting small amounts from each seam. This will allow enough room to lace in the corset as tightly as possible. Cut the pattern pieces out of light-weight, tightly woven canvas, twill, or duck. Cut two layers if the casings for the bones are to be tunneled. Draw the boning diagram onto the pattern pieces. Stitch the corset pieces together and then apply the casings, or stitch through both layers to create tunnel casings. The casings should be narrow enough to hold the bones snugly. Set grommets up both sides of the corset opening. In most instances, stage corsets will be laced up the back.

Do not fit a corset on an actor until the bones and the grommets for lacing are in place. An unboned corset will only conform to the actor's body and give you no idea of the proper fit. Corsets are not comfortable to wear, and many actors will need a good bit of reassurance about the difficulties of wearing them. Explain exactly what movements will be restricted. Provide corsets for the rehearsal period, but advise the actors not to lounge around when wearing them since doing so will result in making their bodies quite sore. It is a good idea to have someone from the costume staff available to lace the actors into their corsets so the lacing will always be done correctly.

Boning for some of the less extreme corseted periods can be accomplished within the bodice itself, without using a separate corset. In this case, the bone casings should be stitched to the underlining of the garment or to a separate canvas underbodice constructed for the boning.

Continuous Placket

A continuous placket is often used in a sleeve or a skirt opening. It may be set into a seam, but it is more often set into a slash. Slash the fabric to the depth of the desired opening and cut a strip of the same fabric on the lengthwise grain, approximately one and one-half inches wide and twice as long as the opening. With right sides together, pin the strip down one edge of the opening. Spread the opening out straight and pin the strip to the other side of the slash. Machine-stitch the two pieces together, stitching about one-quarter-inch from the edge. When you reach the point of the slash, put the needle into the fabric, raise the presser foot, and pivot the garment. Stitch down the other side. Trim the seam as shown in Figure 4.45, tapering off to nothing at the point. Turn the strip to the inside of the garment, turn under the

FIGURE 4.45   *Continuous placket.*

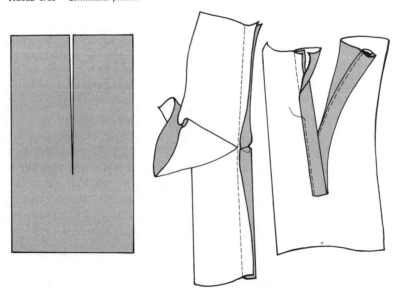

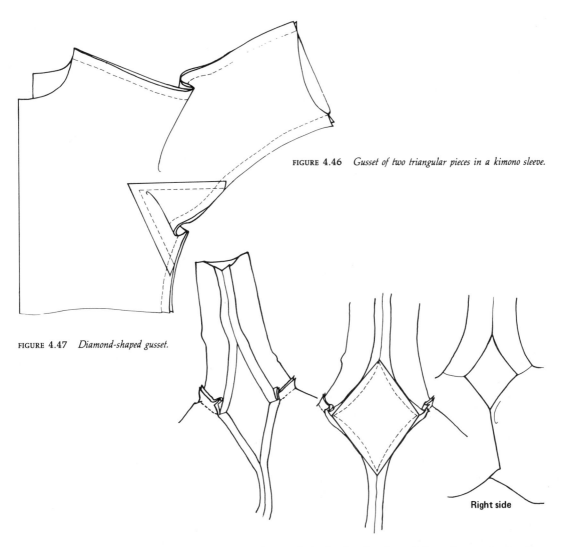

FIGURE 4.46 *Gusset of two triangular pieces in a kimono sleeve.*

FIGURE 4.47 *Diamond-shaped gusset.*

Right side

raw edge, and stitch the strip down over the original stitching line, enclosing the seam. One-half of the continuous strip will form the underlap and the other, folded back into the garment, will form the overlap.

Gussets

Gussets are often used in costumes to facilitate the actor's arm movements. The simplest gusset is the one put in a kimono sleeve. It may be constructed of two triangular pieces of fabric, one inserted into the underarm area of the bodice back and the other in the bodice front (see Figure 4.46). The gussets are stitched in essentially the same manner as the continuous lap. When both gusset pieces are in place, the side seam of the garment may be stitched.

A diamond-shaped gusset can be set into the underarm of a garment with set-in sleeves. Release the side seams to accommodate the gusset. Stitch the gusset to the original seam lines of the garment, as shown in Figure 4.47. Start and end each side of the gusset on a seam, tapering off the stitching

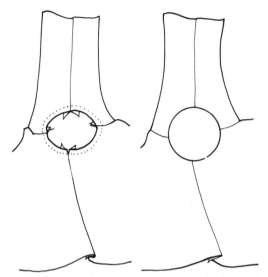

FIGURE 4.48   *Dancer's circular gusset (from outside of garment).*

at each point on the gusset. Be careful not to make a tuck in the seams when you are stitching these points.

There are two versions of the dancer's gusset, or circular gusset, which allows complete arm movement, even in a tightly fitted sleeve. In order to see the theory of the circular gusset, raise your arm and trace around the entire underarm area. The object of the circular gusset is to place a circle this size into the underarm seam of the garment. When the arm is raised, the circular inset will lie flat against the underarm area. When the arm is hanging to the side, the inset will form a small pocket under the arm. The most precise way to make a circular gusset addition to a costume is to slit the underarm seam and have the actor, wearing the costume, raise his or her arm. Lay a piece of muslin over the exposed underarm area and draw a pattern. Depending upon the shape of the underarm, the inset may be a full circle or a flattened circle, more like an oblong. Cut the gusset over this pattern and set it into the sleeve. Most circular gussets have a radius of about four inches.

If the addition of a circular gusset is planned into the garment from the patterning stage, it can be cut as part of a one-piece sleeve (see Figure 4.49 for the pattern shape). Mock up the sleeve in muslin first and fit it on the actor to make sure the gusset projection is large enough before cutting the actual sleeve.

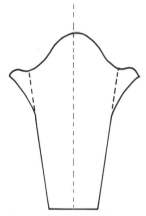

FIGURE 4.49   *Gusset added to sleeve pattern.*

Padding

Almost any part of an actor's body may be padded for the stage. Big bellies, shoulder humps, and enlarged chests are most common. Padding is all executed in essentially the same way. For any padding that involves the upper body or the abdomen, construct a well-fitting canvas, heavy twill, or duck garment that will cover the torso and extend several inches down over the hips. It will probably fasten in the center back with a heavy-weight, separating zipper. Build the padded shape over this body garment with dacron padding, cotton batting, or foam rubber. Dacron fluff makes realistic looking shapes and can be washed and dried in automatic laundry machines without damage. Cotton batting packs down with wear and loses its shape when it is washed. Foam rubber padding can be beautifully and permanently shaped, but it cannot be washed at

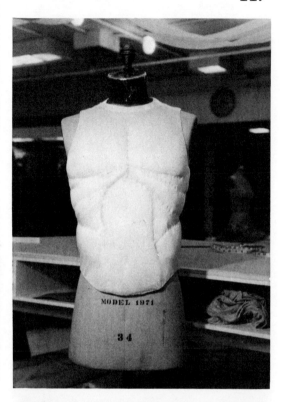

FIGURE 4.50 *Padding being stitched onto a T-shirt in the costume shop at the Milwaukee Repertory Theater. (Photograph by Mark Avery.)*

FIGURE 4.51 *Contoured torso padding. (Photograph by Frances Aronson.)*

FIGURE 4.52 *Tummy padding. (Photograph by Frances Aronson.)*

all. Padding is hot to wear, and if it is to be worn for several performances, its washability is important.

If a very slight padding is required, it can be stitched to a cotton T-shirt and a second T-shirt worn over the top of the padding.

Use a dummy to put the garment on while you are working to shape the padding. Add the padding material in several layers, trimming and arranging to achieve the correct shape. Secure with T-pins. Consult an anatomy book for muscle placement if the chest, back, and upper arms are involved. When the proper shape is achieved, cross-stitch the padding material into place securely and thoroughly. Cover with a thin stretch fabric,

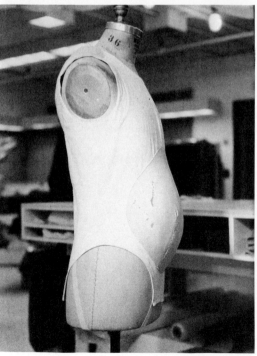

FIGURE 4.53 *Assorted padding and rolls. (Photograph by Jo Brenza.)*

such as nylon tricot. Use an in-and-out quilting stitch through all layers to outline muscle groups and create fine, subtle shapes. Most body padding will require elastic crotch straps to hold it down.

Actors who will be wearing padding should have a good idea of how they will look as it is important to the development of their characters. They should have their padding for as much of the rehearsal period as possible. Measurements for costumes that will be worn over padding cannot be taken until the padding is complete and on the actor.

Scalloped and Dagged Edges

Many medieval garments and hats require dagged edges. Some may be little more than enlarged scallops; others may be extremely intricate. Constructing a simple scalloped edge, or an intricate dagged edge, is essentially the same process. The first step is to figure out how deep and how wide the design

FIGURE 4.54 *Shapes for dagging and scalloping.*

John Mansfield in Androcles and the Lion. *(Elizabeth Covey, costume designer, Milwaukee Repertory Theater.)* TOP RIGHT.

Costume sketches by Susan Tsu. BELOW.

Ruth Anita Bonnie

Jeffrey Tambor in
The School for Wives.
*(Elizabeth Covey,
costume designer,
Milwaukee Repertory
Theater.)* TOP RIGHT.

The Country Wife.
*(Michael J. Cesario,
costume designer,
Krannert Center
for the Performing
Arts.)* BELOW.

*Shirin Devrim Trainer
and Patricia Schmidt in*
Volpone. *(Linda Fisher,
costume designer,
Milwaukee Repertory
Theater.)* TOP RIGHT.

G. Wood in Doctor
Faustus.
*(James Edmund
Brady, costume
designer,
Milwaukee Repertory
Theater.)* BELOW.

Costume design for Touchstone *in* As You Like It. *(Michael J. Cesario, costume designer.)* TOP RIGHT.

Rose Pickering & James Pickering in The School for Wives. *(Elizabeth Covey, costume designer, Milwaukee Repertory Theater.)* BELOW.

Touchstone in As You Like It. *(Michael J. Cesario, costume designer.)* TOP RIGHT.

Daniel Davis and Richard Risso in King Lear. *(Elizabeth Covey, costume designer, Milwaukee Repertory Theater.)* BELOW.

Costume sketch by Susan Tsu. TOP RIGHT.

Daniel Mooney and Montgomery Davis in Volpone. *(Linda Fisher, costume designer, Milwaukee Repertory Theater.)* BELOW.

Virginia Payne in
She Stoops to
Conquer.
*(Janet Warren, costume
designer, Milwaukee
Repertory Theater.)*
TOP RIGHT.

*Costume properties
designed by
Michael J. Cesario.*
BELOW.

Too True to Be Good.
(*Laura Crow,
costume designer,
Academy Festival
Theatre.*)

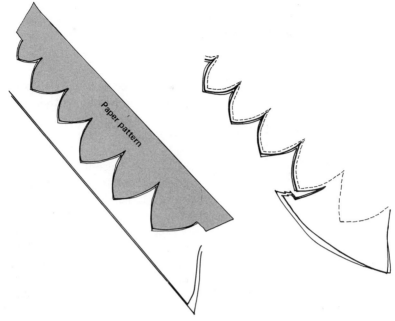

FIGURE 4.55   *Facing a scalloped hem.*

will be and how many individual projections each edge will contain. Draw a brown paper or cardboard pattern to use as a guide. If the edge is a simple, repeated pattern, put several repeats on the guide and move it along the edge of the fabric. Draw in the stitching line with chalk or a pencil. If the projections are not all the same size, as in a hanging sleeve that has gradually enlarging shapes down each side, draw out the entire pattern on brown paper. After it is drawn, show it to the designer to see if the scale is correct. Lay up the garment fabric and the facing or lining fabric on the cutting table with right sides together. If a stiff edge is required, lay an interlining on top of the outer fabric. Pin or baste the layers together along the edge, so they will not slip. Lay on the paper pattern and draw around it. Stitch around the projections. If there is a point between each projection, make sure the stitching line is cleanly pivoted. Trim the seam to one-quarter-inch and notch all the curves. Slash up to one-

eighth-inch of the stitching line on each point. Turn the fabrics back on themselves and work out the edges carefully by hand, gently smoothing and rolling them until they lie flat. Press over the tailor's ham. Pressing on a flat surface may cause wrinkles.

Cartridge Pleats

Many eighteenth- and early nineteenth-century skirts achieve their bell-shaped look with cartridge pleating. Men's gowns from the Renaissance sometimes had flowing sleeves set on with cartridge pleats, and many academic robes today still have cartridge-pleated sleeves. Ruffs can be made with cartridge pleating. This sewing operation has a great many uses and often produces very dramatic effects.

The distance that the pleat is to extend before it begins to fall must be determined first. Measure this distance on the edge of the fabric to be pleated, and fold down. Cut

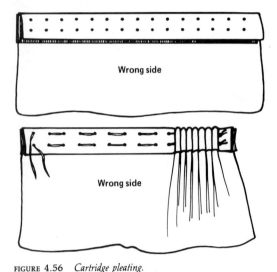

FIGURE 4.56 *Cartridge pleating.*

a strip of muslin, or an even stiffer fabric, the width of the fold-down and insert it into the fold. Calculate the size of each pleat and mark with a series of dots on the wrong side of the garment as shown in Figure 4.56. On many cartridge-pleated skirts, the pleats are larger in the back and on the sides, growing smaller toward the front; often there is a completely flat panel in the center front. If you are doing graduated pleats, you will have to

FIGURE 4.57 *Attaching cartridge pleats to waistband.*

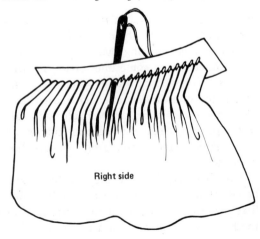

work out the distance between the dots in a mock-up of the pleat sizes.

Using a doubled, well-waxed button thread, do a running stitch through the dots, down through one, up through the next. About one-half-inch down from this original stitching line, do another line of running stitches, corresponding exactly to the top line. If the pleats are to extend more than an inch and a half, do a third line of running stitches below the second. Pull up the gathering threads tightly to form the pleats. If the garment is large, such as a skirt, pleat it in several sections, pulling the threads up separately.

Prepare a two to two-and-a-half-inch shaped waistband that fits the body snugly. This waistband should be very firmly interfaced so that it is quite stiff. Butt the pleats up against the waistband about three-quarters of an inch below the top edge. Hand-stitch the top and the bottom of each pleat to the waistband, very securely, taking care that each pleat goes on straight with top and bottom aligned.

It takes a great deal of time to do cartridge pleating, and garments that are to include this operation should be begun early. Very careful measuring and very careful stitching are imperative for successful cartridge pleats.

Setting Fabric onto Elastic

The procedure for setting fabric on elastic is quite a simple one, yet it is done so often in costume shops, and is so often done poorly, that a quick description of the process seems necessary. The object is to evenly distribute a length of fabric onto a shorter piece of elastic in order to create gathers. Divide both the fabric and the elastic into equal parts (see Figure 4.58). Do this by dividing the fabric and the elastic in half, then in half again, and then again—until the whole length is divided. Pin the elastic to the fabric, matching up the marks made at each section. There may be six inches of fabric between pins and

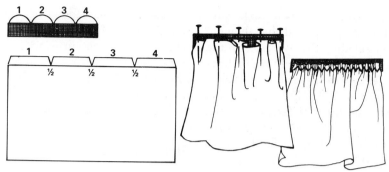

about three inches of elastic, for example. Begin to stitch at one end, pulling the elastic until it lays evenly on the longer fabric. Hold the elastic behind the machine needle, as well as in front, when you are pulling so you will not bend the needle. Use a zigzag stitch for greater flexibility. A tube of fabric may be gathered to a circle of elastic in exactly the same way.

Setting Hook and Eye Tape

Hook and eye tape is a great time saver, particularly when it is used up the back of a

bodice. Make sure that the bodice back is cut with a two-inch-wide self-facing. Place the eye portion of the tape on the left back, with the eyes centered on the closing line, facing away from the center back. Stitch down and turn back the self-facing. Matching up the eyes carefully, sew the hook portion of the tape to the self-facing on the other side, with the hooks facing up and away from the center back, somewhat to the inside of the center back closing line. Turn the facing back, placing the fold about one-quarter-inch to the outside of the closing line. Check to see that the center back closing lines match

FIGURE 4.59   *Setting hook and eye tape.*

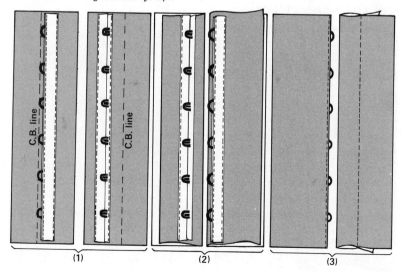

up. Attach the hooks and eyes to make sure they are lined up properly, and that they are completely concealed by the overlap. On the left back, machine-stitch the fold right at the edge. If an underlap is being used, and it usually is, stitch it in with this line of stitching. The inside edge of the self-facing and the underlap can be hand-stitched to the garment underlining. On the right side of the back, stitch through all layers, including the tape.

Setting Zippers

Always use metal zippers in costumes. Nylon zippers are simply not strong enough nor reliable enough for stage use. It is sometimes difficult to find a wide selection of metal zippers in ordinary sewing notion departments, particularly the lighter weights. Contact a local garment factory to find out where they purchase metal zippers. Buy up quantities of metal zippers when you find them on sale. Purchase long zippers which may be cut the correct length. Keep a supply of zipper stops on hand and attach them to the top of cut

zippers with pliers. Inexpensive metal zippers can be made from continuous zipper tape which may be cut in exact lengths. Zipper stops and pulls are relatively easy to attach. Zipper tape is available only in medium and heavy weights, however, and must be purchased in large quantities.

Slot or Centered Zipper

Centered zippers usually occur at the back or front center line of a garment. Turn back the seam allowance on the opening where the zipper is to be placed and press carefully. With the zipper closed, baste in each side of the tape, stitching from top to bottom and making certain that the top edges of the garment match. The top of the zipper teeth should be placed one inch from the top of the garment, allowing for a seam allowance and for sufficient room to turn in a facing or to attach a waistband. The folds over the closing should meet right at the center of the zipper. When you are certain that the zipper is in position, top-stitch it in place.

FIGURE 4.60   *Slot or centered zipper.*

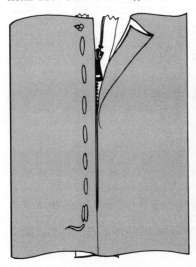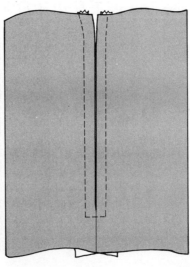

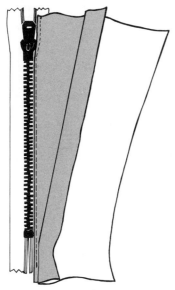 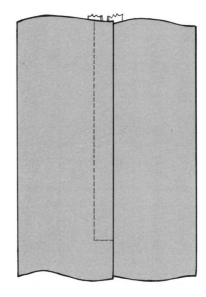

FIGURE 4.61   *Lapped zipper.*

Lapped Zipper

The lapped zipper is always found on a side skirt or pants opening and may also occur in either center front or center back. Fold and press back the left side of the closing (or the side that is to overlap) on the seamline. Fold and press back the right side of the closing (or the side that is to underlap) one-eighth-inch to the inside of the seamline. Stitch down the underlap side as shown in Figure 4.61. Top-stitch the overlap side. Make a right angle at the bottom of the zipper and stitch across to the fold.

When a medium- or a heavy-weight zipper is used in a period bodice for a quick change, create an even wider overlap so there is no chance that the zipper will be seen. The wide lap may be fastened down with hooks and eyes or, if the change is very fast, with small pieces of Velcro.

Separating Zippers

Separating zippers are set in in exactly the same way as either centered or lapped zip-

pers. They may be centered or lapped. In most cases, the bottom of each piece of the separating zipper will be placed slightly above the bottom edges of the garment.

Fly Zippers

Fly zippers are quite simple to set in. There are several methods, all of which are determined by the method of cutting the pants. One way is to use three separate fly extension pieces to create the closing. The fly closing should be done before the front sections of the trousers are attached to the back sections. The lower section of the crotch seam may either be stitched before the fly is done or it may be left open.

Stitch one extension to the left trouser front, right sides of the fabric together. Press the extension out and place the zipper, right side down, on top of the extension with the zipper tape along the side of the seam (see Figure 4.62). On the left side of the zipper, stitch close to, but not crowded against, the zipper teeth; stitch again at the edge of the tape.

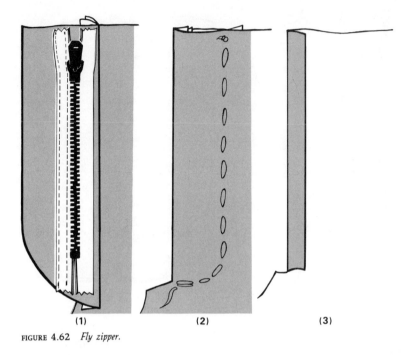

FIGURE 4.62 *Fly zipper.*

Turn the extension under and baste down, then machine-stitch in place. Assemble the other two fly pieces, right sides meeting, and stitch along the curved side. Trim the seam, notch, and turn; overlock the raw edge, or bind with bias tape. This is the fly underlay.

FIGURE 4.63 *Completing the fly zipper.*

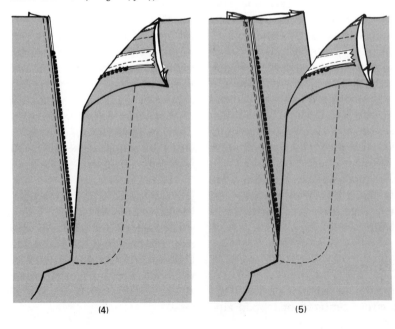

On the right trouser front, turn the seam allowance under and press down. Open the zipper and stitch the free side to the right front so that the fold is quite close to, although not crowding, the zipper teeth. Lay in the fly underlay and stitch it in place, through all layers, close to the first stitching line. Lay the trouser fronts right side up and check the zipper positioning. On the left front, top-stitch the fly facing through all layers. Be careful not to catch the fly underlay in the stitching line until you reach the bottom of the curve. Reinforce the bottom of the zipper closure with overcasting, a bar tack, or a tight zigzag stitch.

Stitching on Leather and Vinyl

Medium-weight and light-weight leathers can be stitched easily on an industrial sewing machine and relatively well on most sturdy domestics. Use nylon thread, lighten the pressure, and set the machine for a fairly long stitch. Leather needles can be obtained for most sewing machines; they are not, however, essential. Many leather garments are created with single top-stitched or welt seams for strength. If the seam is to be opened and

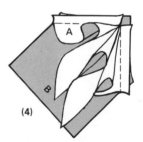

(3)

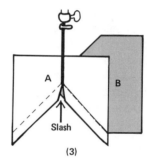

(1)

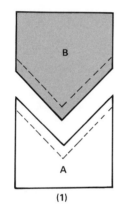

(4)

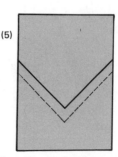

(2)

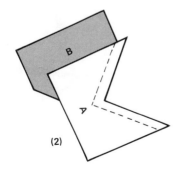

(5)

FIGURE 4.64a & 4.64b *Stitching a point, godet, or decorative detail.*

pressed, use a piece of brown paper between the iron and the leather and little or no steam. The heat setting on the iron should be quite low. Do not let the iron rest in one spot, but move it constantly. In some heavy garments, the seams may be glued down with Barge Cement, a contact adhesive that is particularly effective on leather. Hems in leather garments are usually glued up with Barge. Coat both surfaces that are to be glued. Allow the glue to become quite tacky; then press together. For the best bond, pound the seams or hem with a wooden or rubber mallet. Do not glue down seams in a light-weight leather garment, since Barge does tend to stiffen a bit when it dries.

Vinyl is troublesome to stitch because an ordinary presser foot will drag on its surface, causing wrinkles and puckers. Use a rolling machine foot if one is available. Otherwise,

run a thin path of light machine oil in front of the presser foot as you sew (using the smallest possible squeeze bottle). The oil will allow the presser foot to glide smoothly over the vinyl surface. Wipe off the oil after the seam is stitched.

Stitching a Point

Inserting godets, gussets, and decorative details often call for stitching points. Mark the seam allowances on both pieces as shown in Figure 4.64a. Lay the pieces with right sides together. Stitch from the outside edge to the point. With the needle in the fabric, directly on the point, pivot the pieces and line up the remaining side of the seam. Stitch from the point to the other fabric edge. Do not open the seam. Press up and top-stitch if desired.

FIGURE 4.65 *Swing tack with buttonhole stitch.*

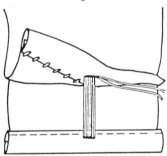 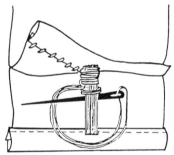

FIGURE 4.66 *Swing tack with chain stitch.*

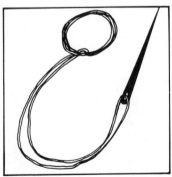 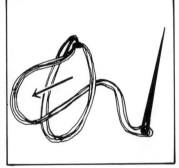 

Swing Tacks

Swing tacks are used to hold two layers of fabric loosely together so there is a significant amount of movement possible. Linings are often fastened to hems with swing tacks. Use silk twist or heavy duty thread, doubled for strength. Sew four or five stitches from one layer to the other, leaving thread lengths of three-quarters to one inch between the two layers. Starting at one end of the threads, execute a buttonhole stitch around the threads and continue this stitch, close together, until it runs the length of the threads.

Swing tacks may also be done with a chain stitch (see Figure 4.66). Form the chain out of doubled button thread and stitch between the two garment layers.

Waistbands

In most instances, skirt waistbands should be stiffened with an appropriate interfacing or with belting. For some reason, there is a great tendency to make waistbands too small. This is probably because the original waist measurement was taken quite snugly and insufficient allowance was made for seaming and stiffening. Cut waistbands three inches longer than the waist measurement. This will leave sufficient room for seaming and for an overlap. Waistbands that are more than two inches wide, finished, should be shaped to fit the body.

When a very heavy skirt must be attached to a waistband, and the waistband is to be covered by another garment, it is often a good idea to set the skirt flat on the outside of the waistband, rather than enclosing it inside. Zigzag the skirt to the band. Two rows of stitching will flatten a gathered skirt and make the waist area less bulky. If several layers of skirts are to be stitched to a single waistband for the layered look, stagger the placements of the skirts on the waistband to reduce the bulk.

FIGURE 4.67   *Waist band—two skirt layers attached to petersham belting.*

Never start to put a costume together without having a plan of action. Certain steps ought to precede others, and one of the most common of all sewing mistakes is to do a step out of sequence and have to rip it out. With planning, sequential mistakes can be avoided. Every shop ought to have a generalized procedure for garment assembly, including the specific stages of completion at which first and second fittings will take place. In addition, special construction steps have to be noted that pertain to each individual costume. If the garment is cut by one technician and assembled by another, both should collaborate on the plan.

What follows is a sample procedure for assembling a lined jacket, coat, or doublet with some discussion of techniques that have not already been mentioned. Steps can be eliminated if they do not apply; steps can be added if necessary. Step 1 begins after the pattern has been developed and the muslin proof constructed, fitted, and altered. In some shops, steps 1 through 5 will be performed by a cutter, with another technician beginning at step 6.

1. Prepare the fabric for cutting.

    a. Straighten grain if necessary.
    b. Shrink if necessary.
    c. Press if necessary.

These steps were covered in Chapter 3. For efficiency's sake, all the fabrics for a set of costumes should be prepared for cutting as soon as they arrive in the shop. Fabrics can be shrunk while patterns are still being developed. Don't wait until the piece is needed on the cutting table before remembering that it must be washed and dried first. After you press the fabric, roll it onto a cardboard fabric tube rather than folding it, in order to prevent creasing and wrinkling.

2. Lay up the fabric on the cutting table.

Some shops only allow single layer cutting. Others cut on the double. When cutting on the double, lay the fabric out smoothly and, if it is at all slippery, pin the selvedge edges together. When working with complicated patterns and designs, it is a good idea not to cut on the double.

3. Position the pattern on the fabric.

    a. Check for nap, design, right and wrong side, plaid, and stripes.

Most costume fabrics are purchased before the specific pattern is developed and it is sometimes difficult to determine from the design alone just how much fabric will be required. If there is any reason to suspect that there is not enough fabric for the garment, lay the pattern pieces out just as soon as they are altered and do not cut anything until you are sure there is enough. If there is not, tell the designer immediately.

The designer will decide in what direction the fabric nap should lie. On most costumes, if the nap runs down the length of the garment, the fabric will appear smooth and silky on stage; if it runs up, there will be greater depth and texture. Lay out all pattern pieces on napped fabric before cutting. Check positioning several times. If a prominent piece is cut incorrectly, it will have to be recut.

A costume is often made with the wrong side of the fabric outside. The designer may want the more subtle effect of the dull side. In some cases, particularly with upholstery fabrics, the wrong side may simply be more interesting under stage lights. The usual practice is for the designer to put fabric swatches on the designs. The correct side of the swatch should be facing up. Check to make sure before cutting.

Placement of plaids, stripes, and large fabric designs should also be worked out with the designer. Sometimes the correct layout will be clear on the design, but often the pattern on the actual fabric may necessitate some adjustment.

4. Cut everything at the same time whenever possible.

    a. Garment, including facings and decorative pieces.
    b. Underlining.
    c. Interfacings.
    d. Lining.

The underlining is the layer that is attached to the wrong side of the garment pieces for body, strength, and shape. In assembling the garment, these two layers will be treated as one. Underlining pieces are cut exactly like garment pieces. Some shops underline virtually all costumes with muslin.

Interfacings are used in the following places: (1) as reinforcement in parts of the garment that will have great strain, such as the button and buttonhole areas; (2) inside collars, cuffs, and pocket flaps in order to preserve their shape; (3) inside collarless necklines, peplums, and the lower part of fitted jackets so as to give them shape; and (4) in belts and waistbands in order to give them firmness and strength. Interfacing fabrics should be firm and they should produce the required amount of crispness. Study the design; consult the designer to determine what degree of crispness is desired; and choose the interfacing material that will produce that effect. In general, the softer looks are achieved by using organdy, batiste, or lawn to interface light-weight cottons, rayons, or crepes. Use muslin, broadcloth, or pellon to interface heavy cottons, linen, or light-weight wool. Use china silk, taffeta, organza, or nylon net to interface light-weight tailored garments that are to be dry cleaned. For a crisp look with washable fabrics (cottons, linens, woolens, and blends), use acro, formite, or siri; with medium- and heavy-weight, tailored, dry cleanable woolen garments, use hair canvas.

Costume garments need not be lined unless there is a reason for doing so. It is no more necessary for the inside of a costume to be aesthetically pleasing than for the backside of a beautiful set to be sanded and painted. However, many garments are lined because they hang better, because the lining will be exposed on stage, or because a slippery lining is necessary so the actor can put on the garment quickly and smoothly. If the lining is a design element, the designer will choose the fabric. If the lining will never show and is purely functional, it may be taken from stock lining materials of the appropriate weight and color.

5. Transfer all pattern markings to the appropriate layer.

If the entire garment is to be underlined, transfer pattern markings to the underside of the underlining, since darts, tucks, seams, and so forth will be stitched through both layers simultaneously. Use a tracing wheel and tracing paper to transfer pattern markings. Tracing boards help make pattern marking quicker and easier. To make a tracing board, cover one side of a sturdy piece of cardboard with a large sheet of tracing paper and tape it down to the under side.

One advantage of using a muslin underlining regularly is that the pattern markings will be clear and easy to follow. If garment pieces are going to be finished off by serging or zigzagging before they are assembled, indicate the match-up places on the pieces with chalk, pencil, or tracing paper markings rather than with notches.

6. Stitch garment fabric and underlining together; serge or zigzag edges.

The garment fabric layer and the underlining must lie flat against each other without any misalignment. In order to match them up perfectly, lay both pieces on a flat surface and make sure the correct side of the garment fabric is on top. Without raising the fabric from the table, pin the two pieces together all around and then baste, either by hand or by machine, a bit to the inside of the seam-line. The basting will be removed when the garment is assembled. Press the two pieces together and overlock or zigzag around all edges.

This construction step is often assigned to inexperienced or student costume technicians because it is so simple. Make sure that the technician understands the importance of lining up the two layers precisely. It is an easy step, but a very important one.

7. Stay-stitch where necessary.

Less stay-stitching is done in costume construction than in fashion sewing. If the pieces are underlined and the edges finished, they do not need stay-stitching at all. If a single layer fabric is being used, which might stretch on a curve, stay-stitch neck curves, armhole curves, and garment bias seams if they are particularly steep.

8. Assemble the garment for the first fitting.

  a. Stitch darts.
  b. Machine-baste main construction seams in body and sleeves. *Do not apply facings.*
  c. Baste on undercollar.
  d. Baste in both sleeves; pin in shoulder pads if they are being used.

Some costumers prefer to fit the garment with only one sleeve basted in. If you do this, bear in mind that the pull across the body will be unequal with only one sleeve in place. Another alternative is to wait until the fitting and pin the sleeves on.

  e. Prepare trim pieces, such as patch pockets, braid, yoke, appliqués, and so forth to be placed on the costume during the fitting.

These are the normal operations that are completed before most first fabric fittings of a coat, jacket, or doublet. In some shops, the seams are not machine-basted, but stitched permanently. The reasons for permanent stitching are that if the seams are correct, they will not have to be restitched, and if they do need altering, it is not a great deal more difficult to rip out permanent stitching than it is to rip out machine-basting.

Many technicians have trouble hanging sleeves correctly. A fitted sleeve that may not show any gathering across the cap is probably the most difficult sleeve to put in. A normal fitted sleeve is approximately two inches larger than the armhole into which it will be set. This extra fabric creates the cup that fits over the top of the shoulder and permits movement of the upper arm.

The top of the sleeve cap, which is on the straight grain, and the top of the shoulder should have been marked on the muslin proof and transferred to the garment pieces. The top of the shoulder is not necessarily where the shoulder seam falls. For example, the shoulder seam on a man's coat that is cut with a fiddle back is well behind the top of the shoulder.

Prepare to control sleeve cap ease by running a line of long machine stitches around the cap of the sleeve from the point on each side where the sleeve head begins to flare out. No easing should be necessary around the bottom of the armhole. Draw up the stitching line slightly to create the necessary fullness in the sleeve cap.

Turn the garment to the inside. The sleeve is right side out. Make sure you are putting the correct sleeve into the correct armhole. Insert the sleeve up into the armhole with the right sides of the fabric together. Pin from the inside of the sleeve. Match up the top of the sleeve cap with the top of the shoulder. Match up the underarm seam on a one-piece sleeve (or the underarm point on a two-piece sleeve) with the underarm seam, or point, on the garment. Pin the underarm portion first; this should fit smoothly. Approximately one-half-inch at the very top of the sleeve should not be eased. There will probably be more ease in the back of the sleeve than in the front. Draw the line of machine-stitching up in order to fit the sleeve cap in the armhole. There should be no large gathered areas. As you work, roll the top of the sleeve over the fingers in order to distribute the fullness evenly. Place pins close together. When the sleeve is completely pinned, turn the garment to the right side and suspend the shoulder from your hand to check the hang of the sleeve. For a more accurate check, place the jacket on a dummy. It is essential that the straight grain in the sleeve be accurately suspended from the top of the shoulder. If the sleeve is hanging correctly, it should cant a bit to the front and not pull across the chest. If the pinned-in sleeve appears to be accurate, hand-baste it into the armhole. It is best not to machine-stitch the armhole seam at this point since there is a good chance that it may have to come out; ripping stitches in this area can cause the armhole curve to stretch out of shape.

9. First fitting.

   a. Check fabric grain throughout.
   b. Check position and direction of darts.
   c. Check seam placement.
   d. Check neck and shoulder line.
   e. Check collar fit.
   f. Check breakline of collar and lapel roll. Mark.
   g. Check closing.
   h. Check sleeve grain, width, and length.
   i. Mark garment length.
   j. Check button and pocket locations.
   k. Check decorative detail.
   l. Mark alterations if necessary.

See Chapter 5 for a detailed discussion of the first fitting.

10. Make alterations and refit if necessary.

11. Remove basted-in sleeves.

This may not be absolutely necessary if the sleeve hang is correct, but it is usually easier to do the next few steps without the sleeves.

12. Permanently stitch all garment seams.

13. Press seams. (Review and use correct pressing techniques discussed earlier in this chapter.)

14. Apply interfacings; tack and pad stitch when necessary.

Lay in the interfacings around the front and neck of the garment and around the bottom if required. Machine-baste to the seam line. If there is an underlining, diagonally tack the front interfacing in place. (Directions for both diagonal tacking and pad stitching were given earlier in this chapter.) Trim the facing back from the seamline. Pad stitch lapels, starting with the roll line.

15. Make pockets.

Construct bound, stand, or welt pockets if called for in the design. Consult directions in a comprehensive sewing instruction book such as the *Vogue Book of Sewing* or the *Singer Sewing Book*. Both of these books have excellent, illustrated, step-by-step directions for these procedures.

16. Make bound buttonholes, if they are being used.

Consult directions in either of the books mentioned in the paragraph above.

17. Construct lining.

Be sure to transfer any garment alterations from the first fitting to the lining pieces. Do not make the lining too tight. Remember that it must move smoothly inside the garment. If it is too tight, it will distort the shape of the garment by pulling. Do not stitch in the sleeve linings; they will be put in later.

18. Join lining front to front facings.

Some technicians prefer to put in linings entirely by hand. Machine-stitching linings to the facings is a short cut and quite suitable in most costuming situations. This seam is usually not opened but pressed away from the facing.

19. Stitch front facing to garment. Stitch both sides of the facing in the same direction.

20. Trim and grade facing seams.

The seam that will lie against the outermost layer of fabric should be the wider of the two edges. Note that in the lapel portion of the jacket front, the facing side is to the outside; below the lapel, the facing is to the inside. Curve the seam grading accordingly.

21. Turn lining and facings to the inside, baste down, and press.

In most instances, the front facings on a jacket will not be understitched. The entire front of the jacket may be top-stitched later. Roll the facings in and baste all around the front. Press the fold line; do not press over the basting stitches. This is not a final press, and lapels should not be pounded here. Turn the jacket inside out and place it on a dummy. Baste the lining flat around the neck and the armholes. Loosely attach the lining seams to the garment seams. This may be done by machine, but it is probably just as quick to do it by hand while the jacket is hanging on the dummy.

22. Construct the collar.

    a. Interface and pad stitch undercollar.
    b. Stitch upper collar to undercollar, trim seams.
    c. Turn collar, baste, press lightly.
    d. Attach collar to garment.

After the interfacing has been laid on the undercollar and machine-basted around the seam line, trim away the interfacing seam allowance. Pin the undercollar to the large end of the tailor's ham and shape it gently around the ham. Leave the undercollar pinned to the ham until it is completely dry, then take it off and pad stitch. Pad stitching creates a subtle shaping and the stitches should never be drawn up so tightly that they cause puckers in the fabric.

The upper collar will be just slightly larger than the undercollar; when the two pieces are attached and turned back on each other, the undercollar will not roll back and be visible from the outside. Grade the seams in such a way that the seam that lies against the outer collar is the widest.

Pin the collar in place; then baste it. Put the jacket, right side out, on a dummy to check it before machine-basting the collar.

23. Put in the sleeves.

    a. Reset if necessary.
    b. Machine-stitch.
    c. Trim sleeve seams.

To stitch in a sleeve, begin just below the point where the easing begins and stitch down and around the underarm. Proceed over the top of the armhole and back around the underarm again. This will put two rows of stitching where the strain will be the greatest. Trim the upper part of the armhole seam to one-half-inch. Trim the underarm portion to one-quarter-inch. Do not slash the armhole seam as this will weaken it.

24. Second fitting.

Recheck everything as in the first fitting. Set bottom and sleeve hems exactly. Make final trim placement. At the end of this fitting, the garment should be ready for finishing.

25. Put in sleeve linings.

Turn the garment inside out and slip the sleeve linings up over the sleeves. Adjust carefully and slipstitch around the armhole. Turn up the hem about three-quarters of an inch shorter than the jacket sleeve hem; baste just above the fold.

26. Put in bottom and sleeve hems.

Lay a canvas or bias muslin strip into the fold of the sleeve hem. Using a hemming stitch, and catching only a thread or two of the underlining, stitch up sleeve and bottom hems. The lining should lie from three-quarters to one inch above the bottom of the jacket and the bottom of the jacket sleeve. Bring the lining, which has been turned under at the appropriate length, down over the hem. Roll back one-quarter to one-half inch to allow for adequate movement and stitch into place. There should always be a little extra fabric in the lining so it will not pull the garment out of shape. When the lining has been pressed down over the hem, there should be no visible stitching.

27. Work buttonholes by hand or by machine, or complete bound buttonholes.

Most domestic machine buttonhole attachments do not operate smoothly with very bulky materials. Make test buttonholes with the correct number of fabric layers before beginning to work on the actual garment.

Be careful to make buttonholes the correct length. If they are too small, the buttonhole is apt to tear when it is being forced over the button. If it is too large, the opening will not stay buttoned. Compute the length of the buttonhole by adding the width of the button to the depth. This is not an infallible measurement, and you should always make sample buttonholes until a perfect size is made. Buttonholes that have been worked on sturdy fabric can be stretched slightly if you carefully insert a small pair of closed scissors into the hole and open them up slowly and gently to the width of the buttonhole. Buttonholes that are too large can be made smaller by taking a stitch or two across each end.

28. Sew on buttons and final bits of trim.

29. Press well.

5

Alterations

For every hour spent constructing garments in a costume shop, an equal amount of time is spent doing alterations to garments that are already constructed. Hems go up and down constantly; pants are cuffed, then uncuffed; buttons always need resetting. Major size, shape, and style alterations are common. Few costume technicians enjoy altering. Most would far rather build a new dress than make substantial adjustments to an existing one. Altering is not considered fun.

This chapter's intention is not to try and convince you that altering *is* fun, but that it is an art, equally as challenging as constructing a new garment, and sometimes even more so. Until the appearance of inexpensive, ready-to-wear clothes, every home sewer was adept at altering. A turn-of-the-century ball gown might have been worn by several women and even a wedding dress often saw more than one woman to the altar. Clothing was altered to keep up with changing fashion,

as well as to fit different bodies. Clothing historians study the alterations made in period garments and often have to undo a series of darts, tucks, and hems before they arrive at the original shape of the dress or jacket.

Today, except for changing hem lengths, few women make alterations to their own clothes. Ready-to-wear clothing is available in so many different sizes that most people can find garments to fit with few, if any, size and shape adjustments. New fashion silhouettes send shoppers to the store and home sewers to their sewing machines.

Yet the fine art of altering still lives in the costume shop and it is a vitally important part of every day's work. Altering is more painstaking than original construction and it is important that costumers master the tricks of the trade. Parts of the garment must usually be taken apart before the alterations can be made. Linings must be loosened or removed, interfacings trimmed, and top-stitching unpicked. There are not many alteration short cuts. In every altering procedure it is important to think through all the steps, in order, before beginning. You must also know what cannot be altered. There comes a time in the life of every costumer when he or she must tell a designer that the size 44-long suit cannot be altered to fit the actor who is five feet, eight inches tall and has a 38-inch chest measurement, even though the suit is the perfect color and texture for the scene.

There are two major reasons for altering costumes: to fit the garment to the actor's body and to change the look of an existing costume in order to be able to use it again. Every actor who goes on the stage in a costume deserves to be as comfortably fitted as the period of the garment allows. Besides causing discomfort to the actor, a poorly fitted costume can destroy the effectiveness of even the most brilliant design. A good fit depends entirely on costume technicians who have good alteration skills.

Re-using costumes is good economics. Why spend money to build a new costume when an existing one can be altered to do the job equally as well? Balanced budgets

are important to all theatre technicians and those who are the most thrifty are always on the lookout for what stock can be salvaged, reworked, and used again another day.

This chapter is divided into four alteration categories. The most common, and the simplest, alterations involve adjustments to garments under construction as they reach the final stages of completion. These are *fitting adjustments.* Alterations to previously constructed costumes or ready-made garments in order to fit them to the actor's body are grouped under the heading, *size and shape alterations. Tailoring alterations* receive a separate treatment because of the special methods involved. By performing *period and style alterations,* the costumer can change a garment in such a way that it will represent another historical period or style from that in or for which it was designed.

Specific alterations that receive detailed explanations in this chapter do not begin to be all the alteration procedures costumers will encounter, although they represent some of the most common. When you are altering, be patient, be methodical, and don't try the impossible.

FITTING ADJUSTMENTS

No matter how carefully the construction and fitting steps discussed in Chapters 3 and 4 are carried out, there are often last minute alterations to make in the final fit of a garment before it is ready for dress rehearsal. Because the garment is essentially complete at this stage, with linings and facings attached, and hems at least basted in place, these adjustments can be called alterations rather than construction steps. It is often the final fitting adjustment that makes the difference between a totally successful costume and a merely adequate one.

The first step in the process is to assess the total fit of the garment and pinpoint the

places where adjustment is necessary. The actor must be wearing the correct shoes and all the undergarments he or she will be wearing when the costume goes on stage. The fitting should take place in a well-lit space before a large mirror (three-way if possible), with the actor standing at least six feet back from the image. There should be sufficient space for the actor to move, especially if the stage action calls for kneeling, falling, stretching, and so forth. Have a chair handy for sitting down. The designer and those technicians responsible for cutting and constructing the costume should take time to look at the costume as a whole, studying the actor's image as well as the actor's person. Make certain the garments are properly adjusted on the body. It always takes a while for new garments to sit comfortably.

One person should be responsible for the actual marking of alterations. If the alterations are to be marked with pins, use safety pins. In a costume shop, never mark alterations with straight pins; safety pins cannot wound an actor and they will not fall out between the fitting room and the work table.

If you intend to mark the outside of a garment, use chalk that can either be brushed away or ironed off. Be sure to sharpen the chalk, or break it, in order to get a good line. Experiment on a scrap of the fabric before marking the garment. The iron-off chalk does leave a discoloration on some fabrics. Stone chalk that brushes off has the maddening property of brushing off too easily on certain soft materials and, like straight pins, may vanish before the garment gets to the sewing machine.

Once the fitting team has determined which alterations need to be made and have marked them, take a last look at the garment. Make sure the body is not overfitted, that the fabric is not straining over the chest, the back, or the belly. Be sure it is not underfitted, that it does not wrinkle or roll where it should not. Look at the sleeves. Do they hang straight from the top of the shoulder with the proper forward pitch? Is the neckline low enough? High enough? Is the waistline in the correct position for the style and period of the garment? Is the hemline perfect? Only when these points have been checked should the costume be removed from the actor and completed.

A word of caution: Garment fit is only part of the total examination being made at the final costume fitting. The designer will also be studying the size and scale of the trim and the suitability of shoes and accessories. It is essential that basic fitting problems be solved before moving on to these other considerations. Handsome trim and pretty sandals will not hide an ill-fitting garment.

SOME COMMON FITTING ADJUSTMENTS

Hems

It is advisable to baste up hems for the final fitting; steam lightly but never press firmly at this stage. Then, if the hemline proves to be either crooked or incorrect, the basting threads can be removed quickly and the correct length marked afresh. A good way to mark hems is with a wide metal yardstick, measuring from the floor up, using safety pins or chalk marks at fairly regular three-inch intervals. Some technicians prefer hem-marking devices that dispense powdered chalk, and some use the right angle, resting the shorter arm on the floor. Use whatever method works best for you, but do mark with care. Always ask the actor to stand up straight and refrain from looking at the floor. When the hem is marked all the way around, pin it up for a final check.

In determining the hem length of a costume, always bear in mind that stages are either lower or higher than the audience. If the stage is lower than the audience, the hemline will appear longer; if it is higher, the hemline will appear shorter. Compensations may have to be made.

Floor length skirts and skirts with trains are more difficult to mark. Usually the floor length skirt hangs one-half-inch to an inch above the floor, long enough to give the illusion of being on the floor, but high enough to minimize the danger of the actor tripping. A seam gauge may be used to measure a floor length hem. Some costumers prefer to mark the skirt with chalk where it hits the floor and hem up the desired one-half to one inch. Pin up the hem allowance and check the mirror image for evenness.

Never try to mark both sides of a trained hem on the actor. Beginning on one side, find the point at which the train begins its descent, mark it and spread out the train smoothly on the floor. Find and mark the longest point of the train at the center back; then connect these two points with the correct shape. When the garment is removed from the actor, lay the skirt out on a flat surface, folded in half, and transfer the right side markings to the left side. (Some adjustment may be necessary if the hang is affected because the actor has a low shoulder or hip.) If the train does not reach the floor, as in certain 1920s gowns, the same principle holds true. Mark only one half of the train in the fitting and the other half with the skirt laid out on a flat surface.

Once the correct hemline has been established, stitch it in place with an appropriate machine or hand-hemstitch.

Tight or Loose Wristbands and Cuffs

It is easier to prevent an ill-fitting wristband or cuff than to adjust it. If the wristbands are too tight at the final fitting, it is usually because the cutter did not allow for the amount of fabric bulk that results from seaming the wristband onto the sleeve. Normally, if the band is to fit the wrist snugly and the sleeve is moderately gathered, the cuff, when cut from light-weight fabric, should have a one-half-inch ease allowance added to the amount of the overlap (which is usually one to one and one-half inches). The amount of ease should be increased if the fabric is medium- or heavy-weight. Cuffs become especially bulky if they must be constructed out of wide wale corduroy, velveteen, or jacket-weight wools. A cuff or wristband that is too tight, having already been trimmed and set onto the gathered sleeve, cannot be altered; it must be recut.

In order to alter a cuff that is only a bit too large, remove the cuff from the back of the sleeve, tighten the sleeve gathers as much as is necessary, and restitch the cuff. The result of this alteration will be a longer overlap. If the cuff is much too large and the sleeve must be gathered in all the way around, the cuff will have to be removed entirely and cut down to the desired length before it is reattached.

On Elizabethan doublets and other garments in which shaped sleeves must fit the wrist snugly without an apparent wristband, cut the bottom of the sleeve just wide enough for the actor to pass his or her hand through, and face or hem the sleeve in a normal fashion. Then the sleeve can be folded back upon itself and secured with a concealed hook and eye, forming a slight inverted pleat at the back of the arm. Final adjustments on this kind of wrist closure only involve changing the position of the hardware.

High or Low Waistline

The position of the garment waistline on the body is a major design and period element. A fashion waistline is always determined in relationship to the natural waistline of the actor, and both natural and fashion waistlines should be marked on the original muslin mock-up of the garment. When the garment is on the actor, it is sometimes helpful to tie a tape around the natural waistline as a guide. If, in the final fitting, the fashion waistline is seen to be even slightly out of position, the entire proportion of the garment will be wrong. Never trim the waist seam before the final fitting. If the position of the waistline has to be changed, this alteration has to be made before the bottom hem is established. Be sure to look carefully at the garment from all angles; it is common for the waistline to fall too low in the back and too high in the front. Measure the distance from the underarm to the side waist and be certain that both sides are identical. Waistline adjustments are often quite small; a quarter of an inch error is enough to be noticeable.

In almost all instances, a waistline adjustment will affect only the bodice portion of the seam, while the seam allowance on the skirt portion remains the same. In other words, the skirt will be moved up or down the bodice. If it looks as though the waistline position might be changed in the final fitting, ask the technician who is constructing the garment to machine-baste the waist seam until after the final fitting. Only when the waistline position has been approved by the designer should the seam be trimmed and, perhaps, bound.

Body of the Garment Too Tight or Too Loose

Costumers are often tempted to put the blame for ill-fitting garments on a devilish tailor who sneaks into the shop at night to restitch all those carefully stitched seams. Why else should a jacket or a bodice, fitted so carefully in muslin, and again in fabric, suddenly be too tight or too loose at the final fitting? The reasons are quite practical. Actors do tend to lose weight in rehearsal (some gain weight as well); costume technicians do not always stitch precisely on the stitching lines and, with a six- or eight-piece bodice or coat, a sixteenth of an inch error, compounded several times, adds up to a bad fit; also, the insertion of zippers, hook and eye tape, linings, and/or facings can make a snug fit too snug. Whatever the cause, there are often seam and dart adjustments to make in the almost finished garment body.

Take care, when releasing or taking in seams at this stage, to decide exactly where the alteration is to be made, and to make certain that the adjustment does not throw off the correct position of the side seams (or side panels) or the center back and center front straight-of-grain lines. If the garment is an inch or less too big or too small all the way around the body, the alteration can probably be made in the side seams, taking in or releasing an equal amount from both the front and the back. If the adjustment exceeds an inch, you will probably want to make small adjustments all the way around, balancing the front and the back alterations in order to retain the correct side seam positions. Pin these adjustments in the fitting so you can see their effect. If the side seams are still positioned correctly, and the front and back grain lines undisturbed, you are ready to remark the seamlines and stitch in the adjustments.

In most instances, stitch in the new seam or dart line before ripping out the old one. Costumers differ in their attitudes toward tools for ripping. Some prefer seam rippers, others single-edged razor blades. Some ban both seam rippers and razor blades from the shop and use small, sharp-pointed scissors. Any tool that is used to rip out stitching can also rip fabric; whichever tool you choose to use, use it with care.

By the time of the final fitting, the garment should fit well across the front of the chest (above the bustline) or across the back. These are crucial areas which involve the armscye curve, and they should have been successfully adjusted long before the final fitting. There is almost nothing that can be done to a bodice that has been cut too narrow across the front or across the back except to recut it. If it is too wide in either or both of these areas, the sleeves can be moved in slightly, no more than three-quarters of an inch on each side, but always at the risk of enlarging the armscye curve and causing the sleeve to bind the actor's arm uncomfortably.

In general, be particularly careful when cutting the upper part of the body garment. Correct as many mistakes as possible in the original sloper. These areas are difficult to alter in the later stages of construction. The girth and waist areas are easier to adjust as long as you keep the important seams and grain lines in position.

Incorrect Sleeve Hang

An incorrect sleeve hang is a very common final fitting problem. A sleeve that is set in too far back will pull against the front of the arm and a sleeve that is too far forward will strain across the back of the arm. *A one-half-inch error in either direction can cause a problem in a fitted or a tailored sleeve.* To check the position of the sleeve, have the actor hold his or her arm down, naturally, to the side of the body. Place your finger on the top of the shoulder, the point from which the sleeve falls (not necessarily the point where the shoulder seam lies), and drop a string with a weight tied to one end of it from your finger toward the floor. The straight grain line of the sleeve fabric should follow the string exactly. If the grain line slants to the back, the sleeve is too far forward; if it slants to the front, the sleeve is too far back. While the garment is still on the actor in the fitting, remove the top of the sleeve from the bodice or jacket and pin the shoulder point precisely. Check to make sure that the sleeve underarm point is lined up with the underarm of the garment.

When these two points are accurately pinned, you can reset the rest of the sleeve once the garment is off the actor.

A Note about Final Fittings

Do not panic when the costume you have built does not fit at the final fitting. Relax. Look the situation over. Find the problem and search for the easiest possible solution. Don't begin marking alterations until you check the following: (1) Does the actor have on the correct undergarments? Is the actor wearing the correct shoes? (2) Is the actor standing squarely on both feet, head up, looking straight ahead? (3) Are the closings correct? The snaps or hooks and eyes lined up? Are the buttons sewed on to match up with the buttonholes? Is the zipper stitched in correctly? (4) Is the garment pulled firmly down on the body, with the waistline in the intended place? These are things you can check in a matter of moments. The more fittings you conduct, the more these steps will become second nature to you.

SIZE AND SHAPE ALTERATIONS

When a costume designer and staff are beginning to plan the costumes for a period production, one of the early considerations is: How many garments can be pulled from the costume stock, and how many must be built? If an established theatre has been methodical about storing and maintaining its costume stock, there are often several garments that can be pulled which will be suitable for the design concept with fitting alterations, additions or deletions of trim, or a change of color.

Re-using even one or two costumes can add significantly to the amount of money available for new costumes. Budget-conscious costumers develop a keen eye for re-usable items. The first step, after a possible costume has been found in stock, is to fit it on the actor. If there are several possible choices from stock items, have them all in the fitting room when the actor is called. Help the actor get into each costume piece that is being considered, making sure it is properly adjusted, and then have the actor stand well away from the image in the mirror so the designer can judge the possibilities of the garment. The designer will be interested primarily in deciding if the garment will fit into the production design scheme, while the technician must consider fit. If alterations are impossible to make, this is the time to speak up. Once all the available possibilities have been tried on the actor and something suitable and adjustable has been selected, each alteration must be marked on the garment and recorded in the fitting notes.

Plays set in the present, or near-present, are often costumed with "shopped" rather than constructed garments. That is, the clothing is bought new from clothing stores, or secondhand from thrift or antique clothing shops. Shopped costumes usually require some size and shape alteration.

Costumers often take actors along on shopping trips to select costume items. Potentially, this saves time because the garments can be tried on for fit and suitability right on the spot. There are, however, some disadvantages to shopping with an actor. Outside the theatre atmosphere, it is sometimes difficult to focus on the clothing needs of the dramatic character apart from the preferences of the actor. Salespersons, who are trained to sell garments to people, not to dramatic characters, are not always helpful, particularly when the item being shopped for is unbecoming, gaudy, or even downright ugly. They may take a dim view of the enthusiastic costume designer who remarks: "How wonderful. That dress is just tacky enough to be perfect." The best solution for acquiring ready-to-wear costumes might be to purchase an assortment of possibilities on approval, try on the garments in the familiar atmosphere of the theatre fitting space, and return the unchosen items promptly.

Raising and Lowering Hems

Altering the hem in a brand new garment is no different from the process discussed in the section on fitting adjustments. Remove the original hem and steam the bottom of the garment lightly before marking the new hemline at the fitting.

Old garments present other problems when hem lines have to be adjusted. What can be done about the discoloration line that inevi-

tably occurs where the hem has been turned up, especially when the garment is made of a washable fabric and the discoloration is marked? Naturally, if the hemline must be shortened, the discoloration will not be a problem; but what if it must be lengthened? Wools, silks, and some napped fabrics like velour or velvet may respond to steam and a lot of brushing. If a wool garment is to be lengthened, it is a good idea to take out the existing hem and send the garment to the cleaners, where all trace of the original hemline may disappear. There is, however, no simple solution for eliminating the stripe that results from severe color fading. A designer can sometimes dream up trim for the bottom of the skirt that will include something strategically placed over the light stripe (think twice before resorting to rickrack!); sometimes a bit of dye may be brushed over the stripe, and then the whole garment may be redyed. Little else. Often it is the presence of a discoloration stripe on the original hem fold that makes an entire garment unalterable. Creases on hemline folds can sometimes be removed successfully by using a pressing cloth that has been dipped in a solution of white vinegar and water.

Hemming wool, silk, and rayon crepe dresses from the 1930s and 1940s can be an especially frustrating experience. Such garments are for sale in antique clothing shops and they are often included in donations to the theatre from attic and basements cleanouts. If the dresses have been packed flat, they will be in better shape than if they have been hanging on a wire hanger for twenty-five years. However they have been stored, the hems will invariably turn out to be grossly uneven. Once the garment has been selected for a specific actor, release the hem stitches entirely and send the garment to the cleaners. Do this even if it comes in a cleaning bag. Complete every alteration, major and minor, before marking the hem. When the garment is not being worked on, hang it on a wooden hanger in a place where it can hang free rather than be squashed by other clothes. (If the garment is a bias cut dress or skirt, do *not* put it on a hanger; instead, lay it flat on a shelf.) While altering the garment, press it as little as possible. Mark the hem at the final fitting, being careful not to pull down on the skirt. Baste up the hem allowance, apply hem tape, and stitch up the hem. Do not press. Steam lightly. More times than not, the hem will still be slightly uneven, but you can be sure that you have tried your best to make it even. If you look at snapshots of women dressed in crepe dresses during the 1030s and 1940s, you will see that nearly all of them had uneven hem lines!

Bodice Alterations

The major difference between altering bodices of existing costumes and making final fitting adjustments is that, when you have cut and constructed the garment in the shop, you have already solved basic body shape problems in the muslin sloper and the mockup. You have, in other words, accounted for the particular shape of your actor. When you alter existing clothes, you must solve these basic shape problems in an already completed garment. This calls for ingenuity.

THE NECK IS TOO LARGE Remove the collar and/or the neck facing. Gather in the excess material at the nape until the neck fits snugly, or as desired. You may distribute this excess material in one of several ways: Two or more darts may be created, radiating from the back neckline. These should be no larger than one-eighth-inch at the top and taper two or three inches from the neckline. If the bodice is too wide all the way down the back, run fine tucks from the back neck to the waistline. If the material is fine, shirr in the fullness.

After the excess material is dealt with, adjust the collar and neck facing and reattach it to the garment.

THE SHOULDERS ARE TOO WIDE If the shoulders are too wide but the fit over the bust or chest is correct, you may create shoulder darts in both the front and the back of the bodice. The back darts should be smaller than the front darts to allow for ease.

THERE ARE WRINKLES ACROSS THE FRONT Front wrinkles occur because the actor has either excessively square or quite sloping shoulders. If the shoulders are high, the wrinkles will move from the shoulder toward the center front; if sloping, the wrinkles will run from the neck toward the armscye. You might be tempted to move the sleeves further in to remove these wrinkles. Don't. It will not work. The adjustment must be made at the shoulder seam. If the shoulders are high, adjust the shoulder seam at the neck end; if low, the adjustment will be at the shoulder end. After the adjustment is pinned in place, you will see that, along with removing the wrinkles, you have restored the correct bodice cross grain line. Adjustments at the shoulder end of the shoulder seam may necessitate an alteration in the sleeve head.

THERE IS EXCESS MATERIAL AT THE UNDERARM This fullness often occurs when a woman has a full bust and a short distance from underarm to waist. The excess material may be thrown in darts which begin near the waistline, on the side seams, and run up toward the bust point. If the extra fullness occurs in the back, it will be necessary to raise the entire back at the shoulder seams. The back neckline may then have to be lowered.

THE FRONT IS TOO WIDE Create lengthwise tucks stitched either on the inside, or on the outside. These should be situated right over the bust point.

THE FRONT IS TOO NARROW   Add an insert of another fabric down the center front or down each side front. This may only be done if the garment will still retain the overall look desired by the designer.

THE WAISTLINE IS TOO HIGH   If the dress is belted, you can insert a piece of closely matching material into the waist seam, in such a way that it will be covered by the belt. Make sure the piecing is well hidden.

These types of bodice alterations require patience, imagination, and a sure knowledge of seamline and fabric grain placement. Take time to study each individual fitting problem. Consider the solution and proceed carefully.

Approach Armscye Alterations with Caution

You should approach armscye alterations with caution. If the armhole in a garment is too tight under the arm but sits properly on the shoulder, you can successfully "scoop out" the underarm portion of the armscye. Some costumers do this while the garment is on the actor, using a small pair of scissors and taking very little material away at a time. Or, you may take an armscye measurement and trim away the armscye of the garment after it has been removed from the actor. Never take away too much material. It cannot be put back.

If the armhole is too big, there are only a limited number of things that can be done to make it smaller. You can raise the shoulder seam slightly, but not so much as to throw off the bodice cross grain. You can take in the side seam, but you must then also trim out the armscye curves front and back, an operation that must be done with care or you will end up making the armhole even larger. If the bodice is cut with a princess line that extends into the armscye, you can take in the curved side front and side back seams.

Avoid armscye alterations that attempt to take in excess width across the front or across the back of a garment by trimming the armscye in toward the body. This makes the armscye larger. The sleeve will no longer fit properly into it and will have a tendency to bind the actor's upper arm.

Men's Shirt Alterations

A substantial collection of men's shirts in many different sizes and styles is an essential part of an adequate theatre costume stock. Shirts can be used over and over again. Certain size and shape adjustments are possible.

Sleeve length can be altered in shirts; cuffs and collars can be turned and refashioned; and body fit can be adjusted. *But* the neck size in a man's dress shirt is virtually impossible to change. Always fit the actor in a shirt with the correct neck size, especially if he must wear a necktie and/or a detached collar. Do be aware that some shirts are cut more skimpily than others and that the actor who wears a size 15 neck in one brand may require a 15½ neck in another. Also, due to laundry shrinkage, a 15½ neck in a shirt that is twenty-five years old will be slightly smaller than a 15½ neck in a contemporary shirt.

In many instances, a costume shirt is worn under a suit with only the collar and cuffs and a bit of the front showing. If the shirt is to be worn in this manner, you can lengthen the sleeve by inserting a strip of fabric in the upper arm of the shirt. In a reverse procedure, the sleeve can be shortened by taking a tuck in the upper arm. Both of these alterations are visible if the shirt is worn alone without a suit jacket, so be absolutely sure, before you do either of them, that there will be no stage business in which the actor removes his jacket. These two alterations have the advantage of being quick and easy.

There is no other way of lengthening a

shirt sleeve. However, a shirt sleeve may be shortened invisibly either from the top or from the bottom. To do it from the top, open the underarm seam that runs from the wrist end of the sleeve to the bottom of the shirt body from the underarm about halfway down the sleeve and down the body. Trim off the top of the sleeve the necessary amount, being careful to retain the correct curve. Stitch the shortened sleeve into the shirt armscye. (The head of the sleeve will probably be slightly smaller than the armscye now.) Restitch the long underarm seam. This alteration is time consuming principally because there are so many flat-felled seams to be ripped.

To shorten shirt sleeves from the bottom, remove the cuffs and the plackets, trim off the sleeves, and replace the cuffs and plackets. This is not a difficult alteration if the plackets are applied and can be removed in a piece. It is a bit tedious if the placket is fashioned with a continuous lap which must be removed and replaced.

Occasionally the shirt you want to use is already showing signs of wear, especially in the collar and cuffs. It is easy to preserve the life of a shirt by turning the collar and cuffs, a mending trick often used by thrifty homemakers. Remove the collar from the shirt by inserting the point of a single-edged razor blade under the stitches joining the collar and the band and gently cutting the threads. Because the stitches are tiny and the shirt collar is usually starched, it is quite difficult to remove these stitches with a seam ripper or with scissors. When the collar is off, fold it in half and mark the center with a pin or a pencil mark. Mend the frayed area with a piece of thin, iron-on mending cloth or with a machine darning stitch. Reverse the replacement of the collar into the neckband so the mended side is to the outside and the unfrayed side to the inside. Pin carefully in place and restitch.

When the frayed cuffs are French cuffs, remove them and mend the frayed areas in the same manner as with the collar. Turn the cuffs over and reverse them. Reattach to the sleeves. Mend simple cuffs by binding the edges with a bias binding that matches the shirt fabric. These simple mending tricks may easily double the life of a fine shirt.

There are times when you will want to alter the shirt body so it fits the actor snugly. Simply create four double-pointed contour body darts, two front and two back, tapering them carefully. Be careful not to overfit. The side seams may also need to be curved slightly.

TAILORING ALTERATIONS

Tailoring is a specialized method of clothing construction. The method is most often used to construct jackets, trousers, vests, and coats. The objective of tailoring is to construct a garment that achieves its shape through interlining, pad stitching, and pressing. This is in contrast to a gown or dress that shapes itself to the body of the wearer. Sometimes tailoring techniques are used in parts of garments: in a man's shirt, for instance, where the collar and cuffs are tailored. Many dresses have tailored collars, and a soft, clinging sheath dress might be topped with a tailored jacket. The desired result determines whether or not a garment is constructed by the tailoring method.

It is necessary to understand certain things about the tailoring method in order to be able to alter tailored garments. There is no section on tailoring as such in this book simply because the techniques are the same whether they are being used to create stage costumes or street wear, and several excellent tailoring instruction books can be found in any library.

Before you begin to alter a tailored garment, hang it up or put it on a dummy and look at it carefully. Your goal will be to alter the garment in such a way that it will end up with the same fine finishing details you can see in its unaltered state. As you study a jacket, for example, note first that the edges of the garment are thin. Thinness at the junction of seams is what all good tailors strive for. There should be no bumps or slovenly, thick areas along the edges of a good jacket. Note also that all the edges curl slightly inward, never outward. This is true of the fronts, the sleeve vents, the pocket flaps, the revers, and the corners of the collar. The seams are all straight and flat without puckers or ripples. The lining is loose and does not interfere with the hang of the coat. The sleeves hang clean with no diagonal pull. The collar sits close without stretching.

Jacket Alterations

The most common alterations to jackets are: raising the length of the jacket (tailored jacket hems are so narrow that it is not normally possible to lengthen them), raising and lowering the sleeve length, and adjusting the body size.

RAISING JACKET LENGTH   Raising the length of a tailored jacket is not a quick alteration. A costume technician may spend an entire work day accomplishing this adjustment. As with most tailoring alterations, work on one side of the garment at a time so you have the other side as a reference.

First of all, mark the new bottom line, which has been arrived at in fitting, with a basting stitch, using contrasting thread. A simple way to reproduce the curve at the bottom edge of the front is to cut a piece of cardboard the shape of the original curve and use the pattern to create the new curve, higher up on the jacket front. One danger in shortening a tailored jacket is that you will end up with a flattened front curve, which will destroy the balance of the garment. Carefully begin to take down the old

hem, loosening the lining first, and then the facing. Observe how the facing and interfacing are placed. Measure the depth of the finished hem allowance and take note of all the places where seams are clipped and trimmed. You must proceed like the inexperienced watchmaker whose only hope of putting the works back together is to keep a careful record of the dismantling process.

Once the inner construction is loose and out of the way (here again, a razor blade is the preferable ripping tool because the stitches are small and well-pressed in and difficult to get at with a seam ripper), turn up the coat bottom on the new hemline and baste it in place, about one-half-inch from the edge. Start at the center back, basting first one half and then the other. Use fairly short basting stitches and be careful not to gather the fabric. End the basting about two inches before the beginning of the front curve.

Making sure the canvas interfacing is out of the way, place the front facing and the front outer fabric face to face and machine-stitch the two pieces together on the new curve line, reinserting seam tape in the same manner in which it was originally used. Stitch only to the edges of the facings. Trim the seam closely. Retack interfacing. Turn the facing to the inside of the jacket and press carefully over a tailor's ham. On most tailored jackets, the stitching line that joins the front facing to the front does not lie exactly on the edge, but slightly to the inside; this causes the front edge to curve in toward the body. By careful steaming you can achieve this effect in the altered edge.

Lightly press the remainder of the hem. Trim the new hem allowance the same width as the original one was. (Once a tailored jacket has been shortened, you cannot expect to be able to lengthen it again.) Cross-stitch the hem in place, taking care that the stitches are invisible from the outside. Hand-stitch the facing.

RAISING AND LOWERING SLEEVE LENGTH
These are the commonest of all tailoring alterations. In the fitting, mark the length of
both sleeves, since very few human bodies
have arms that are the same length. Mark
the sleeve length accurately by placing the
end of a tape measure at the tip of the thumb
and measuring up to the desired length. In
many cases, period research will give you the
normal jacket sleeve length from the period
in which you are working. Five to five and
a half inches up from the tip of the thumb
is an average jacket sleeve length if you wish
the shirt cuff to be visible below. Because
of the disparity in arm length, it is entirely
possible that you will find yourself lengthening one jacket sleeve and shortening the
other.

When shortening a sleeve, place a line of
basting stitches, in contrasting thread, around
the sleeve at the correct length. Be careful
not to allow the sleeve to dip down in the
back. Remove the sleeve buttons and rip out
the lining and the hem. The vent underlap
is cut as part of the sleeve, forming a self-
facing, which makes it impractical to elongate
the vent when you are shortening the sleeve.
Shifting the buttons higher up the shortened
sleeve will acceptably "fake" a longer vent.
The sleeve will have a piece of interfacing
at the bottom. Be sure to move this up to
the new hemline to preserve the proper sleeve
edge. Turn the sleeve up on the new line
and baste it up about one-half-inch from the
bottom. Unless the fabric is very bulky, it
is not necessary to trim away the wider hem
allowance that remains when you shorten a
sleeve. By retaining as much of the fabric
length as possible, you allow the jacket to
be worn by many actors over the years. However, since the sleeve is narrowest at the bottom, you will have to open the sleeve seams
gently, a bit at a time, until the turned-back
material fits inside the sleeve without causing
it to pucker. Cross-stitch the hem into place.
Turn up the lining the same distance as the

sleeve was turned up, and blindstitch the lining into the sleeve, leaving a tuck so the
sleeve will not be pulled up by an overly
tight lining. Be careful when setting the lining
into place that you don't twist it inside the
sleeve.

Lengthening the sleeve is the reverse process of shortening it. In the fitting you will
note down the amount of extra length needed
on each sleeve. Release the lining and the
original hem. Measure the desired distance
down from the original hem and mark this
line with a basting thread. Now proceed as
directed in the paragraph above.

Replace the sleeve buttons after both
sleeves have been altered. A normal placement for jacket sleeve buttons is with the
bottom button one and one-half inches from
the bottom and each button center five-
eighths of an inch up from the one below.

ALTERATIONS TO THE JACKET BODY Modest
size alterations can be made in the body of
a tailored jacket. The center back seam may
be taken in or let out slightly across the
broadest part of the shoulders without harm-
ing the look of the garment. Any alteration
to this seam must be very gently angled back
into the existing seam to avoid puckers. Press
the altered seam well, using a damp pressing
cloth. Avoid center back seam alterations that
must extend into the back neck edge. It is
virtually impossible to alter a tailored collar
without spoiling it. If the jacket is darted,
the darts can be taken in or let out. However,
these body darts are usually clipped in order
to make them lie flat; if so, they cannot be
let out. Side seams may be taken in, but the
seam allowances are often so closely trimmed
that there may be very little left to let out.

Altering Tailored Trousers

Trousers are more easily altered than jackets.
In most costume shops, trouser hems go up

and down all the time, determined not only by the length of the actor's legs but also by the trouser length common to the period in which the costumes were designed.

Uncuffed trouser bottoms are hemmed much like skirt bottoms. There is a limit to how much material can be folded and stitched up inside the legs before the hang of the trousers is affected. The amount will vary according to the weight and character of the material, but anything more than five inches will probably give you trouble.

To shorten cuffed trousers, first clip the tailor's tacks that support the cuff at the side seam and the inseam. Fold the cuff down and remove the hem stitches from the inside of the trouser bottom. Pull the whole leg out straight. Run a line of basting stitches on the original bottom fold (the top of the cuff when it is folded up) and another line of basting stitches on the new fold. Steam out the folds gently; do not steam in a crease. At this point, a tailor would trim away a strip of fabric around the bottom of the leg that equals the distance between the two lines of basting, so that the actual hemline will occur under the cuff. Since the costumer's goal is to retain as much potential hem length as possible for future altering, do not trim away all the excess. Put in the hem with evenly spaced, invisible stitches. Fold up the cuff, press it, and tack it in place. If the hem shows above the cuff edge or pulls at the trouser leg, it can always be trimmed away and restitched under the cuff.

Lengthening cuffed trousers is essentially the reverse. A false cuff can be made if the trouser legs, pressed out, are the right length for the actor plus at least one and one-half inches. Create a one-half-inch deep tuck to simulate the top of the cuff. Turn the hem up one-half-inch. On the underside of the garment, face the hem with a piece of fabric wide enough to meet the bottom of the tuck. Slipstitch hem facing and tuck together. Press.

The center back of most trousers can be altered with relative ease. Usually there is extra material in this seam which extends into the waistband, allowing for greater adjustability. The back seam can be let out in its entirety without disturbing the look of the pants at all. You may also add a triangular insert into the center back seam to let out the trousers even further. Put the trousers on the actor and open the center back seam until there is no more strain on the fabric. Insert a piece of brown paper under the trousers and draw a pattern of the necessary insert. Cut a triangle from a matching, or closely matching, piece of fabric and stitch it into place. A suit or sports jacket will conceal this alteration completely.

Trousers can also be taken in at the center back, but with some care. If the adjustment extends down into the crotch curve, you risk flattening the curve and throwing the trouser crotch length down too far between the actor's legs. This makes an uncomfortable fit that restricts movement.

Wide trouser legs can be tapered successfully if you are careful to take in an equal amount in both the side seam and the inseam. This alteration should begin below the side pockets so as not to involve the inner construction of the pockets.

PERIOD AND STYLE ALTERATIONS

Period and style alterations call for great ingenuity on the part of costumers. Many changes can be made in a garment to integrate it into a particular production style or period, but the trick is to be able to see the potential for change in clothing that is, to the ordinary eye, quite unsuitable. This takes some experience and a willingness to experiment.

Altering for a particular production style often involves reworking trim. A sedate silk gown from the bustle period may be turned into a costume for a dance hall queen by lowering the neckline and by adding rows of thick fringe to the bustle folds and to the bottom of the skirt. Braid may be added to a plain blue blazer in order to costume a naval officer. Trim may always be removed from opulent garments to accommodate a somber production, and added to plain garments for a richer look.

The exact nature of any style alteration depends upon the requirements of the design and should be determined when the actor is in the garment. Achieving the correct scale and proportion in an altered garment is somewhat more difficult than achieving them in the original design. Make sure there is enough time for trial and error. Pin proposed trim in place to study its effect and do not hesitate to try several potential solutions before making a decision. Hastily conceived trim alterations have a great tendency to look tacked on.

Period alterations can be particularly important for costuming twentieth-century plays. A good many secondhand garments that hang in your costume stock or on the racks at Salvation Army stores can be altered to meet a variety of period needs. The smaller the costume budget, the more useful you will find period alterations to be.

Before beginning to search for garments to alter into period shapes, make certain you are absolutely familiar with the period in which the play is set. Each costume period has its own distinctive silhouette, and it is to this silhouette that you must first address yourself. Look at pictures from many different sources until you can make a quick drawing, by memory, of the basic shape of the time for both men and women. Pay particular attention to how much leg is revealed in women's clothing, how wide the shoulders are, where the waist is, and how pronounced

the bust is. As you look at pictures, squint your eyes until you can see the total shape, rather than any detail. In men's garments, check length and width of trouser legs, length of jacket, width of shoulders, and chest prominence.

Once the silhouettes are memorized, begin looking at secondhand clothing to discover which garments can be adapted to the required period look. Once again, use the squint approach. Look at the total garment and assess its shape in relation to the shape you require.

A great many "sack" dresses can be adapted to the early 1920s. A basic Villager shirtwaist dress from the 1960s can receive a new neck treatment and pass very well for a 1930s housedress. A few years ago, young women were wearing high-necked, puff-sleeved blouses that translate easily to the shirtwaists from early in the century by releasing the front waist darts and gathering in the excess material across the center front. Any long gathered skirt can be given an early twentieth-century look by moving the gathers to the back so the front panel is smooth. When you are buying secondhand garments for period alteration, check to see that the darts are unclipped and the seam allowances are generous.

Look at men's suits with the same eye toward adaptation. Ivy League suits from the late 1950s and early 1960s can become suits from the first fifteen or twenty years of this century by the addition of an extra buttonhole or two. A current jacket with wide lapels can pass for a 1940s jacket once you have beefed up the shoulder padding a bit. Wide lapels can be made smaller. Patch pockets can be scrounged from inside facings for a more authentic representation. Pleats cannot be added to pants that do not already have them, but they can be removed by turning the fabric involved in the pleats to the inside of the pants and creating a seam down the length of the legs.

Necklines make major period statements in women's garments. Necklines are not difficult to change. A neckline can be cut away or it can be filled in. Dickey and collar additions can alter a scoop-necked bodice into a Gibson girl look. Perhaps you can find a second blouse with a high neck and collar and simply cut out the portion you need to fill in the low neck.

Collars and neckware are major period signals in men's garments. In each period, take careful note of the shape of the shirt collars, the width of the neckware, and the size of the tie knot. It is easy to change a collar on a shirt. And it is even easier to take the collar off a shirt and add stud holes so a detached collar can be fastened to it. Button cuffs can be changed to French cuffs by removing the cuff, opening it out, lining it with a closely matching fabric, and putting it back on the shirt.

Pay particular attention to lengths: skirt lengths, waist lengths, sleeve lengths, and jacket lengths. Proportion is central to the fashion of any period; and, if you can achieve the correct fashion proportion of the period you are seeking to represent by way of period alteration, you will be well on the way to producing a successful stage costume.

6

Fabric Dyeing and Painting

The first section in this chapter, an overview of fabric dyes and paints for theatrical costumers, was prepared by Deborah M. Dryden, author of *Fabric Printing and Dyeing for the Theatre,* a Drama Book Specialists publication. Dryden is a professional designer as well as a teacher of design and the art of costuming. Her essay provides a sound introduction into the mysteries of coloring and painting fabrics; and her book, with its detailed dye recipes and step-by-step instructions for dyeing and painting processes, is an essential resource tool for costume shops of all sizes and types.

FABRIC DYES AND PAINTS

Dyeing and painting fabrics for theatrical costumes releases the designer from the constricting bonds of commercially available fabric colors and prints. Dyes and paints are used not only to change or tint the original overall color of the fabric but also to print, pattern, texture, or age the fabric to suit the designer's needs. For all the benefits that can accrue from coloring fabrics, these processes are too frequently neglected by costume shops. The busy costumer is often faced with too little time, too little money, and odds and ends of dye in cans and packets, which may or may not be familiar. Equipment for dyeing may be totally absent. Lack of knowledge is almost as common as lack of equipment and supplies. Confusion reigns universally about what type of dye to use for which fabric, about how to set the dye, about whether the dyed fabric may be washed or dry cleaned, and so on.

The proliferation of dye brand names on

the market adds to the confusion of the costume dyer. In actuality, there are only about eight different *types* of dye available, and there are even fewer major manufacturers of dyestuffs. The confusion arises because of the large number of dyestuff distributors, each of whom attaches a different brand name to its dye. The mystery is compounded by the seeming unwillingness of many of these companies to properly identify the dyestuff contained in their own packets.

Perhaps the most frequently used type of dye currently found in theatre shops is the type known as *union,* or household, dye. This dye has a number of familiar brand names: Rit, Putnam, Tintex, Cushings, and others. Union dyes are excellent basic dyes for every shop since they consist of portions of all the other dye types. Therefore, although they do not possess the special characteristics (brilliance of color, for example) of each of their component dyes, they will dye a wider range of fabrics than the individual dye types. Simple to use, their only required chemical assistant is common uniodized salt.

The term "aniline" is frequently used in the theatre almost as if it, too, were a type of dye. This is a common misconception. Aniline is really a substance which is inherent in virtually all synthetic dyes—that is to say, in any dye that is not a "natural" dye. *Acid* and *basic* dyes are two types whose characteristics fall into the realm of those dyes we have been calling "aniline" for so many years. Brilliant in color, these dyes are particularly attractive to the theatre artist, and they are frequently used for scene painting. Their use on costumes has been somewhat more limited due to varied degrees of washfastness. If used correctly, however, both acid and basic dyes can be made relatively colorfast.

Acid dyes are so-called because they require acetic acid (vinegar is a dilute solution of acetic acid) to assist the dye process. Acid dyes are intended for use on protein fibers—silk and wool. Fabrics dyed with acid dyes should generally be dry cleaned rather than washed. Basic dyes can be used on cotton and linen if finishes have been removed from the fabric before dyeing. Both acid and basic dyes can be used to color FEV (French Enamel Varnish).

Direct dyes are a fourth type noted for inexpensiveness and ease of use. Because direct dyes require only salt as an assistant, they are a good general dyestuff. Direct dyes are intended for use on cotton, linen, and viscose rayon, although some will dye silk and wool.

Fiber-reactive dyes have come onto the market relatively recently. They were developed in the 1950s specifically to dye rayon. These are good cold water dyes and are frequently used for the batik process. Known under various brand names (Procion, Hi-Dye, Dylon, Fibrec, Fabdec, etc.), these dyes require common salt and washing soda as assistants, both readily available at a local grocery store. These dyes are most brilliant in color and remarkably colorfast on cotton, linen, and viscose rayon. They are colorfast on silk, although somewhat less brilliant. Fiber-reactive dyes are best suited for dyeing small quantities of fabric or for direct painting with dye pastes. Large quantities of the dyes are necessary for dyeing large amounts of fabric, making the general use of fiber-reactive dyes prohibitively expensive.

Disperse dyes, although in existence for some time, have only just become widely accessible to the consumer. These dyes were developed specifically for synthetic fibers. They are very simple to use and dye acetates and nylon to brilliant, intense colors. They are also effective on polyesters, although the colors that can be achieved are the usual, commercially available polyester colors.

Vat dyes are less familiar to theatrical dyers because they are more complicated to use and require less readily available chemicals: caustic soda and sodium hydrosulphite. These dyes are extremely colorfast on cotton, linen, and viscose rayon. Like fiber-reactive dyes, vat dyes can be used on silk, but with a lessening of color brilliance. Characteristic of vat dyes is their "developing" process. The color of the fabric when it is removed from the dyebath is frequently quite different from the intended color. As the fabric is air-dried, however, the effect of light and air causes the color to "develop" miraculously before the eyes of the observer. Obviously, test swatches are a must for this type of dye.

Vat dyes are available in a thickened form under the brand name, *Inkodye* (from Screen Process Supplies in Oakland, California). This dye already has its chemical assistants within the bottle and is suitable for the direct painting of dye on fabric. The colors go on clear or pastel and then develop in sunlight or under an ultraviolet sunlamp. When applied to the cellulosic fibers (cotton, linen, and viscose rayon), Inkodye is extremely colorfast to washing and dry cleaning without any setting other than the natural developing process and rinsing. Inko products also manufactures an Inkodye for silk, which requires steam setting for fixation. Otherwise, the silk type dye works just like Inkodye Regular. Always store Inkodye in opaque containers, since exposure to light will develop the dye prematurely and deteriorate its strength.

Napthol, or azoic, dyes are not recommended for use in costume shops. They require several dyebaths, complicated processes, and a variety of chemicals. The colors, however, are extremely colorfast and are similar to the rich, earthy colors seen in Javanese batiks. For this reason, some batik artists use this type of dye exclusively.

Pigments differ from dyes in that whereas dyes form a chemical bond with the fabric fiber, pigments rest on the surface of the fabric. Common pigment mediums for use on costumes are generally called textile paints. There are numerous brands: Versatex, Watertex, Aquaset, Britex, and so on. Versatex is an especially good textile paint. Thinned with water or its clear extender, Versatex can be painted, sprayed, or silkscreened on fabric with a water washup. When dry, this pigment can be heat set with a hot, dry iron or an automatic tumble dryer. Versatex pigment is most colorfast when it is correctly heat set. Although generally opaque in nature, colors can be overlaid with some transparency, as is true with dyes. The hand, or drapeability, of the painted fabric may be, depending on the thickness of the pigment used, only slightly affected. Versatex also produces a binder which aids in its use on synthetic fibers. A set of good textile paints, regardless of the brand name, is a wise investment for any costume dye shop.

Acrylic paints are also sometimes used to paint fabrics. They do stiffen the fabric. Once dry, acrylic paints do not require heat setting for fastness.

Dye pastes, made from any of the types of dye already discussed, can be used to paint on fabric. They can be employed either for direct painting or for silkscreening. Each type of dye must be combined with the appropriate chemicals before the paste is made. Virtually all fabrics painted with dye pastes require heat or steam setting for fixation.

DYE STOCK AND MACHINES

If a significant amount of fabric dyeing is to be done in a costume shop, do purchase a stock of union dyes in a variety of colors. Buying dyes in small packets at the grocery store is very expensive. Tintex dyes, with salt included, may be bought by the pound from Knomark, Inc., Jamaica, New York 11434. Bulk union dyes, without salt added, are available from Keystone Aniline Chemical Co., 321 N. Loomis St., Chicago, Illinois

60607. A substantial minimum order is required by both of these companies. Bulk dyestuffs will be delivered in metal containers. Make sure that the cans are clearly marked with the color name. Keep all cans tightly closed, since dyes can deteriorate under light.

Other types of dyes for specific dyeing projects will probably be bought in smaller quantities for a single use rather than being stocked. A craft supply company, or a fabric artist who works with various fabric dyes, can usually help you find sources for obtaining different types of dyes.

The water temperature in most automatic washing machines is not high enough to render most dyes colorfast. Nor will the colors become as deep and as brilliant as they can at higher temperatures. Coloring fabrics in an automatic washing machine may properly be called tinting. Colorfast fabric dyeing can take place either in an open vat of simmering dye solution or in a dye vat, such as one of those discussed in Chapter 1. Whatever vessel is used, however—the tub of a washing machine, a big kettle on a stove or a hotplate, or a steam-jacketed soup kettle—the preparation of the dyebath is the same.

PREPARING FABRIC FOR DYEING

Overcast or zigzag each raw edge of the fabric that is to be dyed. Weigh the fabric while it is still dry and record the weight; this will be used to determine the amount of dye solution needed. (Fabric need not be weighed if it is being tinted in an automatic washing machine.) Wash in a good, low-sudsing detergent and rinse well. If the fabric is heavily sized, soak it in a 5 percent soda ash solution after it has been washed, and rinse again. Soda ash is caustic and should be used with rubber gloves. Fabric should be wet and warm when it is placed in the dyebath.

Sample Dye Swatches

Snip several swatches from the fabric to be dyed. Put a pot of water on to boil, or let the hot water tap run until the water is as hot as possible. Measure a small amount of dye into a glass one-quart measuring cup. Record the amount and colors of dye used. Dye may be measured in teaspoons, but it is most accurately measured in grams; one-quarter to one-half gram of dye is an average amount per one quart of water. Add a few drops of boiling, or very hot, water to the dye and stir it into a paste. Add more boiling, or hot, water to the paste, filling the one-

quart measure. Stir. Pour the dye solution into a stainless steel or enamelware dyeing pan, straining it through a nylon stocking or through several pieces of cheese cloth which have been laid on the bottom of a plastic strainer. Place the swatch in the dyebath. If the fabric is to be tinted in an automatic washing machine, stir the swatch around until it is a shade or two darker than desired; then remove it from the dye. If the fabric is to be boiled or dyed in a vat, place the pan containing the dyebath and the swatch on the hot plate or stove and bring to a boil before removing the swatch. Rinse the swatch until the water running through it is clear. Dry with an iron. Label the swatch with the amount of dye and the color mixture used in the quart of water. If the color is not correct, prepare a new one-quart dyebath with a different amount and mixture of dye.

Dyeing a Piece of Fabric to Match the Swatch

When you have managed to dye a swatch that is pleasing to the designer, you must now color a large piece of fabric to correspond to the swatch. If you are tinting fabric in an automatic washing machine, you need

FIGURE 6.1   *Dye swatches and a garment being painted with dye. (Photograph by Rod Pilloud.)*

only know the number of quarts of water the machine holds in order to multiply the amount of dye contained in the sample quart by the number of quarts contained in the machine and find out how much dye will be needed. Measure this amount of dye into a glass container, add hot water, and make a paste. Pour some more hot water into the container, stir, and strain the solution into the washing machine full of water. Let the machine agitate for a few seconds before adding the fabric.

If you are dyeing in an open kettle or in a dye vat, you must determine the amount of water necessary to make the dyebath. It takes three to four gallons of water to make a dyebath for one pound of fabric. Weigh the piece of fabric to be dyed on an infant scale and calculate the amount of water you will need. Figure out the number of quarts in that amount and multiply the original amount of dye used in the test swatch by that number.

If you are using union dyes to which salt has not been added, you can figure on using about one cup of salt to every eight or ten gallons of dye solution.

Most costumers do not measure as carefully as they might during the tinting and dyeing process. If you are tinting in a washing machine, it is possible to redye the fabric over and over until the proper color is achieved. Simmering fabrics, or processing them in a dye vat, however, is potentially more harmful to fibers, and it is always a good idea to be as precise as possible with dye measurements so the fabric does not have to be redyed. Also, when you keep records of specific dye proportions, you may subsequently save some of the time that would have to be spent on experimentation.

Fabrics should remain in the dyebath for about thirty minutes. Automatic washing machine cycles average about twelve minutes. Set a kitchen timer on the machine and reset the machine in order to retain the dyebath for the full dyeing time.

Costume dyeing is not an exact art, however. There are so many variables in the process that it is virtually impossible to reproduce a specific color every time. Do not be frustrated. There are those times when the unexpected, unplanned-for color turns out to be more perfect than the one you planned to get.

COLOR REMOVER AND BLEACH

Sometimes color must be removed from fabric before it is dyed or, when the dyed fabric must be redyed, color has to be stripped away in order to try again. Tintex or Rit color remover work equally well. Use color remover in an automatic washing machine. Eight to ten tablespoons of color remover in a full tub of hot water is usually sufficient. All color removers have a foul odor and can be irritating if they get on the skin. Use rubber gloves to place the fabric in the machine and try to stay out of the dye room when the color remover is working.

Bleach will remove the color from cottons and linens, but it will often leave a yellowish cast to the fabric. Never use bleach on protein fibers—silk or wool—because they will disintegrate. Bleach has a specific use for ageing and breaking down costumes and for toning fabrics. This will be mentioned again later. After your washing machine has been used for dyeing, run the machine again, on the hottest and longest cycle, with a couple of towels and a cup of bleach in the tub. Scouring powders will remove any traces of dye that are left after the bleach cycle.

EQUIPMENT AND SUPPLIES FOR THE DYEING AND PAINTING AREA

All dyeing and painting activities are extremely messy. They need to be carried on in a protected area, if not in a separate room, where there is as little danger as possible of damaging uninvolved garments with spills and sprays. Even when dyestuffs are handled most carefully, there is always the danger that airborne dye particles will settle on another fabric, particularly a damp fabric, and spoil it completely.

Due to lack of space, many dye shops share quarters with costume maintenance. In these cases, great care must be taken to keep the dye area as clean as possible. Wardrobe assistants should always inspect the condition of washing machines and dryers before stuffing them with laundry, and they should be careful not to place damp laundry on a surface stained with dye. In the best of circumstances, laundry and dyeing should be done in separate places.

The following list of equipment and supplies for the dye area is a lengthy one. It is loosely based on the equipment and supply list from the Tyrone Guthrie Theatre dye shop, a self-contained space separate from the costume shop.

Basic Equipment

steam-jacketed soup kettle dye vat
automatic washing machine
automatic dryer
nonautomatic washer, or Easy
hot plate or stove
gram scale for weighing dyes
infant scale for weighing fabric
drying rack and/or clotheslines
stainless steel or enamelware kettles
smaller stainless steel or enamelware pots
stainless steel long-handled spoons
plastic dishpans
wooden spoons
measuring spoons
quart size Pyrex measuring cups
1-cup size Pyrex measuring cups
wide-mouth jars and lids in assorted sizes
alarm clock or timer
ironing board
iron
dummy covered in plastic
zigzag sewing machine
measuring tapes and rulers
scissors
straight pins and T-pins
laundry marking pens
plastic laundry baskets
terry cloth towels
sponges
cheesecloth and a collection of old nylons
brown paper on a roll
scouring powder
hand soap
paper towels
rubber gloves

Materials for Dyeing

union dyes in an assortment of colors
common salt, uniodized
soda ash for removing sizing
color remover
bleach

low sudsing laundry detergent
other dyes and assistant chemicals as necessary

Supplies and Materials for Fabric Painting

spray gun or atomizer
brushes: 2″, 1″, ½″, fine-tipped sable
hot melt glue gun and pellets
masking tape
textile paints
spray shoe dyes
liquid shoe dyes
shoe polish, liquid and paste
tempera paints
acrylic paints
spray enamels
lacquer and lacquer thinner
metallic powders
white shellac
denatured alcohol
Epoxy adhesive
fixitive spray
dulling spray

Take Care of Dyeing and Painting Equipment

Throw out all old dye solutions promptly and either wash pans and cups with bleach and water or scrub them with scouring powder. Check the filters on the washing machine and dryer often and keep them free of all lint. Automatic dryer filters should be cleaned out after each dryer load. Remember to turn off electric hot plates and stoves when they are not in use. Keep your brushes clean. Dyes and acrylics can be washed out with water. Use denatured alcohol to clean brushes that have been used in shoe polish and leather dyes. FEV brushes can also be cleaned in alcohol.

COSTUME PAINTING

It is difficult to discuss general costume painting techniques, since each individual problem requires its own solution. Before beginning to work with any painting material, make sure you are familiar with its properties and the results you may expect. Always experiment with scrap fabrics before applying paint or dye to an actual costume.

On occasion, you will want to apply a pattern to a piece of fabric before the fabric is cut and fashioned into a garment. Overall fabric printing is best accomplished with a wood, or linoleum block, a silk screen, or a stencil. Use a fabric paint or a dye paste for any of these operations and heat set the pattern.

Smaller pattern areas, such as borders, are often painted on costumes after the garment is cut and assembled. These patterns may be done with a block or a stencil, or they may be painted on with a brush. Some abstract patterns may be done with a sponge. Take care that the paint used for a border pattern does not stiffen the fabric too much. Dye pastes do not stiffen fabrics. Fabric paints, such as Versatex, stiffen only slightly, while acrylics cause the fabric to become quite stiff.

If the garment requires a raised pattern, it may be laid on with hot melt glue and later painted in with a brush. Naturally, hot melt glue will stiffen fabrics and should only be used on heavy garments which are not expected to flow.

Costume Shading

Costumes are often shaded and highlighted in order to give the garments more dimension and to increase their sculptured effect. Shading may be done so lightly and realistically that the garments look completely natural, or it may produce stronger contrasts and a stylized look.

Many costumers use Magix spray leather

FIGURE 6.2 *Jeffrey Tambor and Leslie Gerasi in the Milwaukee Repertory Theater production of* Richard II. *Ms. Gerasi's dress fabric was silk screened. (Elizabeth Covey, costume designer; photograph courtesy of the Milwaukee Repertory Theater.)*

dyes for shading costumes. Choose your colors carefully. Black is rarely used. An assortment of browns and greys is most effective, and otter is a particularly useful shading color.

Shading may also be done with liquid fabric dyes or liquid leather dyes in a spray bottle or atomizer. Dilute union fabric dyes in water and liquid leather dyes in denatured alcohol.

In the smaller areas of a garment, shading can be effectively done with either a brush or a sponge. Blend carefully for a subtle effect.

Painting with FEV

FEV, or French Enamel Varnish, is a versatile theatrical paint that dries with a bright, translucent shine; it can be used for many things. You will find FEV discussed again in Chapter 11 on costume properties. FEV is a mixture of white shellac, denatured alcohol, and dye. Different kinds of dye can be used: acid dyes, basic dyes such as Bazo, liquid leather dyes such as Fiebing or Omega, liquid shoe polish (except white). Bronzing powders may also be suspended in FEV. A mixture of approximately one part white shellac and three to five parts denatured alcohol is suitable for most fabric painting. Experiment with the proportions until you have achieved the correct surface effect on the fabric with which you are working. In general, more shellac will result in a stiffer surface. If too little shellac is added, however, FEV has a tendency to rub off. Unlike most fabric paints, FEV penetrates the fabric rather than lying on top of it; when the mixture is right for the fabric, it remains relatively permanent, even through dry cleanings.

AGING COSTUMES

The process of aging a costume may mean merely to give the garment a comfortable, lived-in appearance, or it may mean virtually destroying the garment shape and portions of the fabric itself, until the whole costume appears in shreds. In between these two poles

FIGURE 6.3 *Michael Tucker and Charles Kimbrough in the Milwaukee Repertory Theater production of* Waiting for Godot. *Both actors are wearing aged garments. (William Wall, costume designer; photograph courtesy of the Milwaukee Repertory Theater.)*

FIGURE 6.4 *Evie McElroy in* Mother Courage *at the Long Wharf Theatre. Clothing was constructed, then broken down. (Rosemary Ingham, costume designer; photograph courtesy of Long Wharf Theatre.)*

and pants pockets and steam the fabric slightly to loosen up the weave. Shiny, new-looking buttons may be sanded down and sprayed with a dulling spray. A dusty look, that is reversable, can be achieved by powdering the garment with Fuller's Earth, a technique particularly suitable for a rented costume.

For more pronounced distressing, scrub the fabric with a wire brush and scrape it with a file or rasp. Holes created with a file or rasp look more natural than those cut out with scissors. File garment edges vigorously for raggedness. Make slashes with a scissors blade or a knife, but never make a straight cut. Cut edges may be singed slightly with a torch, but be careful!

Dirt and food stains can be applied with

FIGURE 6.5 *A scene from* Marat Sade *at the Milwaukee Repertory Theater. Generally stained and ragged garments. (Janet Warren, costume designer; photograph courtesy of the Milwaukee Repertory Theater.)*

lie dozens of different degrees of aging and distressing.

Before you begin to age a costume, be certain of the final effect you wish to obtain. The aging process is not always easy to reverse. Proceed in logical steps. Final touches should only be done after the garment is seen on the actor, under the stage lighting.

Simple wear is best accomplished by removing all sharp creases from the garment, washing it several times if it is washable, or having it dry cleaned and not well pressed. Whenever possible, start with real, secondhand clothing when a worn look is required. Rub elbows and knees with candlewax to give them a worn shine. Use a cheese grater to create slight worn places at hems, cuffs, knees, and around buttonholes, and spray these areas lightly to simulate ingrained soil. To give a man's suit a sagging look, place rocks or other heavy objects in the jacket spray leather dyes or flat enamel sprays, or they may be sponged on with a paste of tempera paint and water. Paste shoe polishes are excellent for greasy-looking stains. Faded areas can be created on cotton and linen fabrics by spattering or spraying with a solution of bleach and water. Undiluted bleach will weaken the fabric and sometimes make holes. Bleach is very destructive to wool and silk, so use it sparingly on these fabrics unless you want extreme destruction. Caked-on dirt can be simulated with flexible glue into which you have mixed paint and sawdust.

Most synthetic fabrics are extremely difficult to age. If you need the look of ragged cotton, make sure the garment you are to distress is cotton and not a cotton and dacron blend. Pure wool ages beautifully, but a wool and nylon blend man's suit will resist all attempts to render it saggy.

Remember that it takes years for a garment to age naturally; never expect to age a costume in a single operation. Whenever possible, put the garment on a plastic covered dummy while you are working on it. Examine your progress from time to time, standing well away from the garment in order to assess its overall appearance. Always be on the lookout for new methods and new materials and don't hesitate to experiment.

7

Footwear, Hosiery, and Tights

In virtually every early conference between actor and costumer, one of the first questions the actor will ask is: "What sort of shoes am I going to wear?" The actor is primarily concerned with the fit, the support, and the general comfort of the shoe. The costumer's task is to create the period look required by the design in a shoe that will not pinch the actor's toes or otherwise cause discomfort. Some actors require arch support in order to be able to stand and walk with ease. Others need additional instep support because of weak ankles. Notations concerning individual foot problems should be included on the actor's measurement blank and carefully considered as the construction and alteration of footwear is being planned.

The style of the shoe is extremely important to the total period look of every costume. The shape of the toe and the height and shape of the heel are the major differences between one period style and another. As with most costume components, a reproduction of an actual period shoe is less important than a strong period suggestion that will appear accurate to the audience and complement the style of the entire production. In many cases, the addition of a specific decorative detail or a change of heel will render a modern shoe suitable for the costume it will accompany.

The following discussion of period shoe styles and the ways in which they can be created for the stage is presented in a loose chronological order. Nearly all the illustrations are of shoes or boots that can either be adapted from easily obtainable modern shoes and boots or be made from scratch. It is not, however, a comprehensive history of footwear (a subject which has already been treated more than adequately in several books which you will find listed in the bibliography); some periods and styles are only touched on briefly while others are omitted altogether. The periods and styles that are covered in some detail are those that the costumer is most often called upon to represent on stage. The sources, from the Middle Ages onward, are predominantly English and American, with only a few exceptions. Once the costume technician has begun to look at the common types of period footwear with an eye toward adapting them from modern shoes or making them from modern materials, it becomes easier to solve the more unique problems and to provide the designer with a reasonable approximation of any footwear from any time or place.

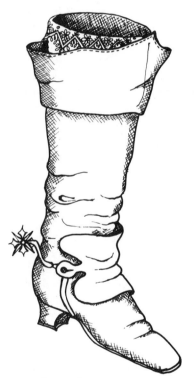

FIGURE 7.1   *Seventeenth-century boot with spur leather.*

Unless they are specifically called for in the text of the play, extreme styles in footwear are usually avoided on stage. No audience member should be found staring at a bizarre shoe when he or she ought to be pay-ing attention to the plot and dialogue. Occasionally, however, a specific dramatic text allows for an outlandish shoe or boot. In Ben Jonson's *Volpone,* the character Sir Politic Would-Be may wear elaborate spur leathers because he is a character much concerned with wearing the most fashionable and up-to-date accessories. On the other hand, the extremely pointed toe worn in fourteenth-century England, a shoe that had to be tied up around the leg, will seldom find its way on stage.

As theatrical footwear, shoes and boots are far more often color-coordinated than they probably would have been in the actual period in which the play is set. This is done so the eyes of the audience will not be distracted by a sharp contrast between garments and shoes. Unless a unique effect is specifically indicated in the script, a harmonious set of colors and a unity of production style is always desirable.

The choice of period footwear is also affected by modern shoe styles. All fashion appears, disappears, and reappears again at alternating points on the historical spiral. Seldom, however, does a style reappear exactly as it was before. In the Victorian period, for example, men, women, and children wore boots for all occasions. The boot was considered the stout and sensible footwear, while

FIGURE 7.2   *Fourteenth-century shoe.*

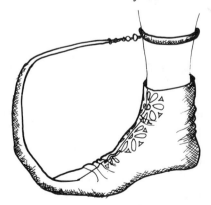

the low-cut shoe was preferred by artists and by the more dashing members of society. In the 1970s, when the most recent boot craze flowered, the situation was reversed: the boot became the high fashion item while the conservative matron continued to wear her sensible pumps. A modern audience's response to a Victorian lady on stage, wearing black satin evening boots, could not help but be affected by current attitudes.

THE PREPARATION OF LEATHER

Through the centuries, footwear has been fashioned from a wide assortment of materials such as knitted and woven cloth, plaited reeds, coconut fibers, and plastic; but leather has been the primary choice since prehistoric hunters first began to wrap their feet in hides. Tanning leather is a craft older than weaving, and the artisan who possesses the skills necessary to prepare fine leather has been valued in every society.

The objectives of leather preparation are the same today as they were for our prehistoric ancestors: to stop the process of decay, to waterproof, to induce suppleness and flexibility, and to strengthen. Primitive man achieved these objectives by drying the hide in the sun, by exposing it to heat and smoke, and by transforming the texture with the use of acid—such as sour milk or urine—and fats for waterproofing. Ancient tanning methods persisted until the nineteenth century. They were very effective; and leather has been widely used over the years for shoes, armor, and some clothing items.

Today, leather is tanned in several ways. In vegetable tanning, the hide is treated with tannin, or tannic acid. Various tree barks are used, including oak, sumac, hemlock, and mimosa, as well as other vegetable substances which contain tannin. In the mineral tanning, or tawing, process the hides are treated with mineral salts, primarily alum and bichromate of potash. Tawing results in particularly light leathers. The chamoising method consists of treating the hides with oils and fats instead of tannin. Chrome tanning was originated in Germany in the second half of the nineteenth century. The skin is impregnated with chromium salts, with or without the addition of other salts. This method converts the pelt quickly and produces strong, durable leather.

Tanneries are excellent places for the thrifty costumer to obtain leather for costumes. In many instances, imperfect hides will be available which can be purchased for a fraction of the price one would pay in a retail store. Leather can be dyed readily, and the tanning imperfection may be completely concealed—if it does not actually add surface interest to a battle-scarred breastplate or pair of boots.

THE PRINCIPAL PARTS OF A SHOE

In order to be able to alter a shoe effectively, it is necessary to be able to recognize the principal parts of the shoe and to know which parts may be changed without causing damage to it (see Figure 7.3).

The *last* is the solid wood or plastic shape on which the shoe is made. Neither the shape of the toe nor the height of the heel can be changed from those of the last on which the shoe was made. Putting on a heel higher or lower than the one on the original shoe will result in a cracked sole at the instep. It is possible, however, to add a higher heel and balance it with an equal addition to the sole, thereby maintaining the original instep curve.

The shoe itself is composed of the *upper,*

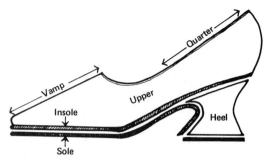

FIGURE 7.3 *Principal parts of a shoe.*

the part which covers the foot; the *sole,* which rests on the ground; the *insole,* which lies between the foot and the sole; the *shank,* a piece of metal sometimes inserted between the sole and the insole which lies along the arch and gives additional support to both the shoe and the foot; and the *heel,* which can be of many sizes and many shapes.

In its simplest form, the upper can be cut in one piece with a single seam up the back. It may also be cut in several pieces according to current fashion. The portion of the upper which covers the front part of the foot is called the *vamp* and the part that covers the back part is called the *quarter.* On some shoes, there is also a *toe cap* which may, in the case of work boots or military boots, be reinforced with a very strong leather or metal. The portion of the quarter that goes around the heel almost always requires some stiffening.

FLAT FOOTWEAR

Heels did not make their appearance on footwear until around 1580, although there are isolated examples of raised or platformed shoes and boots that go back into antiquity. Until the Age of Elizabeth, however, most feet rested firmly on the ground and the footwear was generally soft, nonrestrictive, and gave little support. Soft shoes and sandals from the early fashion periods can be made for stage wear; although, whenever possible, it is better to change existing modern shoes than to start in from scratch. Shoemaking is more difficult than it appears to be, and feet are particularly tricky to fit.

Sandals

Sandals make regular stage appearances in the Greek plays of Aeschylus, Sophocles, Euripides, and Aristophanes; the Roman come-

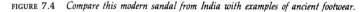

FIGURE 7.4 *Compare this modern sandal from India with examples of ancient footwear.*

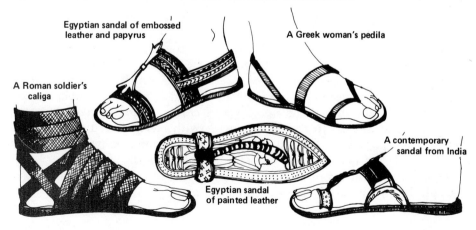

Egyptian sandal of embossed leather and papyrus

A Greek woman's pedila

A Roman soldier's caliga

A contemporary sandal from India

Egyptian sandal of painted leather

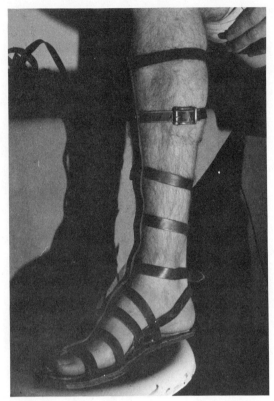

FIGURE 7.5 *Roman sandal which was constructed in a costume shop. (Photograph by Susan Perkins.)*

as the sole and either glued or stitched in place. Most shoe repair shops will do this stitching for you. The sandal straps may be either stitched or riveted in place on the sole and an inner sole glued down on top to protect the actor's foot from the lumps where the straps attach.

Beginning with an already constructed sandal, however, does save time. Sandals have been particularly popular since the mid 1960s and are being manufactured in a great proliferation of styles by large companies as well as by small leather shops. Many sandal styles worn on the street today can be adopted for stage use without any alteration at all, particularly for Biblical and peasant characters. Occasionally a leather shop will provide sandals for a dramatic production for a reasonably low price, or even for a prominent program advertisement. In an amateur or educational situation, the actors may own suitable sandals and be willing to wear them on stage.

The complex strap arrangements that are characteristic of the Roman and Egyptian sandals must be fashioned by the costume technician. The biggest problem posed by strap arrangements that extend up around the leg is how to keep them in place. If they are too tight, they will cut off blood circulation in the actor's legs; if they are too loose, they will fall down around the ankles. If tights can be worn on the legs, the straps will be less likely to fall. Real leather strapping is far easier to keep in place than any of the imitation leathers, which are both slippery and stretchable. When you are planning the construction of sandal straps, prearrange them as much as possible. Points where straps cross can often be riveted together or stitched with a leather needle and extra strong thread. Buckles and rawhide ties work best for holding straps in place. When buckles are used, be sure to provide several holes for the buckle prong to fit into.

dies of Terence and Plautus; Shakespeare's *Antony and Cleopatra, Julius Caesar,* and *Coriolanus;* in more recent works such as Shaw's *Androcles and the Lion;* and in a whole host of Biblical plays and pageants. Sandal styles can range from the simple, primitive sort suitable for a Jerusalem shepherd to the highly ornate creations worn by the Egyptians and the Roman emperors. Materials for researching sandal styles are readily available.

Sandals are the easiest of all the footwear styles to build from the ground up. A very serviceable sole, shaped to the actor's own foot contour, may be cut from stiff leather. It is almost always a good idea to put a layer of rubber on the bottom of the sandal sole. It should be cut in exactly the same shape

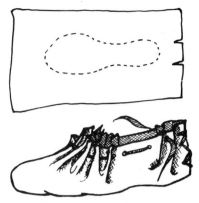

Soft Flat Shoes and Boots

The earliest flat shoe for which we have historical documentation was constructed from a single piece of leather with a narrow leather strip threaded through slashes around the

FIGURE 7.7   *Simple soft leather shoe with the upper cut in two pieces and stitched to the sole.*

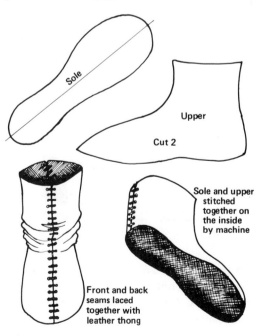

Sole

Upper

Cut 2

Sole and upper stitched together on the inside by machine

Front and back seams laced together with leather thong

outside to draw it up around the foot and a laced seam up the back to hold it over the heel. This simple, one-piece construction, with the later addition of another seam up the front of the foot for better shaping, persisted for many hundreds of years and achieved a great many different forms.

Soft, slipper-like footwear of this type is often used on stage in productions of such plays as the medieval mystery cycles, *Everyman,* and some Tudor and Jacobean histories. When these shoes are built in the costume shop, the uppers should always be cut in two pieces. Cut the sole separately, either from the same leather or from a piece that is somewhat heavier, and stitch the shaped upper pieces up the center back and center front and onto the sole as shown in Figure 7.7. Trim the sole slightly smaller than the actor's foot and the leather from the upper will roll nicely under the foot. Glue an inner sole into the shoe for additional comfort. Arch supports can easily be inserted into these most primitive of shoes for actors who need them.

Certain sorts of slippers can be adapted for this kind of period footwear. Very inexpensive soft slippers can usually be purchased at the hosiery counters of most department stores. Although adequate in shape for a medieval foot, these slippers have plastic soles that make them dangerously slippery and plastic uppers that are difficult to color.

FIGURE 7.8   *Men's contemporary slippers with additional leather lacings. (Photograph by Susan Perkins.)*

Their very cheapness, however, often makes it worth the effort to search for an appropriate color and then to treat the soles and heels to a thorough rasping to score the glass-like finish.

It is possible to purchase soft leather slippers for men that make excellent medieval footwear. These tend to be somewhat expensive, but they wear well and make valuable stock items. Rawhide lacings can be added along faked seam lines to increase the primitive look. If the cowhide from which these slippers are usually made becomes too slippery on the bottoms as they collect dirt, glue a piece of suede onto the slipper bottom for additional traction.

Sometimes the medieval shoe was cut higher than the foot and became a softly fitted boot. If you are to construct soft, flat-heeled leather boots, there is no better way to begin than with a pattern and instructions for making the American Indian "Apache boot." Tandy's, a nationwide firm dealing in leather, leather tools, and kits for leather articles, has a precut kit for Apache boots that makes up nicely. If the boots are to receive hard wear, such as in a long-running pageant or in a Shakespeare festival, glue or stitch a stiff sole to the bottoms. To keep the soft boots from falling down around the ankles, it is helpful to stitch wide elastic inside the top of the boots to grip the leg.

Pointed Toes

After the Norman Conquest, shoes began to lengthen at the front and become pointed. Some of these were made of woven cloth rather than leather, and some were merely the feet of stockings with a sole stitched on to protect the bottoms of the feet. It is difficult to imagine how some of the knights and squires from the twelfth and thirteenth centuries were able to walk without stumbling over these skinny extensions, although it is

likely that the stylization of painting and stonework from that time portrayed the footwear as even more pointed that it was in actuality.

Perhaps the most delightful descriptions of clothing, including footwear, from the fourteenth century can be found in Geoffrey Chaucer's *Canterbury Tales.* Fashions of the well-to-do, the ecclesiastics, and the common folk are all included. Much of this information is elaborated upon and illustrated in Edith Rickert's book, *Chaucer's World,* which contains many contemporary illustrations as well as documentary materials.

The extremely pointed toes are difficult for actors to wear and are always greatly abbreviated for stage use. These styles can be made, much like a sock, from very soft suede or leather, from woven wool, or from a heavy wool or wool blend knit; and they may be pulled on over a ballet slipper or other dance shoe. For an ankle- or calf-high version, it may be necessary to add a canvas stiffener or bones to the tops in order to hold them up. If they are worn over tights, the tops may be attached to the tights with Velcro.

Tights alone, with soles stitched to the bottoms of the feet, do not wear well on stage. There is a lot of strain where the sole is stitched to the tights, and such an arrangement will not last out many performances.

FIGURE 7.9   *Suede rhythm sandal.*

It has become an accepted stage convention, although not historically accurate, to use rhythm sandals for the general everyday wear of characters in plays that are placed in a medieval setting. Robin Hood, Polixenes from *The Winter's Tale,* and Gammer Gurton's manservant, Hodge, might all appear in doublet, tights, and rhythm sandals without creating any reaction from the audience that they are anachronistic. This versatile little suede shoe, purchased inexpensively from a dancer's supply shop, blends well with a wide variety of costumes. Actors find them comfortable and they are seldom ever too slippery for a stage floor. Before putting a rhythm sandal to use, it is a good idea to strengthen the stitching around the soles, particularly at the places where the back and front upper pieces attach.

FIGURE 7.10 *Costume sketch for Marlowe's* Dr. Faustus, *showing pattens. (Laura Crow, costume designer.)*

Pattens

At the beginning of the sixteenth century, the (also called cracow) patten made its appearance. This was a simple wooden sole of varying height with a strap or toe piece into which the soft-shod foot was slipped in order to protect the shoe from mud and garbage while one was walking in the streets. The patten remained in use for quite a long time, sometimes more in vogue than in other times. Properly paved streets and sidewalks alone rendered the patten obsolete.

The costume rendering in Figure 7.10 calls for a pair of pattens. These are quite simple. Pattens for more fashionable characters could be elaborate, with gracefully shaped soles and decorative carving.

Tudor Shoes

The last important flat shoe that was in style before the advent of the heel was the Tudor shoe, worn in England between 1485 and 1558. This style entirely reversed the trend toward a pointed-toe look; the shoe was very broad across the front, comfortable for the toes but clumsy looking. Particularly fine ex-

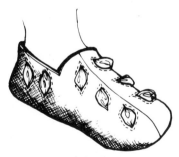

FIGURE 7.11 *Tudor shoe.*

amples of these shoes can be seen in portraits of that much painted king, Henry VIII. The vamp in the Tudor shoe was often cut rather low, and the shoe was kept on the foot by a strap that buttoned across the instep. In the more elaborate examples, the front of the shoe was slashed and puffs of contrasting lining allowed to poke through.

Many of the broad-toed styles that have become popular in the mid 1970s can be adapted to this Tudor look. A strap and slashing added to ballet slippers may also solve the problem of constructing Tudor shoes. Some approximation of the square, boxy footwear is essential when this period is being costumed in order to balance the square, boxy lines of the garments. If the shoe is too delicate, the chest and shoulders of the doublet or the bodice will cause the actor to appear disproportionately top-heavy.

Reappearance of the Flat Shoe

Flat shoes reappear in fashion history in almost every period. They made a widespread comeback just after the French Revolution and were also popular for dancing slippers in the Victorian Era. Schoolgirls in the 1950s wore "flats" to school and in the 1970s, the "negative heel" dropped the heel of the foot below the level of the ball of the foot. In most of these instances, however, flat styles have been worn primarily by young people, while the more conservative middle-aged have stuck with their sensible shoes and moderate heels.

HEELS

Elizabethan diarists have recounted many tales of swollen, painful calf muscles that resulted from the new fashion of heeled shoes and boots that spread like wildfire through the Western world in the last quarter of the sixteenth century. Many of these early heels were not put in the proper place on the shoe to give maximum support, and we can also conjecture that they might have been somewhat wobbly at first.

Actors often suffer similar leg pains when they begin to work with heel heights that are unfamiliar to them. Until very recently, since the popularization of shoes for men with anything other than the standard low, broad heel, male actors had some difficulty learning to work in high-heeled period shoes or boots. Actors should be provided with the shoes they are going to wear, or with a close approximation of fit and heel height, very early in the rehearsal process. A woman who is accustomed to wearing high-heeled shoes will have the same amount of difficulty getting used to a completely flat shoe as the man will who is wearing heels for the first time.

Both posture and gait are affected by the addition of heel height. Women have what has come to be considered a much more feminine walk when they are wearing high-heeled shoes. Steps become shorter and the hips tend to sway. High-heeled slippers and a short, slightly pigeon-toed gait were necessary for the Southern belle who wished to make her hoop skirt sway just enough to be enticing but not so much as to be vulgar. The flat-footed gait is generally considered more aggressive and masculine. Contrary to these stereotypes, however, actors playing the Three Musketeers must appear swashbuckling in high-heeled boots, and Cleopatra has to be elegantly sexy in sandals.

Elizabethan Footwear

Art, philosophy, theatre, and fashion were only a few of the human activities that flourished during the Age of Elizabeth. It was one of the most turbulent of all historical periods, although there was a strong sense of political and social stability and very little warfare. Plays written during this period, particularly the plays of Shakespeare, Marlowe, and Jonson, are so frequently done in the Western world today that theatre artists are almost as familiar with them as with contemporary twentieth-century drama.

The broadest possible knowledge of Elizabethan modes, manners, and dress is invaluable to persons in the costume field. Even when an Elizabethan play is not set and costumed in Elizabethan decor and dress—as is often the case—a thorough understanding of the original period is invaluable in successfully adapting it to another.

Fashion resources from this period abound. Diarists took great delight in describing their own dress and the dress of their contemporaries. Portrait painting flourished, leaving a record of rich gowns, handsome doublets, and painstakingly reproduced fashion details. Painters who paid particular attention to footwear of the period include Antonio Moro (1512–1576), El Greco (1554–1614), Rubens (1577–1640), and Nicholas Hilliard (1547–1619).

The first heels to appear on shoes and boots were modest in height: about one and one-half inches. At the same time (between 1570 and 1580), shoes began to appear with flaps coming up from each side of the upper which tied over the instep with a leather or a ribbon tie. These flaps were known as latchets and provided additional support for feet that were under strain from the arrival of the heel. A rosette or flower was often used to conceal the tie.

FIGURE 7.12   *Elizabethan shoe with heel.*

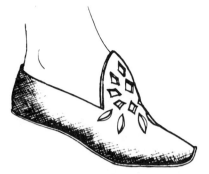

FIGURE 7.13   *Flat Elizabethan shoe.*

The shoe in Figure 7.12 is a remarkably modern looking piece of footwear, although it is sketched from a shoe of the Elizabethan period. A modern shoe could easily be converted into a close approximation of this period shoe by adding the cut-out designs and a colored ribbon tie. The flat-heeled shoe in Figure 7.13 could be constructed from a felt slipper with the additions of a tongue and a cut-out design. The slipper could be sprayed a suitable color or covered completely with another fabric.

Boots were exceptionally popular with the men. In the early part of Elizabeth's reign, boots continued to fit the leg but folded-over tops that became more and more elaborate were added. The fashionable man began to wear boot hose inside his boots in order to protect his stockings and these were made with fancy tops to turn down over his boot tops. Almost always white, the boot hose were often embroidered and lace-trimmed. Until the 1630s, boots were generally reserved for hunting, riding, and other outdoor activities. After that time, boots became the acceptable footwear for all occasions; boots and spurs were even being worn at table.

Several modern boots styles can be used to construct footwear that will complement the costume of a seventeenth-century gentleman. Some cowboy boots (not those with extremely narrow, pointed toes) are excellent to start with because they are built on lasts that will accommodate a heel of one and a half to two and a half inches. The readily recognizable cowboy heel can be exchanged for any of the heel shapes common to the period. If the boot must be made higher in the leg, a leather extension can be stitched on and a turned-back top added which will cover the seamline. Should the budget be strained, and a cheap leather source not be available, imitation vinyl leathers serve admirably for extensions and tops. Currently, high-heeled boots are being made for men which need only a turned-down top to look acceptably seventeenth century. Such boots tend to be expensive but can sometimes be purchased secondhand. Look for the styles that come without zippers. Remember that men with small feet can often be fitted in large-sized women's boots.

For the stage, boot hose may be constructed like false cuffs and fastened just inside the

boot top. Attach the boot hose with Velcro, gluing one piece to the boot and stitching the other to the boot hose. In this way, the boot hose will be easy to remove for washing.

Chopines and Cothurni

Even before the general appearance of shoes and boots with heels, man had revealed his

FIGURE 7.15   *Cothurnus.*

urge to appear taller than nature had made him. In the Greek theatre, the chief actors wore cothurni in order to add to their stature. Chinese emperors signified their power by adding many-layered soles to their shoes. The chopine, which made a relatively short fashion splash in the first half of the seventeenth century, was a ridiculous fashion fad in elevated footwear that has only been equaled in our own century by the gaudy "stacks" worn by flamboyant rock stars.

The chopine originated in Venice. Both Shakespeare and Ben Jonson make mention of it in their plays. An Englishman, John Evelyn, who traveled in Venice during the time, has left us a humorous journal entry in which he describes the ladies of Venice wearing chopines as being "half wood, half human."

The chopine was a shoe whose sole, like Pinocchio's nose, had grown out of all proportion to more than a foot in height. Since

FIGURE 7.14   *Man's modern boot adapted for the seventeenth century with the addition of a leather cuff, boot hose, and spur.*

FIGURE 7.16 *Chopine.*

The Bucket-top Boot

When James I became king in 1603 after Elizabeth's death, men's footwear began to go to extremes. One of the most amusing styles in men's boots that has appeared in all of fashion history turned up then: the bucket-top boot. By 1630, the turned-down top had become so wide that its relationship to the leg was much the same as if one was standing in a bucket. The gaping tops were lined and dripping with linen and lace, and the leather of the boot itself was so soft that the whole affair fell softly in folds around the ankle. Elaborate spurs with fancy spur leathers completed the look.

solid wood soles would have made the shoe too heavy for walking, the stilt was usually made from cork. Venetian ladies, taking the air of an afternoon, were often accompanied by two servants, one on each side, on whom they could lean in order to keep their balance. The fad spread to England, but it is a tribute to the good common sense of the English-woman that it had a much shorter life there than in Venice.

Chopines do not often appear on stage. When they do, their use is primarily comic. The elevated soles are best constructed by an orthopedic shoemaker who can help to balance the shoe and provide the actor with some support. Because of the danger of falling and injuring an ankle, the actor wearing chopines should be able to practice in them as long as possible, preferably with the ankles wrapped in elastic bandages.

Cothurni are often used in productions of the Greek plays. Unlike the inherently comic chopines, cothurni should add majesty to the actors, who are probably also masked, and help them extend themselves to the playing of roles that are larger than ordinary human size. An orthopedic shoemaker, elastic bandages, and lots of practice are again recommended.

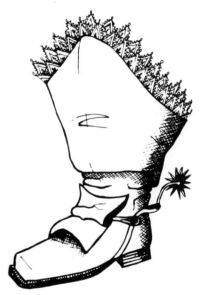

FIGURE 7.17 *Bucket-top boot with spur.*

Costume designers often use the bucket-top boot in productions of Rostand's *Cyrano de Bergerac*, Corneille's *The Cid*, and some early plays by Moliere. It is an essentially comic style and must be adapted with some care to a serious scene. It's difficult to put more than one or two pairs of these boots on the stage at any one time because of the possibility of distraction, and they are only suitable for certain types of characters.

A Wellington-type boot is a good shape to begin with when you are constructing a bucket-top boot. The bucket-top will be cut from another piece of leather and either stitched or glued onto the basic boot. Hoop wire or boning threaded under the boot top will help to maintain the shape. The boot hose should be made from soft cloth, white or cream-colored, rather than from something stiff. Men's dress from this time has been described as "disordered extravagance," and the bucket-top boots with lacy boot hose certainly reflect this feeling.

When planning the size of the bucket top, make sure they are not so wide that they will interfere with the actor's stride. The style is an exaggerated one anyway and its execution for the stage can usually be more modest than the styles depicted by painters of the time. Once again, it is important that actors have sufficient time to rehearse in bucket-top boots, since they are a bit strange to walk in at first.

Spurs should be worn with all boots from this period. The spur leather, often cut in a butterfly shape, was usually decorative and sometimes quite large. The rowels were very fancy. Spur rowels for the stage can be made from heavy, sized industrial felt, wire, or wood. Actual rowels may also be used, although all sharp points must be blunted in order to avoid injury. Lucy Barton suggests, in *Historic Costume for the Stage,* that the wheel portions of tracing wheels make dandy spur rowels; these, too, would need blunting.

Boots and spurs, as well as plumed hats, gauntleted gloves, and swords, were worn by men indoors as well as outdoors, at the theatre as well as on the street, at table as well as on horseback. One does wonder how the gentleman in all his disordered extravagance managed to mount his horse at all.

Shoe Rosettes

Throughout the seventeenth century, shoes continued to be worn by men as alternatives to the popular boot. Both men's and women's shoes were decorated with rosettes. Rosettes were made from strips of ribbon, lace, or leather, and they grew to enormous proportions. Sometimes the lady's shoe had a lace ruffle as well as a lace rosette, as in Figure 7.18.

FIGURE 7.18   *Woman's shoe with lace ruffle and rosette.*

A modern shoe can often be adapted to a seventeenth-century style with a suitable decoration. Avoid extremely pointed toes; a tapered, blunt toe is best. Create the rosettes out of ribbon and back the ribbon with horsehair if a stiff shape is desirable. Hat wire can be stitched or glued to the back of leather strips for the same purpose. Rosettes may be either droopy or perky, depending upon the sort of character who is wearing them.

Red Heels and Brass Buckles

The odd custom of painting boot and shoe heels red arose in England just before the establishment of the Commonwealth in 1649. During the next several years, the wearing of red heels was a part of the identifying dress of Cromwell's opponents, while Cromwell's own men adopted the square-toed black jack boot and a stout black shoe adorned with a brass buckle.

There is a record of Louis XIV receiving a pair of shoes with red heels in 1660, which

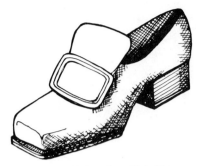

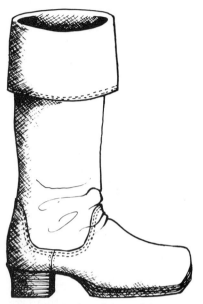

FIGURE 7.19   *Black leather jack boot with heavy top-stitching, similar to styles obtainable today.*

began an instant fad in France. Red heels continued in vogue for quite a long while and were still in use with English court dress until the end of the eighteenth century. After the restoration of the English monarchy, red heels came to be associated with the dandy. A few women affected red heels, but it was primarily a masculine fad.

Red-heeled shoes on stage generally appear to be a bit of frivolous affectation on the part of the character who wears them. They are appropriate for certain characters in Moliere's comedies and in Restoration comedies. Otherwise, it is a fad with limited stage use.

The Puritan shoe with its brass buckle achieved a widespread popularity. In his famous diary, Samuel Pepys notes the exact day, in 1660, when he first put buckles on his shoes. After the Restoration, buckles became highly ornate and very expensive. By the mid-eighteenth century, records show that the town of Birmingham, England, was producing some 2,500,000 shoe buckles per year. The rage for buckles dwindled by the end of the century; they were replaced by ribbon ties and a reappearance of rosettes. England's bucklemakers, who suddenly found themselves out of work, petitioned the Prince of Wales to stop using laces and return to buckles in the hope of reversing the fashion trend. The prince complied, but the populace did not follow suit. Birmingham fell on hard times.

Throughout the buckle craze, many people continued to wear laced shoes. Metal-tipped laces became available during this time. Laces were usually threaded through a single eyelet in each latchet.

FIGURE 7.21   *Brocade Restoration shoe.*

As the century advanced, the shoe tongue grew both higher and broader. Sometimes it swept out on either side of the ankle, producing a handsome line. Sometimes the tongue was backed with a contrasting color and al-

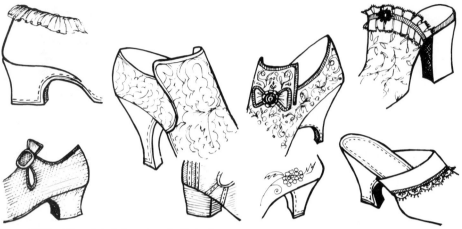

FIGURE 7.22 *Women's heel shapes from the Restoration.*

lowed to fall over. Buckles or ties fastened on top of the tongue.

Restoration plays such as *The Country Wife, Love for Love,* and *The Way of the World* remain extremely popular with audiences and are often produced. Suitable shoes from the period following the restoration of the English monarchy can be created from modern footwear for both men and women. A variety of heel shapes were popular for women's shoes, as Figure 7.22 amply illustrates. Tongues can be added to modern shoes and dyed to match. Buckles, either found or constructed from wood or sized industrial felt, can be stitched on. Men's plain-toe loafers with a medium heel last are excellent choices for this period—with the addition of a tongue, buckle, or rosette—and a new heel shape, if necessary. If the shoes are borrowed and you thus cannot stitch or glue a buckle to the upper, sew the buckle to a circle of elastic which can be slipped beneath the instep.

Until the end of the eighteenth century, the general shapes of shoes remained relatively constant, with some decorative style changes that are easy to research. In the 1790s, women's shoe heels had grown so high that ladies took to using slender walking sticks in order to be able to keep their bal-

ance. Throughout the century, men's shoes were generally less pointed than women's.

Flat Shoes Follow the French Revolution

After the French Revolution, fashion literally collapsed. Clothing shrunk and shoes lost their heels. For about forty years, flat pumps were worn by most young women and by some young men. Women's pumps often had ribbon ties that criss-crossed up the legs. Older women continued to wear plain shoes with a small heel, and many men favored a low-heeled boot that hugged the leg and had a contrasting leather top.

Modern ballet slippers or simple, low-heeled pumps are suitable accessories for the

FIGURE 7.23 *Young woman's flat pump.*

thin, high-waisted dresses of the period. Narrow satin ribbons may be stitched on for laces. Riding boots work well for men; a contrasting leather band around the top can be added, although some riding boots already have them.

NINETEENTH-CENTURY FOOTWEAR

The elastic-sided short boot appeared early in the nineteenth century and was widely worn by both ladies and gentlemen (see Figure 7.24). One variation had eyelets and laces up the side. Most of these boots had stacked leather heels.

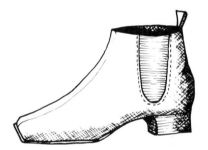

FIGURE 7.24 *Woman's short elastic-sided boot.*

Modern elastic-sided boots with thin soles and heels that are one to one and a half inches high are ideal for most nineteenth-century menswear. The toe should be blunt and not too wide. It is often a thrifty decision to purchase several pairs of these boots in an assortment of sizes for your costume stock. They can be used over and over again. Short zippered boots can be changed to the laced variety by removing the zipper and adding metal eyelets.

During the whole of the nineteenth century there was a vast gulf between the clothing of the rich and that of the poor. Shoes worn by the poor city dweller and the country peasant were shapeless and poorly made out of inferior leather. Soles were thick and clumsy and sometimes made of wood. Search through Goodwill shops and other resale stores for the most broken-down, worn-out shoes in their stocks: These will provide an excellent base for the type of shoe suitable for an impoverished nineteenth-century character.

FIGURE 7.26 *Woman's Victorian laced oxford, similar to "Granny shoes" available today.*

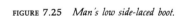

FIGURE 7.25 *Man's low side-laced boot.*

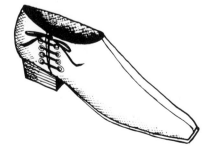

The Victorian Era was lengthy and saw much fashion change, although there is a unifying restrained quality in clothing throughout the period. In the 1850s, machines for stitching leather were developed and shoes became less expensive. Rubber galoshes went on the market in 1844. Both men and women favored boots. The possession of small feet was highly desirable for women; the Victorian lady squeezed her feet into boots that were too short and too narrow and laced them

FIGURE 7.27 *Young girl's Victorian dance pump, similar to the modern "Mary Jane."*

up so tightly around the leg that one can hardly imagine how she walked at all. Boots were fastened with buttons as well as with laces. Shoe buttons sometimes matched the buttons on the garment with which they were worn. Satin boots were popular for evening and soft kid for daytime. Shoes with medium heels and center front laces, similar to "Granny" shoes, were also worn during this time; and young girls favored flat-heeled pumps, rather like Mary Janes, for dancing. These pumps were often embroidered and decorated with bows.

From the last quarter of the nineteenth century until the present, fashion magazines are available for extensive research into contemporary shoe styles. Photography was practiced on a wide scale from the 1860s on. For the first time in the history of fashion,

photographs afford the opportunity to see how clothing really looked, not merely how it was supposed to look or how the painter chose to represent it.

High-button and high-laced shoes from the Victorian Era and from the early part of the twentieth century are difficult to represent on stage. Costume shops that own several pairs of authentic high-buttoned shoes prize them highly. All too often, however, these old shoes are too small, especially too narrow, to accommodate modern feet. Large costume budgets make it possible to have high-buttoned or high-laced shoes built by a specialty shoemaker. With a small budget, the best that can be done is to construct an upper that can be worn over a modern shoe. These can be cut similar to spats out of canvas or soft leather (avoid using stretchy imitation leather) or from a combination of the two. The upper will lace or button around the leg and attach to the shoe beneath it with a piece of elastic under the instep. The difficulty is always to make the upper fit as snugly around the foot and leg as possible so as to conceal the fact that the shoe is built in two parts. Such costuming compromises are more successful when they occur on a proscenium stage rather than on an open stage where the audience is very close to the actors.

Make sure there is a buttonhook available

FIGURE 7.28 *Two women's Victorian boots and three suggestions for spats to be worn over modern shoes with correct heel shapes.*

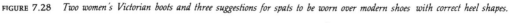

for fastening high-button shoes. A few specialty shops carry buttonhooks and they can often be found in thrift shops or at rummage sales. Some are only utilitarian, while others are quite decorative.

SHOES FOR THE TWENTIETH CENTURY

The secret behind finding and adapting suitable footwear for period costumes from within our own century is to have access to as many different types and styles of shoes as possible. Rummage through attics, secondhand shops, and church bazaars looking for bargains in shoes. Even if the uppers are completely shot, the heels can be used on other shoes. Having a large stock of heels in as many different shapes and heights as possible makes it easier to change the look of a shoe. Pay special attention to acquiring shoes with high vamps.

If you can't depict a period shoe accurately, opt for the style that doesn't look modern, even if it is only an aberrant model straight off the shoe store shelf. When shoes aren't "right" they should be as inconspicuous as possible. Hang onto sensible, lace-up shoes such as those worn by older women. The classic man's wing-tip shoe will serve for many twentieth-century fashion decades.

FIGURE 7.29 *Modern buttonhook and Victorian one with ornate silver handle.*

SHOE COLORING

Leather dyes make it possible to coordinate footwear and garments. They come in both liquids and sprays. Magix brand spray leather dyes are widely used in costume shops and, if used properly, a single pair of shoes can be dyed over and over again without damaging the leather. Before applying a new spray Magix color, all of the old dye should be removed with a deglazing fluid such as Magix Preparer or Dyo-Flex. Mask off shoe soles with masking tape and stuff the inside of the shoes with rags or newspaper. Use a basic color and then mist over that with one or two darker shades so the leather surface will achieve depth under stage lights. It is also possible to create an unavailable shade by carefully misting over one color with one or two other colors. Be careful not to build up too thick a dye layer which will chip or crack. When the shoes are completely dry, apply paste wax and buff lightly. Over an extended production period, shoes may have to be recolored. Remove the old dye completely before applying a new coat. It is a good idea to take off the dye at the end of a production run and apply a layer of neatsfoot oil or mink oil to the shoes or boots before returning them to stock. Shoes cared for in this manner will last for many years of stage wear.

Liquid leather dyes, such as Fiebing or Omega, can be used in much the same manner except that the dye is painted on. A paint-on leather dye has a harsh, flat finish which can be softened and deepened with a misting of spray Magix.

Magix manufactures leather dyes for suede and patent leather in narrower color ranges. Cloth shoes can be colored with Evangeline slipper dye, which is painted on with a swab or brush and which comes in a wide variety of colors.

Less desirable, but often more readily available, are the small bottles of paint-on shoe dye such as Shoe Make-Up and Lady Esquire. These shoe color preparations are not as long lasting as those mentioned above, and they leave a somewhat chalky finish on the shoe. However, the color can be made more lasting by thoroughly deglazing the shoes before applying these products and the surface can be improved by waxing.

Create two-toned shoes with two different leather dye colors. Mask off the area that is to be one color and spray; remove the first configuration of tape, mask off the sprayed portion, and spray again. A two-toned man's shoe with a neat, pointed toe could be the perfect touch for a character in a Noel Coward comedy.

CONCLUDING DETAILS

A shoemaker will be able to put lifts in some sorts of shoes for an actor who wishes, or needs, to be taller. Shoes can be purchased with built-in lifts which will increase height up to two inches, but these are, naturally, expensive. Less extreme lifts are available separately at many theatrical stores. Many short actors have shoes that will make them taller and often ask to wear them on stage. A proper-looking period shoe sometimes has to be sacrificed in favor of increasing the actor's height, although this is a decision that must be weighed carefully by both director and costume designer.

Many stage floors are slippery, and shoes must often be half-soled and heeled with rubber. If this is done in a shoe repair shop, the cost over an entire season of plays can mount up alarmingly. It is quite possible, with a modest investment in equipment, to perform the task in the costume shop. A store that supplies shoemakers can sell you a metal shoe form on which to work, adhesives, and a supply of rubber half soles and heel plates.

The biggest problem you will have is trimming off the edges of the sole and heel. A hand-operated rasp will usually suffice, but an electric Dremyl with a rasp bit makes the work easier and faster. Coarse sandpaper will take care of the final touches.

On the other hand, sometimes actors need slippery shoe soles in order to be able to perform certain stage movements. In these cases, make sure there is no rubber on the bottoms of the shoes and, if necessary, provide the actor with a box of rosin in which the shoes' soles may be rubbed before the actor goes on stage.

The need for arch supports for some actors has already been mentioned. Others will request sponge rubber innersoles or hosiery guards that fit inside the back of the heel. Both of these help to create a better fit. Dr. Scholl manufactures these items as well as many others for keeping feet comfortable in shoes.

Whenever an actor tells you that a shoe is tight, "but I think I can wear it anyway," either have the shoes stretched by a shoe-maker or find another pair of shoes for the actor. A shoe that is tight in a fitting room is absolutely certain to be unbearably tight on stage. No one should have to act with pinched, miserable feet. On the other hand, if the shoes in question are too large, it may be possible to make them work by adding a second pair of socks or a foam innersole.

The correct shoes can add a great deal to a beautiful costume; the wrong shoes can de-tract. Never wait until the last minute to plan and search for suitable footwear. If the cos-tume is being constructed in the shop, a selec-tion of footwear should certainly be available at the first fabric fitting. If the garments are being bought or taken from stock, shoes and clothing should be fitted at the same time. Never set a hem until the shoes are selected and on the actor. Just as soon as the shoes are completed, make them available to the actor so they can become compatible with the feet.

HOSIERY AND TIGHTS

Short socks, probably made from felted wool, were worn for warmth in the ancient world. In *Works and Days,* Hesiod's gloomy epic that dwells on the hardships of life and the inabil-ity of man to escape whatever fate the gods hand out, the dour poet cautions Greek farm-ers to wear socks in order to keep their feet warm on chilly mornings. It is probably safe to surmise, however, that, since socks are not depicted in Greek vase painting or on Greek statues, they were neither widely worn nor particularly fashionable.

Knitted socks, dating from the fourth cen-tury, A.D., and thought to have been worn by an early Christian group called the Cop-tics, have been found in Egypt. The Victoria and Albert Museum in London has examples of these socks in red and brown wool. A par-ticularly interesting child's striped wool sock from the same period is at the Museum of the City of Leicester. All of these ancient socks have a division for the great toe and very modern-looking heel caps.

There is no mention of the knitting process in England before the early fifteenth century, although leg wrappings, short socks, and stockings were being worn as early as the fourth century, A.D. Short socks were made from cloth or leather, wrappings and stock-ings from cloth. Linen and silk stockings were part of the official dress of priests during the fourth century.

FIGURE 7.30 *Costume sketch for Marlowe's* Dr. Faustus. *(Laura Crow, costume designer.)*

In the eleventh century, as European clothing became form-fitting, men began to wear long stockings which reached the crotch and could be tied to the breeches. It was not long before breeches and stockings became a single garment, much like modern tights. These early tights were made from woven fabric and carefully shaped to fit the leg. Doublets grew shorter until, by the fifteenth century, moralists were condemning the show of legs and buttocks. In Venice, certain young men wore very short doublets, coming not much below the waist, and wildly decorated tights with each leg of a different color. Some legs were striped and some were embroidered with patterns that occasionally included small pearls.

Women also wore stockings, but they were not for public display, since skirts covered women's legs completely until relatively modern times. There is an interesting illuminated manuscript from 1306 that shows a lady seated on her bed while a female servant hands her a stocking to put on. Chaucer makes a point of telling us that the Wife of Bath wore red stockings.

In the early sixteenth century, men's stockings and breeches again became two separate garments. Stockings were referred to as "nether-stocks" and were commonly made of wool, cotton, linen, or silk. They were either held up by garters or tied to the breeches. Stockings were expensive items that reflected one's status in society. The types of stockings worn by people in different social classes were often controlled by sumptuary laws. In 1533, for example, Henry VIII decreed that no serving man could wear stockings made from material that cost more than twenty pence per yard, unless the stockings had been given to him by his master.

By the middle of the sixteenth century, hand-knitted stockings were coming on the scene. In 1560, Queen Elizabeth received a pair of black silk knit stockings and was so delighted with them that she never again wore stockings made of woven cloth. The first knitting machine, which was mentioned in Chapter 2, was invented in 1589, and the era of modern hosiery began.

Today, heavy-weight nylon knit tights are used to represent most tights and stockings worn with men's period costumes. Tights are preferred instead of stockings because they eliminate the need for gartering. Danskin is the most popular brand, although other companies make roughly comparable men's tights. They all take dyes well and are easy to launder. Fabric paints and indelible magic markers can be used to put stripes and other designs on tights.

Some production designs will require stockings or tights to be made from woven cloth. Cloth tights can have woven patterns and textures that are impossible to achieve with nylon knits. There is an excellent pattern for cloth stockings in Carl Kohler's *A History of Costume.* The stockings should be cut on the bias for a better fit. In order to eliminate the need for practical gartering of stockings, stitch them onto a pair of worn-out tights from which the feet and legs, up to the place where the stockings are attached, have been cut off. Cloth stockings can also be stitched to dance trunks or bathing trunks. Cloth stockings will never fit the legs as smoothly as nylon tights, but the slightly wrinkled, rough look can be very effective.

Thick, waffle-weave, elasticized cotton tights can be purchased from Eileen Holding, 110 West 18th Street, New York, New York 10011. They are made to order from individual measurements. These tights come in black and white, and the white ones dye very well. If it is necessary to dye each leg a different color, you may ask to have each leg made up separately and sent to you without the crotch seam stitched. Ms. Holding also makes leotards, unitards, shirts, and dance tights from the elasticized cotton, Helanca or Lycra.

Her price list and measurements and order form are available upon request. Her prices are reasonable.

It is relatively simple to find stage hosiery for men for nineteenth- and twentieth-century plays. Modern, dark-colored socks usually do the job. Occasionally, patterned knee socks are required to go with knickers, but these can usually be purchased in golf shops. Girls' knee socks will sometimes fit men with small feet.

Finding women's hosiery to accompany costumes from the past century is more challenging. Nylon stockings did not appear on the market until after World War II. Before that time, women wore cotton and silk stockings and, after World War I, rayon lisle stockings. All of these stockings were seamed up the back, and silk stockings often had designs, called clocking, up the sides. Black silk stockings were generally preferred during the 1890s.

Thin, semi-opaque dance tights are suitable hosiery for late nineteenth-century and early twentieth-century costumes. Clocking can be represented by designs drawn on with liquid embroidery pens, or, if time permits, designs can be hand-embroidered on the tights with silk or pearl cotton embroidery floss. Service-weight, seamed nylons, always available from J. C. Penney's catalogue department look very much like cotton or rayon lisle on stage. If the actor wishes to wear pantyhose, but the period of the play requires stocking seams, the actor may draw a line

FIGURE 7.31   *Clocking.*

up the back of her legs with a brown eyebrow pencil.

In a professional theatre company, where all hosiery must be supplied to the actors by the costume department, hosiery costs can be enormous. Even the best nylon stockings do run, and runs do show up on an open stage. The lifetime of a pair of stockings can be lengthened by careful laundering. Wash them in a mild solution of Woolite or Hosiery Mate and hang them to dry; do not put nylon stockings in a dryer. Investigate the possibility of buying hosiery in large quantities in order to save on the purchase price. In rare instances, a hosiery shop may donate stockings to the theatre in return for a program advertisement. It never hurts to ask.

8

Hats and Hair

Many theatrical costumes demand hats: military uniforms, Victorian ladies' traveling outfits, seventeenth-century Puritan dresses, and mourning costumes from all fashion periods. Playwrights seem to enjoy writing hat business into their plays. The hat-switching sequence in *Waiting For Godot* always draws a delighted audience response, and even the moody Hamlet pokes fun at foppish Osric's manner of wearing his "bonnet." Sight gags that involve a character donning the hat of another character have been common since the early days of comedy.

Building and adapting hats for the stage takes up a significant portion of many work days in a costume shop. Some shops, operating with large budgets, employ a milliner on the staff, but in most shops, costumers share the job of hat construction. Millinery work is often time-consuming and tedious. A patient person who has an eye for detail and a deft and gentle touch with materials will generally make a successful milliner.

FIGURE 8.1 *Trying on hats in a production of* Waiting for Godot *at the University of Virginia.*

TWO MAJOR PROBLEMS WITH STAGE HATS

When the construction or adaptation of stage hats is being planned, it is a good idea to consider the two major problems that can accompany hats on stage: the hat brim that shades or masks the actor's face and the large hat or headdress that is difficult to balance.

Directors frequently complain when hat brims shade an actor's face. This can be a difficult problem to correct when the required hat is a Stetson or a Prussian helmet. Shadows caused by hat brims are particularly troublesome on open stages where most of the lighting instruments hang directly overhead. On a proscenium stage, front and side light help to minimize the problem.

A time-honored solution for eliminating hat brim shadows on the actor's face is to bring the actor on stage wearing the hat, but to have it removed at once. Unfortunately, this ploy isn't always possible; and when it is not, the hat brim must be made smaller or turned up, or the hat must be worn further back on the head. Solve this particular hat problem early, because most directors will eliminate a hat from a production rather than allow the actor to talk in a shadow.

The other problem pertains to large hats, helmets, or elaborate headdresses and has to do with weight and balance. Dramatic characters seldom stand still while wearing their plumed helmets, mitres, or thirty-six inch fantasy headdresses with twinkling lights. They walk, skip, run, bend, jump, and dance. When you are determining what materials and methods to use for a large or elaborate hat, always assume lively stage movement and check with the director to find out ex-

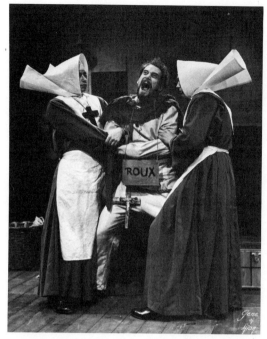

FIGURE 8.2 *Michael Fairman in the Milwaukee Repertory Theater production of* Marat Sade *is restrained by nuns in dramatic headdresses. (Photograph by Gene of Aida.)*

actly what the hat will have to undergo without falling off the head. The use of lightweight materials is important, but even more important is the correct distribution of weight. The only way to check for weight distribution, which is what affects the balance of the hat, is for the costumer to try on the hat at regular intervals while it is under construction. Normally a large hat, helmet, or headdress is heavier in the front than in the back.

HAT MEASUREMENTS

The basic hat measurement is taken around the head with the tape measure just above the eyebrows. This measurement is called the head circumference and it is the only one necessary for hats that merely sit on the head. Table 8.1 is a conversion chart that converts head circumference measurements taken in inches into standard hat sizes. Keep a copy of this information near the hat storage area. It is invaluable for matching hats from stock to actors.

In order to construct coifs, and other head-hugging hat styles, you will also need a forehead to nape measurement, which follows the contour of the back of the head. You may also want a measurement across the head from ear top to ear top.

When you are constructing a hat and calculating the hat size from the head measurements, always allow enough room for the seams, which will thicken up the hat as it is put together, and for the lining, if there is to be one.

HAT SIZES AND THEIR CORRESPONDING MEASUREMENTS

Hat size	Measurement, in inches
5⅞	18¾
6	19
6⅛	19⅜
6¼	19¾
6⅜	20½
6½	20¾
6⅝	21
6¾	21¼
6⅞	21⅝
7	22¼
7⅛	22½
7¼	23
7⅜	23⅜
7½	23¾
7⅝	24
7¾	24½
7⅞	25
8	25¼

BUCKRAM FRAMES, CUT AND STITCHED

Costume hats that have a stiff shape are very often constructed with an inner frame of buckram. Buckram is a stiff, open-weave material which is sized with glue. It normally comes in three weights: light, medium, and heavy. Ordinary fabric shops, when they carry buckram at all, usually have only the light weight. All weights may be purchased from millinery supply shops, most of which are located in New York. Although phone orders can be placed from any part of the country, and shipment is generally prompt, it is a good idea to keep some buckram, in all weights, on hand for unexpected millinery projects. Check the millinery supply shops in the Source Guide for companies who often deal with theatres.

Simple shapes, such as the familiar man's Pilgrim hat, can be constructed from buckram using the cut-and-stitch method. Three pieces are required: the brim, the crown, and the top.

First, make a paper pattern.

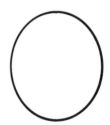

FIGURE 8.3 *Shape for head opening.*

The human head, viewed from above, is not round, but oval. The opening in the brim for the head should be approximately the shape shown in Figure 8.3, and it should correspond with the head circumference measurement, plus about one inch to allow for thickening up when the hat is assembled and covered. The width of the brim will be determined by the design.

The bottom curve of the crown piece and the angle of the sides determine how much slant there will be to the crown (see Figure 8.4 for a Pilgrim hat crown shape). (If the

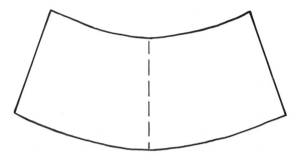

FIGURE 8.4   *Crown shape for a Pilgrim hat.*

with the tabs up inside; backstitch the brim to the crown.

Try the buckram shape on the actor and make a final determination of brim width. Trim if necessary. Stitch hat wire to the edge of the brim, using either a blanket stitch or a machine zigzag stitch. Cover the wire with bias tape and stitch in place.

Cover the entire frame with flannel in order to soften the buckram edges and then cover with a suitable fabric.

FIGURE 8.5   *Pattern pieces for a Pilgrim hat.*

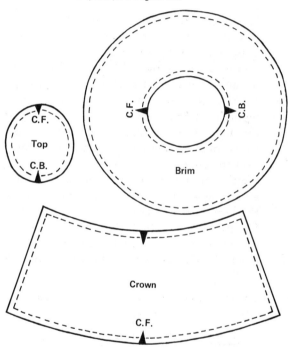

side angles are steeper and go up to a point, you will have the shape for a witch's hat.) The circumference of the top piece must equal the length of the top curve on the crown piece.

Tape the paper pattern pieces together and try the hat mock-up on the actor's head. This will not be a precise fitting, but you can check the brim width and the height and angle of the crown.

Lay the pattern pieces on the buckram and draw around them. Measure and draw in a one-half-inch seam allowance as shown in Figure 8.5. Cut out the pieces. Slash the seam allowances on the top and the brim all the way to the pattern line, forming tabs about one-half-inch wide. Fold tabs up carefully. Using heavy duty thread and a firm back-stitch, sew the crown together to form a cone. Place the top on the crown with the tabs on the inside; backstitch the top to the crown. Put the brim on the bottom of the crown

COVERING THE BUCKRAM FRAME

The flannel cover and the final fabric cover are done the same way. The lining, however, is put in place along with the final fabric cover.

Cut the cover fabric pieces from the original paper pattern and leave one-half-inch seam allowances around each edge of each piece. You will need two cover pieces for the

brim—one for the top and one for the bottom. Cut lining fabric for the top and the crown at the same time.

Cover the top first. Backstitch the top piece to crown as shown in Figure 8.6. Trim wedges from the seam allowance so it will lie flat. Assemble the lining top and crown with machine-stitching. Slip the lining up into the

FIGURE 8.6 *Backstitching top piece to crown.*

hat and stitch it to the crown just below the row of stitches securing the outside top covering. Stitch the bottom of the lining to the bottom of the crown. Pin the crown cover to the top of the hat as shown in Figure 8.7. *Do not* stitch the vertical crown cover seam beforehand. Stitch the crown cover where the top and the crown meet. Trim wedges from the seam allowance and pull the fabric down over the crown. Pull the cover smoothly and tightly around the crown; pin, then blind-stitch the seam. Slash the seam allowance at the bottom of the crown cover so it will lie flat on the brim. Stitch the cover to the bottom of the crown where the crown and brim meet. Attach the top of the brim cover as

shown in Figure 8.8, stitching right at the base of the crown. Smooth the cover fabric over the brim, turn under the brim, and stitch to the tape that binds the edge of the buckram frame. Lay the bottom of the brim cover fabric in place, slashing as necessary in order to turn the seam allowances under. Blind-stitch the outer brim edge first, then the inner brim edge. Add a grosgrain or leather sweat band just inside the crown to stabilize the size.

If you are covering a buckram frame for a hat with a curved brim, the fabric on both sides of the brim should be glued down. A spray millinery adhesive is best, but white glue will also work.

Hats of many shapes can be made from this type of buckram frame: a stovepipe hat, a fez, a cone-shaped hennin, a railway conductor's hat. When a very rigid brim is necessary, use two layers of buckram with a layer of cardboard in between.

If the costume budget is severely limited, some simple hat frames can be made from cardboard, working in the same manner as with buckram, and covered with an appropriate fabric. Cardboard hat frames are not sturdy, however, and should not be expected to last for long.

FIGURE 8.7 *Covering the crown.*

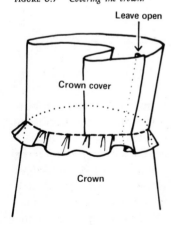

FIGURE 8.8 *Covering the brim.*

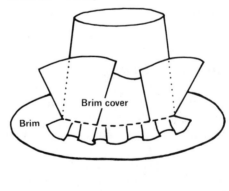

SHAPING HATS ON BLOCKS

Working with hat blocks, it is possible to create a variety of rounded shapes that cannot be made by cutting and stitching buckram. Both buckram and felt may be shaped on a hat block.

Professional milliner's hat blocks are made from wood, either hardwood or balsa, and rest on sturdy bases. Some have removable parts so the completed frame or body may be easily taken from it; some have separate head and brim blocks.

New blocks can be purchased from millinery supply shops, although the mechanization of the hat industry, the limited importance of hats in the modern fashion scene, and the shrinking number of independent milliners are lessening the demand for new blocks. They are costly. Secondhand blocks, however, are often available from milliners who are retiring or going out of business, from antique shops, or from secondhand stores or rummage sales.

If wooden hat blocks are not available, there are workable substitutes. A sturdy padded wig block makes a fine base on which to build hats. Different sizes and shapes may be created with layers of felt, foam, or modeling clay. Styrofoam wig blocks are somewhat less desirable because they are so light, but they can be used. In order to have a sturdy

FIGURE 8.9   *Assorted hat blocks. (Photograph by Richard Bryant.)*

form on which to work, mount the wig block on a piece of dowel and attach the dowel to a wood base.

Some of the most successful of all hat block shapes are "found" objects. A very small pail may be the perfect shape for a medieval page's hat; a basin may be the beginning of a helmet. When you are searching for a shape, look over the property shop storage area and your own kitchen shelves for objects that can be used alone, or in combination, for a hat block. Pieces of foam may be added to round off sharp edges, to fatten out some parts, and to create the proper head size.

Whatever you use for a hat block, cover it before you begin to work. If the frame is to be made of buckram, cover the block with aluminum foil or plastic wrap. Buckram is impregnated with glue and will stick to a bare block after it has dried. If felt is being molded, cover the block with aluminum foil or cloth. Do not use plastic wrap, since felt shaping requires heat as well as moisture, and the plastic wrap may melt.

Shaping Buckram Frames on a Block

To shape a buckram hat frame, first cut a piece of buckram large enough to cover the entire block, with ample to spare. Wet the buckram thoroughly and drape it over the block with the straight grain running from c.f. to c.b. Stretch and pin the buckram at hand firmly on top of the block so that the buckram will not slip sideways. Begin to work the buckram down between the four pins in order to eliminate the folds. This is possible because of the bias pull which allows the loosely woven strands to pack closer together. A circle of wire, forcing the buckram downward, is a useful tool. For most hat shapes, you will be aiming for a frame in which all folds have been eliminated. If the shape, however, must narrow from a bulbous crown to a narrow head opening, remove as much fullness as possible and then arrange

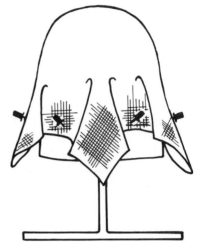

FIGURE 8.10   *Shaping buckram on a hat block.*

the excess buckram in evenly divided folds. When the frame is dry, snip the folds away and cross-stitch the edges together, forming butted darts. Hat frames may also be darted by slashing the buckram and lapping over the excess.

Some frames will not slip easily off the block after they are dry. In these cases, slit the frame to remove it from the block and cross-stitch the pieces together.

Always allow the buckram frame to dry thoroughly before removing it from the block. If too much sizing has been lost in the molding process, resize it before removing it from the block. You can speed the drying by putting the block and buckram frame under a hair dryer on a cool or warm setting.

After the frame is dry and off the block, fit it on the actor, trim as necessary, and bind the edges. Cover the molded frame in the same manner as the cut-and-stitched frame, except that the lining should be stitched in place before the outer fabric is applied. Use a very light fabric to line a rounded frame so that folds may be taken without resulting in too much bulk.

The outer covering should be done with a material that has some stretch so there will

FIGURE 8.11 *Felt body before steaming and shaping, and the block on which it will be shaped.*

be no folds. Do not pull the cover too tight or the buckram frame may collapse.

Shaping Felt Bodies on a Block

A felt hat body shaped on a block is not as rigid as a buckram frame. A felt stiffener, which can be obtained both in a spray can and in a paint-on liquid, is often used to firm up felt hat bodies, particularly the brims.

Felt hat bodies are not usually covered with other fabrics. It is advisable to work with felt that is the desired color since it is virtually impossible to dye a felt hat evenly. Toning and shading, however, are easily done with Magix spray leather dyes or with liquid fabric dyes applied with a spray bottle, an atomizer, a stippling brush, or a sponge.

Moisture and heat are both necessary to mold felt. Wet the felt thoroughly with hot water and then drape it over the hat block. Secure the top of the body to the block with

FIGURE 8.12 *Securing felt body to the top of the block with push pins.*

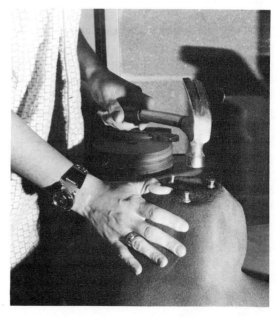

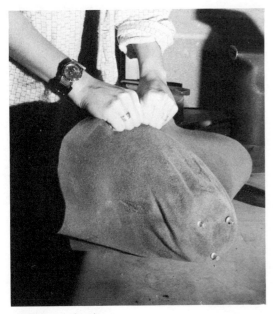

FIGURE **8.13** *Stretching.*

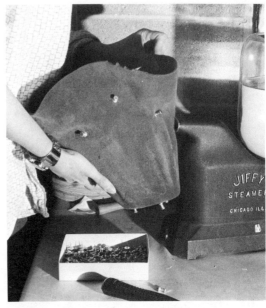

FIGURE **8.14** *Steaming.*

push pins, or hold it in place with one hand while working. Work in alternating steps: apply steam, stretch and mold the felt, apply more steam, and so on. For the steam source, use a hat steamer, a Jiffy steamer, a steam iron, or a steaming tea kettle. Take care not to get your hands in the way of the steam.

If the felt is relatively thin, work it down over the block gently but firmly. Thicker felt can take more vigorous pulling and will stretch a good deal. Molding felt is a bit more time-consuming than molding buckram; the process demands persistence and patience.

Do not remove the felt body from the block until it is completely dry. Then it may be fitted on the actor. Always add a leather or grosgrain sweat band inside the finished felt hat to control the size and to prevent the felt from stretching out.

FIGURE **8.15** *More steaming.*

FIGURE 8.16   *The stretched shape. (Felt shaping photographs by Susan Perkins.)*

READY-MADE FRAMES AND BODIES

Buckram frames and felt bodies are available from millinery supply shops. Buckram frames, and a lighter weight variety made of sized lace-net, come in a wide assortment of shapes, many of which are adaptable to period styles. The edges are already bound and they are ready for covering.

Felt bodies can be purchased in a limited number of shapes that are suitable for blocking and styling. With a minimum of shaping, ready-made felt hat bodies can be adapted to create: Cavalier hats, a whole array of cocked hats, ladies' riding hats from the eighteenth century, American slouch hats, cowboy hats, and many others. Felt hat bodies come in different colors with either a smooth or a furry finish.

Contact a millinery supply company and ask for a catalogue which will list the supplies and the hat styles carried by the company.

FIGURE 8.17   *Tricorn fashioned from ready-made felt body with additional shaping, sizing, and trim. (Photograph by Susan Perkins.)*

USING OLD HATS

The least expensive, and quickest, way to produce a hat for the stage is to refurbish and/or restyle an old hat. Your costume stock should include a collection of as many old hats as can be conveniently stored. They are easy to acquire both through donations and through purchases at local secondhand shops. Many contemporary hat shapes are adaptable to various period styles. Learn to look at old hats with a keen eye to what they can become.

In most cases, you will begin the process of restyling an old hat by stripping all trim from it and beginning with the basic shape. Felt hats can be reblocked into variations on the original shape and, in cases where the felt is not too thin to stretch further, into quite different shapes.

Straw hats can be perked up and can have their shapes altered with steam, although a much gentler touch is necessary than when you are working with felt. A hat block is not always necessary for steaming straw. Work the hat with your hands and set it to dry over wadded up muslin or newspapers. Shape straw brims with hat wire stitched to the edges; cover the hat wire with binding.

For an entirely new look, cover old hat shapes with straw braid. To determine the approximate amount of straw braid needed to cover a hat crown, measure the height of the crown from the center top to the base. Divide this measurement by the width of the braid, then multiply by the circumference of the crown base. For the amount of braid needed to cover the brim, divide the size of the widest part of the brim by the width of the braid and multiply the result by the circumference of the brim. Take the time to make these calculations and you will be saved the frustrating experience of running out of braid before the hat is covered.

Before applying straw braid to a hat, dampen it by wrapping it in a moist towel.

FIGURE 8.18   *Cheryl Anderson and Leslie Gerasi have hats created from store-bought straws with additional shaping, wiring, and trim in a production of* Richard II *at the Milwaukee Repertory Theater. (Elizabeth Covey, costume designer; photograph by Jack Hamilton.)*

This will cause the braid to be more pliable and easier to shape. Straw braid is applied from the top of the crown downward, in a spiral. Notice that the braid has a gathering string along one side that can be drawn up to ease the braid in place. Stitch the braid in place as you apply it to the hat. Use a long milliner's needle and wax the thread heavily.

FIGURE 8.19   *Ronald Frazier, Regina David, and Jacqueline Britten wearing motoring hats in a Milwaukee Repertory Theater production of* Ah Wilderness! *(Susan Tsu, costume designer; photograph by Mark Avery.)*

HAT TRIMS

Down through the fashion centuries, an amazing array of objects, both real and artificial, have been used to trim hats. Embroidery, braid, precious stones and paste baubles, feathers, plumes, whole birds, fruit, leaves, and flowers have been the most common. Check period sources carefully for the types of hat trim favored in a specific era, and try to approximate them whenever possible.

When you are setting up the trim for a particular hat, assemble all the possibilities in order to assess different arrangements and combinations. Hat trims must be in harmony with the hat shape or they will seem to be tacked on as an afterthought. Refrain from using overly large bunches of trim unless the effect is supposed to be markedly comic. Balance the trim, and do not allow the hat to become top-heavy. In most instances, the actor's words should be of greater interest to the audience than a towering bunch of daisies perched precariously on a hat.

Feathers and plumes are particularly popular hat trims on stage. You can purchase plumes already curled, but it is often cheaper and more convenient to do the curling in the shop. One way of curling plumes is by running a scissors blade along each one of the fronds in much the same way certain decorative package ribbon is curled; work very carefully so as not to break the fronds. You can also curl plume fronds by steaming the end of the plume for a few seconds; remove it and wrap the fronds around a broomstick, or some similarly shaped object. Never use a curling iron to curl plumes; the iron will invariably scorch the feather. Old plumes that have grown brittle will not curl.

Two or three thin plumes can be fastened together to produce a thick plume. Run a piece of heavy wire along the spines and wrap

FIGURE 8.20   *Hat trimmings.*

the spines and the wire together with fine wire or nylon thread. This is also a good way to repair broken plumes or feathers.

Plumes can be dyed. In order to obtain deep colors, use a dye that can be dissolved in a nonaqueous solution, such as alcohol or *benzene.* Some feathers may also be dyed, with great care, in a solution of water and Rit or Tintex dye, and then dried in a plastic bag filled with cornstarch. Shake the bag gently and the cornstarch will absorb the moisture. Plumes that have been commercially fireproofed are highly resistant to dyes. Fortunately, you can purchase a wide variety of colored plumes.

At the end of a production run, strip feathers and plumes from the hats they have trimmed and store them separately. Store feathers and plumes in such a way that their spines will not be damaged. Do not put them in air-tight containers such as closed plastic bags. Cardboard boxes and net bags make good containers for feathers and plumes.

Pearls, beads, and sequins are often used on stage hats, sometimes in clusters, sometimes as a overall pattern. For best results, stitch each pearl, bead, or sequin on separately. Although this is a time-consuming process, individual stitching will forestall the loss of many beads should a thread, which holds a large number of them, break.

Grosgrain ribbon is popular for hat bands and for binding hat brims. Shape the ribbon before applying it to the hat. Lay the ribbon on the board, pull the outer curve, and apply steam. The pulled edge will stretch while the inside curve will shrink correspondingly. Sometimes it is helpful to work on a tailor's ham. Only ribbed ribbons, such as grosgrain, can be shaped in this manner.

Make an effort to collect potential hat trims and tuck them away for future use. Keep them sorted and well marked so you can find them when they are needed. Strip feathers, flowers, and leaves from old hats that have no other use. Buy up trims at rummage sales and church bazaars. Save bits of ribbon, lace, and braid from costume construction. Experiment with new materials; often the most successful hat trims are contrived from highly unlikely objects.

HOODS

During the Middle Ages, hoods were particularly popular and were worn by all classes. Some of these hoods extended down over the shoulders and some had long peaks, called liripipes, which were draped around the shoulders or wrapped around the head. Some hoods had dagged or scalloped edges. Simple hoods were adopted by religious orders and are still worn today.

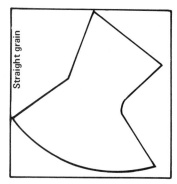

FIGURE 8.21 *Simple hood shape.*

The simplest hood may be cut in two basic pieces from a square or rectangle of cloth (see Figure 8.21). From this basic shape, some subtle shaping can be done. Hoods are often completely lined, both for comfort and for color contrast.

There is an amusing legend to explain the development of the hood into the chaperon. According to the story, an Italian gentleman, leaving a party in a state of inebriation, was unable to find the proper opening in his hood through which to put his head. He placed the opening that had been intended for his face onto the top of his head, allowing the rest of the fabric to fall in folds to one side, and then wrapped his liripipe around his neck. Evidentally, every man who observed him in passing admired his accidental creation, because it became a fad overnight.

At first, men arranged their hoods in this general fashion each time they went out, but eventually their wives stitched the arrangement in place and the chaperon achieved a tidier look. In its final phase, the chaperon was mounted on a stuffed roll which set down on the head and was called a roudelet. The tail, or liripipe, grew to prodigious lengths and was often richly decorated and flamboyantly displayed. This delightful piece of headgear was favored for almost two hundred years, disappearing at the end of the fifteenth century.

A chaperon built for the stage need not start out as a hood. Cut and construct the headband, or the roudelet, the fabric cascade, and the liripipe separately, and then stitch all three parts together. Upholstery piping may be covered for a roudelet, or a fabric tube stuffed with dacron fluff, shredded foam, or cotton batting may be used. The edges of the fabric cascade may be scalloped or dagged (instructions for both of these operations are in Chapter 4) and lined with a contrasting color. Comic effects can be achieved with a liripipe which is overlong. In order to save the actor from becoming entangled in his liripipe, it may have to be fastened onto his costume at strategic points with snaps or Velcro.

Chaperons appear in many paintings and statues of the period and there are countless style variations. They are fun to create and most actors enjoy wearing these highly theatrical hats.

The gentleman in his chaperon was often accompanied by his lady in wimple and veil. Some variation on the wimple was worn by women during all of the Middle Ages. Basically, the wimple is a piece of soft fabric, usually white, covering the chin and neck, drawn up in folds on either side of the face, and fastened just above the ears. Some are

FIGURE 8.22 *Bands for securing wimple and veil.*

band and head band as shown in Figure 8.22. These bands may be secured with Velcro or with a piece of elastic at the closing, so that some adjustment is possible. The wimple and the veil can be secured to the bands with snaps, with hooks and eyes, or with Velcro if a quick change is called for. Some wimples may be cut on the bias and attached directly to the veil or the headdress.

To achieve the graceful folds demanded by the wimple, use the softest possible fabrics: Cotton and silk are best. A very fine muslin weave is excellent. Wool jersey and cotton knits are good if the wimple is to be one of the closer-fitting varieties. Some actors find wimples uncomfortable to wear, particularly if they are close-fitting. It is always a good idea to make a wimple available for rehearsals as early as possible.

more closely fitted than others and almost all are topped with a veil and circlet, or with a more elaborate headdress.

One stageworthy method of securing a wimple and veil is to fasten them to a chin

CAPS

Men began to wear cloth caps at the beginning of the nineteenth century. Many style variations passed in and out of fashion. Caps are still popular today. Recently, the musical, *Oliver*, based on Charles Dickens's novel, *Oliver Twist*, sparked a revival of the big,

FIGURE 8.23 *Cloth cap worn by Tom Blair in the Milwaukee Repertory Theater production of* Never A Snug Harbor. *(Ellen M. Kozak, costume designer; photograph by Jack Hamilton.)*

floppy caps worn by English schoolboys in the mid-nineteenth century. Women as well as men have been wearing the "Oliver" caps.

Modern, ready-made caps are sometimes suitable for a nineteenth-century costume, but it is often difficult to find just the right shape or the right fabric. Caps are not difficult to make in the costume shop. The crown of a cap is basically a circle divided into pie-shaped pieces. Cut the pattern pieces out of muslin and shape the outer edge until you have a suitable shape. You will probably not want equal fullness all around the cap crown. Flatten the circle and take in the seams to reduce the fullness. Make the stabilizing band that goes around the head out of gros-grain ribbon, belting, or leather. The cap brim may be constructed from cardboard, buck-ram, layers of stitched canvas, or sized felt; it may be covered with matching or contrast-

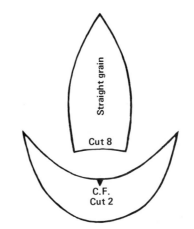

FIGURE 8.24 *Pattern shapes for a cap with eight sections.*

ing material. Once you have developed a pleasing cap pattern, keep it on file for future use.

MEN'S NINETEENTH- AND TWENTIETH-CENTURY HATS

Men's top hats, derbies, soft felts, and straws are called for frequently on stage. None of these styles can readily be built in a costume shop. If you do not have an adequate selection in your own stock, you will probably purchase, borrow, or rent them. Men's hats have changed gradually but decidedly during the nineteenth and twentieth centuries. Be sure you know exactly what style you are looking for when you set out to find a particular man's hat.

Top Hats and Opera Hats

Top hats were enormously popular during most of the nineteenth century. They were worn, in different colors and shapes, for both formal and informal occasions. By the end of the century, however, other hat styles had become more popular for informal wear, and the top hat, along with its close relative, the

opera hat, were being reserved for formal occasions; this remains true today.

The general shape that is associated with the top hat made its appearance with the popularization of the "beaver" in the eighteenth century. The first beavers had slanted crowns, like the Pilgrim or Quaker hats, and flat, stiff brims. Gradually, the slanted crown disappeared, and by 1830, the shape was much like a fat stovepipe. After the depletion of the beaver supply in America around the middle of the nineteenth century, toppers were sometimes covered with grosgrain, merino cloth, shiny silk, or wool; they were also made from stiffened felt. In 1820, the first mechanical felting machine was developed, a boon to the hat makers.

There are two major brim styles for the top hat: the flat brim and the rolled brim. By the end of the nineteenth century, the flat brim had all but disappeared and the rolled brim appeared in many different shapes. Crowns were as high as eight inches and as low as five and three-quarter inches. Some had straight sides, others had gently curved sides flaring into high crowns and large tops, and still others sported deeply curved sides and low, jaunty crowns. Only the most fashion conscious gentlemen remained absolutely current in their choice of top hats. Many men wore a single formal top hat for a lifetime, caring little for the yearly fashion changes.

During the nineteenth century, black felt and rough beaver, as well as fawn, gray, and white top hats were worn with informal clothing. White was favored for the hunt. Brushed beaver, plush, and silk top hats accompanied formal dress.

The faille-covered, collapsible opera hat, or Gibus (the name of its inventor), appeared in Paris in the 1840s. The crown of the Gibus is supported by a spiral spring between the outer cloth and the lining. The spring can be collapsed and the hat folded quite flat. The collapsible opera hat was worn interchangeably with the topper, although it was always much more suitable for formal dinners and the theatre; fashionable weddings and state occasions required the more imposing silk top hat. Opera hats were very popular with the young jet set during the 1920s and 1930s; one might be the perfect choice for a Noel Coward character who is on his way to dinner and a night on the town. Collapsible top hats often provide amusing stage business. Opera hats have relatively narrow brims, gracefully rolled, medium-low crowns, and deeply curved sides. They should always be stored in the expanded position; storing them collapsed will damage the silk covering.

Fortunately, there are a good many old formal top hats and opera hats still in existence. The men who owned them wore them infrequently and stored them carefully between wearings. Some of these hats eventually find their way into costume stocks. The informal toppers, which were worn every day, did not survive in such great numbers. Costumers often re-cover formal top hats with different colored fabrics for informal wear on stage.

You can purchase silk-covered and felt top hats and opera hats new. The felt toppers generally come in black and in only a few colors: gray, blue, brown, and white. Besides being quite expensive, the new models do not have the same style and flair as the hats produced seventy-five or eighty years ago.

Derbies

The first bowler hat appeared in England in 1850. It had a narrow, flat brim and a melon-shaped crown. Over the years, the crown has varied in height and shape and the brim in width and amount of roll. Still called the bowler in England, after its inventor, William Bowler, it is known in America as the derby, from the Earl of Derby, who helped popularize the hat.

The derby is never worn with formal clothes. For several decades it was the most suitable hat to accompany a conservative business suit, particularly in gray or black. In America, the brown derby became identified with the Democratic presidential candidate, Al Smith, and suffered a decided drop in popularity among men of opposing political persuasions.

Some derbies have heavily stiffened crowns and, like top hats, can be permanently damaged if the crown is cracked. Others are softer and more flexible. Store stiff bowlers in individual hat boxes; the softer ones should have wadded paper or cloth stuffed into the crowns before they are put away.

Soft Felt Hats and Straw Hats

From the latter part of the nineteenth century until after World War II, most men wore hats for most occasions. Family photograph albums show straw skimmers or boaters with swimwear, toppers at weddings, caps on the golf course, and derbies or soft felts on the way to business. Even men lined up outside employment offices and soup kitchens at the height of the depression retained the respectability of a covered head. By 1920, the soft felt hat was the most popular of all.

The *fedora,* the *homburg,* the *snap brim,* and the *porkpie* are all soft felt styles. The Stetson, which appeared in the 1870s, has been widely worn both on the ranch and in the city.

The most elegant of the soft felt hats is the homburg. In 1919, a *Men's Wear* feature writer called it the hat of choice of "the cultured, smartly turned-out men of the world who have social position, inherent good taste, and the means with which to satisfy it." The black homburg is quite suitable with a dinner jacket. Most popular in the darker colors, the homburg has a tapering crown and a medium-wide, rolled brim. Homburgs may also be constructed from straw.

Most men's hats stay in style for a long time, with subtle shape changes occurring along the way. An important research source for men's hats in the twentieth century is *Esquire's Encyclopedia of 20th Century Men's Fashions* by O. E. Schoeffler and William Gale. If your character is fashion conscious, this book will tell you exactly what he should be wearing; if he is less than fashionable, you can determine what he might be wearing from the general survey material.

Finding the correct hat size for your actor is sometimes as difficult as finding the correct hat style for your character. Fortunately, hat sizes can be altered to some extent. If the hat is slightly too big, stuff the sweat band with pieces of foam or felt. In a pinch, use Kleenex to stuff hatbands. Most soft felts, straws, and some derbies can be stretched on a hat stretcher to increase their size. Hat stretchers come in wood or metal and are essentially expanding head shapes. Some models supply steam during the stretching process. All hat stretchers should be operated with care; fabric, felt, and leather will stretch only so far before damage is done to the material. Some dry cleaning shops will stretch hats at a modest price.

STORING HATS

The importance of having a hat stock to draw upon has already been mentioned several times in this chapter. Even the smallest of theatres should allot some corner somewhere to a hat collection.

If at all possible, stored hats should be covered to protect them from dust. Store toppers and derbies in individual hat boxes. Plastic bags offer good protection for large women's hats. Soft felt hats, which can be easily steamed into shape before they are worn, can be stored on top of one another in large barrels; they should have some stuffing inside each crown.

Organize the hats according to style and color. Careful labeling will result in less rummaging through the hat stock which, in the

FIGURE 8.25 *Millinery area at the Tyrone Guthrie Theatre in Minneapolis. (Photograph by Rod Pilloud.)*

long run, will keep the hats in far better condition.

During the run of a production, have the actors put their hats on a head block when they are not being worn, except for rigid hats, such as toppers and derbies, which should be placed in hat boxes. Fine hats, well cared for, can have long and useful stage lives.

HAIR

If an inquiry about footwear is the first question many actors ask a costume designer, the second one may well be some variation on: "What am I going to do with my hair?" Most theatrical costumes do require complementary hairstyles. Usually, the actor is able to restyle his or her own hair in order to achieve an adequate representation of the appropriate style; sometimes hair pieces or full wigs are necessary.

It is not difficult to find materials for researching period hairstyles. There are many paintings and drawings to look at and many descriptions to read. Richard Corson's *Fashions in Hair,* which contains drawings of a broad sample of styles from all periods, is a particularly useful resource book for every costume shop to have. A costume designer's sketch usually includes an indication of the hairstyle that will be most suitable for the costume. If the style can be created with the actor's own hair, the designer or costumer will usually help the actor plan how to set and arrange it but will not actually style the actor's hair for each performance. If a wig is called for, however, it will normally be styled, set, and maintained by the costume staff.

Professional hairstyling requires special talent and training. Not every costumer should expect to be able to create sensational hairstyles. Certain processes, dyeing and cut-

FIGURE 8.26   *The wig room at the Tyrone Guthrie Theatre in Minneapolis. (Photograph by Rod Pilloud.)*

ting in particular, will be referred to a professional stylist. On the other hand, a surprising number of hairstyles can be created in the costume shop by novices with a feel for hair. Certainly every costume technician should be able to set and comb a simple style and to maintain wigs properly.

GENERAL PERIOD SHAPES

The height and fullness of fashionable hairstyles throughout fashion history has an interesting relationship to the width and length of the garments worn at any specific time. Whenever ladies' hips widened with panniers, hoops, or peplums, there was a tendency for hairstyles to rise higher in order to keep the figure from appearing squat. On the other hand, the short, head-hugging styles in hair from the 1920s complemented the sleek, skinny dresses. Closely trimmed hair looked best with the narrow lapels and shoulders of men's suits in the late 1950s and early 1960s. The wider lapels and ties, and the flaring shirt collars that followed, demanded longer, fuller hairstyles.

This relationship operates only on the most generalized level, however, for each period always includes many variations on the shapes of the most common hairstyles. Besides, many people from any given fashion period choose not to adopt the prevailing fashion in hair. Some men and women completely ignore what is stylish and prefer to cut and arrange their hair in a manner that they consider attractive. Others retain a favorite hairstyle from their youth, even though it is long out of fashion. When you are choosing a hairstyle for a dramatic charac-ter, consider the personality of that character carefully. Some characters, like some people, would never dye their hair, tease their hair, or change it from straight to curly; others are eager to spend all the hours and all the dollars it takes to be in the forefront of hair fashion.

Out of all the possible hairstyle variations within any fashion period, choose, if possible, a simple style that can be maintained without too much difficulty, and one which the audience will not find distracting. Particularly avoid hairstyles that look as though they might be insecure; also avoid ones that are strangely proportioned to modern eyes. Even some fairly recent hair styles, such as the upsweep, the square-cut, tightly permed look of the early 1940s, and the oversized bouffant, are often softened somewhat for the stage.

CONSIDER THE ACTOR'S FACE

Within the range of styles appropriate for any period, the shape of the actor's face must be taken into consideration when choosing a hairstyle. If the object is to make the actor as attractive as possible, complement the shape of the face with the shape of the hair. A round face should not have too much fullness at the sides, as this would tend to accentuate the round cheeks. Long, straight hair is not good for oblong faces, while medium-length hair is. A square face should have height on the top, but the sides should be away from the jaw line. The triangular face can be broadened at the top with short bangs, while the heart-shaped face might have some fullness at the sides to widen the jaw. Tall hairstyles should generally be avoided by tall people and flaring styles should not be worn by both very large and very small people.

In some cases, however, the object is not to make the actor look merely attractive. Hairstyles can make important contributions to characterizations. A full, fluffy hairstyle that accentuates the round face of a round-faced actor might be absolutely correct for Sister Woman in Tennessee Williams' *Cat on a Hot Tin Roof.* If the actor who requires a lean and hungry look already has an oblong face, the character look can be strengthened by a long, straight hairstyle. Matted, dirty gray wisps of uncut hair can only add to the parsimonious nature of Ebeneezer Scrooge.

HAIR CUTTING

In the 1950s, male actors were reluctant to let their hair grow long enough for certain period hairstyles; in the 1970s, male actors are equally as reluctant to cut their hair short enough for a play set in the 1950s. Female actors who are used to wearing their hair long and straight dislike the thought of having it cut and permed. The whole matter of talking actors into growing or cutting the proper amount of hair for a particular period hairstyle is a delicate one. Many actors want to think they can make do with whatever length hair they have, and a large number of directors, in admirable displays of loyalty to their actors, will agree with them. Costumers who are working on small budgets must learn to be persuasive; those who can afford it may turn to wigs. Wigs, however, will not always solve the problem. Men's short hair wigs are seldom ever successful, and certain short, simple women's styles do not work at all well with wigs.

Fortunately for male actors who are playing a character with close-cropped hair, hair looks shorter on stage than it actually is. Very often, a careful trim around the ears and across the back will give the effect of a very short haircut when, in actuality, the hair is not extremely short.

Whenever possible, it is always best to have haircuts done by a professional. Be certain, however, that the barber or stylist knows that the haircut is being done for the stage and is aware of the exact style that is required. The costumer may want to be present during the haircut and may also want to bring pictures of the appropriate hairstyle for the barber to look at. In most professional situations, the cost of the haircut will be covered by the costume budget.

HAIR COLOR

A specific hair color is sometimes required by the script. If the reference cannot be changed to reflect the actor's own hair color, and if a suitable wig is not practical or preferable, the actor's hair will have to be colored. Hair dyeing should always be done professionally, particularly if the color is to be lighter than the actor's own and if a two-step dyeing process is necessary.

If the coloring process is only to brighten the actor's own natural hair color, a color rinse may be used. There are a great many color rinses on the market, and most are both easy and safe to use without professional assistance.

Gray or graying hair is frequently required on the stage. There are several ways of graying hair. The use of white liquid shoe polish on the hair should be avoided, since it dries the hair and can cause severe scalp rashes. White cake make-up and liquid hair whitener are both good choices. These products can be applied to the hair with a toothbrush and then combed through the hair with a wide-toothed comb in order to break up matted areas.

Stick make-up for graying hair, such as those produced by Leichner and Bob Kelly, does an especially good job of coloring small areas, such as the temples. It has a creamy consistency, is not harmful to the hair, and is easy to control.

Hair-coloring sprays, such as Streaks and Tips, are particularly convenient to use when all the hair must be colored gray or white. Do not cover the whole head with a flat, white spray, however; the result will not be at all realistic. A combination of silver and white sprays will create a more natural look. In some instances, a bit of toning with a blonde spray will also help. No one's hair is ever all one color. Remember this and be subtle when you are using color sprays.

Hair-coloring sprays come in a wide variety of colors. They are generally excellent for highlighting and touch-up work. They are satisfactory for real hair wigs but not on wigs made with synthetic hair.

When you are using any of the spray hair colors on an actor, be careful to protect the neck and face from the spray. Cut a cardboard frame to fit around the hairline. Hold this shield in place while applying the spray. Hair-coloring sprays wash out with ordinary shampoo. They are not, unless they are used to great excess, harmful to the hair. The spray color does rub off, however, and the actor who uses it will probably have to wash his or her hair after each performance.

If the hair color change is required by the role, professional theatre companies must provide all hair-coloring materials for actors who are members of Actors Equity. In addition, if the actor's hair is dyed for a role, the theatre is also financially responsible, should the actor wish it, for having the hair restored to its original color.

HAIRPIECES

Adding a hairpiece to the actor's own hair is often the simplest way to construct a hairstyle for the stage, particularly for women. Hairpieces must be purchased or dyed the same color as the actor's own hair.

The *fall* is the largest and longest hairpiece and is often about the size of half a wig. It is attached to the crown of the head and hangs to the back. It may be as short as seven or eight inches, or as long as thirty-five or

FIGURE 8.27 *Anthony Heald and Susan Monts in the Milwaukee Repertory Theater production of* Ah Wilderness! *Ms. Monts is wearing a fall. (Susan Tsu, costume designer; photograph by Mark Avery.)*

thirty-six inches. Falls may be used on male actors to effect the shoulder-length hair popular in some periods.

Wiglets are small decorative hairpieces, usually curled, that can be added to a style for height and shape. They come in a variety of different sizes. Long *switches* can be made up into braids and chignons. They are among the most useful hairpieces for the stage. *Cluster curls* are also handy to have. You may be able to purchase a single curl or clusters of two, three, or more.

On the stage, real hairpieces are preferable to synthetic hairpieces both because they can be colored to match an actor's own hair and because synthetic hair has a shine under stage lights that does not look real. Synthetic hairpieces are cheaper than real hairpieces, however, and must often be used for this reason. Make sure the synthetic piece is a good color match and integrate it as much as possible into the total hairstyle. A very light dusting

of powder will sometimes reduce the unnatural shine of a synthetic piece.

To attach a hairpiece, make two or three flat pin curls of the actor's own hair and secure them with bobby pins. Slip the comb on the hairpiece into the pin curls, under the bobby pins. Put a few long hairpins through the mesh backing of the piece into the pin curls. If there is no comb on the hairpiece, stitch one in. Sometimes it is necessary to add a piece of the actor's own hair, twisted, around the area where the hairpiece has been attached in order to hide the join. Ribbons and artificial flowers, when these can be worked into the hairstyle, are excellent cover-ups.

Many male actors who are balding have a hairpiece, or a selection of hairpieces, for stage use. If an actor is planning to wear his own hairpiece, ask him to wear it to the costume fitting so the total look can be considered.

FULL WIGS

Wigs that are obviously wigs are required by many plays set during the wig periods of the seventeenth and eighteenth centuries. Men wore wigs in France during most of the seventeenth century, while in England wigs did not catch on until after the restoration of the monarchy in 1660 when Charles II returned from his exile in France. In both centuries, women who were concerned with fashion either wore wigs or added a variety of hairpieces to their own hair. Women's wigs were generally dressed to simulate real hair, while men's wigs were less realistic and were often worn with such a casual attitude that a man was apt to raise his wig to scratch his head, or to remove it and hang it on a fence post before engaging in a fist fight.

Around 1720, powdered wigs became fashionable. The operation was accomplished either with a large puff or with a bellows, and sometimes a special room was designated for

the purpose of wig powdering. In time, people took to greasing their wigs before they were powdered in order to make the powder stick. Wigs were most often powdered white or gray, but there were some colored powders—blue, violet, pink, and yellow being the most frequently used.

By 1760, there was a move to dispense with wigs on men. The destitute wig makers in England marched on St. James to protest this vulgar return to natural hair. For another thirty years, wigs remained relatively fashionable, but they went out of fashion completely as a result of the French Revolution and the association of wigs with the aristocracy.

Altogether, wigs were fashionable for nearly a century and a half. Clergymen, doctors, and lawyers, who considered the wig a badge of their professional importance, continued to wear wigs into the early nineteenth century. Certain members of the English judiciary adopted stylized wigs which are still worn today. Footmen and liveried servants continued to wear wigs as part of their total costumes for much of the 1800s.

Americans never took to wearing wigs as wholeheartedly as the French or English. Southern planters adopted them and so did fashionable Boston; but as the country began to spread westward, wigs were largely abandoned. At the time of the American Revolution, most revolutionists refused to wear wigs altogether, or they wore ones which were not powdered made from naturally colored hair. A man who wore an elaborately powdered wig was immediately associated with royalist feelings. A good many wigs were actually being produced in America, however. In 1769, the small town of Williamsburg, capitol of the colony of Virginia, had eight busy wig making establishments.

Fortunately for the English and French wig makers who fell on hard times when men stopped wearing wigs, in the late eighteenth century, women began to construct hairstyles that required a quantity of false hair. In the 1770s, some ladies sported coiffures that rose more than two feet off the top of the head. These outlandish styles persisted for more than ten years and grew to immense proportions; riding in closed carriages became difficult, as did coming through doorways. In 1774, it was reported that the Duchess of Chartres appeared in a towering coiffure that framed a domestic scene. There was a small figure of a woman seated in an armchair, holding a nursing child; at her right was a parrot pecking at a cherry and on her left a little Negro. Throughout the coiffure, locks of hair from all of Madame de Chartres' relatives were interwoven.

Such fantastic hairstyles were based on an underframe of wool and horsehair over which the lady's own hair, as well as quantities of false hairpieces, were arranged. Along with the small sculpted figures, ornamentation included all manner of vegetables, fruits, feathers, and containers of flowers. Sometimes, fresh flowers were placed in vases which had been attached to the hair and in which fresh water could be kept.

Other than in plays set in specific wig periods, certain other scripts may demand wigs of various kinds. Some of these will be frankly wigs; others will be wigs fitted, set, and dressed to appear as real hair. In Jean Anouilh's *The Rehearsal,* the contemporary characters are wearing eighteenth-century costumes in order to perform a play. A wig of the period is worn for a time and then discarded. Hairstyles of the Gibson girl period are usually achieved with wigs since they are so difficult for the actress to maintain. Some plays call for specialty wigs, such as a monk's fringe and bald pate. The need may also arise for a frankly fake wig, such as the one worn by Thisbe in *Midsummer Night's Dream.*

BUYING, RENTING, AND MAKING WIGS

Bob Kelly Wig Creations in New York City is the largest American supplier of wigs for the stage. All of Bob Kelly's wigs are made from real hair, as are most of those produced by the other theatrical wig suppliers. You may either rent or purchase wigs from Bob Kelly, whereas Alfred Barris, another fine theatrical wig maker in New York, does not rent wigs at all and builds to order each wig he sells. A rented wig may be the right solution for a production that runs for only a few performances; but if the play is presented more than eight or ten times, it may be more economical to purchase the wig, which can then be put into your own stock and used again. Wigs that are purchased for a specific production will come to you already styled. The style is not permanent, however, and a well-made, real hair wig can be restyled, trimmed, and even colored several times during its life.

The basic cost of a wig depends on whether the wig maker already has a suitable wig in stock or must make the wig up especially for your production. In the made-to-order wig, price is determined by the length and color of the hair (a long hair wig is more expensive than a short hair wig; white hair is more costly than black hair), how much of the wig can be machine-stitched and how much must be hand-tied, and whether or not the front of the wig must be tied into fine wig lace. Specialty wigs, such as bald pates with a fringe of hair, tend to be expensive.

For a realistic look, wigs that are to be styled off the forehead, such as the Gibson girl pompadour, must have hand-tied fronts set on wig lace. When the actor puts on the

FIGURE 8.29   *Regina David and Robert Burr in* Long Day's Journey Into Night *at the Milwaukee Repertory Theater. Back view of the wig in Figure 8.28. (Susan Tsu, costume designer; photograph by Mark Avery.)*

FIGURE 8.28   *Regina David and Rose Pickering in* Long Day's Journey Into Night *at the Milwaukee Repertory Theater. Ms. David is wearing a wig with a hand-tied lace front. (Susan Tsu, costume designer; photograph by Mark Avery.)*

wig, the wig lace is glued down to the forehead with spirit gum and make-up is applied on top. If make-up is skillfully applied, the wig lace is quite invisible, even in a small, intimate theatre. A wig that has a fringe of hair hanging over the forehead to cover the hairline need not have a hand-tied front and may be much less expensive.

Some costume supply companies sell period wigs that have already been styled. Most of these are made with synthetic hair. They are less expensive than real hair wigs, but they cannot be restyled. Some are difficult to clean properly. Wool wigs with side curls and queues, suitable for liveried servants and certain eighteenth and nineteenth century comic characters, can be purchased quite cheaply in a variety of colors. Although wool wigs cannot be washed, they dry clean beautifully.

Costume shops often construct frankly fake and stylized wigs from a wide variety of materials: yarn, fur, string, wood shavings, steel wool, and so forth. Real hair wigs, on the other hand, are not often attempted. Wig making is a tedious and time-consuming task,

FIGURE 8.30 *Leslie Gerasi and Rob Lanchester in* The Rehearsal *at the Milwaukee Repertory Theater. Ms. Gerasi is wearing a wig with a forehead fringe and no lace front. (Elizabeth Covey, costume designer; photograph courtesy of the Milwaukee Repertory Theater.)*

requiring specific skills and a high degree of manual dexterity. For those who would like to try their hands at wig making, Richard Corson's *Stage Makeup* includes excellent instructions which are well illustrated and easy to follow.

Measuring for a Wig

When you order a wig from a wig maker, you must send correct measurements so the wig foundation will fit the actor for which it was intended. Necessary measurements may include any or all of the following:

1. Around the head (head circumference)
2. Front hairline to nape of neck (or poll)
3. Ear to ear over the top of the head
4. Temple to temple around the back of the head
5. Temple to temple across the forehead
6. Hairline circumference

Preparing a plastic wrap cap on the actor's head is a very precise way of conveying a head size to a wig maker. The method seems to have been originated by Bob Kelly.

Have thin plastic wrap, Scotch Magic tape, and two indelible markers, in different colors, on hand. Place the actor in a comfortable chair while the cap is being made. If the hair is long, pin it up as close to the head as possible. Cover the actor's head with a layer of plastic wrap, overlapping pieces as necessary. Make sure all the hair is completely covered and that the plastic wrap extends well below the hairline. *Crisscross* the entire head with Scotch Magic tape, covering it entirely and molding the plastic wrap firmly to the head. Place strips of tape all around the hairline. With one color marker, draw around the actor's own hairline and use the other color to mark the hairline that is required on the wig. Remove the cap from the actor, trim away excess plastic wrap, put it in a manila envelope and send it to the wig maker along with a drawing and descriptions of the wig and a sample of the actor's hair, if the wig is to match his or her own hair color.

Styling Wigs

Put the wig on a wig block and set the block on a wig stand. A stand that can be clamped to a table is the sturdiest and most convenient. Pin the wig to the block with T-pins but *do not* put T-pins into fine wig lace. The wig can now be tilted and rotated so you can work on it from every angle. Brush the wig with a wire or a nylon brush and comb with a wide-toothed comb. Always comb down, which is the direction in which the hair has been tied. Work out tangles gently without tugging at the hairs. Use water in a spray bottle to dampen the hair and set, depending on the look and the tightness of curl desired, in pincurls or on rollers. If time permits, let the wig dry naturally; otherwise, use a hair dryer set on a moderate setting. Comb the hair into the appropriate style, using hairpins, bobby pins, barrettes, or other trimmings, and spray lightly with a water-soluble hair spray, preferably one with a lanolin base.

Use a curling iron only to touch up a wig style, never for setting. Prolonged application of a curling iron can permanently damage a wig. Electric rollers are suitable for quick wig setting, but they should not be overused because they have a drying effect on the hair.

How to Put on a Wig

Prepare the actor's own hair for the wig by securing it to the head in one of several ways. If the hair is short, a headband may be sufficient to hold it off the forehead. Medium-length hair may be arranged in large pin curls secured with bobby pins. Always pin the bobby pins downward so they will not snag the wig. Wind long hair around the head and secure with pins. Some wigs will rest more securely if the actor's own hair is covered by a wig cap. Make a wig cap from the top of a stocking from which the lower leg and foot have been cut; stitch or knot the top closed. An ace bandage wound around the head also makes an excellent wig cap. Sometimes it is helpful to stitch a strip of Velcro, the hook side down, to the inside of the wig foundation; the Velcro will grasp the hair or the wig cap and prevent the wig from slipping.

To put on a full wig, grasp the lower back edge of the wig foundation with both hands. Slide the wig over the forehead, leaving the hairline low on the forehead, and pull down snugly. With both hands on top of the wig, move it back until the hairline is in the correct place. Secure the wig to the hair or wig cap with large bobby pins through the wig foundation. Do not put bobby pins through the wig lace.

Take off the wig by grasping it in the same place and pulling it up and over the head. *Never* pull the wig off by tugging at the wig lace and *never* pull it off by the hair. Make sure that the spirit gum holding the wig lace is softened and that all bobby pins securing the wig to the head are removed before taking off the wig.

Washing Wigs

Ideally, real hair wigs should be cleaned with a dry cleaning solution such as carbon tetra-chloride or naphtha. These solutions are flammable and must be used with care. A very mild detergent shampoo and warm water solution will also work, although it will not dissolve make-up that has collected around the edges of the wig. After cleaning a wig in detergent, soak cotton balls in dry cleaning fluid and use them to remove make-up from the edges of the wig foundation.

Wigs can be cleaned on or off the wig block. In either case, swirl the wig around, hair down, in a ceramic or enamelware bowl containing about two inches of the cleaning solution. *Do not* scrub or rub the hair or do anything to cause tangles. Lay the wig on a clean towel and blot gently. If the wig has been cleaned off the block, pin it on the block to dry. Once the wig is dry, apply a good wig conditioner to the hair. Use wig conditioner every time the wig is cleaned. Any traces of spirit gum that remain on the wig lace should be removed with acetone before the wig is cleaned.

Wash synthetic wigs in detergent, pure soap, or in a special synthetic wig wash. Use lukewarm water. Rinse synthetic wigs in fabric softener to combat static electricity. A synthetic wig does not need to be put on a block to dry. For quick drying, put the synthetic wig in a net bag and put it in an automatic dryer on the air fluff setting.

Use very little, if any, hair spray on synthetic wigs. Warm water is necessary to remove hair spray and warm water can damage a synthetic wig set. If the synthetic wig has been sprayed, brush it well with a wire brush before washing.

FACE HAIR

Beards and mustaches made from crepe hair are quite suitable for short-run productions, but long runs require real hairpieces that have been tied into lace. Refer to Corson's *Stage Makeup* for methods of making face hairpieces. Both beards and mustaches may be purchased in a wide variety of styles and colors from theatrical supply houses. They can also be made to order by a theatrical wig maker.

Be sure that actors know and use the proper procedures for putting on a lace foundation beard or mustache. Place the hairpiece on the face to see exactly where it should go. Then put a thin coat of spirit gum on the dry, clean skin, on which there is no make-up. Never apply spirit gum to the lace, and never use latex instead of spirit gum. Allow the spirit gum to become tacky, which takes only a few minutes. Press the lace into the spirit gum with a clean towel. Press straight into the face; do not allow the lace to slide. Use a clean section of the towel for each press. When the spirit gum no longer appears shiny and the towel comes away without sticking, pat a damp cloth over the area. Use a toothbrush, or an eyebrow brush, to lift up any hairs that have been stuck down by the spirit gum.

A full beard may be glued down only by the wig lace around the edges, while a small piece may have to be completely glued down.

Always remove the face hairpiece with spirit gum remover. Apply remover directly to the areas that are glued down in order to soften the spirit gum. Pulling the hairpiece away from the face without using spirit gum

FIGURE 8.31 *Durward McDonald and Bruce Sommerville in* Volpone *at the Milwaukee Repertory Theater. Mr. McDonald is wearing a hand-tied beard on a lace foundation. (Linda Fisher, costume designer; photograph by Jack Hamilton.)*

remover may well damage the piece and irritate the face.

Clean all face hairpieces regularly with acetone to remove caked-on spirit gum. Put the lace foundation in the acetone and allow it to soak until the spirit gum loosens. A soft toothbrush may be used to remove all traces of spirit gum.

9

Costume Accessories

Tasteful costume accessories which are suitable to the period and the style of the play and to the age and station of the characters for whom they are built or chosen are as important to the success of overall production design as fabric choice and well-cut garments. Fine costume accessories contribute texture to the play's action and characterization. Removing a glove, twirling a parasol, brandishing a sword, or rummaging in a purse can all be important bits of stage business. Some occupations are revealed immediately by the presence of a belt, an apron, or a badge of office. Character traits can be indicated by the condition of a cravat or the presence of a pair of oversized sunglasses worn propped on top of the head.

Period stage costume accessories convey controlled historical effect; they are almost never reproductions of museum pieces. Costumers must be able to distill the essence of a period in a single accessory after researching the social, political, religious, and economic pressures that affected the wearing of the item in its own time.

Translating the dramatic essence of an earlier time through the perceptions of a modern audience also requires a keen awareness of today's fashion pressures. Certain modes of dress may be too alien for today's audience to accept; others, although historically accurate, may look so much like a current fad that they fail to convey the intended period look. It is the final effect of the whole set of stage costumes that is important and every detail contributes to that effect: rings, fans, purses, belts, and all the rest. Nothing can destroy the effect more quickly than an accessory that looks wrong, even if it can be proven to be right.

Because a costume accessory carries so many nuances of meaning from the stage to the audience, it is desirable to invite the actor who will be wearing or carrying the accessory

FIGURE 9.1 *Actors in costume with accessories in the Milwaukee Repertory Theater production of* Ah, Wilderness! *(Susan Tsu, costume designer; Photograph by Mark Avery.)*

to participate in its selection. When this is not practical—if, for instance, designs must be complete before the production is cast—the actor and the designer should have ample opportunity to discuss the significance of the accessory and the manner in which it is meant to be used or worn. The designer should be able, when necessary, to give the actor research materials which will describe the handling of certain period accessories. When costuming modern plays, it is often a good idea to wait until the play has been in rehearsal for a while before making final decisions on purchased or found accessories. In some instances, the director and the actor will want to try out several choices before adopting a specific piece.

Practical staging considerations affect costume accessory choice. Is there a suitable spot for the actor to hang his or her hat, cane, or parasol? Will the open parasol fit through the arch that leads into the garden scene? Is the sword suspended in such a way from the gentleman's belt that it will not ensnare the lady's skirt when he passes her? Close cooperation between designer, actor, director, and technician is always necessary in order to produce a handsomely attired production in which each element functions as it should.

ACCESSORY OR PROP?

Costume accessory and costume property are terms that are often used interchangeably.

In most theatre organizations, the responsibility for acquiring or building certain accessory items rests with the costume shop, while others are prepared by the prop shop. Canes, swords, and fans often "belong" to the prop shop, while parasols and purses are provided by the costume shop. Such arbitrary divisions pertain only to individual producing groups; in the long run, it makes little difference who is responsible for which accessory as long as the entire staff is striving for a uniform style.

The costume accessories and costume props discussed in this chapter and Chapter 11 have been arbitrarily divided according to how they are found or produced. This chapter includes items that are normally found in shops (purses, watches, eyeglasses, fans, gloves) and ones that are produced in the sewing room (shawls, parasols, simple belts). Those that require specialized, craft-related building techniques (masks, armor, and costume jewelry) are grouped together in Chapter 11. Accessories that pertain specifically to men's formal wear will be discussed in Chapter 10.

BELTS AND GIRDLES

Belts were used in ancient times, for reasons both fashionable and practical, to bind flowing, shapeless garments to the body. Greek women girdled their tunics in order to achieve a graceful line and to emphasize the body's shape. Leaving off the girdle was a significant part of the mourning ritual. In *The Iliad,* Hector speaks of "the Trojan women with trailing garments" who are weeping for their dead husbands. Greek men seldom

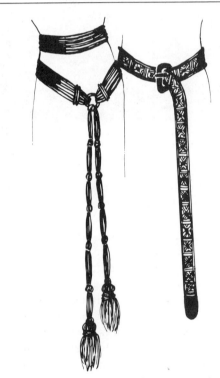

FIGURE 9.3   *Twelfth- and thirteenth-century women's girdles.*

FIGURE 9.2   *Egyptian loincloth.*

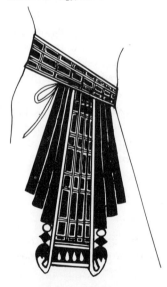

belted their tunics except when in battle. Egyptian upper classes, both men and women, wore elaborate belts that were richly decorated. One distinctive male style was a wide girdle with an apron-like flap in front. Peasants and slaves throughout the ancient world probably bound their garments with thongs in order to keep them out of the way of their work.

In the twelfth and thirteenth centuries, clothes were shaped to the body. Women wore beautiful girdles that hung well below the waist, emphasizing the curve of the hips, with one or both ends of the girdle hanging down in front, in some cases to the bottom of the garment. These belts were made of knotted cords, richly woven fabrics, or squares of gold strung together with links or fastened to a fabric backing for flexibility. Men wore stiff leather belts, sometimes around the hips and sometimes around the waist. Besides being decorative, these belts were used for supporting daggers and, later on, for suspending swords. Sword belts were important to the masculine look for many centuries.

FIGURE 9.4 *Eighteenth-century woman's sash.*

Once women's clothing took on more elaborate shapes, belts lost some of their importance and, except for a short period of popularity for the sash in the late 1700s, did not reappear as a major fashion accessory until the arrival of the shirtwaist in the 1890s. In the twentieth century, women have worn belts with fashion garments whenever the silhouette emphasized the waist. Practical belts continue to be an important accessory for sports clothes.

Sword and Dagger Belts

Throughout the several hundred years during which men commonly displayed weapons, many different types of rigging developed, depending on the shape and weight of the sword and on the fashion that prevailed concerning its wearing. Although there is excellent reference material available for researching the type of weapon common to a specific period, it is often difficult to obtain instructions on how the swords were actually suspended from the belt. In portraits of sword-wearing gentlemen, the rigging is often concealed by a cloak or a sash, or the figure is posed in such a way that the means of suspension are out of sight.

Because it is short, a dagger poses no specific problems. Sometimes daggers are merely tucked into the belt next to the clothing. At other times, a plain leather sheath, or one that is decorated with gold, silver, and jewels, is slipped onto the belt and the dagger placed inside. A modern hunting knife sheath can often be adapted for a period costume.

FIGURE 9.5 *Rigging for broadsword.*

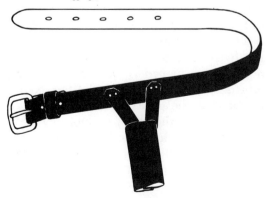

Suspending swords is more difficult. A broadsword, sheathed or unsheathed, should hang relatively straight down at the actor's side. The principal problem costume technicians encounter is that of keeping the sword in place so it does not swing in front of or in back of the actor's legs. Figure 9.5 illustrates a stout rigging for a broadsword. The leather straps supporting the sword should be firm and not too narrow. If the broadsword exhibits a tendency to swing either backward or forward, move these straps wider apart on the belt. In order to hang properly, a stage broadsword must be moderately heavy and well balanced. Some methods of constructing broadswords will be discussed in Chapter 11.

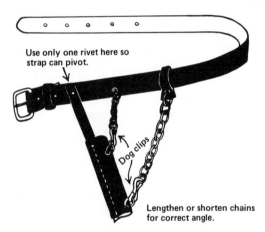

Use only one rivet here so strap can pivot.

Dog clips

Lengthen or shorten chains for correct angle.

FIGURE 9.6   *Rigging for foil.*

Figure 9.6 illustrates one way of rigging a foil. Maintaining the correct angle for the foil is often the biggest problem. This angle will usually have to be adjusted so the foil will not catch on draperies, on furniture, or on other actors. Note the portion of the rigging that controls the angle of the hang. This may be made of a leather strap, a thong, or a piece of chain, and it should be kept as adjustable as possible so changes can be made during rehearsal.

Ceremonial swords, scimitars, and other special weaponry are usually rented for stage productions and should be accompanied by belts and rigging.

Belts with Hanging Objects

Before pockets were applied to clothes, both men and women hung various personal objects from their belts. This custom is frequently represented on stage, often for highly comic effects. A lady's maid may appear with

FIGURE 9.7   *Actor Montgomery Davis wearing sash and belt with hanging objects in a production of* Volpone *at the Milwaukee Repertory Theater. (Linda Fisher, costume designer; photograph by Jack Hamilton.)*

a whole arsenal of equipment for repairing her mistress's appearance hanging down the front of her costume: a brush, a box of powder, a powder puff, scissors, sewing thread, a pincushion, a bodkin, a bottle of scent, a mirror, and so on. Choose these items with care, making certain that none of them can injure the maid or hurt an errant servingman who might chance to give her a buss on the cheek. Scissors should be the blunt, children's model, purchased from a dime store and sprayed gold. The bodkin should not be sharp, and neither the bottle of scent nor the mirror should actually be made of glass. Fasten the objects securely to the belt. Grommets may be put into the belt and the objects tied on with a thong or a decorative cord. Heavy objects may be suspended on a strap and pop-riveted to the belt. Stagger the lengths of the objects and they will be less likely to become entangled. If the objects are too light in weight to hang properly, conceal fishing weights or pieces of hardware in them.

Sashes

Sashes were particularly popular with both men and women in the middle and late 1600s. Throughout the sword-carrying centuries, men often wore sashes under, and sometimes over, their sword belts. Sashes are frequently seen as part of military uniforms or ceremonial outfits. Confederate officers in the War Between the States were particularly fond of sashes; often these were hand-embroidered and fringed by their ladies.

Stage sashes should always be pre-fixed—that is, the knot and hanging ends should be arranged and permanently stitched to the sash, which is then invisibly fastened with hooks and eyes or snaps. Actors should not be asked to tie and arrange a sash for each performance unless it is part of the action on stage. A pre-fixed sash will always look as it was meant to look and will never come untied.

Constructing Belts

Simple belts to match or contrast with costumes can be made by covering a strip of belting with costume fabric. Belting comes in an assortment of widths and weights. If the covering fabric is thin, back it with muslin. Construct a tube of the covering fabric just wide enough to contain the belting snugly. Slip the belting inside the tube so that the seam falls along the center of what will be the wrong side of the belt. Press the covered belt and top-stitch along each edge.

Light-weight metal buckles with instructions on how to cover them with fabric can be purchased in most places that sell sewing notions. Most shops find it handy to keep an assortment of these buckle kits on hand. Follow the directions carefully and always use a light-weight firm backing, such as organdy, if the cover fabric is sheer.

Any buckle that is the correct width for the belt can be taken from one belt and attached to another. Whenever belts wear out, save the buckles for another use. When you are using a slide buckle, one without a prong, you will probably want to secure the end of the belt with a hidden snap. Create holes for a prong buckle with eyelets or small grommets, or by reinforcing the holes with a firm blanket stitch. Clasp buckles are particularly handsome and are suitable for many types of costume. A part of the clasp is fastened to each end of the belt, one part joining to the other to close the belt. Clasp buckles

FIGURE 9.8   *Making a fabric-covered belt.*

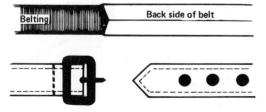

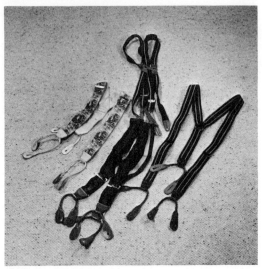

FIGURE 9.9   *Assorted suspenders. (Photograph by Richard Bryant.)*

sers with both belt loops and suspender buttons. Nowadays, the regular wearing of suspenders is rare, although not unknown, and most men prefer belts.

Suspenders are often worn on stage. Tights, breeches, pantaloons, and trousers are all more secure when they are held up by suspenders. Such suspenders are worn for practical purposes only and remain hidden beneath the costume. Wide, elastic, button-on suspenders are preferable. Sew suspender buttons to the inside of the waistband: two sets of two buttons on either side of the center front, about four inches apart, and one on either side of the center back, about five inches apart. Wide elastic may be used instead of ready-made suspenders and stitched directly to the waistband. Dancers will usually want their elastic suspenders stitched in place, and they will want them drawn very tight. Never use clip suspenders on stage if you can possibly avoid it. They are simply not secure enough to do the job. Dancers often use adjustable webbing belts, purchased from an Army Surplus store, to hold up their tights. Once the belt is in place, the tights are then pulled up and rolled over, concealing the belt and securing the tights.

were popular during the 1930s, and a collection of these buckles is nice to have.

Belts or Suspenders

Men generally began to wear leather belts to hold up their trousers in the 1890s. Older men and those with portly figures, however, continued to prefer suspenders. Up until World War I, tailors often constructed trou-

SHIRT COLLARS AND NECKWEAR

The Ruff

The shirt was developed first as an undergarment to provide a soft layer next to the skin. For a long time, it was completely concealed beneath the doublet. About 1530, little ruffles began to appear at the neck. These little ruffles, which were attached to the shirt, caught on and inexorably developed into one of the most remarkable of all fashion foibles, the ruff—certainly the most unique collar ever conceived. The ruff reigned for a bit less than a hundred years.

The earliest ruffs were made out of

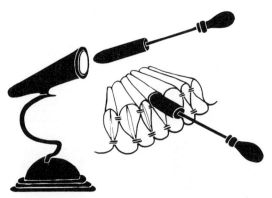

FIGURE 9.10   *Poking stick for ruffs.*

starched linen or cambric. Laundering and starching both the lady's and the gentleman's ruff—for the ruff was a unisex style—were specialized and complex tasks. The starch itself had to be boiled and strained before the scrubbed ruff could be immersed in it. Then the wet ruff was arranged on the setting stick, which was made of bone or wood, to form the pleats or flutes. Wooden sticks were inserted to hold the pleats apart and a heated iron rod used for the finishing touches.

The Christian Church, horrified to see so much human labor going into a secular task, branded starch the "devil's liquid" and condemned the ruff as wicked and sinful. But the fashion persisted. Henry II of France, a particularly meticulous dresser, scandalized his court by applying the ironing rod to his own ruffs personally rather than trusting this important final operation to a servant. Queen

FIGURE 9.12   *Standing ruff.*

Elizabeth was fond of enormous lace ruffs embroidered with gold and silver threads.

The ruff was accepted in every part of the Western world, a fact that actors, who seldom

FIGURE 9.11   *Shirin Devrim Trainer in a large ruff. The Milwaukee Repertory Theater production of* Volpone. *(Linda Fisher, costume designer; photograph by Jack Hamilton.)*

FIGURE 9.13   *Early seventeenth-century falling ruff.*

FIGURE 9.14   *Falling band (Cavalier) collar with band strings.*

enjoy wearing them, have difficulty understanding. Besides producing an unparalleled frame for the human head, the ruff can be one of the most imposing of all accessories.

FIGURE 9.15   *Puritan collar.*

The construction of cartridge-pleated ruffs for the stage was discussed in Chapter 4. This method is not relevant to the later form, the standing ruff. This was a large, fanned-out, stand-up collar that framed the head but did not meet in front. A standing ruff is usually constructed of several gores and is stiffened

FIGURE 9.16   *Preacher's tabs.*

with buckram, cape netting, or Miracle Cloth. (Buckram is the least satisfactory of these materials, since it wilts when wet.) The outer

edge is sometimes wired. A very large or very heavy standing ruff may require narrow solid metal or spiral stays up the seams. For a final touch, paint the finished standing ruff with a coat of the plastic solution which is used to seal fabric window shades. The trick is to produce a ruff that appears to be delicate and airy but is so well supported that it absolutely will not fall.

The Falling Band Collar

The ruff did fall by stages and, in the middle of the seventeenth century, became the falling band collar. This collar was sometimes attached to the shirt and sometimes not. On the stage, the falling band collar is nearly always detachable from the shirt so that collar and shirt can be laundered separately. The band part of the collar lies against the neck, inside the standing band on the doublet, and the collar itself falls out from the top of the doublet stand, creating a sloped line from the top of collar to the shoulder.

Early falling band collars were ruffled and soft; then they became flat. The Cavalier collar spread all the way to the shoulders on each side and was relatively short in the front. The Puritan collar was more like a stiff, white bib. The bib became smaller with time and finally developed into the small preacher's tabs that persisted as part of Protestant ecclesiastical dress well into the nineteenth century.

Band and Stand Collars

It was the growing popularity of wigs in the late seventeenth and early eighteenth centuries that spelled the demise of large collars. The long, elaborately dressed hair covered and hid most of the neck and shoulders; collar and neckwear styles altered to suit the wig. For some time, collars themselves were unimportant, being completely covered by stock and cravats. Shirts were gathered into collar-bands and, in some portraits, these bands are unseen. Soon, however, the collar arose again, high enough to turn down over the stock or cravat. By the end of the eighteenth century, most shirt collars were quite steep and the collar points stood high on the cheeks. Wigs had disappeared; and once again, collar and neckwear were very important parts of a man's costume.

The high standing collars of the early 1800s became fairly low in the middle of the century, only to rise again to new heights until, by 1896, some were fully three inches high. In 1825, the collar became independent of the shirt and was attached to a narrow neckband with studs. Throughout the century, the collar stood straight up, was folded over, or had its points turned down, according to the prevailing fashion mode or to personal preference. The most fashionable of men wore the stiffest collars; men less concerned

FIGURE 9.17 *Assorted collars. (Photograph by Richard Bryant.)*

with such things tended to wear softer ones.

The wing collar, as we recognize it today, with points expressly designed to be turned down, was introduced in 1860 for formal wear. The stand and fall collar was popular at the end of the century, usually with a very high stand and a fall that almost met in front. Both parts were quite stiff.

Modern shirt collars lie close to the neck on a low stand. Style changes are reflected chiefly in the spread and length of the points. Rounded and button-down points have been important variations. Today's casual approach to dress allows men to wear open collars and turtlenecks for all but the most formal occasions.

Choosing the Correct Collar

Doriece Colle's *Collars . . . Stocks . . . Cravats,* published by Rodale Press in 1972, is a good source of collar styles between 1655 and 1900. The drawings are taken from paintings and photographs and amply illustrate the multiplicity of styles popular during these years.

The particular collars and types of neckwear worn by men in the nineteenth and early twentieth centuries are absolutely related to social and economic class. These differences must be taken into consideration when they are being chosen for a stage costume. No working man of the nineteenth century could do his job in the stiff, restricting collars worn by the gentry. Few working men could afford the niceties of neckwear, or the time spent in their maintenance and arrangement, that constituted a fashionable pleasure for the leisure class.

The choice of collars and ties that must be made for Tarleton and Gunner in Bernard Shaw's play, *Misalliance,* is an interesting example of the extent to which class distinction affects clothing and accessories. Tarleton is a successful businessman and a powerful individual whose clothing must reflect his position in life. Gunner is a miserable, underpaid clerk who makes disparaging remarks about his cheap suit; it goes without saying that his collar and necktie must be similarly shoddy and unfashionable.

To discover what was actually worn by farmers and working class folk in any period before photography was commonplace is a real test of the research tenacity and the imagination of stage costumers. Most costume history books dwell on the fashionable modes; but it must always be remembered that these were worn by the few: It always takes a great deal of digging to find out what was worn by the many.

Making or Finding the Correct Collar

Any of the high standing or stand and fall collars from the nineteenth and early twentieth centuries can be made without a great deal of difficulty. The problem is to impregnate them with enough starch to keep them properly stiff throughout a performance. A collar treated with any spray starch or sizing will wilt as soon as the actor begins to perspire. Even though it is troublesome, use a boiled starch. Iron the wet, starched collar between two pieces of soft cotton material in order to avoid scorching. Never make collars that are to be starched out of a cotton and polyester blend fabric; the polyester fibers will not hold the starch properly. A heavy-weight handkerchief linen, backed with muslin, is excellent for collars.

Old collars often turn up at rummage sales and in secondhand clothing stores. Buy them and keep them for future stage use. A manufactured collar is much stiffer than anything you can make in the shop.

Disposable, linen-finish paper collars can be purchased from Gibson Collars, 35 Congress Street, Salem, Massachusetts 01970. Gibson supplies a great many theatres all over the country with handsome collars in a variety of styles. They also sell collar studs, collar bands, and collar band shirts. In most cases, a Gibson collar can be worn for several performances. They are not expensive.

Stocks, Cravats, and Neckties

The bandstrings used to secure the falling band collar at its center closing were the fore-

FIGURE 9.18   *Actor Austin Pendleton wearing eighteenth-century cravat. Cincinnati Playhouse in the Park. (Susan Tsu, costume designer; photograph by Sandy Underwood.)*

runners of the necktie. At first these strings were entirely practical and were often hidden from view. Later they became decorative, were made from colored ribbons, and had tasseled ends. Around 1660, it became fashionable to wear a scarf or piece of cloth around the neck. This form of neckwear is said to have been borrowed by the French from a regiment of Croatians who visited Paris in 1636. The scarf became quite popular and developed into both the stock and the cravat.

Stocks and cravats serve essentially the same purpose: They circle the neck on top of the collar stand. They may provide for some ornamentation at the neck front, which may or may not extend down onto the chest. The stock fastens in the back and the cravat ties in the front. This distinction, however, became quite blurred in the nineteenth century, when it was possible to purchase a ready-made-up cravat which, like the stock, fastened in the back.

FIGURE 9.19 *Late eighteenth-century cravat tied in bow showing shirt ruffles below.*

Until 1815, the stock was pleated or folded. It often had a bow or a knot stitched to the front and was accompanied by a shirt frill or jabot. In the late eighteenth century, the stiff stock began to appear, often achieving

FIGURE 9.20 *Eighteenth-century stock with shirt ruffles below.*

its look with whalebone stays or pig bristles. All styles generally fastened with buckles and straps.

Stocks are the most characteristic kind of neckwear from the eighteenth century and cravats from the nineteenth century, although undoubtedly both styles were worn in both centuries. The stock came to be the more conservative of the two. Most stocks were white, although some black ones were worn.

Webster defines cravat as a "wrapped neckcloth with ends knotted or tied. The term was known as early as 1636." Those early cravats were made of soft cotton and linen and liberally trimmed with lace. Louis XIV wore cravats made entirely of lace, which helped to encourage the development of the lace industry in France. In those days, cravats depended on a profusion of lace rather than the complexity of arrangement which became so important in the early nineteenth century.

FIGURE 9.21 *Early nineteenth-century black full-dress stiffened stock.*

The folded, wrapped cravat first appeared in the 1790s. It was a large piece of fine white cloth, folded diagonally, wrapped at least twice around the neck and tied in front, sometimes with a bow and sometimes with a knot. The knot was favored in France and the bow in both Britain and America. Occasionally, a black cravat was worn on top of the white one.

The name of Beau Brummell, who was the sole arbiter of men's fashions in England in the early nineteenth century, is often associated with perfection in arranging the cravat. In 1828, a pamphlet was published by an H. LeBlanc, describing thirty-two different arrangements into which the cravat might be tied. H. LeBlanc is generally considered to have been a pseudonym for Honore de Balzac, and the pamphlet is thought to have satiric overtones. The matter of correct cravat arrangement, however, was a serious one indeed among fashionable men who had the leisure to be concerned about such things. Other men turned to the more vulgar practice of purchasing pretied cravats, even those made up in colored silks, which helped to disguise the lack of artful arrangement.

Small bow ties for formal occasions and skinny cravats that only went around the neck once and were tied with four-in-hand or Windsor knots began to appear in the late nineteenth century as suitable accessories for wing and stand and fall collars. No doubt all men had become weary with having to pay so much attention to their elaborate neckwear. Certainly the rising middle class, eager to improve its social and economic lot, was much too busy getting ahead to devote an hour or two each morning to the correct arrangement of a cravat.

The term necktie became popular late in the nineteenth century, correctly describing the modern approach to neck adornment. The refinements of the cravat were left behind.

Neckties in the twentieth century have varied little except in width, size of knot, and color. Bow ties and knotted ties alternate in popularity, with neither style ever going completely out of fashion. Compared with the elegant, starched, white cravats of the early nineteenth century, however, these colorful strips of cloth, at some times the only bit of color allowed the darkly suited man, are hardly exciting and are certainly lacking in romance.

Neckwear for the Stage

Virtually all stage cravats are prearranged. Both stocks and cravats are constructed in the same manner, fastening in the back, ex-

Pass the wide end, on the right, over and under the narrow end, then over again. Bring the wide end up through the center and slip it through the loop in front. Tighten the knot by pulling the wide end down and pushing the knot up.

FIGURE 9.22 *Tying a four-in-hand.*

FIGURE 9.23 *Arranging an ascot.*

Start with both ends even and make a loop as shown to form a single knot. Pass the right end over and under the left end to make the second knot. Tighten the knot, then drape the left end over the right one and fasten with a stick pin.

Realism in the theatre has been responsible for a great many plays that require actors to tie their ties on stage. All actors should learn to tie a bow tie, a Windsor knot, and a four-in-hand knot, and to arrange an ascot. This is particularly important for actors at a time when men are not accustomed to wearing ties regularly and may not know how to tie the most ordinary knots. Figures 9.22–9.25 show how to tie these neckties.

When a contemporary necktie must be prearranged for a quick change, tie it on the actor and slit it at the center back. Remove about a half-inch from each edge and bind the edges off with a bit of tape. Add a piece of elastic to each bound end and fasten with hook and eyes. The elastic will ensure a close fit.

Start with the wide end on the right about 12" longer than the narrow end. Make a loop, then bring the wide end around and behind as shown. Pass the wide end over to the back, then bring it across the front, then under again. Finish by slipping the side end through the loop in front. Tighten the knot and shape carefully.
FIGURE 9.24 *Tying a Windsor knot.*

cept that the closing of the stock will be allowed to show, while the cravat closing may be concealed by an additional strip of cloth that extends over the closing and snaps beneath the bow or knot.

FIGURE 9.25 *Tying a bow tie.*
Start with the end crossed over to the right about 1½" longer than the other end. Make a loop as shown. Begin to form the bow with the shorter end and bring the longer end over it. Then push the long end through the knot to complete the bow. Even up the ends, tighten, and shape carefully.

FIGURE 9.26a *Neckwear with assorted accessories. (Photograph by Richard Bryant.)*

Collar Pins, Tie Clasps, and Tie Tacks

Before the beginning of the twentieth century, cravats and ascots were often decorated with stickpins. These ranged from simple gold pins to pins that were decorated with precious stones. Sometimes these pins were

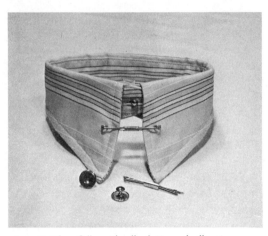

FIGURE 9.26b   *Collar with collar button and collar pin.*
(Photograph by Richard Bryant.)

inserted through the cravat and into the shirt front, which helped to hold the neckwear in place. Sometimes they were merely ornamental.

Although collar buttons were necessary for holding collars in place, and these were often gold or gold and pearl, they did not show. The collar pin came into being when more and more men shifted from the high starched collar to the soft shirt collar early in the twentieth century. These pins held the points or the rounded edges of the collar in smooth alignment. In the late 1920s, the button-down collar made its appearance, although the plain collar, worn pinned, remained popular through the 1930s.

Tie clasps became an important item of male jewelry in the 1920s. In the 1930s, the most common decorative motif for tie clasps was sports. Tennis racquets, dogs, guns, horses, golf clubs, and sail boats all appeared on tie clasps. In the 1940s, tie clasps were bigger and bolder than ever: Some included a chain through which the tie was slipped.

As ties became narrower in the 1950s, tie clasps became shorter and smaller and the tie tack, which looked when in place much like the nineteenth century cravat pin, became popular. The tie tack has a sharp point which pierces both pieces of the tie and a clasp that secures it underneath. Tie tacks were decorated with stones, animal heads, copies of ancient coins, and so on. Like other items of jewelry in the age of mass production, they might either be costly or be priced for the working man.

EYEGLASSES

The need for a method of correcting vision problems has been with the human race at least as far back as records go. Supposedly, the Roman dramatist, Seneca, read his way through all the libraries of Rome using a globe full of water to magnify the texts. Legend has it that the Chinese employed reading lenses as early as 500 B.C. and, in A.D. 1275, Marco Polo reported that he observed many Chinese wearing glasses. In 1268, an English philosopher wrote about using "crystal or glass or other transparent substance" to correct vision problems; and, in 1289, an elderly Italian gentleman spoke of using "spectacles" in order to be able to read. The oldest known work of art portraying spectacles is a portrait painted in 1352.

At first the only lenses made were of a magnifying nature, suitable for correcting farsightedness, a vision problem associated with advancing age. Early in the sixteenth century, the shortsighted, generally younger folk, who could focus on objects close at hand, but for whom distant objects were blurred, could purchase concave lenses for the correction of their particular problem. The degree of correction achieved by all these early lenses was a hit or miss proposition, as it was not until the early 1700s that the grinding of eyeglass lenses was based on sound principles of light refraction.

The widespread use of eyeglasses parallels the availability of reading materials. As long as there were few books, very few people experienced the need for vision correction. After the invention of printing, in about 1440, there were more books to be read, more people became literate, and there was an enormous increase in the demand for spectacles. By the end of the fifteenth century, peddlers sold eyeglasses on the streets of European cities.

For over four hundred years, the wearers of eyeglasses struggled with the biggest problem associated with corrective lenses: how to keep them on. Most spectacles were merely perched on the nose, but some wearers experimented with leather straps tied either around the ears or around the entire head. Others wore a stabilizing piece over the top of the head, and still others tried clipping the spectacles onto their hats. It was not until 1727 that a London optician invented the "temple spectacle," eyeglasses held in place with stiff ear pieces. The frames and ear pieces were steel and the lenses round.

Benjamin Franklin had problems focusing at both close and distant ranges. Rather than contend with switching from one pair of spectacles to another in order to see properly, he invented the bifocal lens: the upper section for seeing distant objects and the lower for reading and writing. Modern optometry has given us the trifocal lens for even more subtle correction.

Perspective Glass, Quizzing Glass, and the Monocle

Many people who require glasses do not enjoy wearing them. Dorothy Parker's bit of doggerel—"Men seldom make passes at girls who wear glasses"—reflects a widespread attitude. Wearing eyeglasses has always been associated with plainness and with old age. In the seventeenth century, the young, fashion-conscious, shortsighted person adopted the perspective glass, a single lens for distance vision that was suspended from a cord or ribbon worn around the neck. The frames and handles were often highly ornate. Elegant poses were adopted for peering through the perspective glass. The farsighted continued to use spectacles for reading and close work, although, more often than not, in private.

In the eighteenth century, a single lens for the farsighted, called the quizzing glass, was much in demand. It had a lovely handle and could be put to elegant use at the card table. At some point, the handle was eliminated and the lens was inserted directly into the eye socket, becoming the monocle. The monocle was particularly popular during the 1820s, when it was worn by both men and women. After its popularity peaked, a certain group of British men remained devoted to the monocle, and it became associated with affectation of character, rather than with the correction of vision.

On stage, the monocle can provide the perfect final touch for an upper-class snob and even a moment of high comedy when it drops from the eye of a startled stuffed shirt. A cord or ribbon is attached to the monocle, and it is worn around the neck to prevent it from falling to the floor.

Lorgnette

The lorgnette developed out of the fad for telescopes and opera glasses in the early nineteenth century. It was a female style, a set of framed lenses, variously shaped, attached to a metal, tortoise shell, or mother-of-pearl handle. The lorgnette handle folded up so the article could be put into the purse when not in use. They became so fashionable during the 1830s that women with no vision problem whatsoever used them. There is a priggish and fussy quality about the lorgnette. One can imagine Lady Bracknell from

FIGURE 9.27 *Actor Robert Burr wearing pince-nez in the Milwaukee Repertory Theater production of* Long Day's Journey Into Night. *(Susan Tsu, costume designer; photograph by Mark Avery.)*

Wilde's *The Importance of Being Earnest* peering through a particularly elegant pair.

Pince-nez

The pince-nez became the first widely worn, truly middle-class style in eyeglasses. In shape it is not unlike the early spectacles that were worn before the invention to stiff ear pieces. Its name describes its manner of attaching to the face: a spring mechanism clamps onto the nose, holding the lenses before the eyes. The style appeared in the 1840s and was widely worn, particularly during the last quarter of the nineteenth century. Well into the twentieth century, the pince-nex remained popular with the farsighted who wore glasses only for reading and close handwork. Elderly stage characters would be much more apt to wear a pince-nez than young characters. One interesting style had a retractable chain that attached the lenses to a

small, decorative pin wore on the lady's dress.

Modern Glasses

Until the advent of plastics, eyeglasses were framed with metal. The ear pieces were thin and the frames gave limited protection to the lenses. Rimless styles, with ear and nose pieces attached directly to the lenses, have been intermittently popular. Plastic frames greatly increased the color possibilities and the varieties of frame shapes. Some modern frames are quite bizarre. Nowadays, even major fashion designers have turned their hand to creating frames for eyeglasses, and a Dior imprint is not unusual. As with all stage accessories, the most outlandish styles must be reserved for specific effects.

FIGURE 9.28 *Assorted twentieth-century eyeglasses. (Photograph by Richard Bryant.)*

Eyeglasses for the Stage

Eyeglasses are often used on stage. As in real life, stage eyeglasses serve both corrective and cosmetic functions. Playwrights sometimes create dramatic characters with faulty vision. In Harold Pinter's *The Birthday Party*, the character Stanley Webber is acutely shortsighted and, in the moments preceding his mental breakdown, his glasses are taken from him and broken. The nature of human

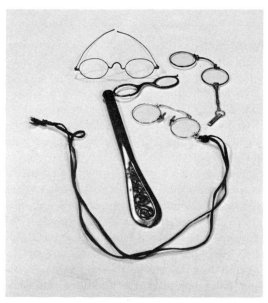

FIGURE 9.29   *Assorted period eyeglasses for the stage. (Photograph by Richard Bryant.)*

perception, central to this play, is succinctly symbolized in this ordinary costume accessory.

With or without specific textual demands, eyeglasses are often given to characters such as scholars, accountants, writers, or others whose ages and personalities seem to require them. Eyeglasses are used frequently on young actors who are playing older characters.

Eyeglasses must fit the historical period of the play, as well as the personality of the dramatic character who is wearing them. Richard Corson's *Fashions in Eyeglasses,* from which some of the historical information in this section was drawn, is an excellent source book for tracking down specific period eyeglass styles. Optical companies can provide a more limited historical perspective. The lens company, Bausch & Lomb, has created a series of illustrations showing eyeglasses down through the ages, with a brief accompanying text. Some opticians can make this series available to you.

Period eyeglasses are often donated to theatres from attic clean-ups and can be purchased from some antique shops. More contemporary frames are to be found in secondhand and thrift shops. An optical firm that has been in business for many years will often have a stock of old frames tucked away in a basement; these can often be bought inexpensively.

When a pair of glasses intended for stage use has prescription lenses, these lenses will have to be removed for the actor to be able to wear them comfortably. Wearing a prescription unsuited to one's own eyes can cause headache, nausea, and, sometimes, poor depth perception. On a proscenium stage that is some distance from the audience, sturdy frames can be worn without lenses. On most open stages, an empty frame will be annoyingly apparent, and plain window glass will have to be substituted for the ground prescription lenses. This must be done by an optician, and it can be fairly costly. Shop around and compare costs. You may be lucky enough to find an optician who will put plain glass into your frames in return for a prominent advertisement in the production program.

If you have a pair of rimless glasses with all the hardware intact—ear and nose pieces—a cooperative optician can make a set of rimless plain glass lenses and fit the hardware to them. Many interesting styles can be created in this way.

When actors are given glasses as one of their costume accessories, make sure they are also provided with a sturdy case in which the glasses can be placed when they are not being worn. When the glasses are put away at the end of the production, see that all traces of make-up are removed from the hinges. Use an old, soft toothbrush to scrub eyeglass frames. With proper care, glasses should have a long stage life.

Fans made their appearance in the ceremonial life of China and Japan before the tenth century B.C., and there has never been a time since when the fan has not been vital to the cultural life of the Orient. Oriental fan display is carried on by both men and women. The largest and the most beautiful fans belonged to the emperors. Fan display plays a significant role in traditional Chinese and Japanese theatre, and great skill is required to execute the subtly controlled symbolic gestures that convey the meaning of ancient stories.

Portuguese sailors brought fans from the Orient to the Western world in the early fifteenth century, introducing a fashion for women of wealth and leisure that persisted for three centuries. The first imported fans were stiff rather than folding. They were constructed of feathers or of fabric and paper stretched on a light-weight frame. The folding fan was brought to Paris in 1549 by Catherine de Medici, where it caught on quickly; it was much more graceful and offered many more possibilities for subtle gesture than the stiff fan.

Fan sticks, which form the frame of a folding fan, can be made of wood, ivory, ebony, and, more recently, plastic. They can be embossed with gold and encrusted with gems; they can be delicately carved or painted with exquisite miniature scenes. The two outer sticks, called the guards, are always thicker than the inner sticks and are often more fanciful.

The fan leaf, which is glued to the sticks, can be made of paper, vellum, kid, silk, or rayon. The découpé fan, made from paper, vellum, or kid, was especially popular from the sixteenth through the eighteenth centuries. Incredibly intricate designs were cut in the leaf with tiny scissors in order to effect the look of fine lace. The most beautiful eighteenth- and nineteenth-century fans were hand-painted, and, in the hands of certain artists, fan painting achieved the level of a fine art.

In fashionable eighteenth-century France, fan display reached an unparalleled peak of frivolousness. Beyond the normal styles, painted, banded in gold, and trimmed with jewels, specialty fans became quite popular. Some ladies had spectacles concealed in the construction of their fans so they could see the opera on stage without anyone knowing that they required visual assistance. The domino fan was a cleverly designed article that included two eyeholes as part of the overall leaf design, so the fan-holder could spy from behind her fan, undetected. The mask fan had a face painted directly on it, as unlike the face of the holder as possible, with eyeholes. Ladies holding such fans could conceal their identities completely.

The fan became the instrument through which a complex courting conversation could be carried on. This practice is said to have grown up in Spain where fan language was a way of getting around the sharp protective eye of the ever-present duenna. Pamphlets teaching fan language first appeared in Spanish but were quickly translated. Here is a version of fan language popular in the nineteenth century.

Placing the fan near the heart: "You have won my love."

Rest the shut fan on the right eye: "When may I be allowed to see you?"

"At what hour?" was answered by the number of sticks shown.

Touching the unfolded fan in the act of waving: "I always long to be near you."

Threatening with the shut fan: "Do not be so imprudent."

To press the half-opened fan to the lips: "You may kiss me."

Clasping the hands under the open fan: "Forgive me."

To cover the left ear with the open fan: "Do not betray our secret."

To hide the eyes behind the open fan: "I love you."

To shut the full open fan very slowly: "I promise to marry you."

Drawing the fan across the eyes: "I am sorry."

Touching the tip of the fan with the finger: "I wish to speak to you."

Letting the fan rest on the right cheek: "Yes."

Letting the fan rest on the left cheek: "No."

To open and shut the fan several times: "You are cruel."

To drop the fan: "We will be friends."

To fan very slowly: "I am married."

To fan very quickly: "I am engaged."

To put the handle of the fan to the lips: "Kiss me."

To open the fan wide: "Wait for me."

To place the fan behind the head: "Do not forget me."

To do so with the little finger extended: "Good-bye."

Carrying the fan in the right hand and in front of the face: "Follow me."

Carrying the fan in the left hand and in front of the face: "I am desirous of your acquaintance."

Placing the fan on the left ear: "I wish to get rid of you."

Drawing the fan across the forehead: "You have changed."

Twirling the fan in the left hand: "We are watched."

Twirling the fan in the right hand: "I love another."

Carrying the fan, open, in the left hand: "You are too willing."

Carrying the fan, open, in the right hand: "Come and talk to me."

Drawing the fan through the hand: "I hate you."

Drawing the fan across the cheek: "I love you."

Presenting the fan shut: "Do you love me?"

FIGURE 9.30 *Colleen Dodson in* The Country Wife *with a lace fan. Krannert Center for the Performing Arts. (Michael J. Cesario, costume designer.)*

This does seem like a less than satisfactory manner of carrying on a conversation, and one can only hope that both lady and gentleman spoke the same language.

Fans for the Stage

Making fans is a specialized craft that should not be attempted in a costume shop unless the fan is purely ornamental and not meant to operate properly in a lady's hand. If strongly motivated by a desire to achieve a specific effect, you may want to cover a fabric fan. Know before you start that this task is delicate and painstaking. It usually requires more time than most costume technicians can afford to devote to it. In most cases, a fine oriental paper fan can be adapted to your purpose with a fraction of the effort.

If you are friendly with your local antique dealers, have them phone you whenever they acquire antique fans. Don't agree to purchase one, however, until you've checked its sturdiness. Antique fans are generally quite costly, and the only ones worth the money must be in mint condition. Fans take lots of wear on stage, even in the hands of the most careful actors.

After true antique fans, the next most elegant ones available are oriental silk fans, which are normally sold in oriental specialty shops. Such shops are located only in large cities. Be warned that silk fans are expensive.

FIGURE 9.31   *Assorted fans. (Photograph by Richard Bryant.)*

Oriental paper fans are the most common stage fans. Some small ones are available in dime stores, and oriental import shops may stock the larger, more sturdy ones. A paper fan is quite stiff when new and must be broken in with some care. Too vigorous a flick in the early stages will rip the paper leaf. Once the fan is broken in, the paper leaf may be sprayed and stenciled, but be careful to use a thin layer of paint. Stain the sticks, or paint them, to simulate the finish desired. If the production is to run more than four or five performances, and if the fan gets lots of use, be sure to prepare back-up fans in case the original one tears.

FOUND JEWELRY

The term "found jewelry" means those pieces of stage jewelry that are bought, borrowed, rented, or adapted from modern pieces. Prop jewelry construction will be discussed in Chapter 1. It is always best to keep the amount of stage jewelry to a minimum. There are, however, certain costumes from certain periods that look unfinished without the proper gold, silver, or jeweled accessories. Use jewelry where it is indicated, make certain it is evocative of the period it is intended to represent, and refrain from using distracting pieces or pieces chosen simply for show.

Earrings

Some of the oldest examples of earrings are in the Cresnola Collection at the Metropolitan Museum of Art. These earrings were found in a Cyprus excavation early in this century and date from 2000 B.C., before the time of the Trojan War. Women who wore these ancient earrings had pierced ears.

Earrings were worn in Egypt, in Mesopotamia, in Greece, and in Rome. Ancient Etruscan earrings, found in tomb excavations, are particularly beautiful and seem to have inspired later Roman designs. Some Greek statues sculpted during the Hellenistic Age have pierced ears, indicating that they originally were adorned with earrings.

In the Western world, earrings were probably not worn at all during the centuries when women regularly covered their heads or wore veiled headdresses. Late in the fourteenth century, earrings became popular and were widely worn by royalty and by the gently born.

In general, the wearing of earrings by men has always been slightly suspect, although there are important exceptions. Sir Walter Raleigh appeared in earrings in most of his portraits, as do other Elizabethan men of fashionable and adventuresome natures.

Until the twentieth century, wearing earrings was restricted to those who could afford these expensive baubles. They were all fashioned of gold, silver, and expensive gems. In 1840, "sets" of jewelry became particularly fashionable: women wore earrings, a brooch, and a bracelet made of black onyx, jet, gold, and pearls. In the 1870s, hanging gold and enamel earrings with gold fringe were popular; and at the end of the nineteenth century, a single diamond stud in each ear was preferred.

The screw-back earring was invented in 1900, permitting women to wear earrings without having to submit to ear piercing. Costume jewelry became popular and acceptable, and earrings began to be worn by women of all social and economic classes. Throughout this century, earrings have been

an important part of female dress. The screw-back and the clip-back earrings were favored until the 1960s, when many women again began to have their ears pierced. Today, most earrings are available in styles for both pierced and nonpierced ears.

There are so many earrings on the market today, many of them copies of ancient styles, that it is often possible, through patient shopping, to find a suitable pair for almost any period play. If not, independent craftspeople who make earrings are often willing to create a pair from the costume designer's sketch. Many costume technicians are also skilled jewelry makers. Beautiful earrings can be created with a few tools and the bits and pieces of old jewelry that collect in every costume shop. Ear wires, posts, screw backs, and clip backs can be bought from most craft stores. A current book on jewelry making such as *Design and Creation of Jewelry* by Robert von Neumann, might be a valuable addition to your shop library.

Pins

Ornamental pins were first used to hold draped garments in place. They were particularly important for Greek and Roman costumes. These particular pins, however, were usually large and ornate; when they are being constructed as costume accessories, they must be built by one of the methods that will be discussed in the section on stage jewelry construction in Chapter 11.

From 1500 to 1700, a great many ornamental pins were worn, even by men, who particularly fancied brooches on their hats. The early nineteenth century saw a great rage for cameos, which were worn at the throat or used to stabilize a shawl. At the end of the nineteenth century, the machine manufacture of jewelry began, to be quickly followed by the widespread wearing of costume jewelry pins in a vast array of shapes and sizes.

Every costume shop should collect and keep costume jewelry pieces. Separate the jewelry according to type and color and store it in boxes or small drawers. One perfect pin can often be assembled from several broken bits.

Beads and Necklaces

Beads are the most ancient of all ornaments. Anything in which a hole could be made was strung on a thong and hung about the neck: nuts, animal claws, bones, shells, and beads formed from clay. Civilization brought more sophisticated adornment. Egyptians were particularly fond of necklaces, preferring deep collars consisting of many rows of strung beads. Great hanging chains were worn throughout the Renaissance.

In 1680, a Paris jeweller invented a process for making imitation pearls, which became very popular. These pearls were formed from blown glass beads which were lined with fish scales and filled with wax. A single strand of pearls, either real or imitation, was very popular. After the French Revolution, necklaces—indeed, most jewelry—went briefly out of fashion. Women took to wearing narrow ribbons around their necks.

A string of beads for the stage must be very securely strung. Not only will a broken strand upset the actor, but it may also create hazardous walking conditions for all the actors on stage. String stage beads on dental floss, fishing line, or jewelry wire. For added precaution, it is a good idea to place a knot between each bead and to glue each knot with epoxy, which will prevent the whole mess of beads from falling off the string, should it break. Long strings of beads, such as those worn by ladies in Queen Elizabeth's day, might be stitched to the bodice front in order to prevent them from swinging loose and ensnaring fans, props, or even other actors.

Bracelets

Bracelets are worn less often on the stage than they are in everyday life. Unless demanded by the script, they tend to be distracting when the actor gestures. Avoid any collection of bracelets on a single arm that would make a clanking noise. Upper-arm bracelets, worn with middle-eastern costumes, are very effective costume accessories, but those worn on the wrist should be considered and chosen with great care.

Rings

Rings are perhaps the most symbolic of all accessories. First, there is the ring as a symbol of power and authority. Included in this group are royal seal rings, pope's and bishops' rings, and the wearing of ostentatious rings by the wealthy and powerful. Rings may also signify agreement, dependence, and protection. Fraternity and sorority rings, marriage rings, and rings that are worn as charms against disease and disaster come under this second heading.

A long tradition lies behind the symbolic wearing of rings. The signet ring, or seal, was common to the Egyptians, the Assyrians, the Hebrews, the Greeks, and the Romans and was adopted by all of the kings in Western Europe. The ring as a symbol of agreement may well be rooted in the ancient myth of Prometheus. After Prometheus was released from the rock to which he had been chained, Zeus instructed him to wear a ring on his finger by which he would remember his former bondage and the understanding under which he had been released.

The marriage ring, worn by women, also dates back to ancient days. It was used by the Egyptians, and by both Greeks and Romans. It was placed on the left hand because that was considered to be the hand of submission, while the right hand was the hand of power. Ancient Egyptian writings explain its placement on the third finger of the left hand because they believed this finger to be connected directly to the heart by a single artery. Early Christians considered the marriage ring a pagan custom but were persuaded to adopt it by 860 A.D. During the period of the British Commonwealth, 1649–1660, the marriage ring was outlawed as heathenish, and some fundamentalist Christian sects still do not accept it. The wearing of marriage rings by men is a very recent custom which has only become widely popular in the twentieth century.

Unlike bracelets, which may detract from the gestures made by an actor, rings seem to be inherently dramatic and will often enhance a performance. Most actors enjoy wearing rings, but they should always be provided with rehearsal rings in order to become accustomed to working with them.

When planning rings for a period production, look at the paintings and whatever other sources are available for the time in order to discover on which fingers rings were worn. Rings can be and are worn on all fingers, including the thumb. The forefinger is a particularly good spot for a ring that symbolizes power.

Many handsome rings can be built from odds and ends of jewelry and set on adjustable finger bands or, as a less expensive alternative, on a circle of elastic. Set the stones or other ornaments onto the band with hot glue or epoxy, perhaps adding additional swirls of hot glue at the sides. Touch up with bronzing powder suspended in the FEV solution.

Wedding bands can be inexpensively purchased at most dime stores. Costume jewelry shops often carry large, adjustable rings that can be adapted for signets. Use your imagination to find and to create costume rings. They are worth the effort.

FIGURE 9.32 *Assorted stage rings. (Photograph by Richard Bryant.)*

WATCHES

Men began to carry watches in the late sixteenth century. These were not especially accurate timepieces but were set in small, handsomely wrought cases and could only be afforded by the wealthy. A century later, men carried watches more commonly, and in the eighteenth century, they played a decided decorative part in the general masculine costume. The watch rested in the waistcoat pocket while a large, fancy fob hung outside. Paintings show some men wearing a watch in both vest pockets, each with a fob; perhaps this custom arose because the watches were still not particularly accurate.

In the nineteenth century, watch cases were quite plain. At mid-century, the machine-made watch was born; and by the end of the century, watches could be bought for one dollar each, and almost every man carried one. The watch was normally worn in the vest pocket, was often fastened to a gold chain which stretched across the chest, and was secured inside the opposite pocket. A fob sometimes dangled from the watch outside the watch pocket.

Women in the nineteenth century wore dainty watches suspended from a chain around the neck. In 1900, and for a dozen years after, women wore small watches made up as pins and fastened to their shirtwaists. The wristwatch was introduced just prior to World War I and gained immediate popularity.

Stage watches do not need to be in working order. Old timepieces that are past repair are often available from watchmakers for very little cost. Many of these are beautiful and are quite suitable for stage wear. Collect watches and take good care of them. They are important stage accessories and cannot easily be fabricated.

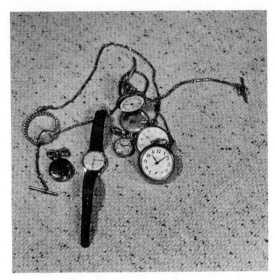

FIGURE 9.33 *Assorted watches for the stage. (Photograph by Richard Bryant.)*

GLOVES

Like rings, gloves started out as symbolic objects. From antiquity, they were associated both with royalty and with ecclesiastical ritual. A king delegated authority to a deputy by sending him his gloves, while early Christian priests wore white linen gloves to celebrate the Mass.

By the fourteenth century, gloves had taken on broader ritualistic qualities. The inclusion of a glove along with a contractual agreement assured both parties of its binding nature. A knight often went into a contest with his lady's glove fastened to his helmet; and throwing down a glove became the correct method of issuing a challenge between gentlemen.

In the fifteenth and sixteenth centuries, wearing gloves became fashionable as well as symbolic. Gloves worn during this period were almost always perfumed. Pamphlets were circulated with instructions for brewing sweet-smelling liquids in which the gloves could be soaked. The Spanish produced par-

ticularly desirable perfumed leather gloves; the scents were said to be permanent.

The period that encompassed the sixteenth and seventeenth centuries was the golden age

FIGURE 9.34a *Leather gloves with gauntlets. (Photograph by Richard Bryant.)*

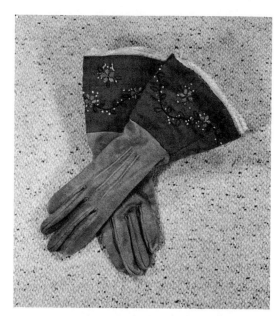

FIGURE 9.34b *Cloth gloves with embroidered gauntlets. (Photograph by Richard Bryant.)*

of gloves. Men's gloves had wide gauntlets that were richly decorated and edged in costly lace. They were an integral part of the fashionable male costume and were worn at all occasions. Women's gloves tended to be small and dainty rather than large and dramatic. Many women preferred gloves made of "chicken skin," the skin of an unborn kid. Queen Elizabeth was especially fond of gloves. It is reported that, during interviews, she slipped her gloves on and off at regular intervals in order to draw attention to her lovely white hands. She was often given gloves as gifts, and she in turn made a habit of giving her own gloves to her favorite friends.

From the seventeenth century to the present, gloves have remained important fashion accessories, although they have become increasingly less flamboyant in design. The length of women's gloves has followed the rise and fall of the sleeve length. Once men adopted the suit, their gloves subsided to the wrist and have remained there until this day.

Gray or white gloves are correct for evening wear, and short brown or black leather gloves are appropriate for protection against the cold. Wool knit gloves have long been practical and popular for sports.

A great many stage costumes require gloves. Fortunately, almost all styles can be approximated from modern gloves purchased in department stores, formal wear shops, and, if you are in a large city, from companies that manufacture gloves.

Gauntlets can be added to many men's gloves, including white cotton formal gloves and suede work gloves. Figure 9.35 illustrates the steps involved in adding a gauntlet to a plain cotton glove. The gauntlet should be stiffened with nylon cape netting or several layers of canvas. Do not use buckram or the gloves will not be washable. Dye fabric gloves with commercial fabric dye and suede gloves with suede-type leather dye. Remember that gloves made of nylon must be dyed with special dyes.

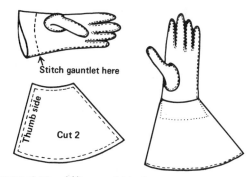

Stitch gauntlet here

Thumb side

Cut 2

FIGURE 9.35 *Adding gauntlet to glove.*

Gloves always come in contact with makeup on stage and should be washable. A gentle hand washing will usually suffice. Ladies' kid gloves can be washed in mild soap. To wash kid gloves, put them on your hands and rub them very gently in soapy water. Lay the gloves flat to dry, turning them several times during the process. Kid gloves that have become spotty and discolored from age can be dipped in a weak coffee or tea solution to give them an overall buff or cream color. Under some stage lights, buff or cream-colored gloves will appear quite white.

PURSES

In order to avoid confusion in this section, "purse" will be the single term employed to mean any container (smaller than a suitcase) carried by a woman (and, less frequently, by a man) to house personal belongings. "Handbag" and "pocketbook" are roughly synonymous terms, but somehow they seem particularly inappropriate when the item being referred to is a dainty, lace drawstring object or an elegant beaded creation from the 1920s. The word *purse* seems the most suitable for all styles.

Until the late fifteenth century, women often wore their purses around their waists, over the underdress and under the overdress. These purses were merely one or two pocket pouches held on with a band, and they were accessible through slits in the overdress. When dresses became too complicated to accommodate the slit through which the pocket purses could be reached, there came the period when women simply hung their belongings from their belts. This use of belts was touched on earlier in this chapter. Small purses of several types were often suspended from the belt for additional carrying space.

Both men and women used purses until the seventeenth century, when men acquired pockets in their clothing. After that, men's purses shrunk in size until they could be tucked into the pockets, and women's purses grew steadily more important to the total costume. The purse did not reach full fashion flower until early in the nineteenth century, when it began to be a coordinated part of the total fashion ensemble. Depending upon the fashion periods, purses may match the dress, the coat, the hat, the gloves, the shoes, or any combination thereof. Ridiculously small purses have been worn on the wrist and monstrous large ones have been slung over the shoulder.

Simple drawstring purses, pouch purses, and clutch purses are regularly made in costume shops, most often out of real or imitation leather or out of the same fabric from which the costume is being constructed. Drawstring purses can be made from a circular piece of fabric which has had eyelets worked in it on the sewing machine, or metal ones set in, through which the drawstring can be threaded (see Figure 9.36). Another

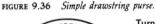

FIGURE 9.36   *Simple drawstring purse.*

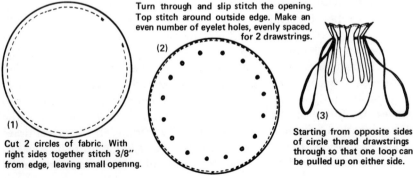

Turn through and slip stitch the opening. Top stitch around outside edge. Make an even number of eyelet holes, evenly spaced, for 2 drawstrings.

(1) Cut 2 circles of fabric. With right sides together stitch 3/8" from edge, leaving small opening.

(2)

(3) Starting from opposite sides of circle thread drawstrings through so that one loop can be pulled up on either side.

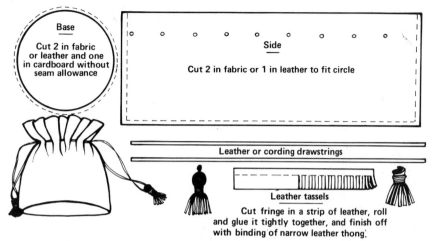

Base
—
Cut 2 in fabric
or leather and one
in cardboard without
seam allowance

Side
—
Cut 2 in fabric or 1 in leather to fit circle

Leather or cording drawstrings

Leather tassels

Cut fringe in a strip of leather, roll
and glue it tightly together, and finish off
with binding of narrow leather thong.

Seam side edges together to form tube. Slip one tube inside the other with right sides together and stitch 3/8″ from top edge, turn through, and top stitch.

Working from the inside, join side piece to one circle. Glue cardboard on top of circle, then
handstitch the second fabric circle to cover it and form lining, or simply glue the second
leather circle to the cardboard. Turn purse to right side and insert drawstrings as in Figure
9.36. Finish drawstrings with small tassels.

FIGURE 9.37 *Purse with stiffened base.*

style is created from two pieces of fabric or
leather with a cardboard circle to stiffen the
base (see Figure 9.37). Make sure that the
drawstrings are long enough for the intended
use and not made from a flimsy material that
will tangle easily.

Construct a pouch from three basic pieces,
as shown in Figure 9.38, plus straps. For a
handmade look, lace the pieces together with
thongs. The seams can also be turned to the
inside and machine-stitched. Pouch purses
are often worn on a man's belt, either suspended from two short straps or from a strap
that is stitched to the back of the pouch,
through which the belt is threaded.

Clutch purses, so-called because they are
usually constructed without straps or strings
and must be clutched in the hand or under
the arm, are common twentieth-century ac-
companiments for a lady's evening costume.
They were popular in the 1930s, the 1940s,

and the 1950s, and often matched the dress.
In construction, they resemble an envelope.
Clutch purses must have an underconstruc-
tion of canvas, perhaps even stiffened with
hair canvas or buckram, over which the outer
fabric is applied. Clutch purses can be fastened with a button and loop, a large snap,
or a clasp.

Although other purse styles are sometimes
built in the costume shop for various special
effects, most are adapted from purses already
in stock or from those picked up in secondhand shops. So many different shapes and
sizes can be found that it usually takes only
patience to find a purse that will lend itself
to being adapted to whatever the designer
wants. Leather purses can be dyed with
leather dyes, and fabric purses can be sprayed
with a fabric dye such as Fab Spray. Old
trim can be stripped away and new trim
added. Do beware, however, of trying to ac-

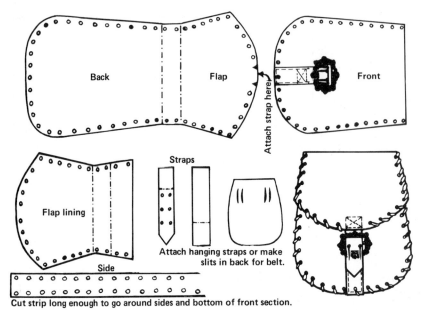

Back

Flap

Attach strap here

Front

Straps

Flap lining

Attach hanging straps or make slits in back for belt.

Side

Cut strip long enough to go around sides and bottom of front section.

Glue lining to flap and attach strap and buckle with machine stitch. Punch holes and join together with leather thong. Be careful to space the holes evenly and match them up to corresponding pattern pieces.

FIGURE 9.38   *Leather pouch.*

complish too many changes on a plastic purse. Whenever you remove an ornament from a plastic purse, you are usually left with an unsightly hole. Most plastic purses will not take any kind of paint or dye successfully.

As a rule, it is safe to borrow purses, since they normally receive gentle use on stage. Some antique shops will even loan beaded purses for a stage production. Before you use a borrowed purse, check it over carefully for damaged links or clasps and repair them if possible. Never borrow a purse if it is to be used roughly.

Stage purses become problems when they must serve a practical as well as an ornamental purpose. It is up to the costume technician to know exactly what items are to be taken from the purse and to arrange the purse inte-

FIGURE 9.39   *Assorted purses. (Photograph by Richard Bryant.)*

FIGURE 9.40 *Penelope Reed in the Court Street Theater production of* Happy Days. *(Joanne Karaska, costume designer; photograph by Jack Hamilton.)*

rior so that the actor can find the required items with a minimum of digging. It is often useful to stuff the bottom of the purse with wadded-up muslin to create a false bottom and eliminate corners into which compacts, combs, and lipstick cases can become lost. Sometimes it might be necessary to create side pockets inside the purse into which such items can be placed. Work these technicalities out with the actor and the stage manager, and make sure the actor has sufficient time to rehearse with the purse and its contents.

Possibly the most complicated stage purse in current dramatic literature is the one belonging to Winnie in Samuel Beckett's *Happy Days.* Winnie is buried in sand and all her belongings are contained in her purse. Toothbrush, toothpaste, clock, nailfile, nail polish, pistol, handkerchief, and other items must be produced from the purse on cue. Organizing a purse for Winnie is a task that tests the ingenuity of both actor and costume technician. Figure 9.40 shows a scene from this wonderfully absurd play.

SHAWLS

At the end of the eighteenth century, foreign travelers began to bring home large shawls made in the Middle and Far East. Indian cashmere shawls were particularly prized. In 1882, France imported cashmere goats in order to produce shawls; and at the same time, artisans in Paisley, Scotland, began to create beautiful adaptations of Indian shawls. These were either five or six foot squares which were worn folded diagonally. The last half of the nineteenth century was the highpoint of shawl popularity.

In the 1890s and the early 1900s, the Spanish shawl was all the rage. These shawls were actually made in the Orient and then shipped to Spain, where the fringe, often a foot long, was added. When they were not being worn by fashionable ladies, Spanish shawls were often used to cover piano backs in Victorian parlors.

Elegant shawls and simple woolen squares or triangles, worn for warmth, are often used on stage. They are easily made but are often troublesome to the actor because movement is restricted. Any actor who is going to wear a shawl should have the item, or a very similar substitute, for the entire rehearsal period. Fringed shawls easily become entangled with furniture, props, parasols, or walking sticks, and they should be used with particular caution. It sometimes helps to spray the fringe with a thin starch solution to deter it from tangling.

The history of umbrellas is a fascinating subject. T. S. Crawford's exhaustively researched and beautifully written book, entitled *History of the Umbrella,* published in 1970, tells the tale with spirit. Crawford's book was the source of some of the information that follows.

Today, the term umbrella usually means an article that affords protection from rain, while parasol refers to a sun shade. This is not an historically accurate use of these terms, however, since they have often been used quite interchangeably. Parasol is the most recent of the two terms and, in the following discussion, it will be reserved for its modern meaning: a lady's long-handled sun shade.

Umbrellas appeared over 3,000 years ago, probably in Egypt, and were first used as religious and ceremonial items. The earliest forms were very likely constructed as a visualization of an ancient concept of the shape of the heavens. They were placed over the head of the monarch, not merely to shade his royal head from the sun but to signify that the king was protected by the sky itself. In certain ancient texts, a hieroglyph shaped like an open umbrella is sometimes used to mean sovereignty. Even the collapsible umbrella belongs to antiquity: The remains of a collapsible frame were found in a Korean tomb that dates from around 25 B.C.

India, the Far East, and Africa all adopted the umbrella as a symbol of reverence. The Buddha is often pictured under the protection of an umbrella; and in Africa, 2,500 years ago, an Ethiopian king was enthroned beneath one. In Greece and Rome, umbrellas took a more practical turn. Ladies frequently shaded themselves with umbrellas, and ancient poets issued more than a few jibes at the effeminate nature of Greek and Roman men who sought similar protection from the elements.

Europe lagged far behind the rest of the world in adopting the umbrella, and England took to it latest of all. The first depiction of the umbrella in England is in a painting of Sir Henry Upton, an Elizabethan diplomat, and shows him with a white umbrella as he rides from the Alps to Padua in the late 1570s. The earliest known use of the word umbrella in the English language, in its proper context, was by John Donne in 1609. In October, 1644, the English traveler, John Evelyn, whose keen observations have been mentioned elsewhere in this book, purchased an umbrella in Marseilles; later, in 1664, he reports having seen the first Chinese paper parasols in Paris.

French ladies took to the parasol in the seventeenth century, but it was a century later before English women adopted it to protect their fair complexions from the sun. In the eighteenth century, the term parasol was the generally accepted one for a fashionable lady's sun shade, and umbrella was reserved for the more utilitarian object.

In the mid-eighteenth century, a plucky Englishman named Jonas Hanway first braved public ridicule and began to stroll about the streets of London protected by an umbrella, which he probably acquired on a trip to France. For thirty years, he shaded his own head from sun and rain, and finally he saw umbrellas come into general use. It was popular, for a time, to refer to all umbrellas as "Hanways."

The church soundly criticized the use of the umbrella in its early days on the grounds that, if God made the rain to fall, then he intended the people on whom it fell to get wet. Reversing this stand completely, it was the English churches who became the first regular owners of large, sturdy umbrellas, which were used to protect the clergyman and the more privileged mourners at a rainy gravesite.

Long before individuals began to carry umbrellas, great English manor houses were equipped with them so guests could be escorted to their carriages beneath a protective cover. Indeed, when a person carried an umbrella on his or her person, it was tantamount to admitting that the owner of the umbrella was not the owner of a carriage.

After the French and American revolutions, umbrellas and parasols were manufactured in greater quantities and were used by working people as well as by the wealthy. Even French fishmongers used umbrellas in the early nineteenth century to protect themselves and their wares from both sun and showers.

The middle of the nineteenth century saw the greatest flourishing of the fashionable parasol. It was a lovely, light accessory which matched the costume of the lady who carried it, and it was outfitted with a long, slender handle. The Germans even produced an oblong model to ape the shape of the bustle. As the Victorian Age advanced, parasols grew less frivolous and more sturdy. The stick was standardized at forty-two inches in length, and the covers harmonized with the clothes but were less gaudy. The popularity of the parasol fell off during the early years of the twentieth century and by the 1920s, the parasol had fallen victim to the new cult of sun worship.

Throughout the same period, the umbrella grew more and more popular as it improved mechanically. Unlike the parasol, however, it was never a high fashion item. Men's models remain so unchanging that one or two will serve most men for a lifetime, and women seldom change their umbrellas with anything like the frequency with which they acquire new hats and purses. An umbrella fashion show in England in 1956 sparked a brief upswing in the popularity of stylish models, and occasional later fads have caught on for a while, but the umbrella remains more utilitarian than fashionable.

Especially good collections of antique um-

brellas and parasols can be found at the Essex Institute at Salem, Massachusetts, and The Museum of the City of New York. In England, old umbrellas and parasols may be seen at The London Museum, The Victoria and Albert Museum, The Gallery of English Costume at Platt Hall, Manchester, and the Birmingham Museum.

Parasols for the Stage

The major difference between a parasol and an umbrella, for practical purposes, is the length of the handle and, sometimes, the size of the top. A perky ruffled parasol demands a long handle which can be balanced on the shoulder, twirled, or held at a rakish angle over the head. Parasol frames are available from a number of costume and novelty companies. The ones that are made especially for dancers are a good deal sturdier than the ordinary ones and well worth the extra cost. Period parasols can sometimes be found in antique shops, but do make sure that the frame is strong and operative before purchasing one.

Parasols present the costume technician with two distinct problems: finding an adequate frame and covering the frame with the proper fabric. Only on rare occasions will you acquire a covered parasol that is the color you require. It is not difficult to re-cover a parasol frame, and the results are well worth the effort.

To re-cover a parasol, remove the original cover carefully and take it apart. Press the old pieces, lay them on the new fabric, matching the grain, and cut around them. Machine-stitch the new pieces together and apply the cover to the frame. Each seam in the cover should pass directly over a spoke in the frame. Secure the cover at the top and bottom of each spoke, stretching the fabric tightly. Add ruffles, fringe, or other decorations to the cover after it has been applied to the frame. The trim can be machine-stitched between the spokes and caught by hand over the spokes. As you work on the frame, open and close it frequently to make sure the cover doesn't interfere with the action.

If the parasol frame comes to you without a cover, you can drape a pattern on it by opening the frame and fitting pieces of muslin between the spokes. Use masking tape to hold the muslin to the spokes. Do not stretch the muslin too tight. The straight grain of the cover fabric should run right down the middle of each pie-shaped section, midway between the spokes on either side.

Most parasols have wooden handles that can be painted to complement the cover and the costume. Use an enamel paint that will not rub off on costume pieces or on the actor's hands.

Umbrellas are not put to practical use on stage as often as parasols. In most instances, stage umbrellas will merely operate as hand props, being carried on or off by a character who has experienced, or is expecting, rain.

If they are not in stock, suitable umbrellas can be borrowed or bought.

Many costume technicians will, however, at some time in their careers, have to find or purchase a matching set of umbrellas for the last scene in Thorton Wilder's *Our Town*. These umbrellas, the large, black variety which are routinely supplied by undertaking firms for rainy day funerals, are as central to the visual impact of *Our Town* as the two stepladders on which the young Emily and George exchange confidences. If your budget is small, you might be able to borrow the required number of black umbrellas from a local undertaking establishment, or possibly from an airline. They can be purchased in most department stores or men's clothing shops, but they are costly. Some directors may want to add the realistic touch of raindrops, and this can be done by spattering them with a thin solution of white glue. Lights shining on the dried glue spots will create a permanent wet-looking sheen. Don't spatter borrowed umbrellas.

WALKING STICKS

In ancient times, the walking stick, or staff, belonged to gods and heroes. From its mythic beginning, the staff became representative of the power of the owner. This significance was fully realized in the king's scepter. Popes, bishops, judges, and military officers have also used the staff in various forms. Modern generals still carry a baton, a swagger stick, or a slender riding crop to indicate their positions of authority.

Except for three periods, late in the fifteenth century, briefly in the eighteenth century, and for a time in the nineteenth century, the walking stick has not been popular with women. Even at these times it was the long, slender staff the women preferred, not the short stick that could double as a weapon.

During the fourteenth and fifteenth centuries, the walking stick was accessory to many

subversive acts and overt displays of violence. It was often constructed with a hollow that might conceal weapons or poison. The quarterstaff was, in the hands of one trained in its use, a deadly instrument. The Puritans carried large oaken sticks which were often put to use as weapons.

In the late sixteenth and seventeenth centuries, the walking stick lost some of its combative nature. The use of bamboo and cane for walking sticks popularized the new name, cane, and the two terms quickly became synonymous. Short canes were very popular with gentlemen in the mid-seventeenth century in France, and they were made of ivory, ebony, whalebone, and lovely woods. Many had richly jeweled heads. In the eighteenth century, the walking stick grew to four feet in length and gentlemen used it to attain elegant poses. Around 1780, ladies affected the shepherdess's crook.

In the nineteenth century, both men and women carried canes; the female version was often the walking stick parasol. At the end of the century, gentlemen's canes again served dual, although peaceful, purposes. They concealed a telescope, a camera tripod, a toilet table, or a footstool, among other things. Except as a walking aid for those who need them, canes have fallen out of favor in the twentieth century.

Stage Canes and Walking Sticks

Walking sticks from the late nineteenth and early twentieth centuries are occasionally donated to a theatre. A considerable number of people, however, seriously collect walking sticks, and they are quite expensive in antique shops and fetch substantial prices at antique auctions. Walking stick collectors can often be persuaded to loan a suitable item for a stage production. If you do not know a collector, advertise your need in the local newspaper. As always, when using a borrowed antique, make certain that it is in good condition when it is borrowed and that it is treated with special care.

Excellent reproductions of period canes, as well as many modern styles, can be purchased from the Giraffe Trading Co., Ltd., 56 Harvester Avenue, Batavia, New York 14020 at surprisingly modest prices. Some styles can also be bought from costume and novelty houses, but these are not especially stout.

The biggest problem with making sticks in the costume shop is that of strength. Hard woods, which are the strongest, are difficult to shape without a wood lathe. Soft wood

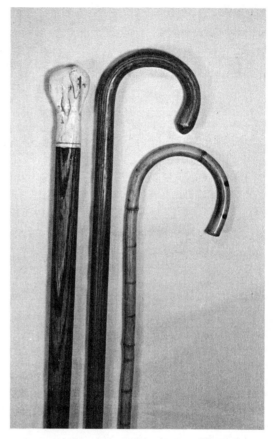

FIGURE 9.41 *Canes and a stick for the stage. (Photograph by Richard Bryant.)*

doweling, which is easier to carve and sand, may not be strong enough. A bannister rod, which is used to construct stairway rails, often makes a handsome walking stick. It will come in a variety of different turnings and need only be cut to the correct length and stained or painted. Rubber tips to keep the stick from slipping are available in most orthopedic supply stores.

10

Men's Formal Wear

Assembling the elements that constitute correct men's formal wear at any one specific time during the nineteenth or twentieth centuries is often a tedious task for the costumer. Some designers do painstaking research and present the costume staff with explicit instructions for the entire formal outfit. Others only indicate the general outline of the clothing and leave the costumer to fill in the details. In some cases, choosing the formal attire for musicians and extras, such as dancers and party guests, is left completely up to the costumer. Since each working situation is bound to be slightly different, every costume technician should know the correct names for formal garments, the major styles from each period, and the correct accessories for each style.

For over a hundred years of fashion history, the outfits worn by men to formal occasions, such as balls, weddings, state dinners, and so on, have been rigidly proscribed by custom and the dictates of fashion. Formal

styles for men have changed less radically than informal styles. The changes that have occurred do, for the most part, form a logical progression of style alternatives that evolve naturally and reflect both social and historical pressures. The style of the coat and the color and choice of accompanying garments are the most important elements to be considered when choosing a formal ensemble for a particular time and occasion.

Men's formal clothing in the eighteenth century was differentiated from informal clothing only by choice of fabric and by the amount and richness of trim. There were no specific coat and trouser styles associated with men's formal garments. This continued to be the case during the early part of the nineteenth century, although gradually the formal equivalent of popular styles tended toward a more uniform color differentiation: Formal wear became chiefly black or dark blue. By the middle of the nineteenth century, the tailcoat with matching trousers had become exclusively a formal style. By the early twentieth century, the cutaway (morning coat) and the frock coat, usually worn with striped trousers, were reserved for formal wear. Today, the tailcoat, the cutaway, and a shorter version of the frock coat are all distinctly formal styles, while the tuxedo, or dinner jacket, remains a variation on the current suit or sports jacket.

The rigid social structure that characterized the Victorian Age encouraged strict rules for dress. Gentlemen paid a great deal of attention to wearing correct formal attire, and younger men were particularly conscious of the most subtle changes in fashion. Americans followed the British lead in formal dress and, at least on the Atlantic seaboard, managed to stay quite up to date, although they remained slightly more casual. During the 1920s and 1930s, the wealthy found many excuses to wear formal clothing, desiring perhaps to isolate themselves from the economic and political upheavals that surrounded them by organizing social functions requiring ritualized dress. After World War II, however, and the declining interest in class and social structure, men found fewer and fewer occasions requiring formal dress. In America, by the 1950s, a dinner jacket or tuxedo served most men for all social engagements except formal weddings. Indeed, a wedding may be the only occasion left today at which American men make regular appearances in tailcoats or cutaways. Attendance at certain balls, dinners, and fraternal functions in England still requires white tie and tails, although such events belong almost entirely to the upper class.

Because ours is a time when fashion choice is commonly left up to the individual and when codes of dress are frowned upon, the costumer must be careful not to take rules of dress in past years too lightly. In real life, as well as on the stage, prospective suitors were once rejected because of ill-chosen garments; business deals did fail and political encounters went awry because the wrong thing was worn at the wrong time. Today, most men find a sense of individuality in dressing uniquely; there were times—and there may be again—when men found strength in adopting the universal, socially accepted styles. Nowhere has the weight of conventionality been heavier than in the area of formal dress.

What follows is a very brief outline of the history of men's formal clothing from the early nineteenth century until the present. For specific details of English and American formal styles, *Esquire's Encyclopedia of 20th Century Men's Fashion* and the Cunningtons' *Handbook of English Costume in the Nineteenth Century* and *Handbook of English Costume in the Twentieth Century* are highly recommended.

THE TAILCOAT

The first version of the tailcoat appeared during the last decade of the eighteenth century. The slanted front skirts of the coat popular at that time were cut away, revealing the breeches and forming squared-off tails that hung down in back. The new style rapidly gained popularity. These early tailcoats were rather loosely cut, but in the 1820s, a waist seam was added and the tailcoat became quite trim. Many variations followed, but by the 1830s, black and dark blue tailcoats were commonly worn for formal occasions. Early in the decade, white trousers were worn with formal tailcoats, but by 1840, the correct trouser color was black. The preferred waistcoat was white satin, velvet, or silk, and the neckwear a large white or black cravat tied in a bow in front, exposing the ruffled shirt front.

In the 1840s, except when it was worn as a dress riding coat (in light colors and tweeds), the tailcoat was an exclusively formal cut. By mid-century, it was no longer worn for riding. In 1853, a contemporary fashion commentator stated that black tailcoats outnumbered any other color twenty to one. The accompanying waistcoat could be white, preferably with embroidered corners, or black. The trousers were always black. Black pumps were preferred over boots. The tailcoat was usually referred to as the evening coat or the dress coat.

From 1860 to 1880, the black tailcoat became totally associated with formal evening wear. A black waistcoat was generally worn with it, although a white quilted one was suitable for "gay" parties. The only exception to the black tailcoat was a wedding version that sometimes appeared in blue, claret, or mulberry and was worn with white trousers; the colored tailcoats remained popular until 1870, when frock coats became more common wedding attire for men.

From the end of the nineteenth century until the present, the tailcoat has remained the most distinctive and least changeable formal coat. It has always been the most rigidly conventional. In the 1890s, white waistcoats took the place of black and have remained correct ever since. A small white bow tie and a stiff-bosomed shirt almost always accompany the tailcoat, although the black bow tie is sometimes required. The tailcoat is worn with matching trousers which, since the end of the nineteenth century, have had a strip of braid down the outseams. The trousers are always uncuffed. The distinctive period changes in the tailcoat have been in: width and style of lapels, width and degree of shoulder padding, and length and shape of tails. These details can be checked by decades in any of the previously recommended sources.

THE FROCK COAT

The frock coat was the most popular man's coat style in the nineteenth century. Like the tailcoat, it was loose-fitting until the 1820s, when it began to be cut with a waist seam and form-fitting darts. At first it was single-breasted with a roll or a Prussian collar and no lapels. The collar and lapels appeared at the same time as the waist seam and, with minor variations, the basic style remained the same for the rest of the century. In the 1870s and 1880s, the informal frock coat was called the "morning frock coat" to distinguish it from the dress frock coat.

The dress frock coat was the first important coat worn for daytime formal occasions. It was black or oxford gray, although a dark blue frock coat was suitable for weddings until the 1880s. The dress frock coat often had a velvet collar and silk facings. Waistcoats worn with frock coats were cut somewhat higher than those worn with tailcoats and were either single- or double-breasted, depending upon the prevailing fashion. Figured white or buff silk fabrics were favored. Trousers seldom matched the frock coat and were usually striped or herringbone.

THE CUTAWAY

Like the tailcoat and the frock coat, the cutaway style began as an informal coat. It appeared in the midst of the nineteenth century and was called a "Newmarket." It was worn either as a suit with matching trousers or as a contrasting jacket. The formal version of the cutaway coat was an alternative to the dress frock coat. Their popularity grew with the growing necessities of daytime formal wear as men began to adopt specific outfits for church, receptions, concerts, and even for walking in the park. By 1870, the cutaway, by now also called the morning coat, had become more and more dressy. It was made up either in black or oxford gray wool with either plain or braided edges. It was always single-breasted. Striped or herringbone trousers and a pale gray, white, or buff waistcoat accompanied the cutaway. Neckwear ranged from a largish black bow tie to a four-in-hand or a striped ascot. Both formal and informal versions of the cutaway style were popular until the turn of the century.

THE TUXEDO

The tuxedo, dinner jacket, or formal lounge coat made its appearance in the United States in 1886 when Griswold Lorillard first wore a "tailless evening jacket" at Tuxedo Park, New York. The new jacket achieved significant popularity in England and on the continent, where it was called the Monte Carlo.

As the latest comer on the formal fashion scene, the tuxedo was, and has remained, the least formal coat style. Both a continuous roll collar or a collar and peaked lapel have been fashionable. At first, it was always black and was worn with matching trousers. In the early twentieth century, the white dinner jacket became acceptable for summer wear and was worn with black trousers. Tuxedos were first worn with white waistcoats, later with black. At the end of the 1880s, some men dispensed with the waistcoat entirely when wearing a tuxedo and, instead, wound a sash around their waists. Although this practice was at first denounced as vulgar, it caught on and was finally formalized into the cummerbund, which is now considered the correct tuxedo accessory.

ASSEMBLING MEN'S FORMAL WEAR FOR THE STAGE

The decade between 1889 and 1900 was the high point of regulated formal dress for men. Fashion magazines and newspapers outlined exactly what was correct attire for business, afternoon receptions, garden parties, and fancy balls. The wedding costume, for instance, consisted of a black frock coat, a double-breasted waistcoat (a light-colored waistcoat if the tie was dark, and a dark-colored waistcoat if the tie was light), gray striped trousers, patent leather boots, gloves made of tan kid or gray suede, and a high silk topper. The tailcoat with matching trousers, white waistcoat, stiff-bosomed shirt, and high collar with a small black or white bow tie was the only acceptable attire for formal evening affairs. The frock coat or the cutaway coat were required for business wear and daytime formal functions. The tuxedo was considered not quite elegant enough for mixed company, but was the perfect dress for all-male formal dinners.

Before and after the so-called "gay nineties," men's formal wear choices were somewhat broader. When choosing a formal costume for a dramatic character, make certain to be aware of all the possible variables. Not only is the date important, but so is the exact occasion for which the clothing is being worn. Is it a daytime or an evening event? Is the character to be dressed in the height of fashion or in a more sedate and conventional style? An older, conservative character might demand formal clothing from the previous decade rather than the absolutely up-to-date fashion. Don't forget that business executives from the last quarter of the nineteenth century until World War I generally wore daytime formal wear to their offices. Some preferred frock coats, but many adopted a uniform business suit that consisted of an oxford gray or black cutaway, striped gray worsted trousers, a light waistcoat, a white shirt with a wing collar, and an ascot, four-in-hand, or bow tie. This outfit was often topped with a black bowler or homburg. Similar clothing was also worn to church. The English businessman was much more formal than his American counterpart, although many prosperous Americans enjoyed wearing the latest British formal styles to work.

Within carefully defined limits, formal wear accessories can provide important character delineations. Although styles are relatively uniform and the correct waistcoat color is imperative, details of neckwear, shirt front decoration, and jewelry can add a wealth of individuality to the formally dressed man.

It is interesting to note that the gowns worn by women to formal events have never become as regimented as the suits worn by men. Throughout the years, wedding gowns have been somewhat distinctive, particularly as to color, but ball gowns and evening dresses in general have tended to follow current styles rather than to develop into styles reserved for formal occasions. There seem to be no readily apparent reasons for this phenomenon, and so it will be left to the consideration of social historians.

11

Costume Properties

Costume properties, as they were defined in Chapter 9 for the purposes of this book, are accessories of dress that are made from modern materials, employing craft techniques. Such properties may be intended to represent realistic articles or ornaments from another era, such as Roman breastplates or Renaissance chains and pendants. They may be stylized versions of modern or period accessories or fanciful objects such as fairy wings or angel halos. Any mask that is worn by an actor is a costume prop.

Every costume shop should have an area set aside in which costume props are constructed. The liquid materials used to make costume props—glues, paints, solvents, and so forth—can all potentially destroy a garment if they are accidentally dropped, spilled, or sprayed on it. Ideally, costume props should not be made in the sewing room. If a separate room is not available, however, create a separate work space by masking off the prop construction area with a curtain, a screen, or a spare flat. There should be a source of hot and cold running water near the prop area, electrical outlets, and, for some of the processes, a hot plate. Nowhere is neatness more important than in the prop-building area. Countless hours can be spent searching for misplaced tools and supplies; a week's work can be destroyed by knocking over an uncapped jar of paint. No matter how late at night or early in the morning the work day ends, leave a few minutes to put away supplies and tools. Liquids should be covered, hot glue guns unplugged, and hot plates turned off.

It is virtually impossible to give step-by-step instructions for making specific costume properties. Each article created for the stage comes from an individual design and will be individually planned and built. There are, however, basic methods which one may employ to begin each project. Once the method

FIGURE 11.1 *G. Wood and Michael Pierce in* A Christmas Carol *at the Milwaukee Repertory Theater. (Elizabeth Covey, costume designer; photograph by Jack Hamilton.)*

Craft instruction manuals may be helpful in learning specific techniques, but these will usually have to be adapted to the specific theatre situation. Do make it a habit to read *Theatre Crafts,* a magazine for theatre technicians, published by Rodale Press, 33 East Minor Street, Emmaus, Pennsylvania 18049. *Theatre Design and Technology,* the publication of the U.S. Institute for Theatre Technology, Inc., 1501 Broadway, New York, New York 10036, is another journal that occasionally has articles relevant to the construction of costume properties.

Begin to create a record of your own work. After you have completed a project, take a few moments to make notes of the process used. Make notations of each step, in order, and the materials employed. A brief record of this sort, put on a file card and kept in a box, can help you or another technician from wasting long hours in repetitive experimentation. For example:

Making imitation leather from felt used to construct a messenger pouch for King Lear

- construct the article from light-weight industrial felt.
- rub entire surface with damp Lava soap, heavy in some places, light in others.
- scrub in brown acrylic paint with a sponge.
- allow to dry.
- rub all over with brown shoe polish; buff lightly.

---

is chosen as a starting point, it may be adapted, altered, and enlarged upon by the costume technician who is assigned to the particular project.

Many of the techniques used to construct costume properties are closely related to techniques used by scenic artists and stage property artists. In a small theatre, tools and materials, as well as techniques, can readily be shared. If the theatre is large and highly departmentalized, costume technicians should make it a habit to visit the property shop often to see what new methods are being employed.

There is very little written material on creating costume properties. Most of the information in this chapter has been learned by experimentation or from instructions passed from one costume technician to another, either in the classroom or on the job.

These are notes for a method that has many specific applications. Real leather might look better, but if the budget will not support the purchase of real leather, this is a satisfactory substitute. The most valuable methods are those that provide a starting point for the creation of individual designs.

The following discussion includes only methods for constructing costume properties that can be carried out by the average costume shop, using tools and materials that are easily available and not overwhelmingly expensive. The most important ingredient in any of these procedures is imagination. Beautiful and functional props can be made from prosaic materials, but only if the costume technician has the ability to see the potential in a piece of felt, a few beads, cork balls, studs, and string.

TOOLS

Many of the basic tools you need for making costume properties will already be in the costume shop. A good way to add to the basic set is to purchase one new tool for each production. Take care of the tools you have and do not allow them to be lost. Be firm with people who wish to borrow tools and see that they are returned as soon as they have been used. Having a specific place for shop tools will make it possible to see at a glance if everything is on hand. Oil power tools as directed by the manufacturer, and keep them clean.

Basic Tools

Many of the following items have already been included in the general equipment lists for the costume shop. It is certainly not necessary to have duplicate tools just for the construction of costume properties. The tools that will be used most often for building costume properties, however, should be stored in that area.

SCISSORS Sturdy, straight-handled paper scissors for cutting paper, cardboard, and celastic. Keep them sharp.

SCREW DRIVERS Regular and Phillips.

HAMMER, TACK HAMMER, AND WOODEN OR RUBBER MALLET The hammer and the tack hammer have obvious uses. You will use the mallet for pounding glued leather seams; nothing else will do the job as well.

WIRE CUTTERS A medium-large cutter that will handle several sizes of wire.

TIN SNIPS For cutting thin sheets of metal. Also useful for trimming hardened celastic.

REGULAR PLIERS AND JEWELRY PLIERS If you have to choose only one pair, choose the jewelry pliers.

MAT KNIFE AND BLADES A mat knife with a retractible blade is safer and the blades will stay sharp longer.

X-ACTO KNIFE AND BLADES Different blades fit different handles; make sure you buy a matched set.

METAL RULER A two-foot rule is a handy size. The metal edge is invaluable as a cutting guide.

CLAY MODELING TOOLS Useful not only for molding clay but also for rubbing and burnishing foil.

PAINT BRUSHES Cheap brushes are only economical if you neglect to clean good ones. Develop the habit of cleaning good brushes before they dry, using the appropriate solvent and then using soap and water. You will find that they have a long life and that you will be spared the annoying propensity of cheap brushes to shed hairs, which stick to newly painted surfaces. Start with a half dozen medium-sized, moderately expensive artists' brushes and add to your collection as you need different sizes.

HOT GLUE GUN AND GLUE PELLETS The hot glue gun has so many uses that it is difficult to imagine a costume shop without one. It is used both for gluing and for creating decorative surfaces. Buy a large supply of pellets; they are cheaper that way. Once you have experimented with a hot glue gun, you will discover a dozen new ways to put it to use. Remember that hot glue will not withstand dry cleaning.

LEATHER PUNCH Buy a hand-operated punch that has several different sized cutters. New cutters may be purchased separately and inserted into the punch when the old ones become damaged or irreversibly dulled.

OTHER LEATHER TOOLS These should include an awl, leather needles (or glovers) in different sizes, and a leather stripper for making rawhide strips.

GROMMET SETTING DYES AND GROMMETS Remember that each size grommet must have its own size setting dye. Start out with one or two common sizes and add others as the need arises. The larger sizes are used more often for costume properties, the smaller ones for costume garments.

VICE GRIP Very helpful for reglueing shoes.

C-CLAMPS In various sizes.

DRAFTING TOOLS Include a chalk board compass.

STAPLE GUN

Desirable Tools

Costume technicians are notoriously fond of tools. A list of special tools that reflect the desires of even half a dozen technicians would be endless. The following few items have been chosen because they perform multiple tasks and are moderately priced.

ELECTRIC DRILL Many shops get on for years punching holes with the leather punch, awls, nails, and ice picks. An electric drill, with an assortment of bits, does the job more quickly and easily. Some drills also include bits that perform other operations, such as buffing.

POP RIVET SETTER Pop rivets are a boon to leather work. They come in various sizes and are easy to insert. Pop rivets may be removed with a drill press, which is usually standard equipment in scenic design shops.

SPRAY GUN Most costume shops use spray paints in pressure cans. Since cans come in a wide assortment of colors, this is usually satisfactory. A spray gun that operates with a pressure canister offers slightly more flexibility, since you can mix your own paint or dye colors.

STOCK MATERIALS

Certain stock supplies should be kept on hand if there is sufficient storage space and if several productions are being planned. Large quantities of paints and glues are cheaper per ounce than small quantities. Even when there is no price differential (e.g., one yard of celastic is the same price per yard as five yards), it is handy to have supplies on hand so construction can begin on a project without having to wait for a mail shipment.

Adhesives

There are several white flexible glues on the market. Sobo is one of the most commonly used. Sobo can be bought in hardware stores, some fabric stores, and always in a craft supply shop. It is available in small squeeze bottles and in gallon jugs.

One of the finest flexible glues, however, is made by Swift Adhesives. It is #3917, which must be ordered directly from the company and is available only in five gallon cans. This glue will not deteriorate. It is thicker than Sobo and can normally be used in a more diluted solution. It is highly recommended.

A special adhesive is necessary to bind foam rubber pieces together. The 3-M Company manufactures one such product, #847, which may either be purchased from a company that sells foam rubber, occasionally from a craft supply shop, or from the 3-M Company itself.

Barge cement is the adhesive of choice for leather work. It can also be used for binding foam rubber pieces when nothing else is available. Keep Barge thinner on hand for thinning the glue, and also for cleaning out brushes that have been used in Barge.

Other adhesives to keep on the shelf might include a good epoxy, Duco cement, Elmer's white glue, a photo spray adhesive, and rubber cement.

Paints and Solvents

FRENCH ENAMEL VARNISH (FEV) FEV produces a lively translucent color that dries very quickly and never fades. It is invaluable for coloring prop jewelry and innumerable other items. FEV is made with one part white shellac to three to five parts denatured alcohol, plus an alcohol soluble dye. Liquid leather dyes, such as Fiebing or Omega, are quite convenient, although some commercial dye pigments are also satisfactory. Make FEV solutions in several colors and store them in tightly capped jars. The solutions are quite stable.

SPRAY PAINTS All spray paints should be used in a well-ventilated area, and it is recommended that the costumers using them wear masks.

Stock basic colors of Magix spray leather dyes and spray enamels such as Krylon and Fab Spray. Black, brown, khaki, tan, and yellow can form a stock supply, with other colors added as necessary. Metallic sprays in bright gold, bronze, and silver should be stocked; Illinois Bronze is an excellent brand.

After spraying with a spray can, turn it upside down and depress the spray mechanism to clear out the nozzle. This will help to prevent clogging. Keep working nozzles from empty spray cans; they can be exchanged for nonworking nozzles. Also save the large plastic caps from spray cans; they make good containers for mixing small quantities of paint. Should you want a small amount of spray paint to use with a brush, spray directly into a plastic cap.

BRONZING POWDERS These powders come in an assortment of metallic colors. They are expensive, but less so per ounce if they are bought in one pound cans rather than in small tubes. Bronzing powders are usually suspended in bronzing liquid, in an FEV solution, in a flexible glue and water solution, or in lacquer. Banana lacquer binds these metallic powders particularly well.

ACRYLIC PAINTS In tubes or in jars, these paints are widely used in making costume properties. The colors are vibrant, they dry rapidly, and they never rub off.

ACETONE Acetone is the most common solvent for celastic. Always have at least a gallon on hand. A five gallon drum is more economical, but keep it tightly capped because it does evaporate.

TURPENTINE For cleaning up.

Fabrics

CELASTIC Celastic is, in its original form, soft and pliable. Soak it in acetone (or in methyl-acetate, in methyl ethyl keytone, or in Celastic 4-Star Solvent) and drape it over a form and it will dry in that form and remain both perfectly hard and water proof. It is used for a variety of costume properties, including armor, helmets, shields, chains, masks, and many other things. Celastic will bond itself to metals, woods, plaster, fabrics, and acetate sheets. It dries in about twenty minutes, and, when hard, it can be sanded.

FELT   Industrial felt is a fabric which can be used for an endless number of costume accessories. It comes in many thicknesses and qualities. The best and the most expensive kind is made from all-wool fibers. Cheaper felts have other fibers, usually of unknown origin, mixed in with the wool. All-wool felt wears much better than mixtures.

Industrial felt is often difficult to find unless you live and work in a large city. Most industrial felt is sold for the purpose of padding large moving pieces of machinery. If you are unable to find a felt supplier, contact a company that uses heavy machines and they may be able to help you. If you do locate a supplier, it is often possible to buy end pieces of industrial felt which may be thinner, less regular, and also less expensive than the regular industrial felt. Felt is sold by the pound.

A particular type of all-wool felt called orthopedic felt may be purchased in orthopedic supply houses. It is used to pad casts and is usually white. Orthopedic felt is approximately one-eighth-inch thick and is excellent for constructing jewelry and crowns.

Decorator felt can be purchased in dime stores and craft supply shops. It can be used for covering certain costume properties, but it is not strong enough to be used without a stout backing.

All felt does tend to shrink, some types more than others. Always steam felt before using it in order to shrink it up as much as possible.

MUSLIN   Medium-weight, unbleached muslin is used in the construction of some cos-tume properties. Muslin can also be soaked in flexible glue and molded into fanciful shapes, such as ears for a mask, or small angel wings.

CHEESECLOTH   Cheesecloth is often used to add both strength and texture to papier mâché masks and latex pieces.

CANVAS   Canvas forms the backing for belts and bandoliers. A somewhat stylized type of armor can be made from two layers of canvas stuffed with batting and painted with flexible glue and FEV.

PADDING MATERIAL   Always keep a bag or two of padding material on hand. Dacron fluff holds its shape well and does not pack down. Cotton batting gives a firm look, but it has a tendency to pack down and lose its original shape. Shredded foam gives a springy look, but it will get lumpy.

Miscellaneous Supplies and Materials

coffee cans
widemouth jars and lids
paper, plastic, and aluminum cups
cake pans
millinery wire
armature wire
plastic screening
tongue depressors
Q-tips and wooden stirrers
foam rubber
leather scraps
liquid latex
aluminum foil
plastic wrap
clothespins
T-pins
push pins
sandpaper
masking and Scotch tape

dental moulage for making life masks
plaster bandages (available from a medical
    supply company)
nonhardening plastic clay (such as
    Roma Plastilina)
imitation gold and silver leaf
silicone protective hand cream
hand cleaners
light-weight rubber gloves

Miscellaneous Decorative Items

Almost anything can decorate a costume
prop. Collect miscellaneous items of all sorts,
including: buttons, studs, string, yarn, rope,
beads, lace pieces, pearls, sequins, cogwheels,
brass and copper wire, eyelets, washers,
shells, pebbles, cork balls, bottle corks, and
broken tile. The list is endless.

SHOPPING FOR A SPECIFIC PROJECT

There is nothing more annoying to a technician working on a costume property than to
run out of a material at nine o'clock at night
or on a Sunday afternoon when no shops
are open. It is almost as annoying to have
to stop in the middle of a step to run to the
hardware store, even when it is open for business. No costume shop that has to work
within a budget will want to overstock an
item that may not be used again for five years.
However, with a little planning, enough materials can be kept on hand so that the work
can proceed efficiently. Most craft supply
stores will sell you several bags or boxes of
a material with the understanding that un-
opened packages can be returned for a full
refund.

Some designers will know exactly which
materials they wish to have a specific costume
property made from. In these instances, the
technician assigned to its construction should
make careful notes, recording brand names
if they are given. Other designers will leave

the decisions about how and of what a property will be made up to the technician. The
technician should make plans for the accessory, but he should always discuss these
plans with the designer before shopping for
the materials. Once designer and technician
are in agreement about method and materials,
the technician should make a list of the stock
materials and special materials needed. Calculate quantities carefully and check stock
materials to make sure enough is on hand.

Shop by phone first. This saves both time
and frustration. Unless you are already sure
of the cost for certain items, check prices from
at least three supply sources. If these three
prices differ a great deal, check some more.
Make sure that the shops you call have
enough of the item in stock. The cheapest
plastic chain in town will do you no good
if the store has only six feet of it and you
need twelve.

Buy everything you need before you start to work.

ARMOR

Many plays from many periods require actors
to be suited up for battle. In some plays, *Macbeth* or *Richard III,* for example, the battle is
actually fought on stage. Most battles before
the end of the seventeenth century were
fought by soldiers in some type of armor.

Since the dawn of civilization, men have
dressed themselves in various heavy shells
in order to protect their bodies from attacks
by other men. Animal skins and leather were
the first protective coverings, .followed in
time by bronze and iron. Early armor was

concentrated on the vulnerable areas of the chest, the back, and the head. Beginning in the twelfth century, men covered their arms, legs, and necks with chain mail and the rest of their bodies with metal plates. From the fifteenth through the seventeenth centuries, complete suits of metal plate armor were worn, even over the face, the hands, and the feet. After the seventeenth century, weapons became so powerful that armor could no longer protect a man from bullets and shells. The character of war changed and individual suits of armor were no longer worn.

Like other costume properties, costume armor may be either stylized or realistic. It is sometimes fiercely real, as in a production of *The Trojan Women,* and sometimes funny, as in *Lysistrata.* Whatever its nature, stage armor must appear to be made out of protective materials. It must look strong and impenetrable, yet it must be light enough and comfortable enough not to create an undue burden for the actor who wears it.

There are several different methods that are commonly employed for making stage armor. The choice of method will be affected by the nature of the material being simulated, the particular style being represented, and the size of the production budget.

Leather Armor

Leather armor can range in complexity from a rough leather jerkin-type chest and back covering to molded leather armor plates made from boiled leather and shaped to the human form. Simple, flexible leather armor of the more primitive variety is always the most successful on stage when it is made out of actual leather skins. Leather is, however, expensive. If you live in an area where leather is tanned, you may contact tanneries to see if they will allow you to purchase small, imperfect skins at reduced prices. If not, you will find the price of skins quite high. Most commercially produced, plastic based, imita-

FIGURE 11.2   *A stylized suit of armor for a production of* Richard III *at the Milwaukee Repertory Theater. (Randy Barcelo, costume designer; photograph by Susan Perkins.)*

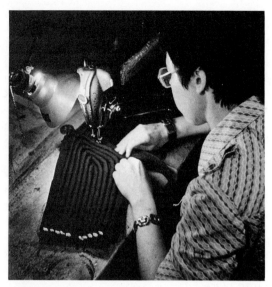

FIGURE 11.3 *Construction of a piece of the armor pictured in Figure 11.2. (Photograph by Mark Avery.)*

Do not leave seam allowances. Remember that felt has no fabric grain and that the pieces can be laid in any direction on the felt. Stitch shoulder seams and side seams by butting the two pieces of felt together and joining them with a wide zigzag machine stitch. Leave the center back open. Fit the felt pieces on the actor and make adjustments.

4. Use the muslin pattern to cut the leather, adding a one-inch allowance around each piece. This will be trimmed or turned under later.

5. Cover a male dummy with plastic and place the felt armor backing on the dummy. Pin it firmly in place.

6. Use Barge cement for gluing the leather to the felt. Barge is a contact cement, which

FIGURE 11.4 *A piece of pigskin armor showing both decorative and practical lacings. (Photograph by Richard Bryant.)*

tion leathers are not suitable for stage armor unless the design specifically calls for a stylized armor with a slick, shiny surface. It is virtually impossible to make commercial, imitation leather look like the real, battle-scarred thing.

The next section contains two methods for making simple, primitive leather armor. The first method requires leather skins; the second creates an imitation leather finish on an industrial felt surface. There were instructions earlier in this chapter for a method of giving an imitation leather surface to a messenger pouch with soap, acrylic paint, and shoe polish. This technique is most successful when it is applied to small items, but it can, in a pinch, be used for simple armor. It is less expensive than either of the two methods that follow.

PRIMITIVE LEATHER ARMOR

1. Develop a muslin pattern from the actor's body sloper, leaving ample ease room for garments which will be worn underneath.

2. Fit the muslin to the actor and make adjustments.

3. Cut armor pieces from industrial felt.

FIGURE 11.5 *A piece of woven leather armor with decorative and practical lacings. (Photograph by Richard Bryant.)*

around the arms, around the neck, and down the center back—trim the leather to one-half-inch from the edge of the felt. At each seam-line, glue each turn-back to the inside. Make sure the turned-back leather meets over the felt seamline. Pound the glued turn-back with a mallet.

8. Make slits or holes for the laces. Lace over each seam. A bodkin for carrying the lacing is a great timesaver.

9. Set grommets up the center back for practical laces. These grommets should go through both felt and leather layers. Lace with stout rawhide thongs.

10. Bevel the edges of the felt at the bottom, neck and arm edges, and up the center back. Glue all leather edges down and pound into place.

The armor piece is now ready to be aged and highlighted with leather dyes.

means that glue must be applied to both surfaces that are to be adhered. With a paint brush, spread a thin layer of Barge on the front of the felt armor backing and on the underside of the front leather piece. Extend the glue to within an inch of all edges and seams. The leather that is not glued down will be used as the base for lacing. Allow the Barge to become tacky, then apply the leather to the felt, working from the center front and moving outward in all directions. Barge sets up very quickly. When the whole piece of leather is applied, pound the leather firmly in place with a mallet. Repeat the gluing process with both back pieces.

The only practical lacings on this particular piece of armor are those that go up the center back. The decorative lacings that appear to lace the pieces of the armor together are placed only through the leather, not through the felt backing.

7. At each seamline, trim the leather away, leaving just enough for a quarter-inch turn-back. At the edges of the armor—bottom,

PRIMITIVE IMITATION LEATHER ARMOR If leather is prohibitively expensive, a relatively realistic looking simulated leather finish can be applied to plain, industrial felt. Construct the felt armor body exactly as was done above and place the armor on a plastic-covered dummy. Put a thick bed of newspaper or plastic drop cloths underneath the dummy, because this is a messy process.

Mix about a pint of flexible white glue with the same quantity of water. In another container, mix the same amount (about two pints) of the FEV solution, using dye that will give you whatever leather color you desire. Coat the felt thoroughly with the glue and water solution. Make sure this layer soaks into the felt. Allow this layer to dry overnight; it need not be completely dry. Alternate several layers of the FEV solution and the glue solution until a leathery texture begins to form. Make sure to coat the felt completely with each layer, including all edges. Do not allow to dry between coats. Afterwards, allow the armor to dry completely, which may take up to two days.

Remove the dry armor from the dummy and rip the seams apart. Trim away rough edges and punch holes along each side of each seam. Lace the pieces together. Set grommets up the center back for practical lacing. The surface will be mottled and uneven and probably will not require much aging or highlighting. If it is too shiny in spots, spray those places with a dulling spray or rub them with soap or brown paste shoe polish.

Molded Armor

Stage armor that simulates leather or metal plates is constructed from a variety of materials that can be molded into firm, strong shapes. These materials must be light in weight and one must be able to add a variety of surfaces, textures, and decorations with paint and glue. Inexpensive, credible armor pieces can be created from papier mâché, but they are completely inflexible and crack or break easily. Fiberglass armor is excellent, and practically indestructible, but it is very expensive and requires sophisticated equipment and technical know-how unavailable in most costume shops. The following discussion is about the three most common stage armor materials: thermoplastic forms molded in a vacuum forming machine, celastic, and sized felt. General directions are for breast and back plates, but armor pieces can be made for any part of the body, using the same methods; only the molds differ.

VACU-FORM ARMOR Unless your theatre has Vacu-form equipment, you will probably purchase Vacu-form armor pieces. They are inexpensive and widely available. A large selection of pieces, including most breast and back plate styles, greaves, helmets, decorative plaques, and insignia, as well as complete suits of body armor, may be obtained at Costume Armor, Hanger E., P.O. Box 6086, Stew-

art Airport, Newburgh, New York 12550. They will send you a catalogue on request.

Simply choose the armor pieces that most nearly conform to the design you are creating. Fit the pieces on the actor and trim if necessary. Most breast and back plates will be fastened at the shoulders and at the sides with straps and buckles. Determine where these straps will go and mark their placement.

Lay the breast and back plates side by side on a large work table and take a few minutes to plan out the decorative steps. Raised areas should be added first. These may be stock Vacu-form plaques or insignia which were purchased along with the armor pieces. If so, glue them to the plate with any good contact cement. Other plaques or insignia can be created from celastic and bonded directly to the armor piece by wetting the celastic edges with acetone and pressing the insignia in place. Many raised designs can be made by gluing rope, felt, string, or yarn to the piece. Others will be done with split cork balls, buttons, or wooden discs. Use the hot glue gun for intricate borders and subtle swirls.

Once the surface is complete, give the entire piece of armor an undercoating of flat spray paint: brown if the surface should simulate leather or bronze, black if it must look like silver or iron. If a rough surface texture is desired, mix a bit of sand or sawdust in some flexible glue and water and lay on a thin coating of this mixture over the base color. Allow texturing to dry thoroughly. The final layer is FEV, colored with an appropriate dye. Shade and touch up as desired, using FEV, Rub & Buff, lamp black, bronzing powders, or oil paints.

There are probably as many ways of painting, texturing, and finishing a piece of armor as there are costume technicians. Use the preceding instructions as the broadest sort of outline guide and develop a specific set of decorative materials and painting techniques for each project.

When the armor pieces are completed, attach straps and buckles with rivets or lace them on with leather thongs.

CELASTIC ARMOR The first step in building celastic armor back and chest plates is to create a mold on which the celastic can be formed. The simplest way to do this is to use a male dummy, padded out to correspond to the actor's measurements—with some to spare. If a dummy is not available, try to find an old shirt display form at a local department store or men's shop. These are usually fairly shapeless, but they can be built up with pieces of foam or padding material.

Once the mold is the proper size and shape (do make sure it is an ample size, since celastic does have a tendency to shrink as it dries), cover it with a good thick layer of heavyweight aluminum foil. Mold the breast plate and the back plate in two separate operations because you will want to extend both shoulders and sides well around the form. They can be trimmed later.

Tear the celastic into strips as long as the full length of the armor and from two to four inches wide. Tear, do not cut straight strips; the torn edges will mold better. Cut a few one- to two-inch-wide strips on the bias; they will go around neck and armhole curves and will bind edges. Tear and cut a good supply of strips before pouring the celastic solvent.

As already stated, the most common celastic solvent is acetone, although others are mentioned earlier in this chapter. Pour out some solvent in a porcelain or a stainless steel bowl. Do not pour out too much; and be sure to recap the container, because these solvents evaporate rapidly. Immerse each strip of celastic in the solvent just before placing it on the mold. It is a good idea to wear rubber gloves when you are working with celastic, since both the fabric and the solvent tend to be irritating to the skin. If gloves inhibit your dexterity, try coating your hands with a protective cream such as Pro-Tek.

Starting at the center front of the mold, lay on a piece of celastic. Following the contour of the chest, lay on the next piece, overlapping it about three-quarters of an inch. Continue in this manner until the entire chest and underarm areas are covered. Use the bias strips around the neck and armholes. The entire molding process should be accomplished quickly. Celastic becomes quite hard in about twelve minutes, and it can be removed from the mold in twenty minutes.

Before removing the breast plate from the mold, however, draw in the neckline and armholes on the piece. At this point, these will be rough approximations. Remove the breast plate and proceed to mold the back plate in the same manner. After both pieces have been removed, fit them on the actor and make necessary trimming alterations with a mat knife or with tin snips. Once the pieces are trimmed, bind the edges with strips of bias-cut celastic moistened with solvent.

After the binding is dry, sand the breast and back plates, using a rough grade of sandpaper and moving to a medium grade. If a still smoother surface is desired, the celastic surface may be covered with a wood filler or with plastic wood.

From this point on, the celastic armor pieces may be painted and decorated in the same manner as the Vacu-form pieces. It will probably be necessary to drill holes to attach straps or other fastenings. Celastic armor is much harder than Vacu-form armor.

SIZED FELT ARMOR Sized felt armor is particularly good for achieving a bulky look. The breastplate in Figure 11.6 was created from this material. Once again, you will need a mold which can be made in the same way as the mold for celastic armor. Cover the mold with sheet plastic rather than with aluminum foil.

Use industrial felt with a high percentage of wool in it. Cut it to fit the actor's body. The fit should be fairly accurate but with

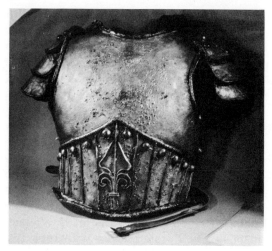

FIGURE 11.6 *Breastplate made from sized felt. (Photograph by Susan Perkins.)*

some allowance for the shrinkage that will occur during the process. Soak the pieces thoroughly with a mixture of two parts white flexible glue to one part water. Place the piece on the mold and work it firmly into place, pushing and stretching until it is smooth. Pin the felt to the mold with long T-pins. Allow the piece to dry; this may take several days. When it is completely dry, remove it from the mold and apply a thin layer of shellac to the inside and to the outside of the pieces.

FIGURE 11.7 *Sized felt armor gauntlet glove with flexible fingers. (Photograph by Susan Perkins.)*

Decorations on sized felt armor are usually larger and simpler than those used on the other two types. After the raised decorations are applied, lay on a base coat of paint and proceed with texturing and finishing. Sized felt is the thickest of the three armor materials discussed; if straps and buckles are being riveted onto the armor pieces, be sure to purchase long shanked rivets and to reinforce from behind.

Chain Mail

Effective chain mail can be made from string knitted on large size knitting needles. If possible, purchase colored string in gray, dark green, or black. This will eliminate spraying the knitted chain mail with a base coat before applying a final coat of bronzing powder mixture or metallic spray paint.

Helmets

Helmets are made from the same materials, and decorated in the same ways, as armor plates. They are more complicated only because the shapes are more intricate and because they must provide a good fit for the head.

Vacu-form helmet shells in a wide variety of styles are available from Costume Armor and some general costume rental and supply companies. After painting, texturing, and the application of decorative elements are complete, create a comfortable fit by gluing a strip of industrial felt or foam rubber inside the helmet. If the helmet is to be removed on stage, spray the inside a flat, dark color that corresponds to the outside surface.

Any style helmet may be created from celastic, once the appropriate mold has been made. Start out with a wig block, a head block, or a hat block and sculpt the desired shape out of modeling clay. Make the helmet

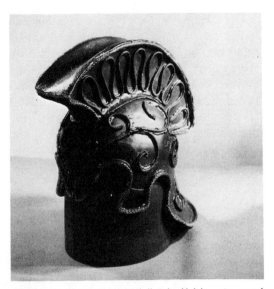

FIGURE 11.8 *Vacu-form helmet shell with added decoration created with rope, string, and hot glue. (Photograph by Susan Perkins.)*

mold somewhat larger than the actor's head; remember that celastic shrinks as it dries. If the design shape is intricate, or if a number of identical helmets will be made over the same mold, put a layer of cheesecloth over the completed clay mold for strength and stability. Hold the mold up and look at it from all angles. Observe it in a mirror. The two sides must be identical. The most common mistake in creating helmets is producing a lopsided mold. Cover the mold with aluminum foil or with a thick layer of petroleum jelly or silicone spray.

Tear straight strips of celastic that are long enough to reach from the front to the back of the helmet. These strips should be about two inches wide. Cut shorter strips of celastic on the bias, an inch wide, for curved areas. Dip each piece of celastic in solvent just before applying it to the mold. Work from the top down each side. Overlap the strips of celastic about one-half-inch. If the helmet includes face flaps, these should be made separately and attached to the helmet after a

fitting. Celastic pieces can be moistened with solvent and stuck to each other. Some celastic helmets must be split in order to remove them from their molds. Split the helmet down the middle and remove each side from the mold. Put the two halves back together with strips of wet celastic.

In addition to the surface already discussed, an excellent helmet surface can be created with Sculp-Metal. Figure 11.9 shows a helmet that was made with a celastic base and a Sculp-Metal surface. Follow directions on the package for mixing and applying the material. Additional designs on the helmet in Figure 11.9 were created with rope and hot glue.

For a particularly comfortable fit, suspend large helmets on plastic workmen's hard-hat liners, which can be adjusted to the head size of individual actors. It is often necessary to purchase an inexpensive hard hat in order to obtain the liner. Fasten the celastic helmet to the liner with rivets or with strips of celastic.

FIGURE 11.9 *Helmet with a Sculp-Metal surface. (Photograph by Susan Perkins.)*

Sized felt is only suitable for very simple helmets with a minimum of shape detail. Construct the felt helmet shape with pieces of felt stitched together, allowing some room for shrinkage. Butt the pieces and stitch them with a wide zigzag machine stitch. The felt shape may be fitted on the actor before it is sized. Make sure that it is not too tight. When shape and size are correct, place the felt helmet on a head block which has been covered with plastic sheeting. Lay on a thick coat of white flexible glue and water: two parts glue and one part water. Let this layer dry. If there is still a fuzzy quality to the surface, add another layer of the glue and water. When the surface is firm and the helmet is completely dry, remove it from the block and paint both the inside and the outside of the helmet with shellac. Add color, texture, and decorations as required by the design.

MASKS

It is difficult to discuss the use and construction of theatrical masks without devoting an entire book to the subject. There are many different kinds of masks and many different methods of constructing them. The mask, as an essential part of the theatre, has a long and a fascinating history, as well as a lively present. Ancient plays and modern plays may require the actors to be masked. The effect of the mask can be frightening, funny, or alienating. The mask may be a realistic representation of a human face or a grotesque interpretation of an imaginary monster. It may be an animal, a bird, or a fish. In fact, it may be anything.

This discussion will cover only the basic steps necessary to begin to build a mask, a description of the most common materials, and a few suggestions for creating special effects. More than with any other costume property, mask-making requires an artist's touch and a sculptor's eye. The techniques are simple, but the outcome depends upon more than the skillful application of those techniques. It is not a task at which everybody will excel, even though it is one that everybody ought to try.

FIGURE 11.10   *Costume sketch for* Oedipus Rex *by Laura Crow.*

Making a Life Mask

The first step in making most theatrical masks is to create a plaster mold of the actor's face on which to mold the mask. This is not a particularly complicated operation, but it is time-consuming, especially if many masks are being made. Some technicians prefer to model the actor's face directly in clay, using

FIGURE 11.11   *Costume sketch for* Oedipus Rex *by Laura Crow.*

A comfortable, relaxed actor is an essential ingredient for a successful life mask.

Place the actor in a prone position, up on a table rather than on the floor. It is best to have the upper body raised slightly on a firm pillow. Cover the actor's clothing with plastic sheeting and construct a cardboard collar that will fit around the neck and catch any drops from the molding material. Tuck the hair into a bathing cap, or cover it with plastic wrap which may be secured with tape. Rub a bit of a silicone hand lotion into the face. Do not use cold cream. The mold material is not harmful to the skin.

The most common material for taking a negative face mold is dental moulage, which is used commercially for making impressions of the teeth and which can be purchased from a dental supply company. Follow the directions on the package for melting the moulage. This is done in a double boiler on a stove or hot plate. When the moulage is smooth and liquid, cool it until it is comfortable to the touch. Apply it to the face, starting with the forehead and working down. The layer should be about three-quarters of an inch thick. Make certain that the actor keeps his or her eyes closed. Cover the entire face except the nostrils. Some technicians put straws in the actor's nostrils as an added precaution. Work quickly. Once the moulage is dry, wet moulage will not stick to it. The moulage will take between twenty and thirty minutes to dry. When the moulage is dry, moisten several strips of plaster-impregnated bandages with water and apply them on top of the moulage. This is to give the mold additional strength. Pay particular attention to the outer edges of the mold: the nose, the forehead, and the chin. As soon as the plaster sets up, which only takes a few minutes, ask the actor to begin to wiggle the facial muscles in order to loosen the moulage. The technician can loosen the moulage around the edges of the mold. When the moulage is free, lift it off the face and turn it, mold side up, into

head and face measurements. For those who do not have sculpting skills, it is best to make a life mask.

The life mask is done in two steps. First, a negative mold is taken from the actor's face; then a plaster positive mold is made from the negative. The two steps should be done consecutively, although the actor's presence is required only for the first step. Schedule an hour for step one. It may not take quite this long, but some actors, particularly those who have not had a life mask taken, may be nervous. Explain the process carefully and offer reassurance that the experience will be neither dangerous nor uncomfortable. The actor's most important task while the mold is being made is to remain still and not to move the facial muscles. If the actor smiles or raises an eyebrow while the negative mold is being taken, the mold will be destroyed.

a box containing several inches of sawdust. Push the mold down into the sawdust, which will support it while the plaster positive is being cast.

Proceed to the second step right away, because moulage tends to shrink as it loses moisture. Pour about two pints of water into an enamelware or stainless steel pan. Slowly sprinkle plaster into the water. It is impossible to give a specific amount for the plaster. Continue pouring, very slowly, until some plaster begins to float on the surface of the water. Carefully knead the plaster with your hand, smoothing out all lumps. Never stir plaster vigorously. The mixture should achieve the consistency of heavy cream. Bang the bottom of the pan several times to release air bubbles and then pour the plaster into the mold, filling it all the way to the top. Plaster becomes warm to the touch as it sets up. As soon as the plaster is cool and set, turn the mold over and remove the moulage. It will come off in chunks that can be saved and reheated for future use. Allow the positive plaster mold to dry thoroughly, for at least twenty-four hours. In order to protect the plaster mold, which will chip easily, give it a coat or two of white shellac before using it. It is always a good idea to mark the back of the mold with the actor's name and the date of casting.

Another excellent material for making a life mold is Flex Wax. Molds made from this wax are incredibly detailed and much stronger than those made from moulage. The process is also quicker. See *Theatre Crafts,* Volume 9, No. 6 (1975) for an article entitled "Plastic People," by John T. Baun and Ernest Foster, which gives specific, illustrated instructions for using Flex Wax as well as information about the company from which it may be purchased.

The purpose of making a mask on a mold of the actor's face is to produce an inner mask surface that will conform to the actor's features and that will, therefore, be comfortable to wear. In order to achieve a good fit, any parts of the mask that are to be grossly enlarged out of proportion to the actor's face will be added after the inner surface of the mask is already complete. Certain mask features can be sculpted directly on the life mold with modeling clay: a bulbous nose, a craggy forehead, high cheekbones. These features will be incorporated in the mask's inner surface and will not affect the fit a great deal. But if the mask is to be broader or higher than the actor's face, these parts of the mask are not sculpted on the life mold; they are added as the mask is being made. Remember that any place on the life mold that is covered with a layer of clay is a place on the inner surface of the mask that will *not* come in contact with the face.

When all the desired sculpting has been completed on the life mold, cover it with aluminum foil and, if the mask is being constructed out of papier mâché, with a layer of petroleum jelly as well.

Papier Mâché Masks

Some of the most beautiful of all theatrical masks are made from papier mâché, and many mask makers prefer it to all other materials. A properly constructed papier mâché mask is quite durable. The process does, however, require several steps and takes rather a long time.

There are two major methods of constructing masks with paper and paste. The first makes use of strips of paper—newspaper, construction paper, or tissue paper—and wheat paste. (A white glue, such as Elmer's Glue-All is sometimes used instead of wheat paste.) The second is done either with a commercial pulp paper mixture such as Celluclay or Shreddi-Mix or with a pulp mix which can be made in the shop.

The costs of producing a paper and wheat paste mask are negligible. The paper may well be free and wheat paste is cheap. Paints will probably be the most expensive ingredients. Pulpy construction paper is a little bit easier to work with than newsprint. Tear (don't cut) the paper into strips of various sizes and shapes. Prepare a good supply of torn paper, since it is difficult to tear more once your hands are covered with paste. To mix wheat paste, put water in a bowl and sprinkle the wheat paste into it. Don't add very much, however; wheat paste swells up a lot as it absorbs the water. Add just a little at a time until the mixture is about the consistency of mayonnaise.

If you are using construction paper, it is a good idea to use at least two colors so you can keep track of the layers you have applied. Four to six layers are good for the basic mask. Spread paste on the paper strips and apply them to the prepared mold, overlapping a good deal. Work continuously. One layer does not have to dry before you add another. When the basic mask is layered in, let it set overnight before you begin to add the height, width, or features called for in the design. Jowls, drooping eyelids, or other bulging areas can be made from rolls or wads of paper, which are then incorporated into the mask's outer surface with additional strips of paper and glue. As you work on the mask, hold it up from time to time and look at it in a mirror. The added distance will give you some idea as to how the mask will look on stage. In general, mask features should be strong and forthright, without a lot of cluttered detail. Make sure that none of the features on the mask interfere with the openings that must be left so the actor can see.

It is difficult to say exactly how thick a paper and paste mask should be. This depends largely upon the complexity of the design. Once you are satisfied with the shape and feel that it is thick enough, allow the mask to dry thoroughly. Drying may be speeded up slightly by setting the mask under a hair dryer set on cool. Be patient. Unaided, the mask may take three or four days to dry

completely. When it is absolutely dry, loosen the mask all around the edges and gently remove it from the mold. Scrape any bits of clay and aluminum foil from the inside of the mask. Rub with a cloth to remove petroleum jelly. Using a mat knife, trim any bits of paper from around the eyeholes, and then fit the mask on the actor. Make the eyeholes larger if necessary. Eyeholes may be masked with screen and the screen incorporated into the paint plan for the mask. Determine the exact outside edge of the mask and mark it with a pencil line. Trim the mask back to the pencil line. Place a piece of soft wire all the way around the edge of the mask and fasten it down with strips of paper and paste to form a binding. This layer will dry quickly. Sand the mask surface lightly with medium-fine sandpaper.

Now the mask is ready for painting. Lay down a base coat first. This is often done with Gesso. Acrylic paints are excellent for masks. Some mask makers prefer tempera colors which are fixed with shellac. Bits of hair, yarn, or feathers may be used for eyebrows or mustaches. Final touch-ups should be saved until after the mask is seen under stage lights. Colors may have to be changed or shadows strengthened so that the features will read properly.

To complete the mask, paint the inside with a layer of shellac and glue in small strips of felt or foam rubber at any of the places where the mask rests directly on the face, such as the bridge of the nose and the cheekbones. Attach whatever fastenings will be used.

Making paper pulp for masks is a bit like playing with mudpies. Newspaper is the perfect material and a large, full face mask can be made with about thirty-five pages of newsprint. Tear the paper into small bits and put it into a pail of warm water overnight. A quicker method is to put paper and water in a pail on a hot plate and let it simmer for two to three hours, stirring occasionally.

Once the paper is broken down, drain off the excess water thoroughly and transfer the pulp to another container, squeezing out more water as you proceed. Sprinkle a half-cup of wheat paste on top of the pulp and knead the whole mixture as if for bread. The pulp is now ready to apply to the mold.

Prepare the mold in the same way as for the paper strip method. Throw a handful of the pulp on the mold and form the mask shape exactly as if you were using clay. Pulp masks are most successful when the features are broad and lumpy rather than finely wrought.

A pulp mask will take up to a week to dry completely. Don't hurry it. If you remove it from the mold too soon, it will surely crack. Sculpted pulp masks are very hard when dry and can be sanded vigorously. They are somewhat porous, however, and should be

FIGURE 11.13   *Michael Pierce and Stephen Stout (as the Lion) in* Androcles and the Lion *at the Milwaukee Repertory Theater. (Elizabeth Covey, costume designer; photograph courtesy of the Milwaukee Repertory Theater.)*

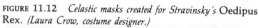
FIGURE 11.12   *Celastic masks created for Stravinsky's* Oedipus Rex. *(Laura Crow, costume designer.)*

undercoated with a layer of shellac on both sides before being painted.

Commercial papier mâché pulp is handled in exactly the same manner. Simply mix the pulp with water as directed on the package.

Celastic Masks

Celastic masks can be created in a fraction of the time it takes to make a paper and paste mask. Some mask makers feel, however, that the material does not allow for the same amount of design subtlety as papier mâché. Nevertheless, a single layer of light-weight celastic, which dries in twenty minutes, can produce a handsome, long-wearing mask. Molding, except for the number of layers involved, and the drying time, is done in exactly the same way as with paper. Painting, decorating, and finishing are also the same.

Other Masks

Masks can, of course, also be made from thermoplastic sheets in a vacuum forming machine, from fiberglass, or from willow caning. Large animal heads are often constructed from wire frames which are padded with foam rubber or sheets of air conditioning foam. A fake fur coat, a yarn mane, buckram ears, and large glass eyes can complete the characterization. Figure 11.13 is a particularly lovable Lion from Shaw's *Androcles and the Lion.*

JEWELRY

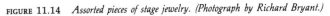

Most prop jewelry made for the stage represents the larger, more roughly made pieces from the earlier centuries. Machine-made, modern costume jewelry is too slick and shiny to project the correct feeling. Rough, prosaic materials and simple methods generally result in the most striking pieces of prop jewelry, whether it is a shoulder ornament for Julius Caesar or a crown for King Lear. In general, prop jewelry is built on a slightly larger than real-life scale with relatively simple, bold designs. For important pieces, designers should always supply the technician with a detailed sketch. Occasionally, however, the technician will receive only an idea of what the piece should look like, and he will be allowed to fill in the details with whatever materials can be made available. Jewelry from all ages is well represented in paintings, on statues, on carvings, and in collections of actual antique pieces in museums, so there should be no lack of research material for ideas and inspiration.

Because they so readily take a variety of

FIGURE 11.14   *Assorted pieces of stage jewelry. (Photograph by Richard Bryant.)*

FIGURE 11.15   *Hot melt glue guns. The holder is made from a piece of cardboard tubing fastened to a block of wood. The small box is to hold glue pellets. (Photograph by Richard Bryant.)*

adhesives and paints, both sized felt and celastic are extremely good for the setting of many jewelry pieces. Pendants and pins can both be built on celastic or sized felt foundations. A flat base coat, FEV, and bronzing powders give the color and finish. In order to attach the pin to a garment, a large safety pin or kilt pin is secured to the back. It can be glued to celastic with a piece of celastic, and it can be stitched to the sized felt with heavy-weight thread.

For prop jewelry that must represent fairly intricate gold work, stiffen bits of lace with white flexible glue and spray with gold paint or brush with bronzing powder suspended in FEV. Build a necklace from individual lace links, stiffened and sprayed, and attached to a chain. Lace can also simulate gold filigree work and be glued over a piece of colored

glass or an imitation pearl. Designs laid on with hot glue and painted gold can represent coarser gold workings.

Instead of painting on a gold or silver finish, some jewelry can be completed with light-weight metallic foil papers, available at craft and artist supply shops. The foil is applied to the object and rubbed firmly in place with wooden clay-modeling tools. Sometimes a toothpick is helpful for work in small areas. Be careful not to rip the foil. Foil papers create a hard, shiny finish that may have to be dulled somewhat for the stage.

Another method widely used for decorating costume props is done with a hot glue gun and imitation gold or silver leaf. Designs are applied to the object (brooch, breastplate, armband, etc.) with the hot glue gun and the glue is allowed to cool slightly. The metallic leaf is then laid on top and patted gently into place with a large, *soft* paintbrush. After the glue has cooled and hardened completely, the excess leaf is brushed away with a *stiff* paintbrush.

After a little practice, all sorts of intricate, raised designs can be accomplished by this method. The metallic leaf will adhere only to the glue itself and can afterward be shaded and painted with magic markers or FEV. Be sure to allow the glue to cool slightly before applying the leaf, as it tends to wrinkle and become dull if the glue is too hot.

Too much glitter on stage must generally be avoided. Stage lights may pick up shiny surfaces and reflect them in a distracting way. Dullcote is a spray enamel finish usually found in hobby shops; it is sold primarily for plastic models. When it is sprayed on prop jewelry, it creates a long-lasting matte finish. A wash of brown, khaki, or gray paint will add both age and a dulling layer to jewelry. Rub and Buff, which is applied in tiny amounts with the finger, creates a similar look. Rub and Buff is particularly good because it reduces the shine without killing it altogether. Paste shoe polish will do essentially the same thing, but it kills more shine. A quick method of toning down and dulling pieces of jewelry is to spritz them with a *flat* enamel spray paint.

Bamboo chains make excellent, lightweight stage chains. Chains can also be made from strips of flexible rubber tubing and from curtain rings. Avoid plastic chain, however, since it does not take paint well. Chains that

FIGURE 11.16 *Michael Pierce and Jeffrey Tambor in* Androcles and the Lion *at the Milwaukee Repertory Theater. Notice the prop jewelry worn by Mr. Tambor. (Elizabeth Covey, costume designer; photograph courtesy of the Milwaukee Repertory Theater.)*

must appear to be roughly forged can be shaped from strips of celastic in much the same way that paper chains are made for Christmas trees.

Stones for prop jewelry can sometimes be recovered from modern pieces of costume jewelry. Often, however, these are too machine-made-looking for a primitive creation. Excellent, rough-hewn-looking stones can be created with clear casting resins, which are sold in craft stores under various brand names, including Klear Cast and Titan. Create your own molds for the resins and layer the mold with sand or sawdust to roughen the outer texture of the stone. Fish bowl gravel, painted with FEV, is useful for smaller stones.

CROWNS

Kings and queens are featured in a great many plays, often wearing their crowns and sometimes seizing them from less fortunate monarchs. Unless the play is farcical, or unless there is some specific reason why the crown should look a bit foolish, a crown must look regal enough, and weighty enough, to represent the power and position of the monarch who wears it. Pay particular attention to the size of the crown in relation to the actor's head: The crown should neither be so small that it looks silly nor so large that

FIGURE 11.17   *Sized felt crown with Klear Cast stones and string and hot melt glue trim. (Photograph by Susan Perkins.)*

out of either of those two familiar materials: celastic or sized felt. Metallic finishes and decorative elements can be accomplished by methods already discussed.

Tooling metals, which have been torched, make particularly handsome crowns. You can purchase these metal sheets in many craft supply shops. They normally come in 36 gauge (.005″) thickness, in twelve-inch-wide sheets that are five, ten, and twenty-five feet long. Copper, brass, and aluminum are all available. In addition, colored aluminum comes in coppertone, goldtone, redtone, bluetone, and greentone. Tooling metals can be cut with heavy scissors or tin snips. It is usually necessary to back the metal with industrial felt or leather to ensure its sturdiness, and care should be taken to turn under, bind, or cover any sharp edges. Before applying the backing, touch the edges of the crown with a propane torch in order to give depth to the metal. Add strips of industrial felt or foam rubber to the inside for comfort and fit.

it overpowers the actor. Always make a scale cardboard mock-up of the crown, which can be fitted on the actor's head and studied for size and shape.

Once the mock-up has been fitted and approved, the crown base can be constructed

A WORD ABOUT SWORDS

Swords are generally produced for the stage by the property department and, as mentioned in Chapter 9, many types of swords will be rented for stage productions. Broadswords, however, are often built in the shop, and the decision as to what sort of metal will be used is an important one which should involve prop and costume technicians, as well as the actor who will wear or bear it.

Swords can always be made from steel in a metal-working shop. Steel is not, as metal goes, very expensive. However, it is very heavy. A long, steel broadsword may simply be too heavy for an actor to manage. Excellent *decorative* swords can be made from aluminum. Aluminum is light in weight; it can be cut fairly easily with a saber saw or a band saw and shaped with a file. For a sword that sim-

ply hangs from a sword belt, aluminum is an excellent material choice.

Aluminum is too light for fighting swords. Practical swords, such as the ones used by Macbeth and Macduff in *Macbeth,* or by Edmund and Edgar in *King Lear* must be capable of withstanding vigorous combat. Steel is too heavy for stage combat. One of the best metals for fighting swords is magnesium. Magnesium can be worked in the shop. It is easily cut with common power tools and files. It is very strong and, when two magnesium swords hit against each other, they make a loud, authentic ringing sound. Magnesium is, however, very expensive. The only method of purchasing which puts it in the range of possibility for the average costume shop is if it can be bought in small end cuts from a company in your area that uses sheet magnesium. Look in the yellow pages under "magnesium." Magnesium is also somewhat dangerous to handle. Sandings and filings from magnesium, if subjected to a spark, react like flash powder. When you are working with it, clean up *all* particles of dust and filings. Sanding disks should be used only for magnesium. If proper care is taken, however, magnesium makes superb fighting swords.

Conclusion

From its conception, this book has been devoted to the practical aspects of costuming plays, to instructions, methods, techniques. So far only passing mention has been made of art. In conclusion, it seems appropriate to speak briefly about art: the art of the theatre, the costumer's art, and the role of visual production elements in the theatre.

Theatre is called one of the lively arts, and it is certainly true that producing a play on the stage is a lively activity, requiring a great deal of human energy. (It is also fervently hoped by everybody associated with the production that the audience attending the play should have a lively experience in the theatre.) Many artists work together to produce a play: playwright, actors, director, designers, technicians. Theatre happens because this group of artists decide to enter into a lively collaboration with one another. A significant difference between theatre artists and artists who work alone, such as sculptors, painters, and poets, is that theatre artists are not only willing to enter into a creative collaboration, but that the collaboration is central to their work.

Theatre artists cannot create alone. The playwright's words are without life until they are spoken, the playwright's world is unseen until it appears on the stage. The task of revealing, performing, exploring, and exploding a piece of dramatic writing falls equally on all members of this unique combine of artists. All are intent upon the same goal, but each approaches that goal from a different vantage point. Their responsibilities are at the same time separate and interdependent. Although actors do not generally design their own costumes and scenic artists do not tell actors where to move on stage, both the actors and the designers working together on a production want the same outcome: a coherent work of art, accessible in every facet to the sensibilities of the audience for whom it is performed. The technician who creates a suitable piece of stage jewelry serves this coherence just as faithfully as the director who is responsible for keeping track of the play's meaning and the production concept.

The success of a theatrical production depends very much on each artist's knowing his or her job and doing it well. Possessing talent alone is not sufficient. Talent must be developed in order to produce a highly trained and disciplined theatrical artist who can participate effectively in the creative collaboration.

Theatre artists acquire much of their training from one another by sharing. Ideas and information are shared whenever and wherever theatre people assemble. This book results from such sharing. A great many costumers, designers, directors, and actors contributed to its contents. But it is only a beginning. For every method of garment construction, every craft technique, every suggestion for economical re-styling and creative making-do, there are a dozen others that had to be omitted because of time and space limitations. Also, there are many, many more ideas, techniques, and methods used by other costumers and unknown to us. The technical literature specifically relating to the costumer's art is poor indeed at present. It is hoped that this book will meet some of the need that exists in this area and that it will inspire others to write other books that will fill in the gaps.

Bibliography

This bibliography is not intended to be comprehensive but rather to present selected examples of the different sorts of books available to costumers.

Broad Surveys

Black, J. Anderson, and Garland, Madge. *A History of Fashion.* New York: William Morrow & Co., Inc., 1975.

Boucher, Francois. *A History of Costume in the West.* London: Thames & Hudson, 1967.

Bruhn, Wolfgang, and Tilke, Max. *A Pictorial History of Costume.* New York: Hastings House Publishers, Inc., 1973.

Contini, Mila. *Fashion: From Ancient Egypt to the Present Day.* London: Paul Hamlyn, 1965.

Davenport, Millia. *The Book of Costume.* New York: Crown Publishers, Inc., 1968.

Garland, Madge. *The Changing Form of Fashion.* New York: Praeger Publishers, 1970.

Hansen, Henny Harold. *Costume Cavalcade.* London: Methuen & Co., Ltd., 1961.

The Hugh Evelyn History of Costume. 5 vols. London: Hugh Evelyn, Ltd., 1968.

Kohler, Carl. *A History of Costume.* Reprint. New York: Dover Publications, Inc., 1963. Original publication date 1928.

Laver, James. *A Concise History of Costumes and Fashion.* New York: Harry N. Abrams, Inc., 1969.

————. *Costume Through the Ages.* New York: Simon and Schuster, 1963.

Payne, Blanche. *History of Costume: From the Ancient Egyptians to the Twentieth Century.* New York: Harper & Row, 1965.

Squire, Geoffrey. *Dress and Society 1560–1970.* New York: The Viking Press, 1974.

Wilcox, R. Turner. *The Mode in Costume.* New York: Charles Scribner's Sons, 1958.

Specific Periods and Countries

Bentivegna, F. C., ed. *Abbigliamento e costume nella pittura Italiana.* Vol. 1, 15th and 16th centuries; vol. 2, 17th and 18th centuries. Rome: Carlo Bestetti, 1962.

Birbari, E. *Dress in Italian Painting: 1460–1500*. London: John Murray, 1975.

Blum, Stella. *Designs by Erte: Fashion Drawings and Illustrations from "Harper's Bazaar."* New York: Dover Publications, Inc., 1976.

————, ed. *Victorian Fashions and Costumes from "Harper's Bazaar": 1867–1898*. New York: Dover Publications, Inc., 1974.

Cunnington, C. Willett and Phillis. *Handbook of English Mediaeval Costume*. Revised ed. London: Faber & Faber, Ltd., 1973.

————. *Handbook of English Costume in the 16th Century*. Revised ed. London: Faber & Faber, Ltd., 1970.

————. *Handbook of English Costume in the 17th Century*. 3rd edition. London: Faber & Faber, Ltd., 1972.

————. *Handbook of English Costume in the 18th Century*. Revised ed. London: Faber & Faber, Ltd., 1972.

————. *Handbook of English Costume in the 19th Century*. 3rd edition. London: Faber & Faber, Ltd., 1970.

Dorner, Jane. *Fashion in the Twenties & Thirties*. London: Ian Allen, 1973.

————. *Fashion in the Forties & Fifties*. London: Ian Allen, 1973.

Earle, Alice Morse. *Two Centuries of Costume in America: 1620–1820*. 2 vols. Rutland, Vermont: Charles E. Tuttle Co., 1971.

Erte, *Erte Fashions*. New York: St. Martin's Press, 1972.

Ewing, Elizabeth. *History of Twentieth Century Fashion*. London: B. T. Batsford, Ltd., 1974.

The Gallery of English Costume. 8 vols. Manchester: Art Galleries Committee of the Corporation of Manchester, 1949–1963.

Gernsheim, Alison. *Fashion and Reality*. London: Faber & Faber, Ltd., 1963.

Gibbs-Smith, Charles H. *The Fashionable Lady in the Nineteenth Century*. London: Her Majesty's Stationery Office, 1960.

Laver, James, ed. *Seventeenth and Eighteenth Century Costume*. London: His Majesty's Stationery Office, 1958.

Mansfield, Alan, and Cunnington, Phillis. *Handbook of English Costume in the 20th Century: 1900–1950*. London: Faber & Faber, Ltd., 1973.

McClellan, Elisabeth. *History of American Costume: 1607–1870*. New York: Tudor Publishing Co., 1969.

The Old West. Multiple volumes. New York: Time-Life Books, 1973–1976.

Peacock, John. *Fashion Sketchbook: 1920–1960*. New York: Avon Books, 1977.

Rickert, Edith. *Chaucer's World*. Oxford: Oxford University Press, 1948.

Schoeffler, O. E., and Gale, William. *Esquire's Encyclopedia of 20th Century Men's Fashions*. New York: McGraw-Hill, Inc., 1973.

This Fabulous Century. 8 vols. New York: Time-Life Books, 1969–1971.

Torrens, Deborah. *Fashion Illustrated: A Review of Women's Dress, 1920–1950*. New York: Hawthorn Books, Inc., 1975.

Vecellio, Cesare. *Vecellio's Renaissance Costume Book*. New York: Dover Publications, Inc., 1977.

Warwick, Edward; Pitz, Henry C.; and Wyckoff, Alexander. *Early American Dress: The Colonial and Revolutionary Periods*. New York: Bonanza Books, 1965.

Theatrical Costume and Design

Barton, Lucy. *Historic Costume for the Stage*. Renewal ed. Boston: Walter H. Baker Co., 1963.

Brooke, Iris. *Costume in Greek Classic Drama*. New York: Theatre Arts Books, 1965.

Christie, Archibald H. *Pattern Design: An Introduction to the Study of Formal Ornament*. Reprint. New York: Dover Publications, Inc., 1969. Original publication date 1929.

Ducharte, Pierre Louis. *The Italian Comedy*. New York: Dover Publications, Inc., 1966.

Meyer, Franz Sales. *Handbook of Ornament*. Reprint. New York: Dover Publications, Inc., 1957. Original publication date 1888.

Motley, *Designing and Making Stage Costumes*. New York: Watson-Guptill Publications, 1964.

Russell, Douglas A. *Stage Costume Design*. Englewood Cliffs, N.J.: Prentice-Hall, 1973.

————. *Theatrical Style: A Visual Approach to the Theatre*. Palo Alto, California: Mayfield Publishing Co., 1976.

Shesgreen, Sean, ed. *Engravings by Hogarth*. New York: Dover Publications, Inc., 1973.

Speltz, Alexander. *The Styles of Ornament*. Reprint. New York: Dover Publications, Inc., 1959. Original publication date 1906.

Occupational Costumes, Uniforms, Arms, and Armor

Ashdown, Charles Henry. *Arms and Armor*. New York: Dover Publications, Inc., 1970.

Brinkerhoff, Sidney. *Metal Uniform Insignia of the Frontier U.S. Army, 1846–1902*. Tucson, Arizona: Arizona Historical Society, 1972.

Carman, W. Y. *A Dictionary of Military Uniform.* London: B. T. Batsford, 1977.

Cunnington, Phillis. *Costumes of Household Servants.* London: Adam & Charles Black, 1974.

———. *Occupational Costume in England.* London: Adam & Charles Black, 1972.

———, and Lucas, Catherine. *Costume for Births, Marriages and Deaths.* London: Adam & Charles Black, 1974.

———, and Mansfield, A. *English Costume for Sports and Outdoor Recreations from the Sixteenth to the Nineteenth Centuries.* London: Adam & Charles Black, 1969.

Ewing, Elizabeth. *Women in Uniform: Through the Centuries.* London: B. T. Batsford, Ltd., 1975.

Funcken, Lilliane and Fred. *Arms and Uniforms Series.* 8 vols. London: Ward Lock, Ltd., c. 1975.

German Military Uniforms and Insignia: 1933–1945. Old Greenwich, Conn.: WE, 1967.

Gough, Henry, and Parker, James. *A Glossary of Terms Used in Heraldry.* Detroit, Michigan: Gale Research Co., 1966.

Mayer-Thurman, Christa. *Raiment for the Lord's Service.* Chicago: The Art Institute of Chicago, 1975.

Oakes, Alma, and Hill, Margot Hamilton. *Rural Costume: Its Origin and Development in Western Europe and the British Isles.* New York: Van Nostrand Reinhold Co., 1970.

Reid, William. *Arms Through the Ages.* New York: Harper & Row, Inc., 1976.

Robinson, H. Russell. *The Armour of Imperial Rome.* New York: Charles Scribner's Sons, 1975.

Stone, George Cameron. *A Glossary of the Construction, Decoration and Use of Arms and Armor in All Countries and in All Times.* New York: Jack Brussel, 1934.

Windrow, Martin, ed. *Men-at-Arms Series.* Multiple volumes. London: Osprey Publishing, c. 1977.

Wise, Arthur. *Weapons in the Theatre.* New York: Barnes & Noble, Inc., 1968.

Costume Dictionaries and Bibliographies

Anthony, Pegaret, and Arnold, Janet. *Costume: A General Bibliography.* London: The Victoria & Albert Museum in association with The Costume Society, 1974.

Cunnington, C. W. and P. E., and Beard, Charles. *A Dictionary of English Costume: 900–1900.* London: Adam & Charles Black, 1972.

Hiler, Hilaire and Meyer. *Bibliography of Costume.* New York: Blom, 1967.

Huenfeld, Irene Pennington. *International Dictionary of Historical Clothing.* Metuchen, N.J.: The Scarecrow Press, Inc., 1967.

Index to British Military Costume Prints 1500–1914. London: Army Museums Ogilby Trust, 1972.

Kyblova, Ludmilla; Herbenova, Olga; and Lamarova, Milene. *The Pictorial Encyclopedia of Fashion.* London: Paul Hamlyn, 1968.

Monro, Isabel S., and Cook, D. E., eds. *Costume Index.* New York: H. W. Wilson Co., 1937.

———. *Costume Index Supplement.* New York: H. W. Wilson Co., 1957.

Snowden, James. *European Folk Dress.* London: The Costume Society, 1973.

Wilcox, R. Turner. *The Dictionary of Costume.* New York: Charles Scribner's Sons, 1969.

Whalon, Marion K. *Performing Arts Research: A Guide To Information Sources.* Detroit, Michigan: Gale Research Co., 1976.

Costume Accessories and Properties

Belfer, Nancy. *Designing in Batik and Tie Dye.* Englewood Cliffs, N.J.: Prentice-Hall, Inc., 1977.

Bowman, Ned A. *Handbook of Technical Practice for the Performing Arts.* Wilkinsburg, Pa.: Scenographic Media, 1972.

Brooke, Iris. *Footwear: A Short History of European and American Shoes.* New York: Theatre Arts Books, 1971.

Bryson, Nicholas L. *Thermoplastic Scenery for the Theatre: Vol. 1, Vacuum Forming.* New York: Drama Books Specialists, 1972.

Colle, Doriece. *Collars . . . Stocks . . . Cravats: A History and Costume Dating Guide to Civilian Men's Neckpieces 1655–1900.* Emmaus, Pennsylvania: Rodale Press, 1972.

Corson, Richard. *Fashions in Eyeglasses.* London: Peter Owen, Ltd., 1967.

Crawford, T. S. *History of the Umbrella.* Newton Abbot: Publishers David & Charles, 1970.

Dryden, Deborah M. *Fabric Printing and Dyeing for the Theatre.* New York: Drama Book Specialists, 1978.

Ewing, Elizabeth. *Underwear: A History.* New York: Theatre Arts Books, 1972.

Gregorietti, Guido. *Jewelry Through the Ages.* New York: American Heritage Press, 1969.

Motley, *Theatre Props.* New York: Drama Book Specialists, 1975.

von Boehm, Max. *Modes and Manners Ornaments.* London: J. M. Dent & Sons, Ltd., 1929

von Neumann, Robert. *Design and Creation of Jewelry.* Revised ed. Radnor, Pennsylvania: Chilton Book Co., 1972.

Wilcox, Ruth Turner. *The Mode in Footwear.* New York: Charles Scribner's Sons, 1948.

————. *The Mode in Hats and Headdress.* New York: Charles Scribner's Sons, 1948.

Wilson, Eunice. *A History of Shoe Fashion.* New York: Theatre Arts Books, 1974.

Patterns and Construction

Arnold, Janet. *Patterns of Fashion.* Vol. 1, 1660–1860; vol. 2, 1860–1940. New York: Drama Book Specialists, 1977.

Bradfield, Nancy. *Costume in Detail: Women's Dress 1730–1930.* London: George G. Harrap, 1968.

Brooke, Iris. *Medieval Theatre Costume: A Practical Guide to the Construction of Garments.* New York: Theatre Arts Books 1967.

Croonborg, Frederick T. *The Blue Book of Men's Tailoring: Theatrical Costumemaker's Pattern Book for Edwardian Men's Costumes.* New York: Van Nostrand Reinhold Co., 1977.

Edson, Doris, and Barton, Lucy. *Period Patterns.* Boston: Walter H. Baker Co., 1942.

Hill, Margot Hamilton, and Bucknell, Peter A. *The Evolution of Fashion: Pattern and Cut from 1066 to 1930.* New York: Reinhold Publishing Corp., 1967.

Hutton, Jessie, and Cunningham, Gladys. *Singer Sewing Book: The Complete Guide to Sewing.* New York: Golden Press, 1972.

Moulton, Bertha. *Garment-Cutting and Tailoring for Students.* Revised ed. London: B. T. Batsford, Ltd., 1967.

Poulin, Clarence. *Tailoring Suits the Professional Way.* Peoria, Illinois: Bennett, 1973.

Smith, C. Ray, ed. *The Theatre Crafts Book of Costume.* Emmaus, Pennsylvania: Rodale Press, 1973.

Tilke, Max. *Costume Patterns and Designs.* London: A. Zwemmer, 1956.

The Vogue Sewing Book. New York: Vogue Patterns, 1975.

Waugh, Nora. *Corsets and Crinolines.* New York: Theatre Arts Books, 1970.

————. *The Cut of Men's Clothes: 1600–1900.* New York: Theatre Arts Books, 1964.

————. *The Cut of Women's Clothes: 1600–1930.* New York: Theatre Arts Books, 1968.

Hair and Make-up

Buchman, Herman. *Stage Makeup.* New York: Watson-Guptill, 1972.

Corson, Richard. *Fashions in Hair.* London: Peter Owen, Ltd., 1971.

————. *Fashions in Makeup.* New York: Universe Books, 1972.

————. *Stage Makeup.* 5th ed. Englewood Cliffs. N.J.: Prentice-Hall, Inc., 1975.

deCourtais, Georgine. *Women's Headdress and Hairstyles.* London: B. T. Batsford, Ltd., 1974.

Miscellaneous

Arnold, Janet. *A Handbook of Costume.* London: Macmillan London, Ltd., 1973.

Glassman, Judith. *National Guide to Craft Supplies.* New York: Van Nostrand Reinhold Co., 1975.

————. *New New York Guide to Craft Supplies.* 2nd ed. New York: Workman Publishing Co., 1974.

Linton, George E., *Applied Basic Textiles.* New York: Lifetime Editions, 1948.

Moss, J. A. Ernest. *Textiles and Fabrics, Their Care and Preparation.* New York: Chemical Publishing Co., 1961.

Sears, Roebuck & Co. *Catalogue: 1897.* New York: Chelsea House, 1968.

————. *Catalogue: 1900.* Northfield, Illinois: Digest Books, 1970.

————. *Catalogue: 1902.* New York: Crown Publishers, 1969.

————. *Catalogue: 1908.* Northfield, Illinois: Digest Books, 1971.

————. *Catalogue: 1927.* New York: Crown Publishers, 1970.

Simon's Directory of Theatrical Materials, Services and Information. New York: Package Publicity Service, 1976.

Shopping Guides

CHICAGO AREA

Accessories

Haren Hosiery
4 S. State
Chicago, Illinois 60603
  312-346-0094
and
1123 Lake
Oak Park, Illinois 60301
  312-386-9400

Adhesives and Tapes

Barney Frankel, Inc.
  1721 S. Wabash
Chicago, Illinois 60616
  312-922-2331
(Barge glue)

Iroquois Paper Co.
2220 W. 56th
Chicago, Illinois 60636
  312-436-7000
(3-M glue system)

Swift's Adhesives &
  Coatings
111 W. Jackson
Chicago, Illinois 60604
  312-761-0100

Tapes Unlimited
2312 Main
Evanston, Illinois 60202
  312-866-6060

Joseph Weil & Sons
1401-43 S. Clinton
Chicago, Illinois 60607
  312-829-7811
(tapes)

Armor

Tobins Lake Studios, Inc.
2650 Seven Mile Lane
South Lyon, Michigan
  48178
  313-449-4444
(vacuum formed armor
  pieces)

Artists' Supplies

Brudno Art Supply Co.
601 N. State
Chicago, Illinois 60610
  312-787-0030

SS Artists Materials
712 N. State
Chicago, Illinois 60610
  312-787-2005

Book Shops

Contemporary Drama
  Service
Box 457, Dept. CAP
Downers Grove, Illinois
  60515
  312-969-4988

Oak St. Book Shop, Inc.
54 E. Oak
Chicago, Illinois 60611
  312-642-3070

Celastic

Maharam Fabric Corp.
420 N. Orleans
Chicago, Illinois 60610
  312-527-2580

Clothing, Secondhand

Briarhouse of Chicago
462 W. St. James Place
Chicago, Illinois 60614
  312-549-9629

Follies
6981 N. Sheridan
Chicago, Illinois 60626
  312-761-3020

S. Hirsh & Sons
621-23 W. Randolph
Chicago, Illinois 60606
  312-263-5213

George Stotis
5308 N. Clark
Chicago, Illinois 60640
  312-878-8525

Costume Rental

Broadway Costumes, Inc.
15 W. Hubbard
Chicago, Illinois 60610
  312-644-4024

Chicago Costume Co. Inc.
1120 W. Barry
Chicago, Illinois 60657
312-528-1264

Costumes Unlimited
814 N. Franklin
Chicago, Illinois 60610
312-642-0200

Dancewear

Capezio Dance/Theatre
Shop
17 N. State
Chicago, Illinois 60602
312-236-1911

Kling Theatrical Shoe Co.
218 S. Wabash
Chicago, Illinois 60604
312-427-2028

Leo's Advance Theatrical
Co.
125 N. Wabash
Chicago, Illinois 60602
312-772-7150

Decorative Items

Leonard Adler & Co.
190 N. State, 3rd floor
Chicago, Illinois 60601
312-332-5454
(trims & feather boas)

International Importing
Bead & Novelty Co.
17 N. State
Chicago, Illinois 60602
312-332-0061
(beads, rhinestones,
sequins, pearls, jewels)

R. Nyren & Co.
2222 W. Diversey
Chicago, Illinois 60647
312-276-5515
(braid, cord, tassel, tape,
fringe)

Progress Feather Co.
657 W. Lake
Chicago, Illinois 60606
312-726-7443

A. Robbin & Co.
321 W. Jackson
Chicago, Illinois 60606
312-939-2240
(sequins, rhinestones)

Dyestuffs

Almore Dye House
4422 S. Wentworth
Chicago, Illinois 60609
312-268-5000

Keystone Aniline Dye
321 N. Loomis
Chicago, Illinois 60607
312-666-2015

Fabrics

Fishman's Fabrics
1101 S. Des Plaines
Chicago, Illinois 60607
312-922-7250

Vogue Fabrics
718-732 Main
Evanston, Illinois 60202
312-864-9600

*Hair, Wigs, and Beauty
Supplies*

Chicago Hair Goods Co.
428 S. Wabash
Chicago, Illinois 60605
312-427-8600

Herman Leis & Son
6729 W. North
Oak Park, Illinois 60302
312-524-0424
(custom-made wigs)

Selan's
32 N. State
Chicago, Illinois 60602
312-782-0331
(wigs)

Make-up

Perle Roland Perfume Shop
946 Rush
Chicago, Illinois 60611
312-944-1432
(Factor and Mehron)

Syd Simons Cosmetics, Inc.
2 E. Oak
Chicago, Illinois 60611
312-943-2333
(make-up artists and
make-up lessons;
cosmetics for sale)

Tech Theatre, Inc.
4724 Main
Lisle, Illinois 60532
312-971-0855
(Ben Nye, Stein, Factor)

*Sewing Machines and
Sewing Supplies*

M.G. Sewing Machine Co.
6448 N. Artesian
Chicago, Illinois 60645
312-764-8188
(machines and equipment)

David Kaplan & Co., Inc.
210 South Des Plaines
Chicago, Illinois 60606
312-454-1610
(thread)

Shoes

John Schoener
2521 W. Berwyn
Chicago, Illinois 60625
312-728-1039
(custom-made clown
shoes)

Miscellaneous

Thunderbird Products Co.
1042 W. Van Buren,
Chicago, Illinois 60607
312-733-2340
(Western novelties, square
dance, etc.)

Wayne's Trick Shop
5413 Hohman
Hammond, Indiana 46320
219-933-9322

LOS ANGELES AREA

Accessories

Hammer
7210 Melrose Ave.
Los Angeles, California
90046
213-938-0288
(custom-made gloves)

Artists' Supplies

Daniel's Co.
2543 W. Sixth St.
Los Angeles, California
90057
213-387-1211

Michael's Art, Drafting &
Crafts
1518 N. Highland Ave.
Hollywood, California
90028
213-466-5295

Standard Brand Paints
124 W. Pico Blvd.
Los Angeles, California
90015
213-748-2933

Book Shops

B. Dalton Pickwick
6743 Hollywood Blvd.
Los Angeles, California
90028
213-469-8191

Doubleday
9477 Santa Monica Blvd.
Beverly Hills, California
90210
213-274-8706

Hunter Books
463 N. Rodeo Dr.
Beverly Hills, California
90212
213-274-7301

Celastic

Maharam Fabrics
1113 S. Los Angeles
Los Angeles, California
90015
213-749-2327

Clothing, Secondhand

Aardvark's
7579 Melrose
Los Angeles, California
90046
213-655-6769

Camp Beverly Hills
9640 Santa Monica Blvd.
Beverly Hills, California
90212
213-274-8317
(international surplus,
antique, and creative
clothing)

Crystal Palace
8457 Melrose
Los Angeles, California
90069
213-653-6148
(ask for Bob and Melodie;
period clothing and
accessories)

Donna's II
7523 W. Sunset Blvd.
Hollywood, California
90046
213-874-9027

Harold's Place,
420 N. Bedford
Beverly Hills, California
90210
213-275-6222

Hollywood Used Clothing
7836 Santa Monica
Los Angeles, California
90046
213-654-4232

Yesterday's Clothes
7424 Sunset Blvd.
Los Angeles, California
90046
213-851-5044

Costume Rental

Western Costume Co.
5335 Melrose Ave.
Hollywood, California
90038
213-469-1451

Decorative Items

A-1 Pleating
8426½ West 3rd St.
Los Angeles, California
90048
213-653-5557
(pleating, covered buttons,
and buckles)

Berger Specialty Co.
413 E. 8th St.
Los Angeles, California
90014
213-627-4855
(glass and wood beads,
shells, pearls, sequins)

Colby Feathers
7932½ W. Third St.
Los Angeles, California
90048
213-653-3054

Handy Buttons
1126 S. Los Angeles St.
Los Angeles, California
90015
213-747-5349
(grommets and dyes,
durable snaps)

Hollywood Fancy Feathers
Co.
512 S. Broadway
Los Angeles, California
90013
213-625-8453

Klein's Bead Box
314 N. King's Road
Los Angeles, California
90048
213-651-3595

Pacific Coast
745 San Julian
Los Angeles, California
90014
213-624-3982
(floral supplies)

Dyestuffs

Screen Process Supplies
1199 E. 12th St.
Oakland, California 94606
415-451-1048
(Inkodye)

Fabrics

Beverly Hills Silks &
Woolens
417 N. Canon Drive
Beverly Hills, California
90028
213-271-8389

Dazian's Inc.
165 S. Robertson Blvd.
Beverly Hills, California
90211
213-657-8900;
213-655-9691
(novelty fabrics, muslin)

Homesilk Shop
330 S. La Cienga Blvd.
Los Angeles, California
90048
213-655-7513

International Silks &
Woolens
8347 Beverly Blvd.
Los Angeles, California
90048
213-653-6453
(ask for Marco; boas,
beads, and buttons)

Left Bank Fabric Co.
8354 W. Third St.
Los Angeles, California
90048
213-655-7289
(imported and designer
fabrics)

Levine Bros.
530 W. Los Angeles St.
Los Angeles, California
90013
213-624-6541
(woolens and trims)

Standard Felt Co.
115 S. Palm Ave.
Alhambra, California
91801
213-282-3165
(industrial & decorative
felt; $100 minimum
order)

George Tewes
2619 E. 8th St.
Los Angeles, California
90023
213-269-0435

Leather

Macpherson Leather Co.
200 S. Los Angeles St.
Los Angeles, California
90012
213 626-4831
(skins, dyes, sprays,
buckles, etc.)

Make-up

Ben Nye, Inc.
11571 Santa Monica Blvd.
Los Angeles, California
90025
213-478-1558

Millinery Supplies

California Millinery
Supplies
718 S. Hill St.
Los Angeles, California
90014
213-622-8746
(third floor has flowers,
ribbons, felts, and
buckram bodies)

Sewing Supplies

Keller
345 N. La Cienga,
Los Angeles, California
90048
213-655-5577
(scissors, chalk, seam tape,
etc.)

Shoes

The Folk Motif
2752 E. Broadway
Long Beach, California
90803
213-439-7380
(mid-Eastern shoes,
imported and custom-
made)

Shoe Repair

Dan Dee
1713 N. Vine St.
Hollywood, California
90028
213-464-4082

Di Fabrizio
6276 W. 3rd St.
Los Angeles, California
90036
213-936-6883

Willie's Shoe Repair
5326 Melrose
Los Angeles, California
90038
213-463-5011

NEW YORK AREA

Accessories

Albert's Hosiery
609 Madison Ave.
New York, New York
   10022
   212-755-6483

Gibson-Lee,
35 Congress St.
Salem, Massachusetts
   01970
   617-745-9190
(disposable collars and
cuffs, shirt fronts, collar
buttons)

The Giraffe Trading Co.
56 Harvester Ave.
Batavia, New York 14020
   716-344-1900
(walking sticks)

Eileen Holding
110 W. 18th St.
New York, New York
   10011
   212-242-4797
(tights and unitards)

Conrad Mandel
59 Orchard St.
New York, New York
   10002
   212-925-1740

Parklane Hosiery
2A Penn Arcade
New York, New York
   10001
   212-594-2047

Morris Trenk
90 Orchard St.
New York, New York
   10002
   212-674-3498
(hosiery and underwear)

Preger & Wertenteil
333 Grand St.
New York, New York
   10002
   212-925-5710
(hosiery)

Uncle Sam Umbrella Shop
161 W. 57th St.
New York, New York
   10019
   212-582-1976
(umbrellas, parasols, canes)

Adhesives and Tapes

Beacon Chemical Co., Inc.
125 MacQuesten Parkway
South
Mount Vernon, New York
   10550
   914-699-3400

H. G. Pasternak, Inc.
225 Lafayette
New York, New York
   10012
   212-925-4865

Armor

Costume Armor, Inc.
P.O. Box 6086
Hangar E, Stewart Airport
Newburgh, New York
   12550
   914-564-7100
(vacuum-formed armor
pieces)

Excalibur
25 Brightside Ave.
E. Northport, New York
   11768
   516-757-8888
(swords and scabbards)

Artists' Supplies

Pearl Paint
308 Canal St.
New York, New York
   10013
   212-431-7932

Book Shops

British Information
Services
845 Third Ave.
New York, New York,
   10022
   212-752-8400
(publications from the
Victoria and Albert
Museum and H.M.S.O.)

Drama Book Shop
150 W. 52nd St.
New York, New York
   10019
   212-582-1037

Hacker Books
54 W. 57th St.
New York, New York
   10019
   212-757-1450
Celastic
Alcone Company, Inc.
Paramount Theatrical Sup-
plies
575 8th Ave.
New York, New York
   10018
   212-594-3980
*Clothing, Ready-made, New,
and Secondhand*
Barney's
111 7th Ave. (at W. 17th
St.)
New York, New York
   10011
   212-929-9000
(discount suits, new)

Bogie's
201 E. 10th St.
New York, New York
   10003
   212-260-1199
(used clothing, furs, quilts)

Syms
45 Park Place
New York, New York
   10007
   212-791-1199
(discount suits, new)

Unique Clothing
   Warehouse
718 Broadway
New York, New York
   10011
   212-674-1767
(used clothing)

J. Wippell & Co., Ltd.
P.O. Box 456
Fair Lawn, New Jersey
   07410
   201-796-9421
(clerical and choir
garments)

Corset Supplies

E. deGrandmont
50 W. 17th St.
New York, New York
   10011
   212-242-5122

K. M. Jacobs
172 Madison
New York, New York
   10016
   212-683-7675

Laufer
50 W. 29th St.
New York, New York
   10001
   212-685-2181

Nathan's Boning Co.
336 W. 37th St.
New York, New York
   10018
   212-244-4781
(continuous steel boning)

Costume Rental

The Costume Collection
601 W. 26th St.
New York, New York
   10001
   212-989-5855
(rents only to nonprofit
organizations)

David's Outfitters, Inc.
36 W. 20th St.
New York, New York
   10011
   212-691-7388
(military and civilian
uniforms, new and used,
rental and sale)

Eaves & Brooks Costume
   Co., Inc.
423 W. 55th St.
New York, New York
   10019
   212-757-3730

Dancewear

Capezio
755 7th Ave. (at 50th St.)
New York, New York
   10019
   212-245-2130

Herbet Dancewear
902 Broadway (3rd floor)
New York, New York
   10010
   212-677-7606

Selva
1776 Broadway at 57th
New York, New York
  10019
  212-586-5140

Star Barres
206 Pierron St.
Northvale, New Jersey
  07647
(mail order only; catalog
  upon request)

Decorative Items

Abetter Cork Co.
262 Mott St.
New York, New York
  10012
  212-925-7755
(cork beads and balls)

Cinderella Flower &
  Feather Co.
57 W. 38th St.
New York, New York
  10018
  212-947-4302

Duplex Novelty Co.
315 W. 35th St.
New York, New York
  10001
  212-564-1352
(wooden beads)

Hyman Hendler & Sons
67 W. 38th St. (between
  5th & 6th)
New York, New York
  10018
  212-947-6670
(ribbons)

M & J Trimming Co.
1008 6th Ave.
New York, New York
  10018
  212-244-7072
(ribbons, buckles, buttons,
  etc.)

Miligi
58 W. 56th St.
New York, New York
  10019
  212-582-2337
(pleating)

Ben Raymond
611 Broadway
  (at Houston)
New York, New York
  10012
  212-777-7350
(lace trim)

Sheru
49 W. 38th St. (between
  5th & 6th)
New York, New York
  10018
  212-565-0766
(beads, flowers)

Tinsel Trading Co.
47 W. 38th St.
New York, New York
  10018
  212-565-2460
(antique trims)

Dyestuffs

Aljo Dyes
116 Prince St.
New York, New York
  10012
  212-226-2878

Fabrics

Art-Max Fabrics
250 W. 40th St. (between
  7th and 8th)
New York, New York
  10018
  212-563-6686

B. & J. Fabrics
263 W. 40th St. (between
  7th & 8th)
New York, New York
  10018
  212-736-6255

S. Beckenstein, Inc.
130 Orchard St.
New York, New York
  10002
  212-475-4525

Far Eastern Fabrics
171 Madison Ave. (near
  34th)
New York, New York
  10016
  212-683-2623

FE-RO Fabrics
147 W. 57th St.
New York, New York
  10019
  212-581-0240

Gladstone Fabrics
16 W. 56th St. (between
  5th & 6th)
New York, New York
  10019
  212-765-0760

Grand Silk House
357 Grand St.
New York, New York
  10002
  212-475-0114

Inter-Costal Textile Corp
480 Broadway
New York, New York
  10013
  212-925-9235
(drapery and upholstery
  fabrics)

Kessler Upholstery
  Supplies
3952 Broadway (between
  165th & 166th)
New York, New York
  10032
  212-568-2344
(dacron batting)

C & F (Liberty Fabrics)
250 W. 39th St. (between
  7th and 8th Aves.)
New York, New York
  10018
  212-354-9360

Orchard Fabric Center
189 Orchard St.
New York, New York
  10002
  212-777-6457

Paron Fabrics
140 W. 57th St.
New York, New York
  10019
  212-247-6451

Poli Fabrics
132 W. 57th St.
New York, New York
  10019
  212-245-7589

Rose Brand Textiles
517 W. 35th St.
New York, New York
  10001
  212-594-7424
  toll free: (800-223-1624)
(muslin)

Weiss & Katz
187 Orchard St.
New York, New York
  10002
  212-477-1130

Weller Fabrics, Inc.
54 W. 57th St. (between
  5th & 6th)
New York, New York
  10019
  212-447-3790

Central Shippee, Inc.
35 Hamburg Tpk.
Bloomingdale, New Jersey
  07403
  201-838-1100
(industrial felt)

Continental Felt Co.
22 W. 15th St.
New York, New York
  10011
  212-929-5262
(industrial felt)

Hair, Wigs, and Beauty
Supplies

Alfred Barris
165 W. 46th St.
New York, New York
  10036
  212-354-9043
(sells wigs and hair pieces,

Bob Kelly
151 W. 46th St.
New York, New York
  10036
  212-245-2237
(sells and rents wigs and
  hair pieces)

Ray's
721 8th Ave.
New York, New York
  10036
  212-757-0175
(beauty supplies)

United Beauty Supply
49 W. 46th St.
New York, New York
  10036
  212-582-2324

Hats and Millinery Supplies

Feldman Machines
1032 6th Ave. (at 39th)
New York, New York
10018
212-947-1662
(millinery wire, hat
steamers)

Gampels Millinery Supply
Corp.
33 W. 37th St.
New York, New York
10018
212-398-9222
(millinery wire)

Haentz Hat Crafters
20 N. Springfield Rd.
Clifton Heights,
Pennsylvania 19018
205-623-2620
(hats)

Manny's Millinery Supply
Co.
63 W. 38th St.
New York, New York
10018
212-279-4917

Leather and Leather Goods

A & B Leather & Findings
500 W. 52nd St. (at 10th
Ave.)
New York, New York
10019
212-265-8124
(supplies and tools, Magix
spray dyes)

Mac Leather
424 Broome St. (off
Broadway)
New York, New York
10013
212-964-0850
(leather, supplies, and
tools)

Minerva Leather Co., Inc.
78 Spring St. (between
Broadway and Lafayette)
New York, New York
10012
212-925-6270

National Leather & Shoe
Findings
313 Bowery
New York, New York
10003
212-982-6227
(supplies and tools, Magix
spray dyes)

Make-up

Garden Pharmacy
1632 Broadway
New York, New York
10019
212-265-3546

Bob Kelly Cosmetics
151 W. 46th St.
New York, New York
10036
212-245-2237

Leicher Makeup
599 11th Ave.
New York, New York
10036
212-246-5543

Make-Up Centre, Ltd.
150 W. 55th St.
New York, New York
10019
212-977-9494

*Sewing Machines and
Sewing Supplies*

American Trading Co.
599 6th Ave. (18th St.)
New York, New York
10011
212-691-3666

Continental Sewing Supply
Co.
104 W. 25th St.
New York, New York
10001
212-255-8837
(machine parts and
attachments and
machines)

Fox Sewing Machine
307 W. 38th St. (between
8th and 9th)
New York, New York
10018
212-594-2438

Greenberg & Hammer
24 W. 57th St.
New York, New York
10019
212-586-6270
(sewing supplies)

A. Smith & Bros.
555 8th Ave. (between 37th
and 38th)
New York, New York
10018
212-594-0056
(sewing machines and used
tailor's dummies)

Steinlauf & Stoller
239 W. 39th St. (between
7th and 8th)
New York, New York
10018
212-869-0321
(sewing supplies)

Wolf Form Co.
39 W. 19th St.
New York, New York
10011
212-255-4508
(new tailor's dummies)

Shoes and Boots

La Ray
320 W. 48th St.
New York, New York
10036
212-757-4545

McCreedy & Schreiber
37 & 55 W. 46th St.
(between 5th and 6th)
New York, New York
10036
212-582-1552

Miscellaneous

Gordon Novelty Co.
22nd on Broadway
New York, New York
10011
212-254-8616

Index